VIDEO VORTEX

READER III

INSIDE THE
YOUTUBE DECADE

INC Reader #14
Video Vortex Reader III: Inside the You Tube Decade
Editors: Geert Lovink and Andreas Treske

In Memoriam Thomas Elsaesser (1943-2019)

Copy editor: Jack Wilson
Cover design: Berkay Donmez
Design and E-Pub development: Tommaso Campagna
Toolkit: networkcultures.org/digitalpublishing/

Published by the Institute of Network Cultures, Amsterdam, 2020
ISBN E-Pub: 978-94-92302-60-1
ISBN Paperback: 978-94-92302-61-8

Contact
Institute of Network Cultures
Phone: +31 (0)20 595 1865
Email: info@networkcultures.org
Web: www.networkcultures.org

Download this publication freely at: networkcultures.org/publications
Subscribe to the INC newsletter: networkcultures.org/newsletter

This publication is supported and funded by the Amsterdam University of Applied Sciences (HvA), produced during the corona crisis of March-May 2020. Thanks to all the authors for their contributions, Jack Wilson for his keen copy-editing job and Tommaso Champagna for hacking it all together. A great thanks in particular to the organizers and contributors of Video Vortex #12 in Malta (September 2019), which extraordinary level motivated all of us to produce this publication.

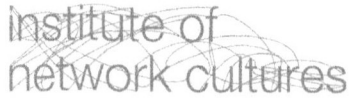

VIDEO VORTEX

READER III

INSIDE THE YOUTUBE DECADE

EDITED BY
GEERT LOVINK
AND **ANDREAS TRESKE,**
INC READER #14

Previously published INC Readers

The INC Reader series is derived from conference contributions and produced by the Institute of Network Cultures. The publications in this series are available in EPUB, PDF form, and a print run of 2000 copies. All INC Readers, and other publications like the Network Notebooks series, INC Longforms, and Theory on Demand, can be downloaded and read for free. See networkcultures.org/publications.

INC Reader #13: Miriam Rasch, Let's Get Physical, A Sample of INC Longforms 2015-2020, 2020.
INC Reader #12: Loes Bogers and Letizia Chiappini (eds), Critical Makers Reader: (Un) Learning Technology, 2019.
INC Reader #11: Inte Gloerich, Geert Lovink and Patricia de Vries (eds), MoneyLab Reader 2: Overcoming the Hype, 2018.
INC Reader #10: Geert Lovink, Nathaniel Tkacz and Patricia de Vries (eds), MoneyLab Reader: An Intervention in Digital Economy, 2015.
INC Reader #9: René König and Miriam Rasch (eds), Society of the Query: Reflections on Web Search, 2014.
INC Reader #8: Geert Lovink and Miriam Rasch (eds), Unlike Us: Social Media Monopolies and Their Alternatives, 2013.
INC Reader #7: Geert Lovink and Nathaniel Tkacz (eds), Critical Point of View: A Wikipedia Reader, 2011.
INC Reader #6: Geert Lovink and Rachel Somers Miles (eds), Video Vortex Reader II: Moving Images Beyond YouTube, 2011.
INC Reader #5: Scott McQuire, Meredith Martin and Sabine Niederer (eds), Urban Screens Reader, 2009.
INC Reader #4: Geert Lovink and Sabine Niederer (eds), Video Vortex Reader: Responses to YouTube, 2008.
INC Reader #3: Geert Lovink and Ned Rossiter (eds), MyCreativity Reader: A Critique of Creative Industries, 2007.
INC Reader #2: Katrien Jacobs, Marije Janssen and Mateo Pasquinelli (eds), C'LICK ME: A Netporn Studies Reader, 2007.
INC Reader #1: Geert Lovink and Soenke Zehle (eds), Incommunicade Reader, 2005.

CONTENTS

APPENDICES

INTRODUCTION

GEERT LOVINK
AND ANDREAS TRESKE

INTRODUCTION

GEERT LOVINK & ANDREAS TRESKE

'There's truths you have to grow into.' H.G. Wells

What's online video today, fifteen years into its exponential growth? In the age of the smart phone, video accompanies, informs, moves, and distracts us. What started off with amateur prosumers on YouTube has spread to virtually all communication apps: say it with moving images. Are you addicted yet? Look into that tiny camera, talk and move the phone, show us around, and prove the others out there that you exist!

With this third reader the Video Vortex community — initiated in 2007 by the Institute of Network Cultures — proves that it is still alive and kicking. No matter its changes, the network is still driven by its original mission to develop a critical vocabulary for this rapidly spreading visual culture: what are the specific characteristics of online video in terms of aesthetics and political economy of image production and distribution, and how do they compare to film and television? Who is the Andre Bazin of the YouTube age? Honestly, why can't we name a single online video critic? Can we face the fact that hardly anyone is using the internet? What are you going to do with that 4K camera in your smartphone? Have we updated Marshall McLuhan's hot and cold media for our digital era yet? Who dares? We see the *Woman with a Smartphone Camera* in action, but who will be our Vertov and lead the avant-garde? Who stops us? Let us radically confront the technological presence as it is and forget the pathetic regression to past formats: radical acceptance of the beautiful mess called the net.

From its inception, Video Vortex dealt with a broad range of topics. In part, these were inherited from the old days of video art, tactical media, and new media arts contexts such as ISEA, Transmediale, and the net.art/net criticism circles like Rhizome and nettime. Think of the question: what is the status of the museum and gallery, and what it could it be when if it engaged with the virtual and the network. As the call for Video Vortex #8 in Zagreb put it, 'spatial issues and exclusivity are put in relation to the constant virtual presence of the artwork. Fast changing technologies are undermining the very sense of the preservation of the moving image in an online context.' What we have witnessed is a constant production of new genres and techno-spatial assemblies. Just think of changing role of the music video, from MTV to YouTube as a music-on-demand service (image free!), but also consider video activism and the disturbing trend circa 2015 of ISIS propaganda videos, that Donatella Della Ratta writes about her 2018 *Shooting a Revolution* book.[1] Have you ever watched on the millions live webcams that are open and freely accessible online? Or the surveillance capacity of online video drones that inspect

---

1   Donatella Della Ratta, Shooting a Revolution, London: Pluto Press, 2018.

and protect properties? Or the once private 'revenge porn' images and films that have been put online without consent? Do you remember the use of livestreaming during the Euromaidan in Kiev or in the Nuit debout of Paris? And what about the video evidence, recorded on the streets of Hong Kong, that document police brutality or the videos of health workers at the forefront of the exhausting fight against the coronavirus, recorded with their smart phones inside sealed-off intensive care units?

Given its ease of access and use, video has historically been aligned with media activism and collaborative work. Now with video's ubiquity across social media and the web, its dominance of the internet of things, and the role of the camera in both the maintenance and breaking down of networks — in addition to the increasing capacity of digital video to simulate that which has not occurred — we require novel theories and research. This is to say that rapidly changing technological formats underscore the urgent need to engage in practices of archiving and curation, modes of collaboration and political mobilization, as well as generating fresh comprehensions of the subject-spectator, actors, and networks constituted by contemporary video and digital cultures.

Let's go back when it all started. In 2008, in his opening essay of the first Video Vortex reader, Thomas Elsaesser wrote:

> Thanks to all of them, I have found on YouTube ways of knowing and ways of being that are ludic and reflexive, educational and participatory, empowering and humbling, in short: marking an unusually soft dividing line between creative design and hard-core engineering, art and technology, singularity and repetition: preconditions if one wants to come to an understanding of the possibility of new 'life-forms' emerging at one of the sites of the post-human: the electronic world of algorithms and statistics, of contingency, constraint, and collapse, in short: of constructive instability and performative failure, in a world divided, but also held together by Rancière's "double heteronomy".[2]

He emphasizes two primary and very productive ideas: constructive instability and performative failure. Elsaesser, in a Benjamin attitude of *flâneurie*, moves along a path with a certain distinction of an avant-garde merging art and life with joy and curiosity: making failure an advantage, enacting poetics of a praxis, recalling the human element. Elsaesser's citation of Kathrine Hayles points to the starting phase of the Video Vortex project:

> As N. Katherine Hayles argued some years ago: "What [...] is already happening, is the development of distributed cognitive environments in which humans and computers interact in hundreds of ways daily, often unobtrusively." the terminology of Marcus Novak, quoted by Hayles, we are moving from "immersion" (our old-

2   Thomas Elsaesser, ''Constructive Instability', or: The Life of Things as the Cinema's Afterlife?', in Geert Lovink and Sabine Niederer (eds), *Video Vortex Reader: Responses to YouTube*, Amsterdam: Institute of Network Cultures, 2008, p. 13.

fashioned cyberspace) to "eversion" (localized virtual reality environments, like wi-fi hot-spots or other information-rich niches).[3]

Fast forward to fall 2016, the first day of the new academic year at Bilkent University in Ankara (Turkey), at an orientation meeting for more than fifty first-year students of the Department of Communication and Design. The students were asked: 'what is "video"?'. Although some of the students' answers were effectively general knowledge about 'video', the majority were surprisingly heterodox, indicating that the students had a more reflective and personal relationship to video.[4] Instead of offering a single definition, we believe the answers of these students from 2016 gives us a more holistic sense of how our relations to 'video' developed and changed inside the YouTube decade. They described video as a 'moving image', 'hundreds of images one after another', 'recordings with sound', an 'assemblage of image and sound', an 'occasion of self-expression', the 'recording of life', an 'illusion that consists of many images', the 'creation of visual conditions in digital environments...constituted by cell phones', a 'flow of knowledge', that which is 'shaping the real world', a 'platform transferring chosen thoughts and emotions', the compression of reality into 'what is wanted to be seen' or the result of 'extracting a dream'. As one student wrote: 'What is 'video'? In simple man's definition video is moving pictures, but for me, it is of showing much more just with few pictures...'

What did change in the past decade is the total takeover of visual culture by the smartphone. Images taken with the smartphone are never stand-alone, sovereign (data) objects. They are classified, measured, rendered, tagged and automatically processed and optimized to a photographic standard — or, in laymen's terms, beautified' — and then they are stored in the 'cloud'. Computational photography combines multiple images with sensory data. Apple's 'Deep Fusion' stitches pieces from multiple images together instantly to render precisely pixel-deep skin tones and details to create an expensive studio look that fits in your pocket. The single image does not technically exist. The single photograph has been lost in the smartphone.

Hito Steyerl opens her text on proxy politics in 2014 with reference to smartphone image processing. She describes a dialogue she had with a software developer, where he explained to her that the phone compensates for its technical deficiencies of tiny and low-quality lenses etc. through rendering the image by way of an instant search and access to all other similar images or meta-data available in social media.[5] Through noise of the initial snapshot, the photograph is cleaned through algorithmic processing, or let's say that the image is dis-/re-covered. Such a process, however, is only possible if the image is converted to something machine-readable.

---

3   Idem.
4   The average age of the students was around 18, and nearly all of them came straight from Turkish or international high schools. 5% were international students.
5   Hito Steyerl, 'Proxy Politics: Signal and Noise', e-flux Journal 60 (2014), https://www.e-flux.com/journal/60/61045/proxy-politics-signal-and-noise/.

Advances in pattern recognition algorithms notwithstanding, it is still the case that the computer cannot accurately recognize what the photograph contains. By re-writing the image as machine-readable text, metadata facilitates the identification, discovery, retrieval, (mis)use, exploitation and dissemination of images online.[6]

Image technology has become highly political. The implications of facial recognition technology combined with selfie aesthetics create — per Mitra Azar — new forms of human and machine agency. He proposes the selfie become an 'Algorithmic Facial Image' with this as a new phase of selfie culture.[7]

What has changed with online video in the past decade is the excess in the availability and mobility of moving images, which are no longer pure recordings but are subject to a similar instantaneous algorithmic processing in their flow from the phone of the user to various social media outlets or platforms in the global data cloud(s). A continuous digital signal allows any text to be either video or image, in flow and flux, or 'Stilleben'. The purpose is to free what you want to see from the noise the machine actually senses. And what we want to see is ourselves, alive. Through the cloud, any image — still or moving — is comparable and replaceable. With stitched-together images as the baseline, fakes are part of the nature of ultra-fragmented super modernity. Deepfake is the new normal. My image is part of an archive, which exists at the fingertip of machines to be rendered out of data clouds for whatever purpose by whoever or any-something. I am young and I am old, I am here and I am there. Robert De Niro and Al Pacino in *The Irishman*. Online video is not photographic. It is not cinematographic. It is a modular scan of data to build a gesture, a signal, a form of speech, mood, temperature, and climate (to refer to a notion of Peter Sloterdijk). What has changed is our image of the world. What has changed is the world itself. The fragmented live video images made by drones, satellites, ALPR cameras, together with Google's live view and search algorithms reflect a world build out of algorithmic belief. Nicholas Mirzoeff in his book *How to See the World*, writes on the massive impact that visual information has on us and our perception.[8] The photo of earth by the 1972 Apollo mission called 'The Blue Marble' made us to see the world for the first time as a whole. It was 43 years after that moment, in 2015, NASA shot another full photograph of earth. All the images we received from our planet before that were, and are still, built out of parts and pieces, constructed out of satellite scans closer to the earth's surface.

There is an image of a gigantic, abandoned open-air cinema on the web. Somebody built a cinema in the desert.[9] A screen, chairs in rows, and projection room. The wooden chairs

---

6   Daniel Rubinstein and Katrina Sluis, Notes on the Margins of Metadata; Concerning the Undecidability of the Digital Image, Photographies 6.1 (2013): 151-158.

7   Mitra Azar, 'From Selfie to Algorithmic Facial Image', paper presented at Video Vortex XII, Malta, 28 September 2019, https://networkcultures.org/videovortex/wp-content/uploads/sites/8/2019/09/Final-Video-Vortex-Program.pdf.

8   Nicholas Mirzoeff, How to See the World: An Introduction to Images, from Self-Portraits to Selfies, Maps to Movies, and More, New York: Basic Books, 2016.

9   Jeremy Fugelberg, 'An Abandoned Cinema in the Egyptian Desert Where the Only Show is Sunset', Atlas Obscura, 26 March 2014, https://www.atlasobscura.com/articles/sinai-peninsula-abandoned-theatre.

remind one of the opening sequence of Vertov's *Man with the Movie Camera*, when the audience enters the cinema. The dispositive cinema is laying down, rotting, its architecture are disappearing in the dust. The technological and discursive shift it created was a blink of a bit more than a hundred years. But was it not the mission of the 19th century to develop the transportation and transformation of image worlds by any means? Cinema was just a faster technological application of mass-communication than the electronic image, which took 50 years more to become broadcast television, and now we are abandoning that for digital video. So, since the mid-19th century image technology is in a continuously evolving avant-garde practice. It supports the war for space which — according to Sloterdijk — is lost as we came to the knowledge that we have only this world, and no other alternative.[10] To escape we need to construct a *sphere*, Pavel Florensky's space medium, where space and things are becoming inseparable.[11]

In 1956, Günther Anders noted in his essay *The World as Phantom and Matrix* that when the world comes to us, it is a phantom image, and when an event occurs in this world and is televised it becomes a kind of ubiquitous object in an assembly line, a commodity we pay for. And so, per Anders: 'When the actual event is socially important only in its reproduced form, i.e., as a spectacle, the difference between being and appearance, between reality and image of reality, is abolished'.[12]

In early 2019 Yu Ran, a professor from Beijing, moved his cinema course to the short video platform TikTok, a popular image platform known for its funny, absurd, cute videos, typically consumed by swiping through the autoplaying 'For You' feed. Surprisingly, in a world of shrinking screens, ultra-short videos with the elements of comedy and drama tell new stories of an edited daily life. These videos create massive online open footage, building miniature interactive narratives. Yu Ran points out four characteristics for the platform, it's users, and the ultra-short videos: Updated loyalty, a like/match role, an interactive topic, and the ability to comment. An account producing these popular videos is more or less like a company or a factory. While Yu Ran is teaching his course, he has to guarantee to be not only informative and keeping a specific quality, but also be humorous and to reply on every comment. Every account follower needs to be researched. The one account produces a team of content producers, identity managers, customer service, production manager and supervisor. Online video has become a product and an event on the digital assemble line, which pushes for automation. As Hito Steyerl cynically noted in 2019, this change has taken place not only on the production side but also the viewer, becoming 'Some sort of machine cinema in which even the spectators are machines'.[13]

10   Funcke, Bettina and Peter Sloterdijk, 'Against Gravity: Bettina Funcke Talks with Peter Sloterdijk', *Bookforum*, February/March 2005, https://www.bookforum.com/archive/feb_05/funcke.html, retrieved at http://dev.autonomedia.org/node/4584.

11   Pavel Florensky, as cited in Lev Manovich, *The Language of New Media*, Cambridge, MA: MIT Press, 2001.

12   Günther Anders, The World as Phantom and as Matrix, http://marcuse.faculty.history.ucsb.edu/projects/anders/Anders1956DissentWorldPhantomAndMatrixOCR.pdf.

13   Hito Steyerl in Alex Greenberger, "Is Shakespeare Fake News?': Artist Hito Steyerl Ponders Tough Questions in an Interview About Experimental Filmmaker Harun Farocki', *ARTnews*, 6 February

Have we been blind? Is there any canonical text of the past decade that defined the depth and spread of online video? The demise of theory becomes apparent here. Thirty years into its unprecedented growth, critical internet studies is still marginal, sitting between chairs. While film and television studies have been caught in the day-to-day operations of their institutional players, online video remains a victim of the 'remediation' thesis and the reproduction of the high-low culture divide. Making a bad start as 'participatory culture', the DIY television channel approach was soon taken over by semi-professional content and remediated content from 'old media', including mainstream music. During our long Video Vortex decade, we have closely followed the creation of 'influencers', something Google initiated with its 2007 ad revenue sharing 'partner program' to make their video service profitable after their purchase of YouTube in November 2006.

In 1993, during the transition from analogue to digital video, Sean Cubitt claimed that there will never be a video theory because video prevents a theoretical approach by being something we don't wish to know about.[14] Joshua Neves spoke on Video Vortex #9 in Lüneburg about video's resistance to theory, arguing that the absence of a theory was a result of video's lack of an essential form.[15] But, online video in its multiplicity and ubiquity challenges our understanding of contemporary media cultures, screen studies, audiovisual aesthetics and the project of media theory. Namely, that in online video there is the complete eradication of the discrete media object. Why? Online video is not only spatial in terms of a spatial practice of various forms, but it also as a bodily intimacy. With video, we have developed an intimate relationship with the network and the booming platforms dominating it. Online video is the driving force. The network itself is video. We are living in and with an ocean of online video. This is a metaphorical image used many times in the discussion of data. But as data is procedural, means it is in constant flux, the stream of data visualized is online video in too many instances. Theoretical approaches from artists and filmmakers like Harun Farocki and in his footsteps, Hito Steyerl, are deeply grounded in an appreciation of a cinema, and are theorizing the image and image politics, and therefore reflect the crisis of a dispositive. The bond between reality and the photographic image is broken. Audiovisual culture calls to new modes of existence. Online video is closer to forms of life.

In his chapter in the previous *Video Vortex reader II*, Stefan Heidenreich challenged Friedrich Kittler's position that media determines our situation. They don't, rather media has ceased to exist in plurality: 'The situation resembles an ecological system, where the conditions of climate and terrain define an environment for very many different species. In the same sense, a technological system provides an environment for many different types of data, formats, and contents'.[16] Media Do Not Exist![17] Traditionally we want to see stable entities and describable

　　　2020, https://www.artnews.com/art-news/artists/hito-steyerl-harun-farocki-thaddaeus-ropac-interview-1202677179/.
14　Sean Cubitt, Videography: Video Media as Art and Culture, London: Palgrave Macmillan, 1993.
15　Joshua Neves, 'Video Theory', presented at Video Vortex #9, Leuphana, 1 March 2013, https://vimeo.com/66055799.
16　Stefan Heidenreich, Vision Possible: A Methodological Quest for Online Video', in Geert Lovink and Rachel Somers Miles (eds), Video Vortex Reader II: moving images beyond YouTube, Amsterdam: Institute of Network Cultures, Amsterdam, 2011, p. 16.
17　Jean-Marc Larrue and Marcello Vitali-Rosati, Media Do Not Exist: Performativity and Mediating

objects. But, as fledging fields like media archaeology have discovered, there have never been stable mediated objects. When the cinema was established, television was more experiment than media, and now both are overrun by other parallel technological developments. When television was at its peak, analog video was conquering the western art establishment, and the internet was in its early youth, the textual medium switched already to a multimedia practice. Indeed, in her groundbreaking *Videoblogging Before YouTube*, Trine Bjørkmann Berry argues a new cultural-technical media hybrid that anticipated our current media ecology had emerged long before YouTube,.[18]

It is a pity that it took nearly 20 years to translate Maurizio Lazzarato's book *Videophilosophy: The Perception of Time in Post-Fordism* in English, as this is a text that has — in its critical reflection on the politics of media and the commodification of the self through the exploitation of time — not lost its power and relevance in the post digital era. We are all 24/7 workers. To quote Lazzarato:

> The introduction of real-time by the new technologies has detonated the concept of action and replaced it with the event. Video technology was involved in this becoming. By deterritorializing subsequent flows, digital technologies push and encourage us toward a knowledge, thought, and action of the event and situations, a knowledge and action of assemblages and multiplicity—a knowledge and action in which consciousness is devalued, in which it is no longer the highest element of the human but rather a form of communication. It was always within the limits of our perception, starting from the impossibility of consciousness to see beyond divisible space and time—and therefore the impossibility of seeing other temporalities—that the concepts of action and actor have been constructed.[19]

Lazzarato ends his book citing Walter Benjamin, stating that 'in order to construct a "new barbarism," we have to first testify to our relative poverty of experience within the new conditions of capital'.[20] News barbarians need to rise up. Deleuze and Guattari discuss the barbarian in relation to the nomad. The nomad crosses any border continuously and freely, and with the nomad, now, today comes a non-thing: online video, a language, a signal, a system. It is something we are living with,[21] and it is something, a memory technology, which has gained its own autobiography.[22]

Conjunctures, Theory on Demand #31, Amsterdam, Institute of Network Cultures, 2019. In a crude variation, relevant here for the Video Vortex context, we could pose: Platforms Do Not Exist.

18   Trine Bjørkmann Berry, Videoblogging Before YouTube, Theory on Demand #27, Amsterdam, Institute of Network Cultures, 2019.

19   Maurizio Lazzarato, *Videophilosophy: The Perception of Time in Post-Fordism*, New York: Columbia University Press, 2019, p. 162.

20   Ibid. p. 223.

21   Andreas Treske, *The Inner Life of Video Spheres*, Amsterdam: Institute of Network Cultures, 2013.

22   Ina Blom, *The Autobiography of Video: The Life and Times of a Memory Technology*, New York: Sternberg Press, 2016.

The transformation of the functions of art, widely anticipated by video and further expressed by digital technologies, is summed up in Guattari's formula, which states that art should not only tell stories but create apparatuses in which the story can exist. Aesthetic practices thus become highly productive, as verified in the information economy, because here too the distinctions between art and life, between art and work, tend to lose their unilateral character, as Benjamin had announced. Therefore, we end as we began, hoping for the emergence of a new type of barbarism in which power-time opens an incommensurable field of action with the time that has been lost.[23]

In *The Social Photo*, Nathan Jurgenson discusses the merits of 'social video', a term that accurately describes that digital file is never a monad, always deeply relational, linked in a machinic algorithmic kinship with similar digital entities, both human and non-human. According to Jurgenson, stillness is more informative and documentary in nature. 'For viewers, the photograph affords a sense of total control over the small slice of the visual reality it depicts. Video, by contrast, has limitations that stem from more closely mimicking how experience unfolds. In this way, the photo suggests the knowing; the video, observing'.[24] Despite its differences, much of what Jurgenson writes about the social photo can be applied to online video in that they appear quick, cheap and abundant. We agree that social video should be described as a cultural practice, yet the real challenge here is not YouTube culture but to generate a 21st century social theory that is fully compatible with software-assisted video. The poverty of sociology over the past decade is taking a toll. These days, the social is technical and not merely a factor that the remainders of the welfare state are administrating. The 'social' in 'social video' beyond the control phantasms of the big data/AI regimes?

With Jurgenson, we can note that social video has become something lighter and more immediate. Thinking of the 50 years journey from the Sony Portapak to the 4K smartphone and the 50 shades of mobile video, all of them assisting us on the run, all of them deeply private and public in their own ways, from Betacam, VHS, digital camcorders to today's pocket cameras.

According to Jurgenson, today's acceleration is such that the immediacy transcends the journey: 'it is not rapid transit but rather an always imminent closeness. The locomotive is the symbol of mechanical speed, the struggle to overcome distance. Digital connection, on the other hand, transcends space. The train wins a battle against space that digital connection does not have to fight'.[25] In this line, Jurgenson qualifies social video, first and foremost, as an experience (in contrast with art, information, or documentation). The aim of social video is, then 'to experience something not representable as an image but instead as a social process: an appreciation of impermanence for its own sake'.[26]

23 Lazzarato, p. 226.
24 Nathan Jurgenson, *The Social Photo: On Photography and Social Media*, New York: Verso, 2019, p. 113.
25 Ibid, p. 22.
26 Ibid, p. 50.

The canonical text on online video has not yet been written, but with the Video Vortex network, bits and pieces have — and are being — aggregated to construct a set of tools to help reflect on practices in a perpetually-evolving sphere. The latest conference of the Video Vortex Network in rejecting universalism emphasized contributions addressing the use of video in activism and political mobilization, artistic practices, technological developments. The 11th conference and exhibition in Kochi, India, reflected on the global South and the existence of video across the uneven conditions of 'other' video cultures. Video Vortex XII, back at Europe's border in Malta, focused particularly on art and aesthetics, brought to the foreground in geopolitics, AI, and online video cultures on social media platforms. Still, many of the questions formulated for the announcements from Video Vortex IX in Lüneburg, Germany, echo and call for further exploration:

> What is underlying aesthetics and what are the specific interface contexts? What are the new possibilities of collaborative production? Does the future of film museums and cinematheques lie in online cinematic databases? What are the existing cinematographic visions of the future of the moving image in public space? What are the standards and alternatives for sharing, licensing and hosting moving images on the Web? How does moving image production relate to cultural, technological and political dominance? Have amateur and professional video grown closer further erasing the ability to distinguish between distinct visual tropes and operating within similar economic arenas, or are they still in competition? Furthermore, how do mechanisms of monetization on many video platforms effect the collision between professional and amateur content and its creation? What techniques aesthetics, genres, structures and practices exist in the realms of amateur and professional online video creation, and where through the maze of the internet are unique forms and practices emerging? Do specific interfaces privilege specific forms of content and practices? What could new methodologies and epistemologies for the unfolding video-grammars in the global videodrome look like?[27]

With the contributions in this reader, we continue to respond to the broad, emerging and urgent topics, from YouTube bias algorithms to TikTok, the role of Netflix, the use of video in messaging, the politics of conservation, the rise of deep fakes, synthetic intimacies, ISIS videos, but also indy servers, censorship, geo-blocking and the invisible 'moderation' factories, as well as discussing amazing artist videos and the role of influencers and their silly nihilist routines. Please note our love and sadness while watching video on the run, our passion for online video theory in the bitter age of platform capitalism, but also video as online activism and the rise and rise of streaming... Klick, browse, swipe, like, share, save and enjoy!

---

27   Post-Media Lab, 'Video Vortex #9: video re:assemblies', *Mute*, 31 May 2012.
      https://www.metamute.org/editorial/lab/video-vortex-9-video-reassemblies

References

Anders, Günther. The World as Phantom and as Matrix, http://marcuse.faculty.history.ucsb.edu/projects/anders/Anders1956DissentWorldPhantomAndMatrixOCR.pdf.

Azar, Mitra. 'From Selfie to Algorithmic Facial Image', *Video Vortex XII*, Malta, 28 September 2019, https://networkcultures.org/videovortex/wp-content/uploads/sites/8/2019/09/Final-Video-Vortex-Program.pdf.

Bjørkmann Berry, Trine. *Videoblogging Before YouTube*, Theory on Demand #27, Amsterdam: Institute of Network Cultures, 2019.

Blom, Ina. *The Autobiography of Video: The Life and Times of a Memory Technology*, New York: Sternberg Press, 2016.

Cubitt, Sean. *Videography: Video Media as Art and Culture*, London: Palgrave Macmillan, 1993.

Della Ratta, Donatella. *Shooting a Revolution*, London: Pluto Press, 2018.

Elsaesser, Thomas. ''Constructive Instability', or: The Life of Things as the Cinema's Afterlife?', in Geert Lovink and Sabine Niederer (eds), *Video Vortex Reader: Responses to YouTube*, Amsterdam: Institute of Network Cultures, 2008, pp. 13–32.

Fugelberg, Jeremy. 'An Abandoned Cinema in the Egyptian Desert Where the Only Show is Sunset', *Atlas Obscura*, 26 March 2014, https://www.atlasobscura.com/articles/sinai-peninsula-abandoned-theatre.

Funcke, Bettina and Peter Sloterdijk, 'Against Gravity: Bettina Funcke Talks with Peter Sloterdijk', *Bookforum*, February/March 2005, https://www.bookforum.com/archive/feb_05/funcke.html, retrieved at http://dev.autonomedia.org/node/4584.

Greenberger, Alex. ''Is Shakespeare Fake News?': Artist Hito Steyerl Ponders Tough Questions in an Interview About Experimental Filmmaker Harun Farocki', *ARTnews*, 6 February 2020, https://www.artnews.com/art-news/artists/hito-steyerl-harun-farocki-thaddaeus-ropac-interview-1202677179/.

Heidenreich, Stefan. 'Vision Possible: A Methodological Quest for Online Video', in Geert Lovink and Rachel Somers Miles (eds), *Video Vortex Reader II: moving images beyond YouTube*, Amsterdam: Institute of Network Cultures, Amsterdam, 2011, pp. 13–24.

Jurgenson, Nathan. *The Social Photo: On Photography and Social Media*, New York: Verso, 2019.

Larrue, Jean-Marc and Marcello Vitali-Rosati. *Media Do Not Exist: Performativity and Mediating Conjunctures*, Theory on Demand #31, Amsterdam, Institute of Network Cultures, 2019.

Lazzarato, Maurizio. *Videophilosophy: The Perception of Time in Post-Fordism*, New York: Columbia University Press, 2019.

Manovich, Lev. *The Language of New Media*, Cambridge, MA: MIT Press, 2001.

Mirzoeff, Nicholas. *How to See the World: An Introduction to Images, from Self-Portraits to Selfies, Maps to Movies, and More*, New York: Basic Books, 2016.

Neves, Joshua. 'Video Theory', from *Video Vortex IX*, Leuphana, 1 March 2013, https://vimeo.com/66055799.

Post-Media Lab, 'Video Vortex #9: video re:assemblies', *Mute*, 31 May 2012, https://www.metamute.org/editorial/lab/video-vortex-9-video-reassemblies.

Rubinstein Daniel and Katrina Sluis. Notes on the Margins of Metadata; Concerning the Undecidability of the Digital Image, *Photographies* 6.1 (2013): 151-158.

Steyerl, Hito. 'Proxy Politics: Signal and Noise', *e-flux Journal* 60 (2014), https://www.e-flux.com/journal/60/61045/proxy-politics-signal-and-noise/.

Treske, Andreas. *The Inner Life of Video Spheres*, Amsterdam: Institute of Network Cultures, 2013.

VIDEO VORTEX AND THE PROMISE AND PERILS OF ONLINE VIDEO ART

GEERT LOVINK
AND SABINE NIEDERER

VIDEO VORTEX AND THE PROMISE AND PERILS OF ONLINE VIDEO ART[1]

GEERT LOVINK & SABINE NIEDERER

How can we study online video? In 2005, we had recently launched the Institute of Network Cultures, a research group at the Amsterdam University of Applied Sciences. Shortly after, as online video emerged, students began approaching us to borrow books about YouTube. It is easy to make fun of such a demand for instant theory, but the question was—and still is—a legitimate one: Is it possible to develop a critical analysis of current developments as they unfold? Inspired by these students and dismayed with the dominance of starry-eyed rhetoric that seemed to be in awe of high uploads and rapid technological change, we decided to start organizing serious research. Despite its non-existence in the official reality of museum spaces, cultural policies, media regulations, education and academic research, we were confident that online video would take over the world.

With the launch of Vimeo (in 2004) and YouTube (in 2005) just behind us, we wanted to join this history-in-the-making and participate in the development of this technological field through artistic, activist and critical practices. Together with Melbourne-based artist Seth Keen we launched the Video Vortex project in late 2006. Since then, Video Vortex has become a lively research network of artists, activists, coders, curators, scholars and critics convening in conferences in Brussels (October 2007), Amsterdam (January 2008), Ankara (October 2008), Split (May 2009), Brussels a second time (November 2009), Amsterdam (March 2011), Yogyakarta (July 2011), Zagreb (May 2012), Lüneburg (February 2013), Istanbul (September 2014), Kochi (February 2017) and Malta (September 2019). The network has produced three anthologies (including this one), a website, a mailing list, and several exhibitions, with more to come as internet and video continue to merge.

Prehistories of online video

Online video is frequently understood as something new and unprecedented, only emerging in the 2000s. But this medium always comprised a multitude of prehistories, historical forerunners that have yet to be adequately unpacked. One potential history would examine how online video challenged the art institution and the archive. As media players became embedded into web browsers, video was suddenly liberated from the material constraints of the VHS tape and the DVD disc, initiating a shift in distribution with profound implications for accessibility and the democratization of media. A second historical thread could take this one step further by investigating dedicated online media players such as RealPlayer, Flash, and VLC. As the YouTube behemoth engulfed the web, allowing anyone to embed video into her personal or professional homepage, these online media

---

1   Previously published here: Geert Lovink & Sabine Niederer, Video Vortex and the Promise and the Perils of Online Video Art, in: Sanneke Huisman & Magda van Mechelen (ed.), A Critical History of Media Art in the Netherlands, Jap Sam Books, Prinsenbeek, 2019, p. 333-341.

players became obsolete, fading into the media ether. A third history might deal with the tradition of video and its potential to intervene in mass media television. From international performances by Nam June Paik to local Dutch public access video art infrastructures like Salto, Park 4DTV, and Deep Dish, this historical perspective would consider the rise of YouTube in tandem with the looming death of cable television. A fourth historical angle might zoom in on video as a tool for documenting live events. Here we might reexamine the collections of Montevideo and Time Based Arts for video registrations of happenings and performances from the 1970s. Interestingly, these videos, due to their long duration, did not work on early versions of YouTube. Today, we see live performances like events or concerts documented or sometimes live-streamed through Periscope or Facebook, and then chopped into short clips and shared online. Such documentation provides 'coverage' of an event while deeply altering our sense of duration and 'liveness'. A fifth genealogy could consider the network ('social') aspect around video art, acknowledging that online video is situated in a broader terrain of other practices such as experimental film, documentary filmmaking, new media art, electronic art, and net.art. Each of these 'disciplines', loosely understood, fosters its own space of collective creativity—its own codes, customs, and techniques of medium-specific audiovisual experimentation. In this realm, net.art can be considered the more conceptual, often abstract and online strand, whereas media art functions as a broader, catch-all category comprising audiovisual art installations and experiments in sound, image and performance. In the current 'post-digital' era, a return to materiality brings the digital back to the tangible installation. In retrospect, we may ask how the aesthetics of the medium have changed with the advent of new technological formats, platforms, and audiences. Yet even as online video strives to slough off these older formats, it constantly comments on them and refers back to them. The question then becomes: How can we do away with this rearview mirror and develop medium-specific concepts when the development of online video is inextricably bound up with these other media?

After years of chatter about 'digital convergence' and 'cross-media platforms', it was only in 2006 that we actually began to witness the merger of internet and television at a spectacular pace. Darting from the desktop to the tablet, from the mobile phone to the urban screen, the speed with which moving images were created and then shared across the internet has become rapid and unrelenting, creating a media condition within society that seems as omnipotent as it is omnipresent. In those innocent early days of online video, Video Vortex saw a tremendous potential for the democratization of media. Video art had previously been confined to the white cube of the gallery—stamped, certified and curated by the art world. Far from simply being an example of online 'fan culture' described by academic Web 2.0 pundits like Henry Jenkins and Jeff Jarvis, this new openness and accessibility was a potentially revolutionary shift in the production and distribution of video art. Yet the revolution was never realized. Over a decade into the history of this new medium, the opening up of video art still has not transpired. Instead, we notice a schism: on the one hand, we have the audiovisual-art-that-makes-it-into-the-museum; on the other, we have mainstream online video culture. In the place of openness, we have a gap that is constantly policed: high culture and 'low', the gallery and the browser, the artists and the rest of us.

Critical online video research

So if online video has enormous potential, it is yet unrealized. In the Video Vortex network, we ask ourselves questions such as: What platform-specific concepts can capture the aesthetic, political and cultural aspects of online video? How can we surpass or redirect the recommendation economy and its algorithms? Why do people 'Like' certain videos and why do others remain unseen? What role do users play in the realm of online video, whether through uploading, recommending, commenting or tagging? Our goal has always been to critically and systematically develop the work produced during the conferences. Driven by this vision, the 'organized network' produced three Video Vortex anthologies, in 2008, 2011 and 2020, while also contributing to projects such as *The YouTube Reader* edited by Pelle Snickars and Patrick Vonderau.[2]

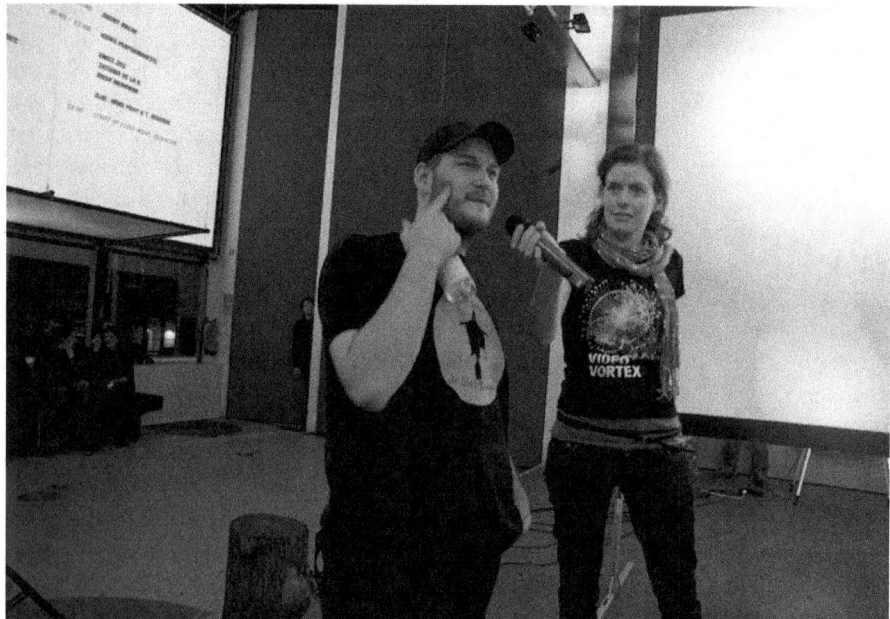

Fig. 1: Interview with Emile Zile. Video Vortex #2, Amsterdam (2008). Photo by Rosa Menkman

Video Vortex research stresses the particularities of the platform. One might recall, for example, that YouTube originally limited uploaded videos to lengths of 3 minutes or less. It was this early technical limitation, rather than user preference, which led to the bite-sized, ephemeral video associated with the platform today. Or consider the 'channel', a feature that allows users to create their own collections, but also significantly reconfigures how

---

2   See Geert Lovink and Sabine Niederer (eds), *Video Vortex Reader: Responses to YouTube*, INC Readers #4, Amsterdam: Institute of Network Cultures, 2008; Geert Lovink and Rachel Somers Miles (eds), *Video Vortex Reader II: Moving Images beyond YouTube*, INC Reader #6, Amsterdam: Institute of Network Cultures, 2011; Pelle Snickars and Patrick Vonderau, *The YouTube Reader*, Stockholm: National Library of Sweden, 2009.

online video is packaged, curated and consumed. The rise of the database as the dominant form of storing and accessing cultural artifacts also has a rich tradition that needs further exploration. Alongside these conditions that shape production and consumption, video platforms also have lesser known, more-or-less automated restraints. What is the role of filtering bots, the invisible army of cleaners, or the self-regulatory model also known as 'user-generated censorship'? How can a theory of filtering and flagging take shape like the one presciently introduced by Minke Kampman back in 2009?[3] While YouTube established its reputation by encouraging users to 'share' freely, it now intervenes more and more. Recently it has become very strict about nudity and copyrighted material. Soon it will begin organizing content around curated channels, aiming to compete with streaming services such as Netflix, Hulu, Amazon's Prime Video or Apple's iTunes. As a platform for artists, film and video professionals and researchers, Video Vortex responded to this emerging field with themes like aesthetics, media activism, platform alternatives, video as social practice, and heritage. In the space that remains of this essay, we'll touch on three themes—presentation, distribution and curation—concluding by highlighting some ways forward for the study and conceptualization of online video.

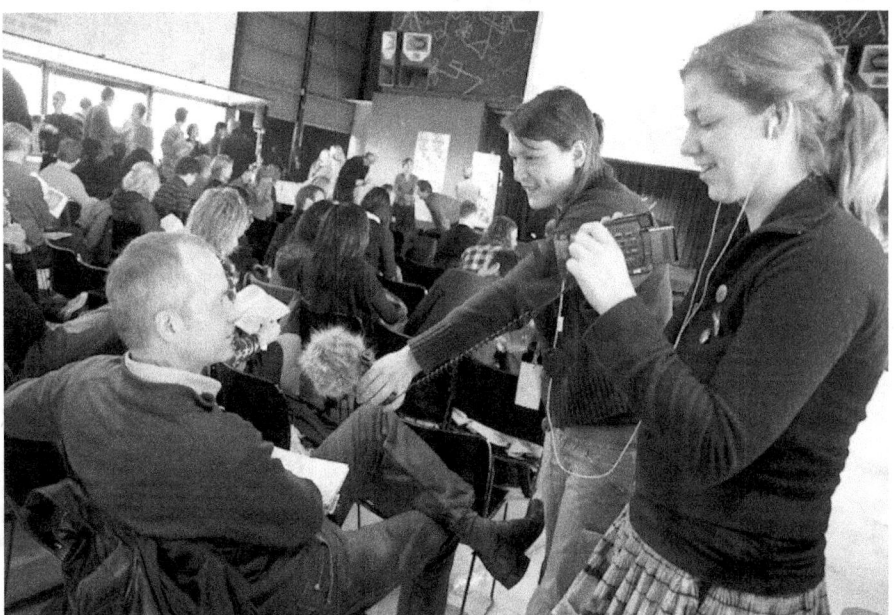

Fig. 2: Videoblogging. Video Vortex #2, Amsterdam (2008). Photo by Rosa Menkman

First, presentation. Tapping, swiping, staring at YouTube, what do you see? Is there a homogeneous style that mainly builds on eyewitness TV, candid camera formats and webcam diaries? Have we already forgotten how YouTube professionalized its producers

---

3   Minke Kampman, *YouParticipate: The politics of the YouTube flagging system*, MA thesis, University of
      Amsterdam: Amsterdam, 2009, http://scriptiesonline.uba.uva.nl/document/147177.

by creating channels back in 2013, thereby creating the new sociological figure of the 'influencer'? And now that music videos and commercials increasingly resemble video art, can we define how artistic practices influence the look of online footage? Is YouTube an artistic medium in itself, or is it merely used as a (self) promotional device? Video production is no longer the rare privilege of a handful of artists that managed to get access to expensive video gear and professional editing suites. Think of Snapchat, the use of video inside WhatsApp, and Instagram stories and their influence on our aesthetic vernacular—a now ubiquitous visual language of selfies, point-and-shoot, and point-of-view. Alongside this phone-centric perspective is the rise of drone aesthetics and the after-movie. Digital image manipulation has gone mainstream.

This mass uptake of video experimentation ultimately leads to a liberation of reality. With the increase of computational power, 5G wireless networks, 4K cameras and seemingly limitless cloud-based storage, a video is no longer merely a documentation tool for communication purposes. Veracity is in the eye of the beholder; authenticity in the age digital media has been thoroughly undermined. Think of artist responses such as Mark Leckey's YouTube-based *Proposal for a show* (2010) or Richard Grayson's *Posessions_inc* (2016-2018), which surpass reality through absurdist dummies, tangible objects and ranting puppets. These artists are not recreating reality, but instead present alienating material objects with a mind of their own.[4] Given these conditions, a reality watermark or a team of factcheckers are not the answer. Deep fake is here to stay.

If these are the aesthetic techniques and treatments available to video creators today, how might they be taken up by art practices? These issues are important for both users and art professionals and are an extension of the worlds of video art and documentary filmmaking which have seen a progression from analog to digital as well as from VHS to DVD to online distribution. What aesthetic strategies do artists like Natalie Bookchin and Perry Bardemploy when integrating the 'video of the crowds' into their work?[5] Their question is strategic: how can user-generated content transcend the individualized level of the remixing citizen who re-appropriates culture, and how can we make sense of it as a co-created but still coherent artwork? Bookchin's 2009 gallery installation/Vimeo work *Mass Ornament*, for example, uses the database aspect of online video canonically. We see teenagers who have turned their homes into theaters, dancing alone but together. These solo acts, self-portraits that are exhibitionist in nature and processed by the digital craft of the artist, thus become part of a collective statement. If we agree that all such artworks are collaborative, multi-authored efforts, how can they transmit a unique style and message? And how might we formulate a web-specific theory of such online aesthetics?

---

4   For a discussion of Leckey's work on YouTube and other examples of (online) video art that comments on digital culture phenomena see Sabine Niederer and Raymond Taudin Chabot. 'Deconstructing the Cloud: Responses to Big Data Phenomena from Social sciences, Humanities and the Arts', *Big Data & Society*, 2.2 (2015).
5   See Natalie Bookchin's works *trip* (2008), *Mass Ornament* (2009), and *Testament* (2008–2017) (http://bookchin.net/projects.html); also see Perry Bard's global remake of Dziga Vertov's *Man with a Movie Camera* from 1929 (http://dziga.perrybard.net/).

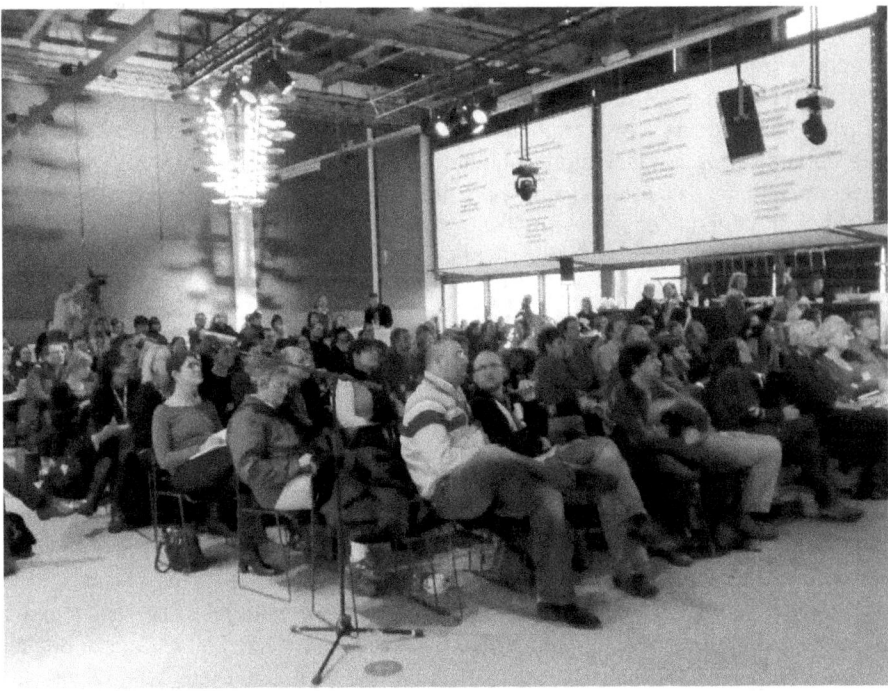

Fig. 3: Audience. Video Vortex #2, Amsterdam (2008). Photo by Rosa Menkman

For artists, online video enables new aesthetics, but also foregrounds new issues. In the late 1970s, as unions disintegrated and social movements proliferated, UK socialist feminists Sheila Rowbotham, Lynne Segal, and Hilary Wainwright back in 1979 issued a new rallying cry, urging us to go 'beyond the fragments.'[6] The same demand has now arrived in the context of digital culture. How can a patchwork of dispersed videos be transformed and synchronized into a lucid work of art? How can a multitude of individualized expressions be brought together into a coherent image? We could ask the same questions of Lev Manovich's cultural analytics.[7] Can a multiplicity of cultural artifacts viewed as data express the unity and Zeitgeist of art? How can we balance the individual voices with the general outcomes that are processed? Is there a place for anomaly, outliers and the casual witness? At what point does complexity unravel into an incoherent mess?

Secondly, distribution. This theme investigates developments in the field of open source software in creating alternatives to proprietary software such as media players. From 16mm film and video to the internet and back, artists have always used moving images

6   Sheila Rowbotham, Lynne Segal, and Hilary Wainwright. *Beyond the Fragments: Feminism and the Making of Socialism.* London: Merlin Press, 1979.
7   Lev Manovich, 'Cultural Analytics.' *Software Studies Initiative* (blog), September 2008, http://lab. softwarestudies.com/2008/09/cultural-analytics.html.

to produce critical and innovative work. The default device for producing moving images is now the smartphone. Can there ever be a free software video camera? Think of the 'change is in our hand' Fairphone, which, like any smartphone, has a 12MP CMOS sensor dual flash built-in camera.[8] When will we have user-friendly open source video editing software installed on each smartphone? If information wants to be free, it also wants the appropriate software architectures and hardware infrastructures. For years, users and programmers have envisioned a truly distributed network, one realized by alternative software and open licenses. Here, it was imagined, content might finally float freely, decoupled from the dictates of centralized servers and the nasty legalese of corporate license agreements. What happened to such promises?

Thirdly, curation. How do curators respond to the new conditions that YouTube brings, apart from using it as a private research tool? With unlimited uploads and a massive audience, online video platforms seem to provide the ideal artist portfolio. But why don't video artists and filmmakers occupy YouTube? In fact, in some respects, we see video platforms moving away from the arts. Video art and online video have become separate worlds. We might find high-production video installations on display and gallery spaces dedicated to post-digital art and pushing the boundaries of photography and film, but where is the social embedding and aesthetics? In 2016, the first-ever YouTube exhibition was organized in Beeld en Geluid in Hilversum, entitled *Let's YouTube*.[9] For nine months, all aspects of YouTube were covered in monthly themes: Your Life, Games, Music, Beauty & Fashion, Journalism/Opinion, Food, DIY, Entertainment, and the Future. Why is the museum so absent in the current situation? If we want to overcome this classic high-low divide, we'll have to reassess the relevance of the network and open spaces for experiments, in galleries, at festivals, support collectives and other forms of the image commons.

If the art world and online video are estranged, curating has nevertheless become a buzzword, a vital skill in the age of information overload. However, the gallery curator and the platform curator appear to be two distinct roles, with zero overlap. For YouTube and its online video siblings, the consensus is that the role of curators in the 'collaborative filtering' process is key. But where are the star curators specialized in the aesthetics and culture of online video? What's the role of online video in curatorial programs and education at-large in art academies, apart from being a de facto tool for hosting images that struggle to draw attention? And how can we incorporate the social aspects of online video back into this art education realm? These days, online video is all about being social—the more 'Likes', comments, and followers, the better. If there is no feedback, there is no right to exist. Social embedding of the video clip is the *a priori*. Without 'Likes', no one sees it. Literally. Can we as a network of artists, makers, and theorists put forward an interesting alternative to the dominant logic of the influencer?

---

8   Fairphone, https://shop.fairphone.com/en/.
9   Instituut voor Beeld en Geluid, 'Let's YouTube',
       https://www.beeldengeluid.nl/bezoek/agenda/lets-youtube.

While curation is now acknowledged as key, it can rapidly slide into censorship. The pictorial turn still has the internet in its grip. But instead of the innocent, funny 'user-generated content' we know from its early days, we're confronted with content that reflects the growing tensions in society. Comments have become a playground for trolls, with popular channels such as PewDiePe putting out content that is not consistent with what YouTube wants to be.[10] At some point, this flood of content must become unmanageable. We may soon reach the limits of popular online culture. After all, video is no longer the medium of a handful of vloggers. In 2018 there were 2000+ YouTube channels with one million or more followers. How does one even begin to summarize such content flows?[11] Automated controls are dialed up; content gets filtered, shaped, or erased before it is ever seen. As a result, YouTube might become less social. The 'open' platform becomes a walled garden with powerful editors. Such a scenario could be highly profitable for YouTube (and therefore Google). The formula becomes simple: more viewers, watching more videos = more ad revenue. Elite channels with high production values will certainly get a boost; niche online video communities might be left in the cold. But would this shift to more centralized control also lead to a new underground of online art practices?

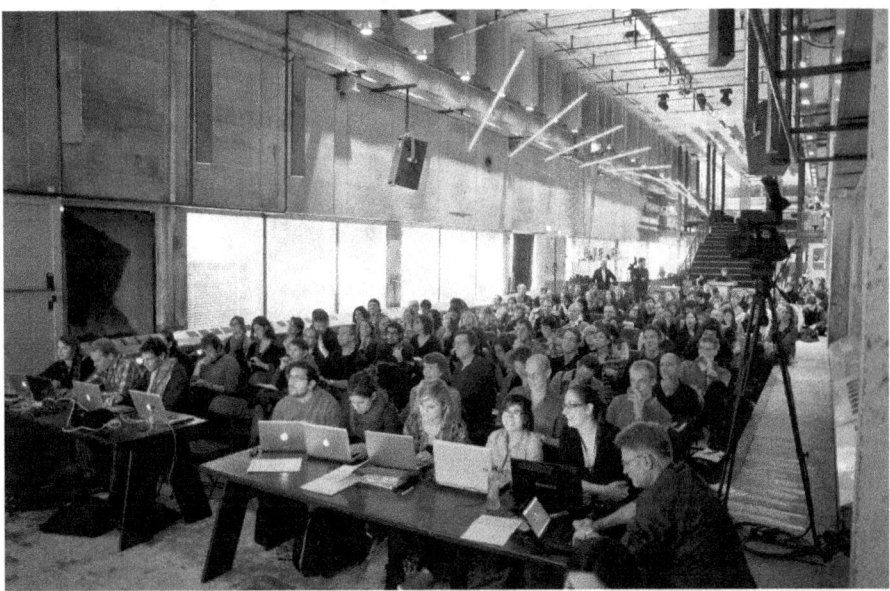

Fig. 4: Audience. Video Vortex #6, Amsterdam (2011). Photo by Anne Helmond

---

10   Rajiv Rao, 'PewDiePie versus T-Series silliness reveals battle for the soul of YouTube', *ZD.net*, 28 December 2018, https://www.zdnet.com/google-amp/article/pewdiepie-versus-t-series-silliness-reveals-battle-for-the-soul-of-youtube/.

11   Like 2018's 'YouTube Rewind' video controversy, which became the platform's most-disliked video of all time. See Todd Spangler, 2018. 'YouTube Rewind 2018 Officially Becomes Most-Disliked Video Ever', *Variety*, 13 December 2018, https://variety.com/2018/digital/news/youtube-rewind-2018-most-disliked-video-ever-1203088810/#!.

Countering platform economies

The internet itself will not absorb this inevitable shift from the model of YouTube to that of Netflix. The perception of what an internet 'professional' is will revert (back) to those capable of producing high-end television and film. Artists who choose to experiment with other visual languages and technologies risk becoming excluded. Galleries, art spaces, and festivals are the vanguards of visual experimentation. Where is the critical content going to be produced to feed these places?

To conclude, then, we urgently need to establish new places and communities for audiovisual experimentation. It was in this spirit that we celebrated online video culture at the Video Vortex II video slamming evening, with a collaboratively curated playlist modeled after Dagan Cohen's *Upload Cinema*.[12] Many of those videos have now been taken offline, but what remains is the inspiration to get together and develop alternative celebrations that surpass this limiting platform logic. YouTube should not be given free rein to dictate the future of a medium that is influential at so many levels—artistically, politically and culturally. If you are an artist, a curator, a researcher, a student who wants to do experiments, we urge you to come together with others. Connect, organize, and create infrastructures aimed at autonomous revenue streams. Claim the image commons in the post-digital era. Let's create and collaborate, collectively exploring the endless possibilities of online video. Bring your own beamer.

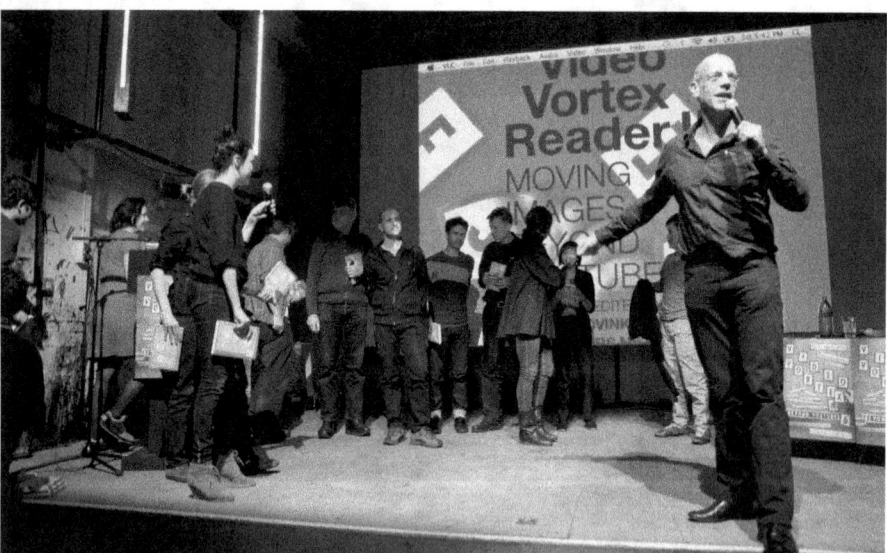

Fig. 5: Book Launch: Video Vortex Reader 2. Video Vortex #6, Amsterdam (2011). Photo by Anne Helmond

---

12   Dagan Cohen, 'Wat is Upload Cinema', *Upload Cinema*, http://uploadcinema.nl/press/64/upload-cinema-how-to-dagan-cohen.

References

Bard, Perry. http://dziga.perrybard.net/.

Berry, Trine Bjørkmann. *Videoblogging Before YouTube*, Amsterdam: Institute of Network Cultures, 2018.

Bookchin, Natalie. http://bookchin.net/projects.html.

Burgess, Jean, and Joshua Green. *YouTube: Online Video and Participatory Culture*, Cambridge: Polity Press, 2018.

Campanelli, Vito. *Web Aesthetics: How Digital Media Affect Culture and Society*, Rotterdam: NAi Publishers and Amsterdam: Institute of Network Cultures, 2010.

Cohen, Dagan. 'Wat is Upload Cinema', *Upload Cinema*, http://uploadcinema.nl/press/64/upload-cinema-how-to-dagan-cohen.

Fairphone. https://shop.fairphone.com/en/.

Flusser, Vilém. *Ins Universum der technischen Bilder*. Göttingen: European Photography, 1985.

Grayson, Richard. 'Possessions_inc', *Matts Gallery*, 2016, https://possessions-inc.mattsgallery.org/.

Institute of Network Cultures. 'About', *Video Vortex*, http://networkcultures.org/wpmu/videovortex/about.

Instituut voor Beeld en Geluid. 'Let's YouTube', https://www.beeldengeluid.nl/bezoek/agenda/lets-youtube.

Kampman, Minke. *YouParticipate: The politics of the YouTube flagging system*, MA thesis, University of Amsterdam: Amsterdam, 2009, http://scriptiesonline.uba.uva.nl/document/147177.

Leckey, Mark. 'Prop4aShw', 1 June 2013, YouTube video, https://www.youtube.com/watch?v=v5XCscE-CpAo.

Lovink, Geert. *Networks Without a Cause: A Critique of Social Media*. Cambridge: Polity Press, 2011.

Lovink, Geert, and Sabine Niederer (eds.) *Video Vortex Reader: Responses to YouTube*, INC Readers #4, Amsterdam: Institute of Network Cultures, 2008.

Lovink, Geert, and Rachel Somers Miles (eds.) *Video Vortex Reader II: Moving Images beyond YouTube*, INC Reader #6, Amsterdam: Institute of Network Cultures, 2011.

Manovich, Lev. 'Cultural Analytics', *Software Studies Initiative* (blog), September 2008, http://lab.softwarestudies.com/2008/09/cultural-analytics.html.

Niederer, Sabine and Raymond Taudin Chabot. 'Deconstructing the Cloud: Responses to Big Data Phenomena from Social sciences, Humanities and the Arts', *Big Data & Society*, 2.2 (December, 2015).

Rao, Rajiv. 'PewDiePie versus T-Series silliness reveals battle for the soul of YouTube', *ZD.net*, 28 December 2018, https://www.zdnet.com/google-amp/article/pewdiepie-versus-t-series-silliness-reveals-battle-for-the-soul-of-youtube/.

Rowbotham, Sheila, Lynne Segal, and Hilary Wainwright. *Beyond the Fragments: Feminism and the Making of Socialism*. London: Merlin Press, 1979.

Snickars, Pelle, and Patrick Vonderau. *The YouTube Reader*, Stockholm: National Library of Sweden, 2009.

Spangler, Todd. 2018. 'YouTube Rewind 2018 Officially Becomes Most-Disliked Video Ever', *Variety*, 13 December 2018, https://variety.com/2018/digital/news/youtube-rewind-2018-most-disliked-video-ever-1203088810/#!.

Treske, Andreas. *Video Theory: Online Video Aesthetics or the Afterlife of Video*. Bielefeld: Transcript Verlag, 2015.

NOTES TOWARD A GENERAL INFINITY OF DIGITAL IMAGES

RAHEE PUNYASHLOKA

NOTES TOWARD A GENERAL INFINITY OF DIGITAL IMAGES

RAHEE PUNYASHLOKA

I.

It would not be too hyperbolic to suggest that all of the history and *techne* [but especially the metaphysics] of the image that has governed the human civilization can be encapsulated by a single idea: a frame put upon varying densities of *swirls, waves,* and *movements*; so as to simultaneously capture the everything and nothing, the sum of all parts and the smallest part itself: the infinite and the infinitesimal. While it is ubiquitously present, the metaphysical preponderance on this particular idea of 'capturing infinity within a frame' moves in and out of the foreground, emerging with various artistic *schools* [such as the works of Bosch, the many intersecting planes and frames of Raphael's frescoes, pointillism, Malevich, the entire history of abstract expressionism *et al*] and receding with the next. Several contingent factors have led to the emergence of this 'question concerning the infinite' in our current modernity, yet again, with a near total disruption/destruction of the figurative/figural in lieu of the abstract; the abstract which organizes itself in space in (seemingly) hitherto unimaginable ways, so as to make us directly confront the infinite.

The several possible reasons for the foregrounding of this 'question concerning infinity' within our collective psyches have been demonstrated by many historians, philosophers, and theorists in one way or another: diagnosed by most as some form of 'crisis of modernity' that we suddenly are forced to confront: the emergence of mediatized realities and cybernetic actualization of 'too much data': an 'archive fever' if you will, of the most infinite kind.

While the puzzle pieces regarding the infinite vis-a-vis the image have been laid out with considerable force and elaboration, my thesis is that there is one indispensible piece that is yet to be fully *placed, i.e., the emergence of the digital*

When I speak of 'the emergence of the digital' into the image, I do not mean to merely suggest what seems like a commonsensical — yet not necessarily untrue — fact today: that there is a proliferation of 'the digital' in the image (as with everything else, as part of our move toward a 'digital society') in our contemporary times. What I mean to suggest is that 'the question concerning infinity' within the image, in its very being, is incontrovertibly tied to the idea of the digital; and what we see today is but a logical accumulation of both 'the infinity question' as well as 'the digital' in a process that is simultaneous and correlative, with one *causing* the other, and both of them operating in an ourobouros like structure; as a dyad.

Thus, the predominance of the digital in the image — as the final iteration of research into 'the digital' in the long twentieth century[1] — is not a phenomenon unique to our current modernity, even though the 'digital image' gets actualized as part of it for the first time. It is but the latest re-iteration of the dyad mentioned above: whenever there is an emergence of the question concerning infinity within the history of the image, there is a simultaneous emergence of the digital lurking besides it.

It is indeed possible, and maybe even necessary to conduct a thorough research elsewhere so as to demonstrate how this dyad exists and *coincides* at each moment in the history of the image when one (i.e. the digital) or the other (i.e. the infinite) *becomes* an issue.

[Perhaps this can be abstracted further, beyond our immediate preoccupation with the image, to show a metaphysical contiguity of 'the digital' and 'the infinite' and develop a more concrete philosophical idiom elsewhere]

But, *naturally,* we shall have to do so in a roundabout manner, only after a definition of 'the digital image' has been reached.

II.

[As part of my 'artist's talk' in Video Vortex XI, I tried to open up an investigation into what could be the definition of a 'digital image' while also simultaneously providing an overview of my own practice-based foray into similar questions through a series of works that I call *Noise Reduction*. The next couple of sections are a summary recap of the same. (To this effect, they ought to be seen as coupled together, rather than one being an extension or effect of the other, or vice-versa)]

In order to investigate what 'the digital image' could be, first we need to arbitrarily latch on to a semblance of a fixed idea as to what an image itself is. But it would seem that we are stumped at the very outset, as 'what is an image' and 'what is the essence of an image' has indeed been a complex philosophical problem for several centuries, with a recorded inception in Western philosophical tradition toward the end of the Greek civilization and before the Roman empire and Christianity[2], inevitably yielding several interpretations. Given this very complex and various philosophical history of the image, means that we cannot stick to a single authoritative definition regarding the same. However, in order to make a minimal attempt toward an understanding of the idea of an image, we could start with the most immediately accessible that is present at hand to us-i.e. the dictionary definition of 'image'-and work backwards therefrom. The term 'image' is originally seen as coming from the Latin *imāgō,* which is in turn from Proto-Italic *imā* + *-gō*, from Proto-Indo-European *$h_2$eym*-('to imitate'). The several meanings that are ascribed to this originary

---

1   As we very well know, digital image processing occurs only after all other aspects of research into the digital had been exhausted, be it computational, mathematical, musical, or otherwise.

2   i.e. in the works of the late Greek atomists and following them, Lucretius, who provides the earliest 'definition' of what an image is in his On the Nature of Things.

'form' of the term 'image' include an imitation, a likeness, a representation, a statue, a picture, a mirroring, semblance, apparition, shadow, echo, a conception or thought, and a copy.

Thus, we see that, even within its originary understanding, we find the meaning of the 'image' to be several. To be an 'image' is thus, on the one hand, to be a copy or imitation or even a spectral shadow of some 'thing' or 'being', and thus, to originate from that thing or being as a *post-facto image*. On the other hand, an image is also the absolute, essential core from which, and on the basis of which, the thing or being is given birth to, for example, when 'Man is created in the image of god' in the Bible, or when the Platonic ideal image[3] is taken as a symbolic form to create material entities, and so on. The 'image' thus exhibits a peculiar duality that renders it as paradoxical: it originates from some being while being the origin of that very being. It is like an interface that is perpetually at an interface with itself. At the point of origin, *it is its own being, even though it is not.* The 'original image' is always already complexly structured in a double bind with itself, where the origin is differential and in a *mise en abyme*, so as to produce itself. To this effect 'the original image' can only be seen as a split, divided being, and as a *not-yet-image*, or an image-qua-image, an *imagined image*, if you will.

One is forced to contend that the reason why the philosophical tradition spanning several centuries has been unable to come up with an essential definition of the 'image' is precisely because of this vexing character that it possesses. Where one tries to assign meaning, the image approaches an abyssal configuration. To draw an analogy immediate to this book (i.e. *Video Vortex*), the image functions akin to an uncontrollable 'vortex'.

By insisting for so long on this paradoxical doubleness of the image I am trying to hint at the fact that the image appears to have a surplus, uncanny logic that cannot be adequately conceived through mere analogy of any kind. This 'doubleness' can indeed be put in Hegelian terms to suggest a dialectical nature to 'the image', but what is crucial to remember is that the *nature* of the parts that form this dialectic cannot be pinned down to belonging to any absolute being or beings. The dialectic nature can only be thought of through abstract, pre-historical, pre-ontological non-entities i.e. the not-yet-images which undergo a 'reduction' or sublation (*Aufhebung*) in order to form the 'image' in synthesis. What we deduce, thus, is that *the image is essentially synthetic.*

The implications that can be drawn from this deduction are manifold, especially when one considers the spirited discussions that have occurred in recent years vis-à-vis the

---

3   Indeed it would be quite easy to demonstrate that Plato's conceptions of image (which he interchangeably refers to as eidolon, phantasma, and eikon) exist as a kind of ontological 'ground' or basis, as 'categorical imperative' for his theorization of the idea of idea (eidos) that he took as an ideal beyond the 'image'. And this is also a key problem which he seems to have been wary of because of which he was so terrified of the image and wanted to throw all of its agents out of the ideal republic. This demonstration of the eidos' dependence on the eidolos is something I have sidelined here and taken as an axiomatic, although such a demonstration is indeed possible and necessary and should perhaps be attempted elsewhere.

question of the film image vs. the digital image. Indeed, a familiar 'accusation' thrown at the digital image given its indexical quality contrary to the analog nature of the film image[4], is that it is immaterial and synthetic. To intervene into this debate through the deduction that we arrived at would be to say that, 'yes, precisely, the digital image is indeed synthetic, and it is precisely because of its purely synthetic nature that it is truer to the essence of the image-in-itself'. As counter-intuitive as it may sound at first, what we derive from the discourse presented above is that *the originary idea of the image is in fact something approximately digital in nature*, even though we may have become accustomed to the idea of the filmic image as essential over the past century or so.

Conversely, and to think of this within more generalized or abstract terms, our civilizational discomfort with the dyad of 'digital I infinite' can be posed as a more fundamental, metaphysical bias that we seem to have carried with us all this while: a preference to what Yuk Hui calls 'natural objects'[5] in lieu of our inability to deal with the digital: with the inevitable emergent properties of the digital in our current modernity resulting in collective melancholia and, in more practical terms, a drive toward 'high definition' and '4K' in order to *restore* the 'natural objects' thus displaced by the digital.

III.

My own work, especially the series, *Noise Reduction (1, 2,* and *3)* is based in this matrix of the digital image 'fighting', as it were, the *natural order of things*. The title of this series is intended to contribute to the same effect. 'Noise', as we know is the quintessential 'impurity' that simultaneously deteriorates as well as enables the transmission of any message through media.[6] In case of the digital image, anything that is purportedly *not-the-image-in-itself* is classified as 'noise'; the most significant representative of 'digital noise' in an image are the pearly dots and speckles that lurk beneath the background, at dimly lit or poorly focused margins, and so on. Given that the digital image has hitherto largely been seen as a purely functional object, whose sole function ought to be to capture the thing in itself without any distortion, there has been a parallel drive within prosumer as well as media industry circles toward various applications and techniques that can 'reduce noise' and produce a *pure image* as it were. Even as we follow on the footsteps of Shannon's theorization regarding the irreducibility of noise, and a (almost) century shaped by this principle that founds information/digital technology, it is rather peculiar that a demand is made from the visual component of the digital landscape to 'purify' and produce the 'in itself'. This curious concurrence of the digital image and a metaphysical re-emergence of the 'in-itself' (contrary to the past few centuries in the history of ideas, where there have been endless attempts to eradicate the 'in itself' in favor of 'multiplicities', 'perspectivisms', and the 'subjective') deserves more attention elsewhere.

---

4   D. N. Rodowick, The Virtual Life of Film, which presents a detailed investigation and elaboration
      regarding how the digital image is 'indexical' and the film image is 'analogical'
5   Yuk Hui, 'What is a Digital Object'
6   C. E. Shannon, 'A Mathematical Theory of Communication'

[What is remarkably odd is also the fact that some of the most staunch antagonists in the tale of the digital image are people one expects to be the most open to the 'new' and the 'avant guard' i.e. experimental filmmakers. A lot of their critiques are based on the nature of the digital image not being 'tactile' or 'material' vis-a-vis the film image; and there has been an astonishing proliferation of experimental films that primarily deal with this material quality that is unique to the film reel in recent times]

My own hypothesis, of course, is that this entire discourse is a 'false movement' that hides the truly radical potential that only the digital image engenders: multiple 'reductions'[7] of drastically different themes and planes in hitherto unimaginable ways so as to eventually give way to a consolidated critique of 'natural objects' (i.e. the image, in our case).

IV.

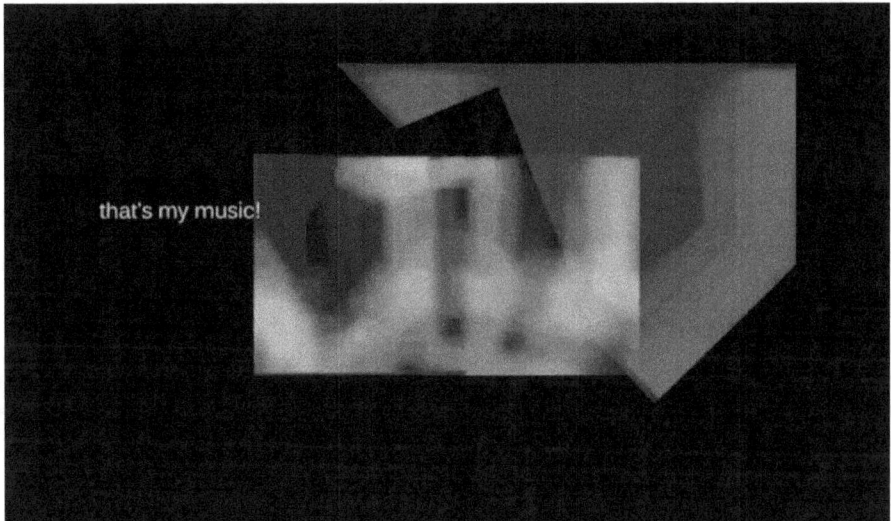

Fig. 1: Still from Noise Reduction 1: The Big Combo.

The first work, *Noise Reduction 1: The Big Combo*[8] is an attempt at abstracting a 'filmic text', i.e. the classic noir film *The Big Combo*, as well as a documentary on Amos Vogel, and trying to represent it through an alternate scenescape where several digital abstractions float in and out of the frame and interact with each other, as if in a simulated reaction to the events that occur in the narrative of the original films. Simultaneously, what is attempted in the work is to conceive of a digital minimalism wherein the abstract computer-generated images are of an almost lowest possible resolution, contrary to the drive toward HD and 4K that the digital image has become associated with. This is so due to my contention that the preoccupations of the digital image, as well as its true radical

---

7   i.e. in the Hegelian sense of sublation or Aufhebung which can also be translated as 'reduction', and
     which is hinted at, through my title.
8   https://vimeo.com/74388770

potential is to some degree divested from the mere facilitation of high quality 'cinematic images'.

The digital minimalism of the first work is taken to its logical extreme with *Noise Reduction 2: Chinatown*,[9] where the most 'material' image of the digital medium, i.e. the 'Media Offline' sign that we get within our editing suites in case of an absent image is juxtaposed with the material qualities of the filmic medium, such as splices, dirt, scratches, sprocket holes etc.

The titular Chinatown of course refers to Roman Polanski's *Chinatown,* whose narrative events are 'reduced' to abstract noise that interacts on the Media Offline sign (in a similar vein to *Noise Reduction 1*), but it also alludes to, and tries to imagine the digital image-scape as something of a veritable 'Made-in-China' entity i.e. plastic and cheap, but ultimately the most accessible

The third film of this series is *Noise Reduction 3: Z*,[10] which tries to take further the interactibility of the material nature of the film image with the digital apparatus by probing inward. The clip used for this film is one of the first tracking shots along the Z-axis in the history of cinema i.e. The Miles' brothers' *The Trip Down Market Street*, which is further continually zoomed into while selectively running digital algorithms over it to identify differential 'noise' undergoing within it. An added soundtrack of a video game, 'Unreal Tournament' decontextualizes and suspends the image even further. The context which forces such an examination is the obvious problem which the digital image is seen as having, i.e. flatness, as opposed to the film image, which, due to its inherent celluloid imprint, is often conceived of as having near infinite planes of image forming a kind of 'volume image' which gives the perspective of depth and hence a purportedly organic seeming quality.

[One could cite Erwin Panofsky, who, in *Perspective as Symbolic Form* points out that it is only following the Renaissance artistic tradition that space itself came to be seen as having a 'volume-like' structure: the eventual governing direction through which the 'volume image' of the film reel is now seen. This indirectly ties in with my first thesis regarding the image being originally digital: here, with the image as being originally *flat* with perspective and volume being applied to it after the Renaissance. We can draw several interesting insights into the question concerning the digital image, flatness, infinity, and their respective antitheses vis-a-vis the direction that Panofsky opens up for us.]

---

9   https://vimeo.com/75490662, password: chinatown
10   https://vimeo.com/142070581, password: marketstreet

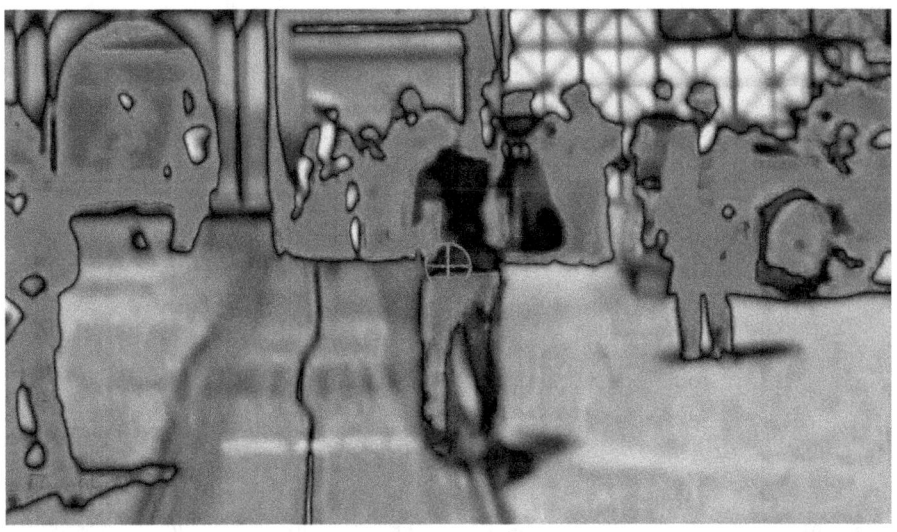

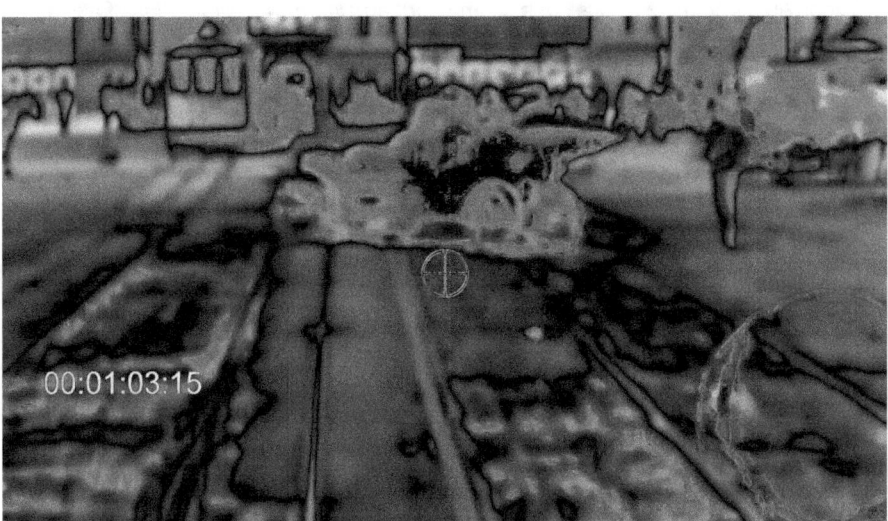

Fig. 2 : Stills from Noise Reduction 3: Z

In *Noise Reduction 3* the surfaces, edges, and margins are algorithmically located as having secret and violent underbellies which erupts out as noise when it is made to interact with a digital apparatus. These noisy eruptions become more and more pronounced as one traverses deeper and deeper along the z-axis, i.e. as the field of 'natural objects' on the screen gradually diminishes with time. For the 'narrative' purpose of the work itself, the exploration of these noisy underbellies culminates when the original Miles brothers' travel across the Z-axis ends. But this does not stop us from engaging in a speculative exercise: that is, to imagine an infinite travel along the z-axis, toward the 'centre' of the noise.

By 'travelling' sequentially from *Noise Reduction 1* to *Noise Reduction 3* — and therefore conceiving of this particular idea of "infinite cinema" — I have been able to find a minimal but meaningfully singular axiom regarding the being of the digital image.

V.

If one were to engage in the premise of an infinite travel along the Z-axis for any given 'non-digital' image within the schema of natural order of things, what inevitably happens with any given cross section of the image, no matter how dense or detailed, is that the image would zoom on and on to a point of absolute invisibility, *an absolute black screen of nothingness.* However, a similar zoom-in in case of the digital image produces drastically different results (and this obviously includes any *originally* 'non digital' image that is *treated* through the digital apparatus). Given the indexical nature of the digital image, any zoom in along the z-axis is *not a zoom in but an algorithmic simulation* of a zoom in. Thus, what we get even after multiple (and, in theory, infinite) attempts at zooming in into the smallest cross section of an image, and making it undergo a 'noise reduction' are clear 'residues' of visible image that are remarkably diverse *representations of the abstract-in-itself.*

VI.

The 'flatness' of the digital image is not the lack of depth but the *actualization* of infinite depth within any given image. Here, there is no dispersing or deconstruction of the image required so as to confront the infinite. There is only a *re-encoding*: a *noise reduction.* Thus, it is in the infinite re-encodability of even a minimal cross-section or *component* that the digital image varies from hitherto existing 'natural images', and by taking this property as an axiom we can postulate a thing or two about the future of the image-as-such.

The following images on the next pages are a demonstration of a series of 'noise reductions' that have been made to operate over a single cross section of the footage of Noise Reduction 3, i.e., a demonstration of the speculative exercise of travelling deeper and deeper into the z-axis of the same, single image.

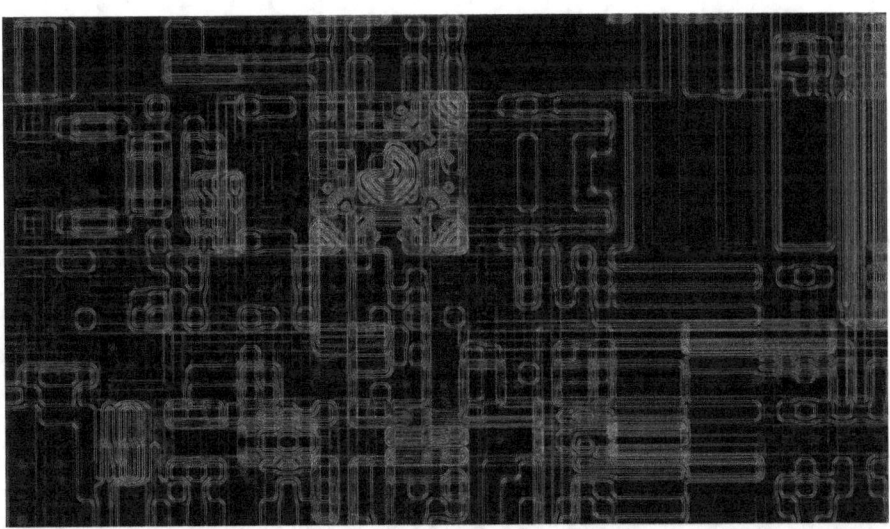

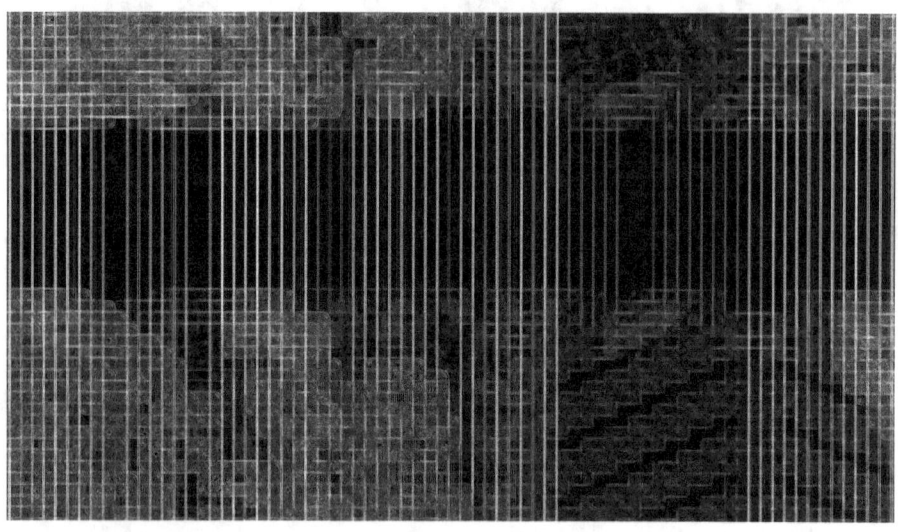

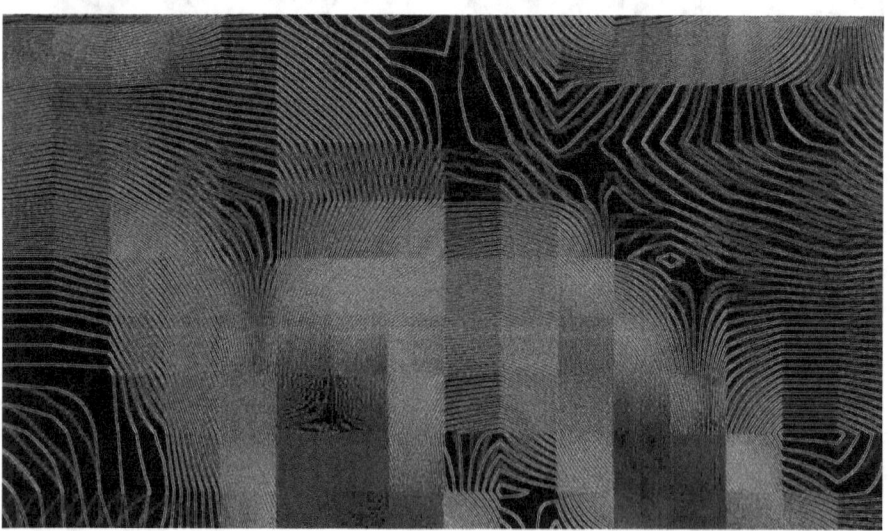

THE OBJECTIVES OF DIGITAL IMAGES AND FILM
IN TIMES OF AI, AUTOMATION, CALCULATION, AND (HYPER)CONTROL

COLETTE TRON

THE OBJECTIVES OF DIGITAL IMAGES AND FILM IN TIMES OF AI, AUTOMATION, CALCULATION, AND (HYPER)CONTROL

COLETTE TRON

Introduction

Here, I would like to propose a contribution to a critique of digital images: from their conception and production to their diffusion and use, including the web as one of the devices where many apparatus coincide and compose a 'vision of the world', which is a large part of the question concerning online images and films. What is the purpose of these images, considering the environment in which they exist: is it technological, social, or economic? What politics support their aesthetics, if, indeed, automation, artificial intelligence, big data and intensive computing still allow a sensible dimension? To this end, we will look to the history of art and to philosophy for some possibilities of thinking and interpreting the role played by technics in the conception of images of this kind. And we will look to some artists and their work in terms of the aesthetic and political positions they adopt, and in relation to the historical and social context in which they take part in order to critique the making process of digital images. How these artists trust or keep at a distance from the 'intelligence of the machine', to use Jean Epstein's formula?

To sustain our topic: what's the matter, or to what end some images, in times of calculation, automation, data, and artificial intelligence, the starting point of this analysis will be the *Kino-Eye Manifesto* (1923) by the Soviet filmmaker Dziga Vertov, in which he defends a cinema of truth, a realist cinema, where the camera becomes a 'mechanical eye', more objective than human subjectivity. Vertov's context is obviously the project of the Soviet revolution and the invention of a new man it hoped to bring.

We will then examine the series of films by the German artist and critic Harun Farocki, called *Eye/Machine* (2000), leading to quite a different analysis of the relationship between eye and machine, with his concept of 'operational images' serving a critique of total automation and, above all, of the project by which such technologies, in the service of industrial capitalism, become the operator of man, rather than the other way around.

The history of the apparatus associated with the visual organ that is the eye has now reached a complete and unprecedented stage, with the development of digital technologies, where computing and calculation form and inform images. This is their reality, and their truth. But which reality is involved with this truth, and is it the one of the real world ? And how, really, should we go about reintroducing the question of truth?

These cases would be related to the history and theory of images made by calculation, from the Renaissance to the virtual turn, and would involve the question of artificial intelligence, the intelligence of machines, compared to human perception and sensibility, []{#_Hlk38359230 .anchor}amounting to a fundamental readjustment of the role of science and technology, and their end. What we need is a practical and theoretical structure with which to think — and to lay the poetic foundations for — an art of making digital images as an art of (hyper)control. To de-measure the world. This is a political project for a 'non-inhuman world', according to Bernard Stiegler's expression.

'I am kino-eye,
A mechanical eye.
I, a machine, show you the world as only I can see it'
Dziga Vertov, *Kino-Eye Manifesto*

In his 'Kino-Eye Manifesto' written in 1923, the filmmaker Dziga Vertov proposed a cinema of truth (Kino Pravda, cine-truth), a realistic, objective cinema through which the camera could show life in itself: replacing the sensibility and subjectivity of the human point of view on everyday life and work, with a 'mechanical eye' bearing universal characteristics: 'Free of the limits of time and space, I put together any given points in the universe, no matter where I've recorded them. My path leads to the creation of a fresh perception of the world. I decipher in a new way a world unknown to you'.

A new point of view on the world to serve the ends of revolution, and in order to create a new man, was the political objective of communism. 'We,' wrote Vertov, 'that is the Kinoks, bring people into closer kinship with machines, we foster new people. The new man, free of unwieldiness and clumsiness, will have the light, precise movements of machines, and he will be the gratifying subject of our films.' Thus, 'Long life to life in itself!', cried the Manifesto, the camera expressing itself through Vertov, or replacing him: 'Long life to the kino-eye of the Revolution!'

Some decades after this history of cinema and 'its revolutionary practice', at the beginning of the twenty-first century, the German filmmaker and critic Harun Farocki — a Marxist who had been a child during the Second World War, then grew up in the Cold War (witnessing and possibly involved in its coming to an end), conscious of the ideological and economic struggle that followed it particularly after the fall of Berlin Wall and the collapse of the Eastern bloc that saw communism in Europe swept away (its specter having haunted it, according to Marx and Engels in *The Communist Manifesto*, whose first sentence was discussed by Jacques Derrida in *Specters of Marx*).

So, Farocki with his *Eye/Machine* trilogy and with his concept of 'operational images', opened up a new question of the relationship between eye and machine: these new kinds of images no longer aim to show life and work, and have nothing to do with the work of revolution — unlike the project of cinematic truth of Vertov and the Soviet avant-gardes — but they are effective in the sense of efficient and also destructive. Farocki examined the relationship of the means of production to the means of destruction. His film series was born in reaction to the simulated images of the first Gulf war and showed how, then, they were entering civil society and the economic world, finding applications for military operations or for automation processes in various domains of industry, and even in everyday life.

Thus, don't they — machines, technology — take control? Here, we could talk again about 'societies of control' (Deleuze), or even of 'hypercontrol'. Bernard Stiegler defines hypercontrol as a stage beyond control – 'the control-through-modulation discovered and analyzed by Deleuze', allowed by data technologies, and automatic treatment of information: 'Formalized by applied mathematics and realized concretely through algorithms devised to capture and to exploit the traces generated by individual and collective behavior, interactive, reticular automatisms are systems designed to capture behavioral expressions'.

I continue with another quote from the paper by Stiegler, 'Ars and organological inventions in societies of hypercontrol': 'Given that digital technologies, in particular after the exposure of the immense problems posed by 'big data,' constitute an age of hyper-control — in societies that have become hyper-industrial (rather than post-industrial) — is an art of hyper-control either conceivable or desirable?' It would be a kind of politics and poetics inventions to struggle against hyper-industrial development and applications of digital technologies and the dispositives that lead as well as follow peoples' behavior.

Actually, what is the function of these images? What is the aim of technics? The camera, this machine of vision, has become digital and 'intelligent', or 'smart' — a term that first appeared with 'smart weapons' — and decides and acts according to the dictates of a computer program and at an advanced stage of automation.

According to Farocki, images are no longer made by or for the human eye. Images with neither author nor spectator are merely technical operations, or functions in a system of operations. They are (auto)generated, automatic, and autonomous. They are no longer animated, put in movement by a spirit (in Latin, *anima* means 'spirit'), but are programmed and activated. The program and the 'intelligence of the machine' record and treat the data of reality without the least human intervention. And they determine by themselves, as smart devices, what decisions to take and what actions to accomplish. That the machine undertakes such operations does not mean that they are related to human faculties and abilities such as thought, reflexion, or sensibility and sensation, or reason and knowledge. It means only that they are capable of recognition. 'To recognize and to pursue', or to control – this was what saddened Farocki: such are the aims and ends of these images.

The history of eye and its devices, the history of cinema (as images in movement), and of cinema's technological development thus converge here through the digital (computer program, simulation, automation). Where binary numbers and calculation are what *form* and *inform* images: these are what structure, program, and give rise to them. Is it their truth? And what is the relation of this truth to that of reality? This is what Farocki has tried to understand, to show, and to critique in most of his films and to do this via the history of the technologies of the image and their objectives.

Measures and images of the world

In Book I of his treatise *De Pictura*, Leon Battista Alberti explained:

> To make clear my exposition in writing this brief commentary on painting, I will take first from the mathematicians those things with which my subject is concerned...I beg you to consider me not as a mathematician but as a painter writing of these things. Mathematicians measure with their minds alone the forms of things separated from all matter. Since we wish the object to be seen, we will use a more sensate wisdom.

When painters use their organs and senses of sight to apprehend reality and with their ingenuity, mind, and instruments; imitate it, reproduce it, represent it, interpret it, and even invent or imagine it — meaning to put it into images. First in their mind and afterwards onto or into artefacts where these, too, have a history which is the history of art and technics.

To which knowledge, acknowledgment, perception, sensation, apprehension, comprehension of reality does each practice call, along with its technics? A multitude of knowledges are required, particularly in the Renaissance and with the invention of perspectival drawing: arts and sciences support one another in the technical and aesthetic history of the relationship between eye and mind (or spirit), and with the mediation of instruments, which become the instruments of scientific knowledge.

Harun Farocki: 'The mathematician artists of the Renaissance' are the pioneers of what will come to pass with digital technologies. He continues: 'Erwin Panofsky has written that we can interpret the conception of perspective both in terms of proportion and objectivity and in terms of chance and subjectivity'. About this visual order of the Renaissance, Farocki concluded: 'If we conceive an image as an instrument of measurement, we will be forced to lose touch with chance and the subject.'

Objectivity and/or 'objectality': technics seems to embody, or to contain, a universal point of view. That was the wish, or the utopia, of which Vertov dreamed. The truth of the real. And in this way, Vertov seemed to trust in the machine. But for Farocki, this seems to have turned into distrust, in another age of the history of images and their technics, the age of their digital condition, which refers both to their materiality and their technological functioning. I would like to add that this distrust is also a reflection of another historical and political context: the end of communism, the globalization of liberalism, and the market economy, a market and marketing from which images cannot escape especially since in this way they become one of the factors of production and productivity.

'To apprehend an image,' wrote Farocki, 'as an instrument of measurement is to push it towards a mathematization, a calculability, and ultimately a "digitality" of the Image world'. And in return, the instruments of measurement and calculation rationalize images, images of the world, and the world itself. Farocki has described the history of calculated images starting from the technics of photogrammetry: from their role in measurement and calculation, through to digital transcription applied to the devices of vision, from photography to virtual and computer-generated images, all these form a continuity in a history running from the invention of perspective, to modernity, and beyond through which the representation of the visible becomes the paradigm of its edification, where science and technology establish themselves as factors of objectivity, but also of truth.

This modelling, based on calculation, is valid up until the processes of digital simulation and automation, of increases in the capacity to store and treat data, of the development of artificial intelligence, and thus the feedback loops between the measurement of the world and its calculated representation all being to scramble reality itself, its existence, in a surfeit of simulation and simulacra, which Jean Baudrillard perceived as a loss of the referent and an evacuation of the real, becoming 'the desert of the real itself'. Yet, said Günther Anders, quoted by Farocki: 'Reality would have to begin'. For this, wouldn't it be necessary to show of what this reality is composed, and how it is made?

To see or to measure?

That is the question, and the problem, introduced by Alberti and taken on by Farocki.

In a commentary on Farocki's analysis of digital images, based on the technics of photogrammetry — invented by French engineers and developed by the German engineer Albrecht Meydenbauer (1834–1921) — the French philosopher Jacques Rancière wrote: 'an inhuman image that is only the effecting of a calculation and leads itself to inhumanity. It is here that the history of Meydenbauer gains its whole meaning...the evil of images is the evil that subordinates them to the operation of mastery by excellence: the operation of measurement'. And here is the shift, the overthrow in the order of things, and thus a revolution — but it is not one of a kind predicted by Vertov — because, Rancière continues: 'Meydenbauer doesn't see: he measures. And in this way his inventions announce a future where the images of the world will be numbers'. So, what is becoming the vision? And in which relation to reality?

This last sentence repeats Farocki's final observation in his film *Images of the World and the Inscription of War*. The military-industrial turn and its objectives or ends transform the project of a new man, discovering the world under a new eye, produced by the machine and specific to the apparatus, in a 'process of the self-abolition of the human being', according to Farocki, or of the 'obsolescence of mankind', according to Günther Anders, one of Farocki's references. The senses are obstructed, the mind is absent, and the gestures are relegated. Man and his organs are inactive, unemployed. This autonomy of the machine perhaps tends towards complete automation, to a situation in which the system is closed and autoproduces itself. It is generative. Sui generis. Maybe, as a technological parody of autopoiesis. We can perceive artificial intelligence as a paroxysm of this technical tendency. And we may also perceive calculation as a technological paradigm, from the 'measuring of the world' in the Renaissance to today's intensive and automatic computing.

Poietic

Tekhne, in its ancient Greek meaning, refers to making but also to production in a higher sense: art. 'It is something poietic' said Heidegger in his famous text 'The Question Concerning Technology'. It is also a kind of knowledge as an unveiling, an unconcealment. It creates 'openness'. About the means and ends of technics, he writes: 'We will, as we say, 'get' technology 'spiritually in hand'. We will master it. The will to mastery becomes all the more urgent the more technology threatens to slip from human control.' Does the growth of the complexity of technology mean that it tends towards its own autonomy? Heidegger questions the implementation of technics and its causality with regard to 'what operates'. So, what is an 'operational image' and could we ask for Heidegger's help in defining Farocki's terms concerning the automation of the process of visibility? What activates the appearance, the unveiling, the unconcealment of an image? Could we not do so, given that technics is related to a 'making appear', as Heidegger phrased it?

According to Heidegger, once again, every production, linked to technics, must be 'an act to which we must answer', which implies responsibility. To make come, to make appear, in a presence of the thing, of the object, of the production, that opens and reveals, 'in the exactness of representation'. This exactitude becomes its truth.

Here is causality redefined, and the coming of 'being there', but which would vanish at the hands of modern technics. And let us save a place for spectrality (Derrida), or disappearance (Pérec). This is the 'logic of haunting', which led Jacques Derrida to conceive the term 'hauntology', beyond an 'ontology or a thought of being', absent, or coming back as a spirit, virtually, and of which the virtual and teletechnologies would be the production in the form of simulacra, without real opposition between presence and absence, 'non-presence' wrote Derrida, 'life and non-life'. But also 'life and death of truth'. According to the philosopher, these kinds of inscriptions would create a 'spectrography', and where it would be possible to invent a 'spectropoetics' of new media and their technologies.

But let us come back to Heidegger. Making and unveiling are modes of production of technics. Its truth. But Heidegger still worried about 'modern technology' which would be 'based on modern science' and 'motorized'. The human being itself is provoked by industrial technology born from this exact science. This human being no longer acts directly or fully on its milieu, for now it is technics itself that is the operator. It is technics itself that transforms matter for its exploitation. What Heidegger calls *Gestell* becomes the master and possessor of nature, undermining every anthropocentrism, and amounting to a form of rationalization. Here, production needs to undertake many operations, through which technics is removed from poietics and from making, revealing the object by gathering the elements, matters and parts, and transforming them through a complex system that becomes a technology: the machine interferes, imposes its presence and its action, its operations, between man and production. 'Thus,' according to Heidegger, 'modern technology is not a pure human act'.

In a process, or set of operations which present themselves as the industrial production chain, or an assembly line — and this is also characteristic of the technics of cinema and its poetics — it becomes important to rethink the function of the technical dispositive (a dispositive, according to Foucault, being an organisation that stands between knowledge and power) of the instruments, of the causalities and above all of the ends of technics; the relations of dependence and autonomy between man and technics; of tools with which to access knowledge; and of the modes of production of presence, appearance and disappearance, visibility and invisibility, of things and of being. The possibility or impossibility of their being-there, as a presence to the world. Or, at least of its return. The aim is to rethink the formalizations — the ways of modelling reality— in relation to digital technologies that bring together data capture, algorithmic simulation, intensive computing, artificial intelligence, full automation and possibly autoproduction which could produce an abstract reality, where we can no longer understand who is the author or the controller, and maybe with no signification and no direction.

Hence, concerning 'what should be done', to again cite Farocki: to (re)deploy the interactions between man and technics, science and art, towards a conception of co-responsibility in poietics. Towards a new art of making, producing 'non-inhuman' forms of life. And, if possible, towards a poetic appearance of the truth: that was, according to Heidegger: the question concerning technics, the question concerning its essence more than its aims, and the question of the meaning of the relation between art and technics. Art: as a domain both similar and different from technics. 'Such a realm is art', wrote Heidegger at the end of 'The Question Concerning Technology', 'But certainly only if reflection on art, for its part, does not shut its eyes to the constellation of truth after which we are questioning.'

Such questions should be asked anew, in the framework of digital images, data production and automatic processing, and considering the increase of artificial intelligence. Adding the dimension of the web and its continuous flow, all these elements give rise to another economy of the images, where quantity and computation could disqualify the principles of poetics: and thus, in the words of Heidegger, the access to 'the dimension'. Which is to say the immeasurable measure, impossible to calculate, always to be evaluated by a poetic taking of measure, singular, neither generic nor systematic, not scientific, not 'mere geo-metry', and, 'by which only the human receives the measure suitable to the whole extent of his being'.

References

Alberti, Leon Battista. *De Pictura*, Paris: Allia, 2007.

Baudrillard, Jean. Simulacras and simulation, Paris: Galilée, 1981.

Derrida, Jacques, *Specters of Marx*, Paris: Galilée, 1993.

Farocki, Harun, dir. Eye Machine, http://www.harunfarocki.de/installations/2000s/2000/eye-machine.html

Farocki, Harun. *To recognize and to pursue*, Paris: Pompidou Center editions, 2002.

Heidegger, Martin. The man habitats as a poet, 1951.

Heidegger, Martin. *The Question Concerning Technology*, 1953.

Stiegler, Bernard. 'Ars and organological inventions in societies of hypercontrol', *Leonardo* 49.5 (2016): 480–484.

Vertov, Dziga. *Kino-eye Manifesto*, Modern review, 1923.

ALGORHYTHMIA

PATRICIA G. LANGE

ALGORHYTHMIA

PATRICIA G. LANGE

YouTube is a juggernaut of online video. Viewers collectively watch 5 billion videos per day, while an estimated 500 hours of video are uploaded every minute.[1] Many factors have contributed to its success, but particularly the efforts of early vloggers who used the site in creative and social ways. The same is largely true now, with creative video makers bringing visibility to the site and benefitting from the income that arises from the advertisements placed on their videos. YouTube uses automated 'search and discovery' recommendation systems that deploy algorithms which are designed to suggest videos to users in an effort to increase their engagement with the site. For some video makers, algorithmically driven recommendation systems complicate their video-creation and sharing experience. Rhythms of their interactions vis-à-vis the site have become difficult to navigate, resulting in a condition that I refer to as algorhythmia: or, arrhythmic anxieties caused when they cannot keep pace with the demands of algorithms and audiences.

The corporate entity of YouTube reportedly uses 'hundreds of signals,'[2] including 'watch time' and 'average view duration' to provide recommendations designed to keep people watching videos on the site — and thus experience more advertising. Watch time is the amount of time a viewer watches a video, measured in minutes. Average view duration refers to the average time that content is viewed before viewers click away. Pundits say that on average viewers watch about 50% of most videos, and if viewers watch 70% to 80% of a video, the video is said to be doing well.[3] . Such metrics help determine which videos will be promoted in users' recommendation lists, and the conglomeration of these signals constitute a set of algorithms, that are deployed to increase the user's time on the platform.

The technological landscape between video creation and viewership on YouTube is constantly in flux, and this to such a degree that many users feel as though they and the site are in a state of 'permanent beta'.[4] In this conditions, it is sometimes difficult for creators to keep up with the temporal demands of automated recommendation systems, as these systems constantly demand — and reward in the form of visibility — new content. However, as creativity takes time, human pacing may not always map onto the platform's need for novelty.

1   Salman Aslam, 'YouTube by the Numbers: Stats, Demographics & Fun Facts,' Omnicore, February 10, 2020, https://www.omnicoreagency.com/youtube-statistics/.
2   See YouTube Creators. 'How Long Should Your Videos Be?', YouTube video, 16 January 2020, https://www.youtube.com/watch?v=G1tHzUGdMwY.
3   Peter Lang, 'YouTube Average View Duration – The 50% Rule.' Uhurunetwork, https://uhurunetwork.com/the-50-rule-for-youtube/.
4   Gina Neff and David Stark, 'Permanently Beta: Responsive Organization in the Internet Era', Working Paper, Institute for Social and Economic Research and Policy, Columbia University, 2002, https://academiccommons.columbia.edu/doi/ 10.7916/D8G44X47.

The sociologist Henri Lefebvre argued that we must pay attention to the rhythms of life, which provide clues about how societies function.[5] He engaged in what he called 'rhythm analysis' which refers to exploring different types of societal rhythms, including interactional and behavioral patterns that may become irregular and thus produce 'arrhythmias.' When two rhythms are arrhythmic, they are out of sync. Such irregularities may produce problems worthy of investigation. Taking his ideas into consideration, we may study arrhythmias of creative production and viewership within automated assessment systems in order to understand potential areas of anxiety or conflict that occur when we attempt to express the self through media—in this case through posting videos on YouTube.

What is Algorhythmia?

Algorhythmia is defined here as a condition in which the needs, abilities, and pacing of human creators are out of sync with the evaluations, assessments, and metrics of automated systems that are used to determine participatory parameters and profitability in commercialized, interactive, media-sharing environments. Algorhythmia is a special type of arrhythmia. It results when people participate in systems that demand more than humans can reasonably provide while maintaining their own level of creative integrity, authenticity, and satisfaction.

The new term proposed here, 'algorhythmia,' helps us investigate what happens when the rhythms shaped by the pace of creating videos fall out of sync with the expectations of algorithms and audiences. The term joins the idea of an algorithm—or formula for assessing videos' performance and position on recommendation lists—together with Lefebvre's notion of arrhythmia, or instances in which actions fall out of sync in a way that creates problems.

Case studies of video makers show that algorhythmia can produce distress among creators and audiences, and pacing and quality of videos may decrease as a result of this productive misalignment.[6] If videos decrease in quality *en masse*, this also adversely affects the site itself, which risks becoming associated with videos that work for algorithmic parameters rather than producing novel, creative works. As algorithms are increasingly becoming part of daily life, we should work to understand how to identify instances of algorhythmia.[7] We must learn to recognize its effects and explore whether or not there is a realistic 'cure' for this societal 'condition.'

What Are Its Symptoms?

Signs of algorhythmia may visibly appear in media environments like video sharing sites.

5   Henry Lefebvre, Rhythmanalysis, London: Continuum, 2004.
6   Patricia G. Lange, Thanks for Watching: An Anthropological Study of Video Sharing on YouTube, Louisville, CO: University Press of Colorado, 2019.
7   See especially Tarleton Gillespie, 'The Relevance of Algorithms' in Tarleton Gillespie, Pablo Boczkowski, and Kirsten Foot (eds), Media Technologies: Essays on Communication, Materiality, and Society, Cambridge, MA: MIT Press, 2014, pp. 167–194.

Indicators include viewers noticing a drop in the pace of production by video makers or creators taking breaks due to physical exhaustion or lack of creative inspiration. In response to a slower pace of production, algorithms lower the ranking of less prolific video makers in recommendation systems, putting even more pressure on them to perform in order to to generate income. Videos may be hastily produced, receive less attention, and thus find themselves ranked poorly in recommendation systems. Symptoms of algorhythmia manifest when human creators need to take a break, or viewers notice breaks, or there is a decline in the quality of the videos being posted.

In one case study, a video maker named Roberto Blake posted fewer videos for a couple of months. Blake has over 300,000 subscribers and his videos typically receive thousands of views. His YouTube channel focuses on providing trips on growing YouTube viewership as well as general graphic design. After Blake began posting at a slower pace, members of his viewing audience became concerned about the drop in the number of his videos. They wondered if the reason for the decline was related to his history of depression. Blake made a video reassuring his viewers that he simply had the flu. But he argued that during his absence, YouTube's algorithm had downgraded the ranking of his work. Blake made a video response to his viewers explaining that he was not burned out, but he believed that his brief hiatus had cost him his position in the algorithmic ranking system. In his video 'WHY I TOOK A BREAK FROM YOUTUBE', posted on April 9, 2018, Blake stated:

> Doing less content and prioritizing other things, whether it's my health or whether it's the growth of my business, I'll be real with you, that has hurt me a little bit in the YouTube algorithm. I know that and a lot of other creators are experiencing exactly the same thing. And it's not great, it sucks, but you know what? Our supporters, our viewers can always help us beat the algorithm with doing one simple thing, sharing videos that you think deserve more views, that you think deserve support, or that you think can entertain or educate or motivate people.[8]

Viewers may notice when a video maker's pace has slowed, and video makers believe they can see that their rankings have dipped according to the YouTube algorithm. As Blake points out, taking human breaks from the relentless pace of video making is often vital not only for one's immediate health but to long-term avoid burn out and maintain creative inspiration. In addition, diversifying one's income-generating portfolio is often advantageous.

Many video makers on YouTube gain income not just from sharing revenue with YouTube earned from advertisements posted on or alongside their videos, but also from their own businesses, merchandising, and special appearances at events. At times these income-generating opportunities—as well as the basic maintenance of one's human health—inevitably take precedence over continually producing new video content. In sum, symptoms of algorhythmia surface when watch time of a video maker's work decreases

---

8   Roberto Blake, 'WHY I TOOK A BREAK FROM YOUTUBE', YouTube video, 19 April 2018, https://youtu.be/hrQoMlnu7Wo.

due to a slower pace of production wherein the satisfaction of audiences also declines if they expect or demand a faster pace of creative production than a video maker can realistically provide.

What Are Its Effects?

Effects of Algorhythmia include burnout, attempts to reverse engineer the algorithm, and an overall decrease in satisfaction among viewers and creators regarding their media. Attempts to reverse engineer the algorithm do not always guarantee better videos or improve the creative aura of the site. Early YouTubers who used the site socially complained that even the introduction of monetization systems created an environment that resulted in competition and prioritization of commercialism over human sociality.[9]

Burn out among video makers is common, an observation that has been widely reported.[10] In the case study mentioned above, Blake stressed to his viewers that although he was not burned out, if one does YouTube 'long enough,' one is likely to experience some form of it. Burn out results from responding to the relentless pace of making videos while being continually assessed by vast audiences and automated search and discovery recommendation systems that rank creators within a landscape that is constantly changing in technical features. In another example, the famous YouTuber Olga Kay noted that she began posting twenty videos per week, and was afraid to slow her pace lest she 'disappear' from the YouTube viewing landscape.[11] She reported feeling that her work pace became oppressive.[12] Life activities all became fodder for video production for the site which continually put pressure on her to constantly record her life events to keep up with algorithmic rankings.

A key effect of algorhythmia is the practice by video makers of attempting to 'reverse engineer' the algorithm.[13] This means that video creators hypothesize which particular characteristics are being used to assess and rank them and their work in YouTube's recommendation system. However, algorithms are composed of many variables and not all assumptions may produce widely desirable results for creators, viewers, or the site in general. For example, YouTubers speak of a '10-minute trick' on the site, in which videos that are longer than 10 minutes are perceived to retain viewers longer, and thus expose them to advertising for a longer period of time. Reports indicate that for videos longer than

9   Hey Watch This! Sharing the Self Through Media (dir. Patricia G. Lange, 2020).

10   Julie Alexander, 'YouTube's Top Creators Are Burning Out and Breaking Down En Masse,' Polygon, June 1, 2018. https://www.polygon.com/2018/6/1/17413542/burnout-mental-health-awareness-youtube-elle-mills-el-rubius-bobby-burns-pewdiepie.

11   Leslie Kaufman, 'Chasing Their Star, on YouTube.' New York Times, February 1, 2014, http://www.nytimes.com/2014/02/02/business/chasing-their-star-on-youtube.html.

12   Chris Stokel-Walker, 'More than a Decade Later, How Do Original YouTube Stars Feel about the Site?,' Ars Technica, June 11, 2017, https://arstechnica.com/features/2017/06 /youtube-changed-my-life-a-pair-of-original-videostars-ponder-a-life-lived-online/.

13   Matt Gielen and Jeremy Rosen, 'Reverse Engineering the YouTube Algorithm: Part I.,' Tubefilter, June 23, 2016, https://www.tubefilter.com/2016/06/23/reverse-engineering-youtube-algorithm/.

ten minutes, more ads may appear, thus generating more revenue for video makers (and the site, which shares advertising revenue with creators).[14]

In response, YouTube has seen instances of 'temporal padding,'[15] or adding extra time to videos' length in a way that does not provide substantive content. For example, YouTubers might take a break and walk away from their computer but leave the camera rolling just to make sure they have reached the 10-minute mark. Video content showing no one there and nothing happening is hardly a marker of personal creativity.

YouTube has responded in part by releasing materials such as video tutorials that warn against making long videos just to gain views. YouTube spokespersons claim that such a practice often 'hurts' rather than 'helps' video performance. In the video, *How Long Should Your Videos Be?*, YouTube says that although length of time is admittedly a factor that the site pays attention to through its algorithms, it is better to have a high quality video rather than a longer video that ultimately leaves the viewer 'less satisfied'. The corporate entity of YouTube does not want people to feel dissatisfied after a video and thus leave the site. Their advice is that 'run time should match content' such that a short message would deserve a brief video, whereas a message that takes time to convey merits a longer video. They warn creators not to 'over-think' a video's length. Algorhythmia may lead to reverse engineering practices that may not always yield high quality or creative work.

Is There a Cure?

Finding a cure for algorhythmia is arguably beneficial to the website's performance given that the needs of creators, viewers, and the corporate entity of YouTube are at least in partial alignment to maintain viewership, including supporting a creative aura for the site. All of these entities desire producing interesting material that keeps viewers engaged. Potential solutions to algorhythmia on video sharing sites include demystifying the algorithm, turning to other mechanisms of assessment, encouraging diversification in income-generation for creators, paying creators a base salary, and turning to human moderators and evaluators for assessing video acceptance and popularity.

Transparency in algorithmic assessment may reduce perverse incentivizing that creators engage in to satisfy what they surmise to be successful assessment metrics of their work. Although video length is a factor of assessment, for instance, there are many other evaluation variables which are not always made plain to creators. However, implementing complete algorithmic transparency is not likely to happen in the foreseeable future. Algorithms are considered to be proprietary corporate secrets and making them plain is seen as revealing potential competitive advantages. 'Gaming the system' once algorithms

14   Amanda Perelli, 'How Much YouTube Pays Creators for 100,000, 1 million, and 4 million Views,' Business Insider, September 22, 2019, https://www.businessinsider.com/how-much-youtube-pays-for-views-100-thousand-million-2019-9.
15   Patricia G. Lange, Thanks for Watching: An Anthropological Study of Video Sharing on YouTube, Louisville, CO: University Press of Colorado, 2019.

are known might also intensify as creators may work to satisfy particular variables, rather than considering video creation holistically. Further, algorithms are quite complex, and may not be easily understood by video producers or even engineers, given that they are implemented in real time by automated systems. Even if algorithms were made available, their complexity may not render them easily digestible or actionable to the lay person.[16]

'Cures' for algorhythmia might also focus on humanizing or at least bringing humans back into the equation of designing metrics for assessment. YouTube creators propose using 'satisfaction surveys' in addition to algorithms for understanding the user experience. Human moderators might call out videos of interest so that the pacing of human assessment is not left to unrelenting automated tactics. At the same time, surveys themselves may not necessarily solve the problem. Surveys may simply be automated for instance, by offering evaluations that can be read and interpreted by algorithms. What might be beneficial are surveys that require human parsing, and subsequently human responses and interactions.

At the same time, it is important not to oppose humans to algorithms, given that algorithms are created and implemented at least in part by humans. Scholars warn that portrayals of algorithms as 'unsupervised' or possessing some kind of 'wicked autonomy' that manages to excise humans from the equation misrepresent how humans routinely intervene in their creation and implementation, and thus should be held accountable for their operations.[17] It is incumbent upon researchers and analysts to locate the humans in the system who are shaping algorithms and their effects.

In Blake's case study mentioned above, he exhorts his audience to 'beat the algorithm' by making the human decision to collectively forward worthy content. Although this is one understandable strategy, it is important to recognize that individual tactics place the burden on audiences rather than on corporations that benefit from creative labor. Offering base salaries and engaging in income diversification are additional tactics that might assist creators, given the challenges and human toll of algorhythmia. One option that might counteract the relentless pace and dependence upon algorithmic assessment might include paying a minimum, baseline salary to qualified creators. In this way creators are guaranteed insurance benefits and a steady income, even during slow creative periods or times of illness. However, in digital environments that are increasingly dependent on the gig economy, the idea of stable salaries and benefits has effectively given way to on-demand, task-oriented models of calculating compensation.[18]

Successful commercially-oriented YouTubers long ago learned that financial security comes from having a diverse portfolio of income streams, rather than relying only on receiving money from advertisements placed with videos. YouTubers earn money from paid endorsements and sponsorships of products, special appearances, and merchandising. YouTubers discuss diversification as one strategy to avoid burn out. By focusing on a variety of activities, it is

16   Gillespie, 'The Relevance of Algorithms', pp. 167–194.
17   Nick Seaver, 'What Should an Anthropology of Algorithms Do?,' Cultural Anthropology, (2018): 375-385.
18   Mary L. Gray and Siddharth Suri. Ghost Work, New York: Houghton Mifflin Harcourt, 2019.

possible to receive steady income, even during times in which video productivity or pace of creativity slows. Salaries and diversification enable humans to have a safety net that arguably assists in providing the resources to find inspiration for future creativity. These strategies arguably not only benefit the individual creator in dealing with algorhythmia but also provide mechanisms to encourage participation and ensure more positive experiences for creators and viewers. Of course they require tremendous effort themselves, and a certain level of celebrity to emerge as viable options.

Conclusion

Algorhythmia is a specific type of arrhythmia, in which creatives cannot keep pace with the demands of algorithmic assessment systems, which are created to satisfy audience demands. Symptoms emerge when productivity of video slows, audiences become disappointed, and algorithmic systems demote videos and their video creators in automated recommendation systems. Key effects include a wish to reverse engineer the system and follow sometimes seemingly perverse incentives in order to maintain one's position in algorithmic ranking systems. Additional effects include a decline in creative inspiration and quality of videos, which impacts creators, viewers, and the site as a whole. Creators often experience burn out as a result of trying to keep pace with automated assessments in an environment that is constantly changing in terms of features, technological infrastructure, and viewers' tastes.

The impacts of algorhythmia are felt across multiple entities and thus it is arguably to everyone's advantage to deal with this societal condition in creative spaces. Media-sharing platforms like YouTube are seen to have little role in content creation, but the choices made by their agents and infrastructures have considerable effect on what kinds of creative works may be produced and circulated, and how this work is organized, promoted, and monetized.[19] Potential solutions are not easily identifiable but we should work as a society to envision next steps. Problems may not be adequately addressed if solely left in the hands of individual companies. If we are concerned about ensuring equitable access to production and distribution of novel content, it is vital to ensure that venues in which content is circulated enable the pulse of creativity to thrive.[20]

References

Alexander, Julie. 'YouTube's Top Creators Are Burning Out and Breaking Down En Masse,' *Polygon*, June 1, 2018, https://www.polygon.com/2018/6/1/17413542/burnout-mental-health-awareness-you-tube-elle-mills-el-rubius-bobby-burns-pewdiepie.

Aslam, Salman. 'YouTube by the Numbers,' *Omnicore*, February 10, 2020, https://www.omnicoreagency.com/youtube-statistics/.

Blake, Roberto. 'WHY I TOOK A BREAK FROM YOUTUBE', YouTube video, 19 April 2018, https://youtu.be/hrQoMlnu7Wo.

---

19   Tarleton Gillespie, 'The Politics of 'Platforms,' New Media & Society 12.3 (2010): 347–364.
20   Patricia G Lange, 'Participatory Complications in Interactive, Video-Sharing
      Environments,' In Larissa Hjorth, Heather Horst, Anne Galloway, and Genevieve Bell (eds), The
      Routledge Companion to Digital Ethnography, New York: Routledge, 2016, pp. 147–157.

Gielen, Matt, and Jeremy Rosen. 'Reverse Engineering the YouTube Algorithm: Part I', *Tubefilter*, June 23, 2016, https://www.tubefilter.com/2016/06/23/reverse-engineering-youtube-algorithm/.

Gillespie, Tarleton. 'The Politics of 'Platforms,' *New Media & Society* 12.3 (2010): 347–364.

_____. 'The Relevance of Algorithms', in Tarleton Gillespie, Pablo Boczkowski, and Kirsten Foot (eds.), *Media Technologies: Essays on Communication, Materiality, and Society*, Cambridge, MA: MIT Press, 2014, pp. 167–194.

Gary, Mary L. and Siddharth Suri. *Ghost Work*, New York: Houghton Mifflin Harcourt, 2019.

Kaufman, Leslie. 'Chasing Their Star, on YouTube', *New York Times*, February 1, 2014. http://www.nytimes.com/2014/02/02/business/chasing-their-star-on-youtube.html.

Lang, Peter. 'Youtube Average View Duration – The 50% Rule', *Uhurunetwork.com,* https://uhurunetwork.com/the-50-rule-for-youtube/.

Lange, Patricia G. 'Participatory Complications in Interactive, Video-Sharing Environments', in Larissa Hjorth, Heather Horst, Anne Galloway, and Genevieve Bell (eds.), The Routledge Companion to Digital Ethnography, New York: Routledge, 2016, pp. 147–157.

_____. *Thanks for Watching: An Anthropological Study of Video Sharing on YouTube,* Louisville, CO: University Press of Colorado, 2019.

_____. dir. *Hey Watch This! Sharing the Self Through Media*, 2020, view at https://vimeo.com/394007182.

Lefebvre, Henri. *Rhythmanalysis*, London: Continuum, 2004.

Neff, Gina, and David Stark. 'Permanently Beta: Responsive Organization in the Internet Era', Working Paper, Institute for Social and Economic Research and Policy, Columbia University, 2002, https://academiccommons.columbia.edu/doi/ 10.7916/D8G44X47

Perelli, Amanda. 'How Much YouTube Pays Creators for 100,000, 1 million, and 4 Million Views', *Business Insider*, September 22, 2019, https://www.businessinsider.com/how-much-youtube-pays-for-views-100-thousand-million-2019-9.

Seaver, Nick. 'What Should an Anthropology of Algorithms Do?', *Cultural Anthropology* 33.3 (2018): 375-385.

Stokel-Walker, Chris. 'More than a Decade Later, How Do Original YouTube Stars Feel about the Site?', *Ars Technica*, June 11, 2017. https://arstechnica.com/features/2017/06 /youtube-changed-my-life-a-pair- of-original-videostars-ponder-a-life-lived-online/.

YouTube Creators. 'How Long Should Your Videos Be?' YouTube video, 16 January 2020, https://www.youtube.com/watch?v=G1tHzUGdMwY.

THE ABSENCE OF TELEPRESENCE

DAN OKI
(SLOBODAN JOKIĆ)

THE ABSENCE OF TELEPRESENCE

DAN OKI (SLOBODAN JOKIĆ)

The aesthetics of telepresence were conceived through telephone conversations. For today's fifty-year-olds, this was a sense of communication with a person outside the physical reach of voice and vision. The feeling grew stronger when you knew someone was very far away or that they were in some other time zone: that it was nighttime over there when you are calling in the daylight. Just over a hundred years ago, the first intercontinental radio call was conducted from Arlington, USA to Paris, France by radiotelephone, which was spectacular at the time. Today, the existence of telepresence is something quite commonplace.

Earlier, regular calls were always made from the same phone and received on a single phone within the family or work community. Intimate calls were those when someone called someone who, in some certain hour, somewhere else, was eagerly awaiting a call. When a house was full of people, they made group calls to another home, most often full of close persons. Often both groups have already visited other houses they were talking to now and they knew exactly where the phone was located at the other end of the wire. Phone calls for teenagers were confusing, when their parents answered and handed them the handset, and then listened to intimate conversations spatially anchored in a wire within a wall outlet. The calls from an unknown voice that had penetrated into privacy with unpleasant contents or excited breathing at the other end of the wire were disturbing. The privacy of one's own home did not necessarily mean the intimacy of a telephone conversation, so intimacy was sometimes only granted by going to the public space of a post office or telephone booth. In any case you could be alone in the phone booth, unlike your own home where you had to hide from your family. As a boy I was often in the post office with parents who called my father's sister, from Zadar to Paris. We did this even though we already had a phone at home. It was cheaper and everybody did it. Calling overseas from home was a great convenience that was expensive, which was the reason why people, aside from the post office, also telephoned from work, making private conversations at their workspace. This has diminished the difference between private and business telephone conversations.

In post offices, there were phones but also phone directories, which people used a lot if they wanted to call someone whose phone number they could not reach. However, the completion of phone directories of individual cities was much slower than the growth of telephone subscribers themselves. Communication was helped by personally written phone books, where people, along with the names of persons and fixed telephone numbers, carefully marked addresses, post office boxes, and later on mobile phone numbers and internet addresses. In written address books, just before the end of their widespread existence (which, by the way, already look like the dinosaurs of network culture), there were various forms of written recording of data related to telepresence. Address books have this importance even more so since they have been used for many years, as opposed to planners. Planners actually always lasted a single calendar year. Like address books, planners have become an integral part of computers, and later mobile phones and smartphones. In this transitional period, address books and planners connected the physical mobility with fixed telepresence through the functions of mobile telephony.

Telepresence spread into everyday public space, first through mobile phones as audio devices in the nineties, and then through multi-media devices in the second decade of this century. The telepresence before cellphones, visible in the interior of the home and in offices, moved from the privacy of home or the business of work on to the streets and squares, waiting halls, boats, planes, trams, buses, mountains, coasts of the sea and the lakes, along the rivers, on meadows or in remote forests.

I took the first series of photos of people with mobile phones in 1997 —when Sony was one of the world's leading mobile phone manufacturers — with the then old analog Minolta camera in Tokyo. Twenty years later, during the shooting of the second series of smartphone people in 2017 Samsung was one of the leading mobile phone manufacturers in the world as well as in the Far East. The epicenter of the mobile fever has moved from Tokyo to Seoul. I am convinced that cities and countries that produce a certain technology simultaneously produce a specific part of human reality mediated by that same technology. This is reflected most through the frequency and nuances of using technology in everyday life, whether it is technological anthropological novelties, social engagement, or psychosocial pathologies that have infected society. Following these observations, it was logical to photograph the mobile callers in Seoul, just as I had photographed them in Tokyo twenty years ago.

The 1997 photo series was taken from a distance and the 2017 Seoul series from up close. Why? Twenty years ago, it was difficult to get close to *phone people* because they looked around as they talked, unlike today when they mostly look at the screen of a smartphone, so they do not notice what's happening around them. That's why I recorded long shots in Tokyo, unlike the recordings in Seoul where I recorded medium shots and close-ups. Then, in 1997, after a few shots, I found that I could not accurately focus the photos, nor set the exposure, so I was left with a sensory and experimental approach to photographing. I was most fascinated by the number of mobile phones in Tokyo, which were hardly ever used in Europe, while they were everywhere in Tokyo, in the most varied forms and colors. The mobile phone apparently became a new status symbol, especially among younger generations, but what was much more interesting is its anthropological-technological impact on the way of communicating, face gestures and behavior in the public space. People were staring absently at the space that was surrounding them directly, while they were acoustically driven to another space through telepresence. That was strange at first, especially if someone had a headset and a cell phone hanging around their waist, so at first glance they seemed to be speaking to themselves. Phones rang, played, sang, made sounds, inviting the owners to pick up the phone and accept the conversation, or make an appointment. The look was pointed at the phone only when dialing a number of another mobile phone, or by structuring simple settings. At the time, there were no contact lists or text messages in mobile phones, let alone cameras or the internet. The mobile phone at that time was actually an audio device so the audio mode of communication through telepresence was the first to entertain the everyday visual perception of public space. And now, the 'telephone' part of a telephone is the least important. The intensity of inclusion and exclusion from a given space occurred in the intensity of communication on the cellphone.

When the intensity of audio telecommunications was at its peak, the absence of looks and surprising reactions that were not related to what was happening in the public space were intensified, occasionally completely excluding those who became the repetitions of mirroring different telepresence from the physical space. When the conversation ended, they would return from the space of virtual and psychologically conditioned absence to the space before the conversation, and that was often the moment when they noticed the photographer.

Twenty years later, in Seoul in the spring of 2017, I did not intend to shoot people with phones, but I remembered what I had previously photographed in Tokyo. This series of photos and videos was shot with a Canon DSLR digital camera, which is different than the Minolta camera, as it can capture a motion picture in HD and in full resolution, which makes it actually similar to a movie camera. It was not just the digital camera that replaced the analog camera, but the technological change followed even in front of the camera, within smart phones that evolved from an audio device to a multimedia device, computer, camera and video camera in one.

Photographing people with smart phones was simpler, as the core of their presence and the dominant awareness of consciousness was no longer where they were physically located. Mostly, I photographed the minimal expressions on their faces with specific expressions of the most diverse psychological states. Activities of people with smartphones have been multifaceted into a spectrum of quite new protocols: chatting, surfing, texting, GPSing, reading, recording, addressing, scheduling, posting comments and images, listening to music, photographing, taking selfies in all directions, making videos, as well as watching and sharing a wide variety of photos and videos. At some moments I felt as if I was shooting the meta-synchronization of new chips, with the creation of neurons and synapses in young human brains that were simultaneously flowering with petals and the buds of cherry blossoms. It all seemed like a fascinating blend and unity of technology, human and nature in Seoul in 2017. But is that really the case?

For the past two decades we have been using the mobile phone to make calls from anywhere, to anyone, to any place covered by the network. All that civilization has communicated by telepresence, mediated through the global structure of the telephone connected to the wire, has been transformed within the same *disposition* framework into the new stored mobile media architecture of a global character, but this time with much greater coverage of the virtual presence and availability phenomena. Additionally, a whole new field of media creativity was open, and the masses have hurried toward cheap or free communication that was suddenly more accessible and faster. But this massive participation in communication also meant the prosperity of third parties - the owners of global web platforms. Monopolies on social networks, across a wide variety of Internet services, have been realized almost imperceptibly through presentation and storage of audiovisual content on the *web*, and are 'stored' even more imperceptibly in the cold shadow of private capitalist interests. Of course, they number in the billions.

Communication distributed as a digital database is different from a telephone conversation, the digital picture is different than a fax sent out in paper rolls. The chronotopes made through the interlacing of private and public, business and secret are still present in the public space, but their former contents have been completely blended through various social-media protocols in the technologically different everyday life of newly established mobile media architecture of the 21st century. Humanity, a linguistic animal, came to the border they are just overcoming by becoming a *cinotelematic* animal.

As a person is not born with the ability to speak, she learns to do so in her early years and perfects it through life; we can say that in this century speech and digital text are increasingly coming under the *disposition* of mobile media protocols. The multiplication of psychological, ethical and aesthetical manifestations opened up new questions about models of self-consolidation, and later about ecological aspects of presence. It is astonishing how fast children master these protocols and how deeply and tactually they pierce them with their tiny fingers and brains. Parents are struggling with children to regulate the amount of time they spend on these so called 'smart' phones; a new generation of cell phones that have been referred to (in this context with a lot of irony) as *smartphones* - why would you fight with the child to use or surround itself with something that's really smart? Since much of the time devoted to play, creativity, communication with others and dealing with different environments is now happening in the smartphone domain, the question is how it will affect the younger generation, but adults as well.

Perhaps in this search of answers to these questions, we will be helped by a kind of paradigm shift in the scientific approach to the problem. Thanks to neural coding (a field of neuroscience), we have found that tuning curves of neuronal activity during sensory encoding of the brain (displayed on a coordinate system, when looking at footage of a walk past a river on television or a video projection) strongly coincide with tuning curves of neuronal activity of people who are really walking past that same river.[1] However, the tuning curve following the actual walk along the river in the coordinate system is significantly above the one following people watching the footage, although they are very similar. The difference between the tuning curves lies in the amount of engaged neurons, the intensity of the experience, but there is no significant diversity in the tuning curve itself within the coordinate system. What is questionable is precisely this diminished number of neurons, attention reduced by media technology, limited experience of a pre-mediated world that until now belonged solely to duality of anthropological and philosophical aspects of language in relation to reality. Another good example of media contaminating the awareness of a situation is at a dinner at a restaurant where two people communicate using a smartphone and send food photos to social networks. Why do they not want to look at each other's faces? Namely, the process of looking at a human face requires complex neuronal activity as one of the most demanding processes of brain activity. Frequent and everyday media reduction of neuronal use easily makes people avoid physical situations that require neuronal effort and complexity they are not accustomed to, which they have systematically avoided through universal *medialization* of different aspects of life. This logically results in the reduction of communication predispositions in *non-medialized* reality as well as increased attention contamination.

---

1   Vittorio Gallese and Michele Guerra, 'Embodying Movies: Embodied Simulation and Film Studies',
     Cinema 3 (2012): 183–210.

In the twenty-year timespan with technological and anthropological changes, there has also been a change in the internal view into the *disposition* of a smartphone as an art tool. This change is realized through the following: the viral nature of photography and motion pictures, *telematic* dissemination of the camera *disposition* from paper, screen or projection onto social networks, direct visual communication of telepresence through mobile devices, and thus in a new contextualization of photography and film art as an artistic expression. Watching people with smart phones makes it clear that the cinematographic *disposition* works through their absence in the public space, and how it interacts with the gallery articulation *disposition*.

The motion picture in articulated gallery spaces as a *disposition* of visual arts is perceived through the physical presence of the body moving in space, unlike the cinema where the audience is in a state of rest and silence. In the exhibition context, the observer always knows where she is located and from what point she is viewing the work, often also aware of other visitors in the space, architecture, surrounding sounds, etc. In a cinema, the audience has literally been emptied of the awareness of the space and the audience focuses together and gradually synchronizes with the time-space features of the projection in darkness. It would be wrong to say that when someone is moving and speaking, recording or tracking mobile navigation on a smartphone, this is in line with the *disposition* of exhibition articulation, while someone sitting in a restaurant, airplane or tram and watching video on a mobile device would suit the cinema. Why? Simply because we are speaking about the emergence of a new complex *disposition* of multimedia mobile communication.

The instantaneous but also non-instantaneous possibility of various ways of communicating by smartphones has provided, unlike the computer, the sudden mobility that is achieved through the many modes of self-styling, self- activating, self-emitting and self-documenting. The intimacy in front of the networked screens is now visible in public space, during the performance of character, personality, and the construction of interpersonal relationships. Media creativity is often its own goal, in the direction of shaping social plastics as an instantly created and a simultaneously *networked* autobiography. This immanent aspect of instantaneity and a new kind of autobiography is a significant feature of the *disposition* of multimedia mobile communications.

The gradual incorporation of artistic design processes of the 1920s and 1930s avant-garde into computer programs for design, drawing, graphics, photography, sound, film, etc. occurred in the eighties and nineties of the past century, as Lev Manovich claims.[2] We can say that the same thing happened afterwards with conceptual and media art of the sixties and seventies. It has been built into the technological communication protocols of smartphones. Unlike the works of avant-garde art from the 1920s, where key objects were paintings and sculptures, in the conceptual and media art of the 1960s, there was a shift towards the intangible aspect of communicating with the audience, towards virality and social plastics that were realized in the smartphone, half a century later. In both cases, it is about digital technological synthesis of artistic processes. Certain art movements, that appear very diverse in a certain point in time, are visibly becoming similar and placed under the common denominator of digital through

---

2   Lev Manovich, *Soft Cinema*, Karlsruhe: ZKM Center for Art and Media Karlsruhe, 2002.

this technological synthesis of creative processes. From a temporal distance this fusion of plastic mental contents seems entirely logical and obviously does not include the complete individual artistic act as such, but realizes the general artistic process.

The question is what will happen with the art of today, the artistic process of which is still not seen from the necessary distance, nor has it been technologically mapped. It is not about whether the chip as a material is smarter than a rock or whether the latest medium erases the meaning of the one preceding it. Of course, people will work with both rock and chip, they will continue to use radio or watch television while using smartphones. The new material and the new media, of course, do not wipe out the ones preceding them, but they place them into a new context and give them new meaning. The development of art and technology in this way works through constant innovations, and their simultaneous overcoming is determined by the establishment of infinitive regression or the simultaneous return to old materials and old media. The source of one and the other is human self-awareness, perception and reflection of the world mediated by generation changes, their methods of evaluation, creation and reconceptualization of new and old technologies.

The union of planners and address books, writing and publishing, cameras and screens, recording and broadcasting, creative work and audience is realized in the smartphone. How do we use this device? It seems to me that the best answer to this question is related to direction, because all these activities unify the life-changing protocol that is happening following our personal directorial conception that is simultaneously documented in the smartphone and its *network*. Broadcasting the personal communication of speech and writing is gathered through the automatic scanning of once-immaterial language manifestations. Automatic photo albums or movie diaries are edited by erasing or new recordings within the established viral database of audiovisual data where capturing, montaging, and archiving are united in a multimedia autobiography. In this instantly documented and broadcasted autobiographical displacing of the self, there are frequent narcissistic disorders due to the vast media mirror found in the many blind points of the individual's reflexive (in)visibility, which is seen or unseen by the individual, but is visible to others who are also most often burdened and tangled within the network of narcissistic machines.

Therefore, at the end of this text, I suggest that we replace the media direction of autobiography with the direction of bioautography, as the basis of attention ecology, structure and action in the context of smartphones. What do I mean and what are the sources of such a proposal?

The word bioautography is most often mentioned in the pharmaceutical context.[3] Therein, it means using cells to detect their attachment or other reactions in the presence of a particular substance. Bioautography is a biotest that not only allows the detection of compounds in plant extracts more efficiently than ever before, but also a test based on the ability of some compounds (e.g. Vitamin B12) to increase the growth of some organisms or compounds

---

3   Saikat Dewanjee, Moumita Gangopadhyay, Niloy Bhattacharya, Ritu Khanraa, and Tarun K. Dua, 'Bioautography and its scope in the field of natural product chemistry', Journal of Pharmaceutical Analysis 5.2 (2014): 75–84.

and to suppress the growth of others. When this definition, or even better, its process, is transposed into the context of general human life as a kind of technological narrative-visual realization (i.e. autobiography - self-writing), we come to the definition of self-writing. It is actually an attempt to write out life, or the only letter we write the moment when we try to overcome a certain medium and introduce ourselves as the content. In this context, we come to the concept of the ecology of attention, analyzed by Yves Citton in his book *The Ecology of Attention*.[4]

This ecological self-writing or auto-medialization as the introduction of the self into the space of one's own environment with constant reflection related to the awareness of the possibility of (self)observation from outside and continuous adaptations to discursive assumptions corresponds to the concept of bioautography. In the case of the approach we're discussing here, it is about self-testing reactions that are, within ourselves, creating the use of new technologies such as the smartphone. The techniques of the self, such as recognition, separation, and the reduction of certain elements of telepresence, are an integral part of everyday life that leads to the ecology of attention. As the testing of technology on humans is increasingly spreading (and preventing the inclusion of the ecological contents of attention into everyday life for a good part of users), the principle of bioautography is more clearly depicted on the horizon as the subject, performance and object of contemporary *homo sapiens*. The feature of each new medium is somehow to dazzle the user in a self-test of reality, and this (the medium) is realized as a temporary purpose in itself. Here, together with the narcissism of media prestige as a self-produced technology (genre), the user's narcissism rises as the logical consequence.

This narcissism is the consequence of access to media. It is interesting that this approach is not defined as socially, but generationally conditioned. Thus, Katharine Hayles separates the *deep attention* of older generations from the *hyper-attention* of younger generations, raised in the digital environment.[5] Reading a book or watching a movie in the cinema requires deep attention, and a good part of the younger generation is no longer able to do so because they do not have the ability of focusing on one content. More so, such content is described as boring because they need a lot of different stimuli to keep them focused for a longer time period. It is mathematically logical that a consciousness divided into several channels of attention can't be as profound as 'one-channel' consciousness, but the contemporary person of the 21st century should certainly still have to master both types of attention recognized by Hayles. In fact, it is remarkable that the rise of new media is recontextualizing the usage of older media. We could say that hyper-attention actually recontextualizes deep attention, giving it not only a new meaning but also new modes of existence.

Acknowledgements Text is a result of PhD research at ASCA - University of Amsterdam. Funded in part by Centre for Cross Cultural and Korean Studies, University of Split. Practice based artistic research was helped by VN Gallery in Zagreb and HULU in Split.

4   Yves Citton, The Ecology of Attention, Cambridge: Polity Press, 2017.
5   N. Katherine Hayles, 'Hyper and Deep Attention: The Generational Divide in Cognitive Modes', Profession (2007): 187–119.

References

Citton, Yves. The Ecology of Attention, Cambridge: Polity Press, 2017

Dewanjee, Saikat, Moumita Gangopadhyay, Niloy Bhattacharya, Ritu Khanraa, and Tarun K. Dua, 'Bioautography and its scope in the field of natural product chemistry', Journal of Pharmaceutical Analysis 5.2 (2014): 75–84.

Gallese, Vittorio and Michele Guerra. 'Embodying Movies: Embodied Simulation and Film Studies', Cinema 3 (2012): 183–210.

Hayles, N. Katherine. 'Hyper and Deep Attention: The Generational Divide in Cognitive Modes', Profession (2007): 187–119.

Manovich, Lev. Soft Cinema, Karlsruhe: ZKM Center for Art and Media Karlsruhe, 2002.

THE SELF-SPLINTERING EVOLUTION OF MUSIC VIDEOS IN THE ERA OF DIGITAL (DIY) AUDIO/VISUAL STREAMS

ALBERT FIGURT

THE SELF-SPLINTERING EVOLUTION OF MUSIC VIDEOS IN THE ERA OF DIGITAL (DIY) AUDIO/VISUAL STREAMS

ALBERT FIGURT

'For the new music we can stay home' *ADILKNO, The Dominant Ear, 1992*

What exactly is a 'music video'?

A visual narrative that *illustrates* a pre-existing audio content? A short film *modeled on* the pace of a song? An emotional trip *evoked* by sounds? Or simply some bare historical [or historicizable] *video-recording artifact* of specific people playing specific instruments in specific spatio-temporal set[ting]s? And for what concerns the medi{a}eval times before the advent of commercial television - with its particular flowering of dedicated video_music channels in the '80s & '90s, did the cinematic industry ever come out with relevant or isolated *ante litteram* (maybe we should say: *ante picturam*) musically-infused snippets? What about *silent cinema*, notoriously rarely silent at all (a live soundtrack was supposed to be played in sync with moving images, not to mention the habitual loud and collaborative response from early movie theater crowds) or — vice versa — the once glorious genre of *musical films*, triumphant fetishes of the 'sound era' (where any mundane chore could be millimetrically rearranged into some happy-go-lucky socialite chore+ografy, whilst adjacent ordinary actions are gently dunked into meta-narrative singing & dancing [a pretty disorienting, chewing-gum-flavoured version of late-Brechtian 'verfremdungseffekt' aka 'estrangement'])?

In a nutshell: how much *actual music* or *musical equipment* are we supposed to see or be confronted with, while experiencing some kind of music-related visual media content? And how deeply are we (spectators or synesthetic listeners) and they (fictional characters, players or narratees within the very content) supposed to be aware of such *wriggling inner musicality*, oscillating between flamboyant visibility and allusive opaqueness (in academic jargon: between the *infra-* and the *extra-diegetic register*)?

Whip panning to the [near] present: what happens to this already *slippery balance* when autonomous yet unorganized music video production becomes the norm (see under: post-Mtv user-generated wilderness), a lot of celebrated YouTube personalities are musicians or performers and *most of the top-ranking, billion-views-plus videos are strictly audio/visual [read: language-no-problem] or somehow music-related?*[1]

---

1   en.wikipedia.org/wiki/List_of_most-viewed_YouTube_videos
     en.wikipedia.org/wiki/List_of_viral_music_videos
     https://en.wikipedia.org/wiki/List_of_viral_videos

I certainly have a lot of doubts: some of them will be addressed, problematized and partially solved here; all the rest is a mixture of chaos and creativity, a breeding ground particularly dear to yours truly (videoartisan and musician), but also almost inevitable while working - as in this case - at the crossroads of *languages*, *[new?] media* and *devices*. In short: most of the questions will remain itching fissures, but they're meant to positively in/af_fect you (hoping for further understanding via mutual brain-rubbing).

What follows is therefore a *colloquial rollercoaster* of scratchy, open-ended reflections accumulated throughout the years - interspersed with some scattered creative samples of exponentially demanding complexity (or, conversely, a tasty omnivor{aci}ous buffet of *video-tarts*, with some spicy theoretical sauce to dress and taste them - as you wish, and until sated).

SwINGIN' BREVI{ral}TY

I guess the first aspect worth focusing on (while tentatively addressing the decisive transition of video_musical material into the participatory web) is time-related, and has to do with *shortness*. When talking about a *music video*, indeed, we're usually referring to something between 3 and 5 minutes long:[2] that's because of the original fabrication and distribution of commercial pop songs, in turn shaped around the physical limitations of the legendary 45 vinyl record - aka 7''. Interestingly enough, not so much has changed from the revolutionary introduction of that double-sided hit single(s) aural[3] support: considering its friendly and emotional usability, an album-extracted pop song remains probably (since the 50's, and with very limited exceptions..) the *fastest disposable cultural object* in the whole mass media supermarket[4] - not including ads. Cinematic or televisual[ized] items, on the contrary, are generally way longer and thick to digest; still, even nowadays, they also tend to keep *vestigial yet prescriptive container-related lengths* (notwithstanding the growing pressures of deep remediation, on demand flexibility and online repurposing).

In this perspective, the introduction of YouTube changed everything - dramatically scrambling formats and frame[work]s of reference with an initial *upload limit* set at 10 minutes (the typical duration of..?), slowly expanded to the inescapable Warholian standard of 15 min (more or less ephemeral, when your potential audience is the whole world - but distracted?), in the end technically removed altogether - thus creating the ultimate pachyder{ando}mic video repository, with astonishing long takes that could range from a *4-hrs live feed* of a Tesla Roadster floating in outer space

---

2   As bizarre as it may *sound*, in some languages (like Italian, Spanish, French or Dutch) the word for a *promotional song-related short* is simply a generic but appropriate 'videoclip' (sometimes even 'clip').

3   The adjective is ambiguous - or even *amphibious* - since it could be referring to both *hearing purposes* or to a *long obliterated Benjaminian totem* with some deep analog added values, like prescribing a set of compulsory bodily habits (*stand up and flip me, please*) whilst establishing a phantomatic unspoken hierarchy (*I also have a B-side!*).

4   We shouldn't forget that precisely atomized *.mp3 files* have been the driving force of the *lossy compression goldrush*, started with the Napster-gate and now all around us in the (almost totally commodified) form of a multistranded peer-to-peer / streaming culture.

(but with a stereo unit on!) to a plethora of *10-hrs HD windows with mesmerizing soundscapes* (indiscriminately luring the user into relaxing eco-systems like dripping rain forests, crackling fireplaces or vaguely counterintuitive vacuum cleaner epics).[5]

Let's now analyze some of the most popular web videos of all times, starting from the very beginning (Fig. 1): on the left we have the (in)famous 'Numa Numa Guy',[6] haphazardly partying in his room in 2004 / on the right, one of the first internet celebrities - Matt Harding,[7] 'dancing badly around the world' (according to his own slogan) in 2008; two almost complementary memetic videos, both entertaining because goofy but strikingly different when it comes to authoriality, proxemics and spatial coordinates...

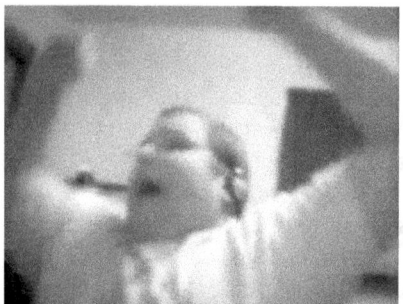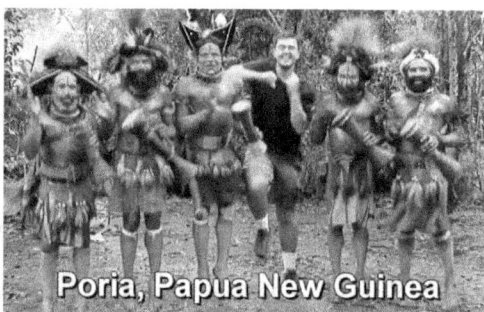

Fig. 1: 'Home sweet home' vs 'Mi casa es tu casa'

If we abruptly skip to 10 years after that uncannily poignant *lip-sync seated-ballet*, right at the apex of the YOLO/FOMO-fueled integration between online video platforms & social media ones (with YouTube establishing itself as the brand new [paradoxically not-so-normative] standard in terms of *desirable visua*clickabi*lity*), another twofold example - strangely resonant with the first one - can be spotted (Fig. 2). On one side the 'Harlem Shake' phenomenon[8] - dated 2013, seemingly unplanned but very intriguing in its lighting quick 2-act storyline: roughly 15 seconds of autarchic dancing + 15 seconds of collective madness (something like a perfect cocktail of our lonely numa numa hero metamorphosing into the convivial globe-trotter shaman) / on the other side Pharrell Williams' 'Happy' videos' playlist[9] - dated 2014: an overwhelming 1-day marathon, composed of 24 different 1-hr videos, where the same song is repeated over and over again (crushing the limits not only of an ordinary hit single, music video or feature film but of segmented video consumption in general).

5   https://youtu.be/mVpfOQ1N3aM
6   https://youtu.be/KmtzQCSh6xk - *originally uploaded on newsground.com*
7   https://youtu.be/zlfKdbWwruY
8   https://youtu.be/8vJiSSAMNWw
9   www.youtube.com/playlist?list=PLKPi39tTpkdpjBVQZo5oFLWjFjIOMkd2A

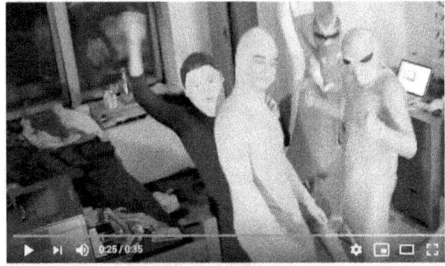

DO THE HARLEM SHAKE (ORIGINAL)

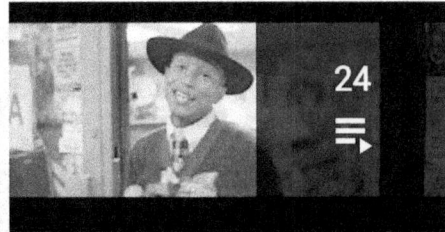

24 Hours of Happy

Fig. 2: 30" vs 24 hrs

Two highly debated video-memes, boosting their way out of a brutally reorganized media environment, yet - once again - two emblematic face[t]s of the same coin: the first one harsh, site-specific, steadily captured and ultrarapid / the second some sort of explorative endless take, recorded with a stabilized professional camera in constant fluid motion. A couple of *bewitching dancing acts*, cartoonistically *stretching or compressing space-time limitations* while inviting our sensory system (eyeball in primis) to *join the party* - incidentally, both Dawkinsian carriers gave then birth to an incredible proliferation of gloCALLy disseminated responses, parodies, mash-ups and emulations (a bunch of collateral relics that afterwards, in their abundance, feel even more relevant or contagious than the 'originals').[10]

This is to say that pop songs and popular web clips go hand in hand since the very rise of digital video hosting services: first of all because they share a *limited length* as well as a desperate need to catch the attention of the viewer/listener (read: *captivating attitude*), but also because *music is a universal trans-cultural language* - so virality can be guaranteed by purely audio/visual streams of information, not necessarily infiltrated by words (and anyway: if you don't know how to play, at least you can dance!).[11]

MULTIPLIERS of SOLITUDE(s)

Turning the disc: have you ever seen this man?

He has variously been described as 'the mysterious Chatroulette piano-player' or the 'impromptu singer/songwriter' (Fig. 3); around 2010 he quickly gained an impressive cult following by improvising *customized melodies & ready-made lyrics* while looking at his

10 Can we otherwise index them as wannabe 'musical flash-mobs' or 'calls to action' (particularly after the initial *incubation*)? Not sure, but it's vital to notice that while the first one is literally accidental and not promotional, the second one is conceived to be an exuberant sensation - talking 'bout the difference between a *seasonal flu* and *bacteriologic guerrilla*...

11 See the prolific current, in the following years, of *clubbing [video]hits*: Psy's 'Gangnam Style' (first video to reach 1 billion views in 2015 - now they're 3.5 bln), Bruno Mars' 'Uptown Funk' (uploaded on Nov, 2014 - 3.7 bln as I write) and Luis Fonsi's 'Despacito' (uploaded on Jan, 2017 - 6.67 clicks in just 3 years); is the secret ingredient to be identified somewhere in the prescribed / warmly suggested [massively ornamental] *dance steps*?

random Interlocutors' [re]actions during *real-time serendipitous sessions within videochat websites*. Originally perceived as an evanescent human juke-box (unpretentiously free-styling his days away in front of a screen), he was actually carefully recording and skimming the best takes in order to repost them on his private channel via a selection of fresh and unique super-cuts.[12]

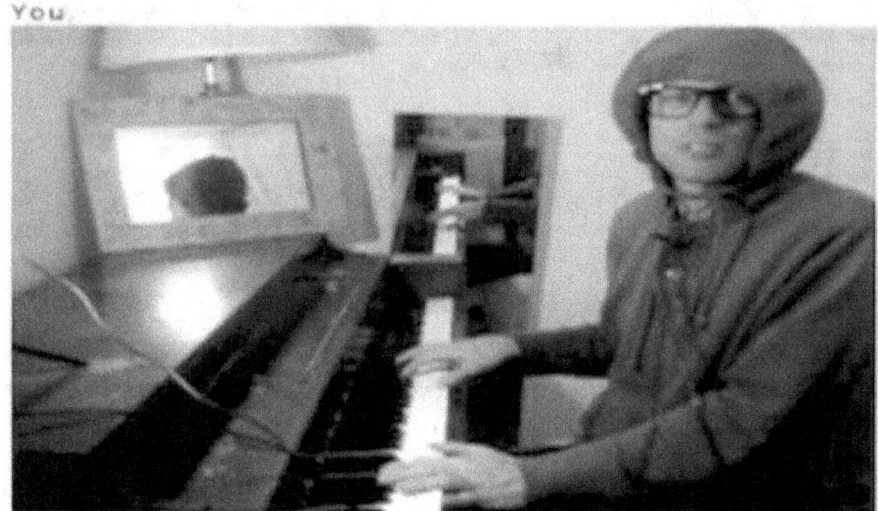

Fig. 3: *Me² = Me-Me*

However, what stands out for me here (apart from the obvious [and abused] metaphorical 'from bedroom to stardo{®}m' upgrade, or the undercurrent gradual tendency - especially in the last decade - to con/fuse creativity with exhibited interactivity [or interpassivity]) is our hooded man *self-framing mise-en-scène*: as you can see, there's one mirror replicating the pianist's head and another one virtually extending the piano he's busy playing - just an inventive way to optically enlarge the tiny borders of that average bohemian attic, or a subtle (even unconscious) allusion to the way sound sources are [re]com_bined/piled during accurately diligent, handmade and mindful musical work?

Multi-tasking (or better *'task-switching'*) is an inherent factor in music: you have *polyphony, harmony, counterpoint, chords, arrangement* and so on - all words meant to describe an organized array of different soundwaves, emitted simultaneously by one or more inter/dependent muscle, limb, instrument, sound source or sonic channel. Note that this is not so convenient with mere spoken words (let's say: not artistically pleasant) - the only way to accept more than one voice at a time being in a choir, unison, or Gregorian chant. *Multiplicity of output(s)* is therefore peculiar to musical evolution, a stunning arborescence from single notes to monophonic melodies to symphonic scores to, eventually, ∞-track recording.

---

12   https://youtu.be/JTwJetox_tU

And here it comes again some piece of *tech-machinery*, playing a crucial role: before the advent of phonography, the *multilayered package of an elaborated symphony* was to be silently conceived in the head of the composer, then transcribed *on paper*, then played somewhere, sometime, by some orchestra (maybe); after the advent of phonography, there was the possibility to directly *record live sound* without being obliged to produce or use a *side sheet* (that's what jazz & early rock 'n' roll musicians used to do) - but just as a *single track*, meaning that no consecutive intervention was allowed. Then *multiple-track recorders* arrived, and it was a shock: just as musical history & practice tellingly changed while slowly evolving towards polyphony, musical notation and phonography, also the giant step of *shifting from single-track to multi-track recording* generated unprecedented re/percussions in the affiliated industry. All of a sudden futuristic knob-riddled *mixing desks*, almost mystical in their design and potentialities, opened not only a complete new galaxy of 'recording craftsmanship' - with records wholly imagined & built directly in *audio engineering facilities* (up to the studio itself becoming at times the *overriding instrument* - to be virtuously 'played'); they also ultimately refreshed the composer position, crowning an already gifted ensemble swiss-army-scribe as the *ultimate cybermaster of extensive cathedrals of sounds* - finally able to manipulate frequences, weave intricated sequences, baptize convoluted sonic scaffoldings and even (after the introduction of MIDI workstations) mimic all possible oscillatory entry in the wavelength-cyclopedia (or synthesizing unheard ones) with the simple touch of a fingertip on a plastic keyboard.

\\\ Case scenario: what if you're not only a composer, but also a *talented multi-instrumentalist* (read: you can master several instruments)? Augmented case scenario: what if you want to give it a try at *self-sufficient multi-playing* (read: work on introspective, stratified pieces of music)[13]? Case scenario on [a]steroids: what if you also would like to *showcase a visual outcome of your lively efforts*? ///

Well, you basically have to choose between two radically diverse options:

1) become a traditional *one-man band* (sometimes also referred to as 'one-man orchestra'), thus opting for a *body-related, live or performance-based approach*: travel the world as a gipsy busking artist, with all your equipment physically tangled on you [..a happy but somehow goofy gesture?] simultaneously activating different portable instruments via a series of skillfully coordinated gestures[14]

---

13 Many famous multi-instrumentalist musicians, also because of their unrestrained selfish attitude (difficult to cope with when you're in a band, almost impossible to handle if you happen to be the *band leader*), have fallen back on this: some notable examples of one-man-band-recorded songs (or entire LPs) can be found in the discography of Paul McCartney, Frank Zappa, Stevie Wonder, Phil Collins, Sting, Lenny Kravitz, Prince, Billy Corgan or Burzum.

14 An assembly-line alternative could be relying on a loop station, either enclosing yourself within a circle of selected inter-connected instruments (i.e. https://youtu.be/n2eD4GcLohE) or recording modular units with just a single instrument and incrementally piling them up (guitars, basses and drumming kits feature prominently in this subculture, but maybe a unique properly trained voice [aptly amplified and effected] is the ultimate surprising option (i.e. https://youtu.be/0gKWfvd-chA).

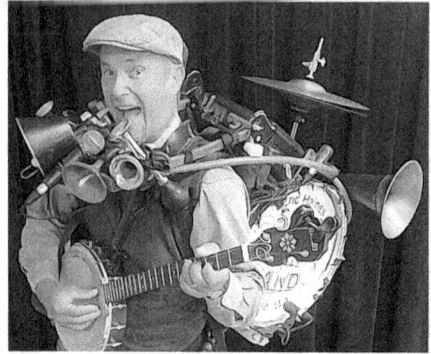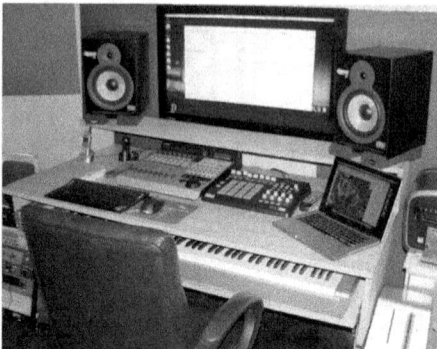

Fig. 4: Body vs So[ftware]ul

2) become a transhumanist *self-replicating musician*, thus relaying on a *meta-physical, recorded & remixed or interface-based approach*: apply your multi-tasking skills to intimate, sparkling audio/visual sampling [..hypershaking the numa numa rehearsal bedroom!] to simultaneously present your many converging talents, both music and video-related, through some unsettling yet thought-provoking *multi-channel [digital] installation*

LIV(e)ING WITH YOURSELF

Introducing Jack Conte, a popular Bay Area independent singer-songwriter, filmmaker, polymath virtuoso and recently (not by chance) founder and CEO of the crowdfunding venture 'Patreon': back in 2008, along with the weekly release of quirky split-screen extravaganzas[15], he was busy formulating the notion of 'VideoSong' (Fig. 5) - an *inspiring transversal format* characterized by 2 very basic [but quite disruptive] rules:

1) What you see is what you hear (No lip-sync for instruments or voice)

2) If you hear it, at some point you see it (No hidden sounds)

Does this ring a bell [various puns intended]? This is exactly the opposite of what usually happens in ordinary, classy, glamorous music videos - where everything is *artificial* or *contrived* (cable-less guitarists soloing on top of the mountains, singers chanting underwater) and a lot of additional texture sound is *undercover on purpose*.[16] Moreover, conventional music videos are normally constructed around the appeal and/or the beauty of the singer - inserted in some narrative or conceptual context, while in this kind of humble homely recordings *expertise* is the key and narration (even in the form

---

15   See www.youtube.com/playlist?list=PL73323A5328141496 (coincidentally, something I was also experimenting with, nearly at the same time: https://youtu.be/RYydNcwvPAw).

16   Unfortunately, this is increasingly happening also during [fake or faded] live concerts - where the band is concealed / parceled out, leaving the floor to [often auto-tuned] singers overacting on stage with BOOMbastic postures & gestures.

of lyrics) is more or less absent. Here *creative cleverness* (often blissfully released from withered structures, humorously self-referential and imbued by witty avant-gardism) is way more important than reassuring or glittery features, thus the *bare functionality of the performative musical body* [in real-time motion] finally overcomes the *pop iconography of the fictionalized spectacular body* [in playback-aided moves].

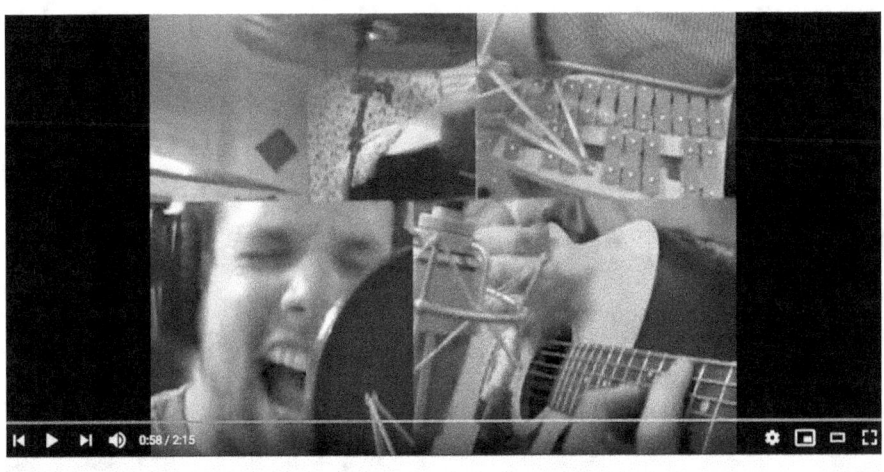

VideoSong 1 - Push - Jack Conte

VideoSongs Volume I

Mar 9, 2008   LIKE   DISLIKE   SHARE   SAVE   ...   Jack Conte - 2 / 8

Fig. 5: Me, myself (h)and I

Outlining it: musicianship meets DIY video practice, multi-track recording (coupled with multi-tasking software abilities) becomes multi-screen performance and *standardized music clips are fatally re-shaped as split-screen audio/visual egotrips*. Yep, 'cause for some reasons - as if a third unwritten rule was surreptitiously added overnight, most of Conte's VideoSongs out there (and the same applies to the vast majority of his subsequent copycats) are de facto adopting a visual *self-replicating strategy*.[17] The result, at first glance the umpteenth unanticipated online video craze, has proved to be a rather *exquisite [corpse] game-changer*.

With just a little research, you may infact discover that in the latest period many influencial musicians on YouTube & [Dolby] surrounding territories are embracing (consciously or not, occasionally or on a continuous basis) the *VideoSong self-replicating flavor* as a viable tool to present, modernize or promote themselves. Take Giulio Carmassi's dome{sophi}sticated smooth-jazz ballads,[18] Diego Stocco's self-assembled chordophones' compositions,[19] Publio Delgado's absurdist loop-sketches or 'destroyed jazz standards',[20] Gianni Luminati's ska rendition of 'Yesterday' in a clones'-crowded Lynchian-living-room,[21] Jacob Collier's

---

17   Slightly self-indulgent or exhibitionistic, but still - a *skilled and sonorous (!) reponse* to the deluge of mute
      selfies, adrenalinic go-pro stunts, unboxing charades, flirty camgirls and chatty commentators.
18   www.youtube.com/user/giuliocarmassi/videos
19   https://youtu.be/2MNb118Yp60
20   www.youtube.com/user/vendidou/playlists
21   https://youtu.be/TWHnqqVvarw

psychedelic n-Instruments jo{yful}urneys or reharmonized R'nB covers,[22] Harry Miree's kaleidoscopic 'Drummin #SELFIE' groovy patterns,[23] Davie504's bass bets and challenges (up to a gifted 13-billion-clicks stringless solo),[24] Louis Cole's vaporwave-drowned programmatically 'short songs'[25] and Pupsi's vegetable-only vibes[26]: this is just a partial scanning of the most successful, brilliant or crazy results emerging from an ever-enlarging club of tinkering adepts.

Some of these performers are already established click-millionaire or music professional, some have been in the meantime noticed by producers and put under contract, some are converting their reclusive endeavor into live shows (touring alone with the aid of complicated apparatuses or treading the stage with good old bandmates if not newcomers recruited for the occasion), some others are just hidden gems ready to be discovered and words-of-mouthed. Either by following, reworking, spreading, renegotiating or maximizing Jack Conte's *seminal thread/trend*,[27] it's like any proficient web musical videographer (or videoartist-turned-musician) wants at this point to test such specific recipe on his/her very digitized skin, like a customary *rite of passage* that can guarantee a *qualitative leap* - or a *piece of bravura* that has to be accomplished to proudly enter some re{de}fined élite.[28]

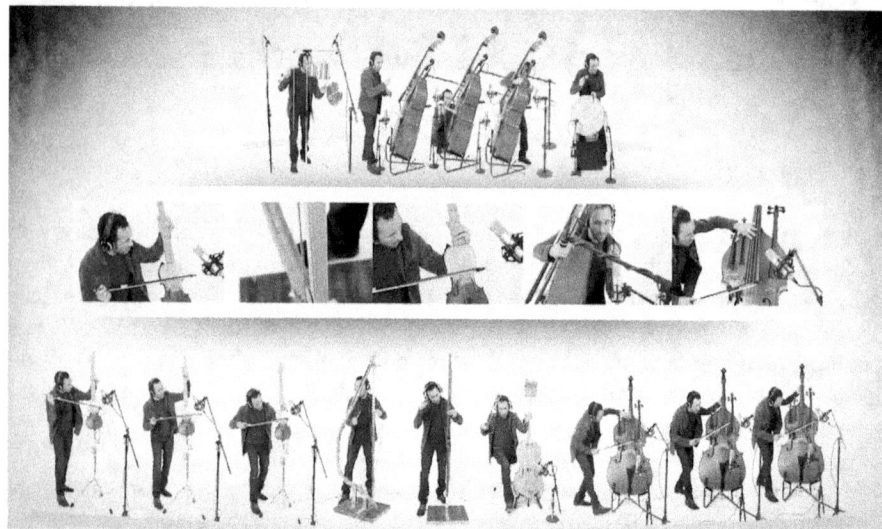

Fig. 6: Me ad-lib[idinem]; Diego Stocco, 'Custom Built Orchestra' (2012)

22   https://www.youtube.com/playlist?list=PLHX_dBxnc8z-gRnsslod1XrlQzKQqvRwp
23   https://youtu.be/d5sKsEqkoy8
24   www.youtube.com/user/Davie504/featured
25   www.youtube.com/user/louiscolemusic/videos
26   https://www.youtube.com/channel/UCftm4VNxngya7wjl_ZtLMPw/videos
27   Please refer to the 'Atlas of Clones' at the end of the article for a provisional taxonomy of self-splintering videos' aesthetic, editing choices and development.
28   Even Dave Grohl (former drummer of Nirvana / actual lead guitarist-singer of Foo Fighters - so an already notorious chairs 'n' roles swapper) felt the need to contribute to such undeclared match with a 23-minute progressive-rock sonata for 7 instruments: https://youtu.be/e05H80-k0mY.

WHAT THE HECK IS GOING ON(line)?

Apparently, we're standing at the [busy] intersection of *live_set* and *videotutorial*, *backstage* and *documentary*,[29] *videoart* and *installation*, *promotional content* and *vernacular creativity*, *online video dialect* and *new media crossover template*. One thing is for sure: often quite experimental, definitely variegated and professionally-inclined, *multiple iterations of this uncertain format* flourish every day at any corner of the web - all manifesting a similar trajectory towards a fragmented yet simultaneous *polyphony of the body image & sound(s),* all displaying an implied yearning for *media multiplicity & expanded artisticity* in the prosumer, user-generated-content arena.

I suggest to provisionally label the above-mentioned audio/visual UFOs as '*Self-Splintering Multi-Channel VideoSongs*', and to possibly scrutinize or (re)interpret them as a metaphorical representation of [corpo_real?] daily routine, solitude/solipsism, artistic production, social pressure, competition and talent in an heavily accelerated [post?]digital domain. These and other *video_mosaics* are indeed clearly symptomatic of impalpable epistemic feelings zigzagging within the online (video_musical) underbelly;[30] however, they cuncurrently popularize - in a refreshing and challenging way - the idea that *transmitting both a message & its generative process* could be not only transparently instructive but also extremely engaging.

With a sharp swerve from the golden age of televisual music videos, today's free-lance musicians (or video_song-writers) seem more interested in showing how unconditioned art is *created & assembled* in their sumptously-wired garage/mini-flat rather than [dis] playing or re-enacting formulaic earworms in fancy scenarios for monetary purposes;[31] the *work-in-progress*, hard-core (yet immaculate) musical moment appears to be more important than its discursive or commercial counterpart, so with VideoSongs (and derivative hybrids) moving images don't simply complement or suffocate the musical score with the only imperative of better selling it out, but are employed precisely to unveil or celebrate its *fascinating intricacies* and *compositional labor*.

Last but not least: most of these clips are nakedly presented or proposed as straightforward (but seldom simplistically played) *instrumental pieces*; sonic sculptures to audiovisually contemplate, so that the whole focus is for once (and/or for a change) totally on *the real thing* - with no more language barriers, technical restrictions or intoxicating paraphernalia.

---

29 To be fastidiously nitpicking, since it's biologically impossible to gather a living orchestra of selves (so far), mockumentary would be a better choice of word. On the flipside, albeit confusing, a *serialized selves' band* videoclip is just the *visual equivalent of a soloist recording enterprise* (see footnote 13); the perceptive dissonance is of course greater if the video presents contiguous [SFX-obtained] or fast-paced sequential *self-replication framing* (check Atlas' tables for more info).

30 ..full of *hyper-connected loners* & *not-so-beautiful losers* mass-turbating with sci-fi gizmos?

31 Sneaking afterthought - in some cases it could also be (sadly) the other way round: the general lack of money (or proper remuneration), so common in the art world, is forcing performers to capitalize solely on themselves and their isolated-dens' resources.

HAPPY (never)ENDING (story)

So, are videosongs of any kind destined to become the next reference embodiment of the elusive, chimeric 'music video'? Are they going to be, in parallel, among the opening decade's *viral delicacies* (after all, they could easily result funny and appealing also for non-expert or non-musician viewers)?

I don't know, I can't really tell - and honestly also not so interested about that.

As a musician (artistically grew up during the web infancy), I'm simply too excited to care: being able to regularly acknowledge via this subgenre the existence + expressive paths of dozens of *talenteDadaist individuals* (exploding their [master]minds out to my laptop with such a level of *insiders' pornographic detail*) is already compelling enough. For what concerns the filmmaking implications of all this mess, let's conclude instead with a wildly meta-referential / second layer kicker.

Remember Pharrell Williams' optimistic jingle? And what about Vine (¤ 2013 / † 2017), the gone-too-soon [and as-easily-forgotten] Twitter/ing app enabling smartphone users to share 6-second-long video-loops? Coming full-circle, here you have Rob Scallon's 'Vine Symphony'[32] - a very curious homage to the 24 hrs video-epidemic.

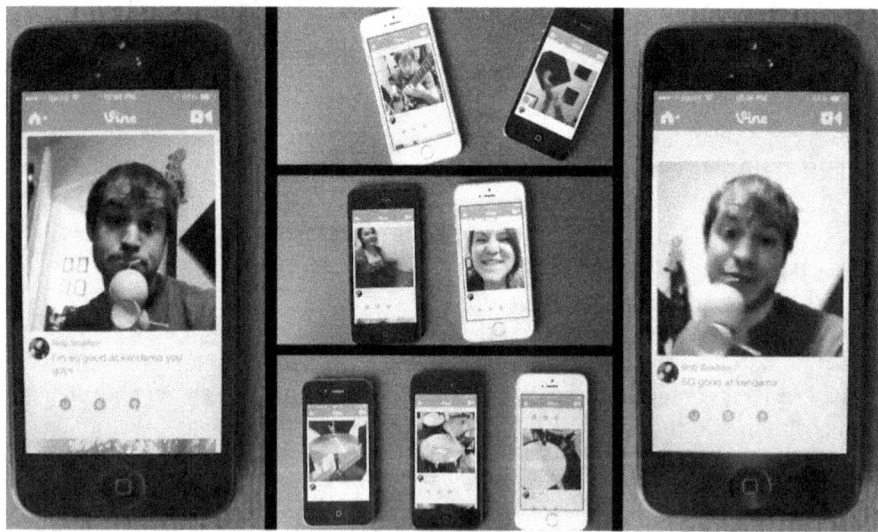

Fig. 7: [Me, myself (h)and I] *device(s)*

Reading from the video caption: 'I discovered that one measure of 'Happy' is exactly 6 seconds. So this happened.' From extreme lenght to extreme fragmentation, then - a squared *multi-channel-turned-multi-[smartphone]-screen installation*, at a time tangible

---

32   https://youtu.be/87OAf5siak4

& digital: tangible because of the interrelated assemblage of meticulously synchronized devices in physical proximity / digital because little by little their proliferation is further segmented by applying the usual post-productive split-screen trick(s).

__Closing distressful head-scratchers__

Should we expect an upcoming automation of simulacrum-splintering videos? Why can't underground geniality still get completely rid of gregariouSharing or mainstream danceable fads to be noticed or discussed? If a measure of 'Happy' lasts exactly 6 seconds, what's the measure of happiness in our frantic anthropoceniCircus?

Are we doomed to get stuck / stay [b]locked in our solitary *room-verse*, never enjoying a proper *living-room-chorus* again, multiplying ourselves for the sake of art but also to alleviate a meta_static personal or hetero-directed loneliness?[33]

Hoping all this question{able}s' listing won't inadvertently splinter your reading & videosurfing mind, too - or perhaps just leave you with some unwanted, *dis_concerting aftertaste* - that's all (for now).

---

33 Writing from Milan, Italy, 18 March 2020. End of the first week of 'national quarantine': social distancing is a painful necessity, outdoor activities are severely reduced (when not legally punished), fear is a foggy but sticky beast; in return, the MEDIcAI brew of late-to-the-party smart working + gaping balconies' concertStreaming + countless citiZENshipped CO{llaborati}VIDeos + free charity GigaBytes (to remotely divvy up, while emprisoned in aseptic bunkers by the state [of affairs]) sounds like a terrific, maybe mildly terrifying *UN_reality show* - still out of focus the showrunner's credentials, gloomy plot twists, perplexity and insecurity within the network(s) about the possibility to confirm next season of the series...

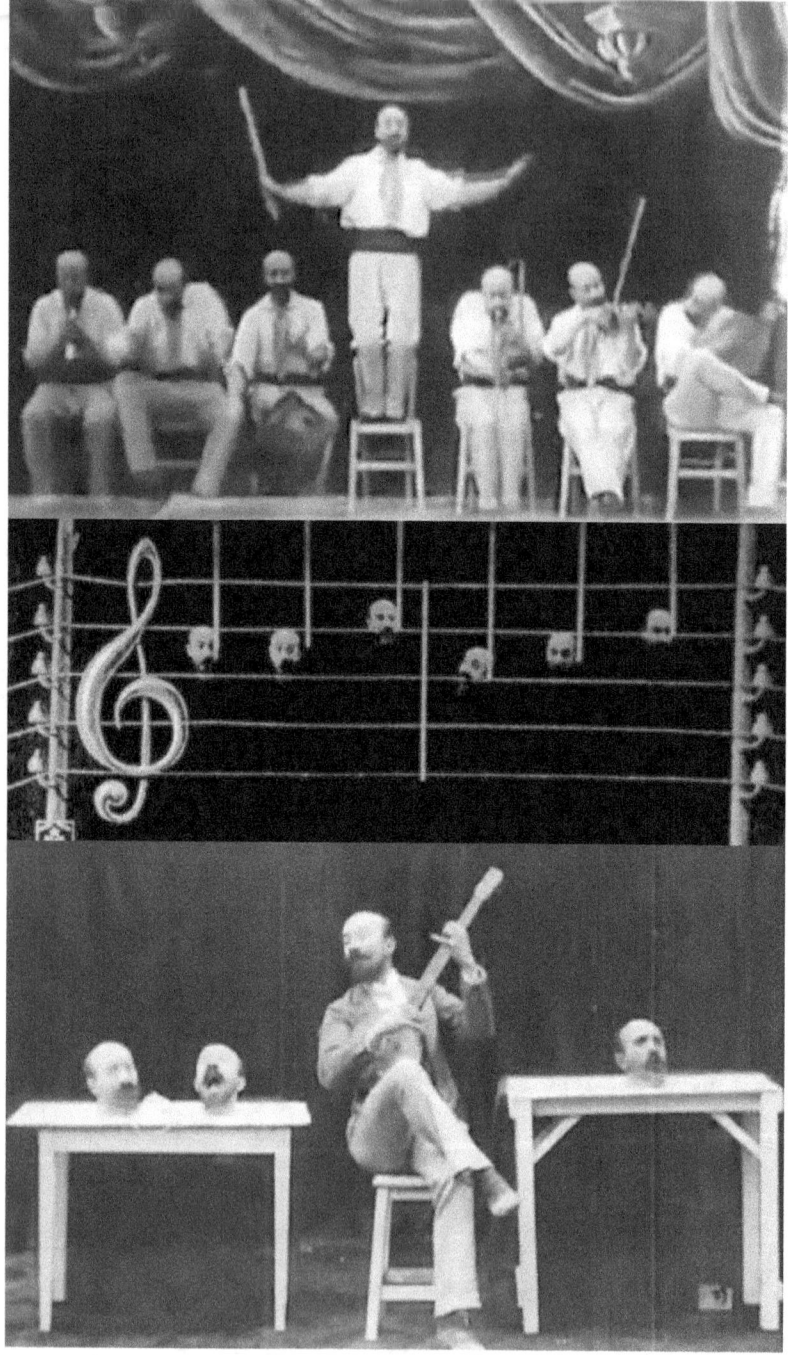

1. The GODFATHER
a former magician starts tinkering with multiple exposure and compositing techniques

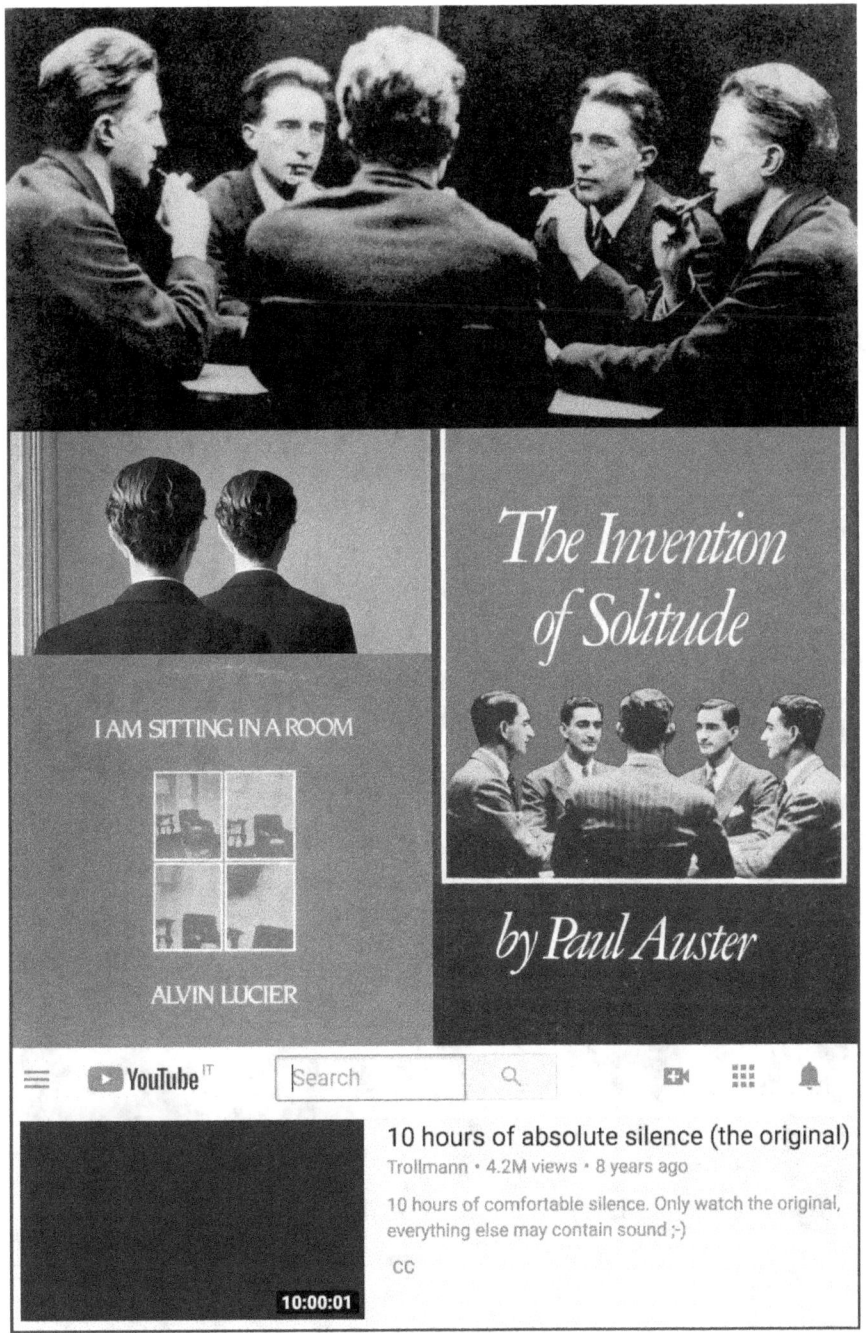

2. CONCEPTUAL SESSIONS
creative meetings with one's own demons

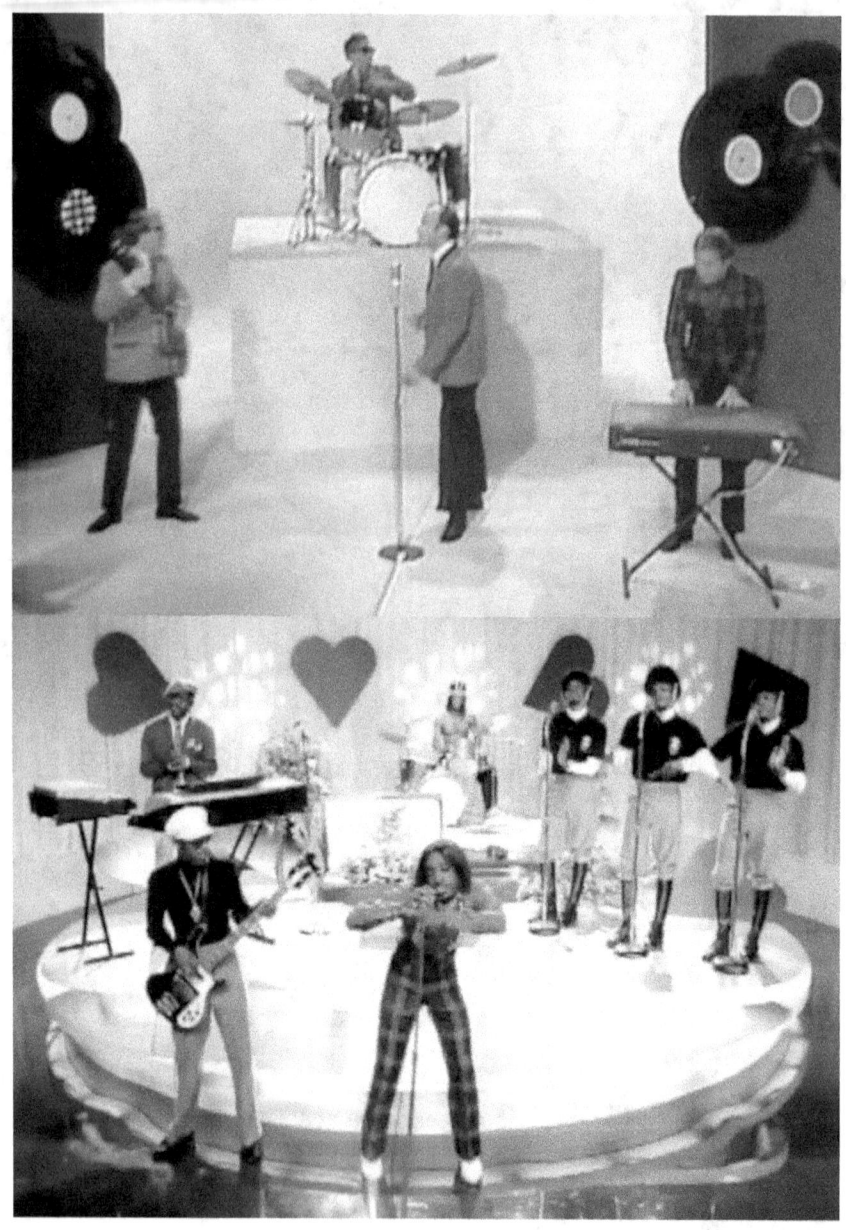

3. SIDE by SIDE (A)

metaphysical editing [pop version]

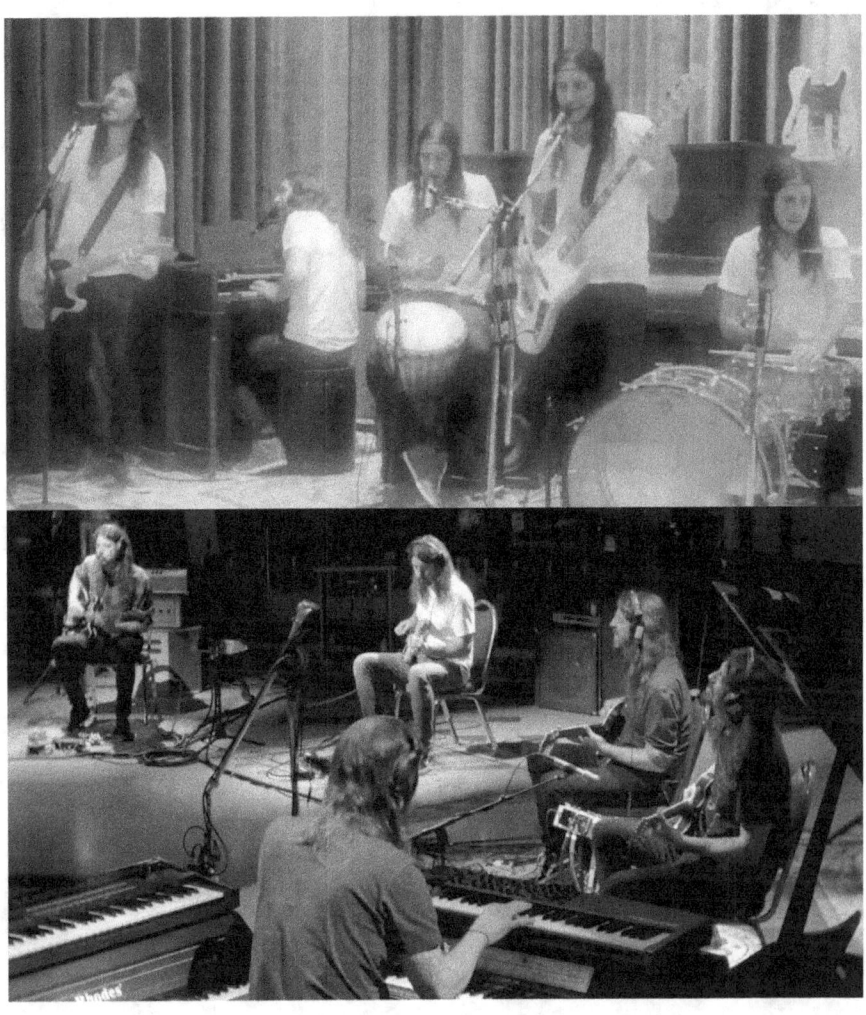

4. SIDE by SIDE (B)
metaphysical editing [indie-rock version]

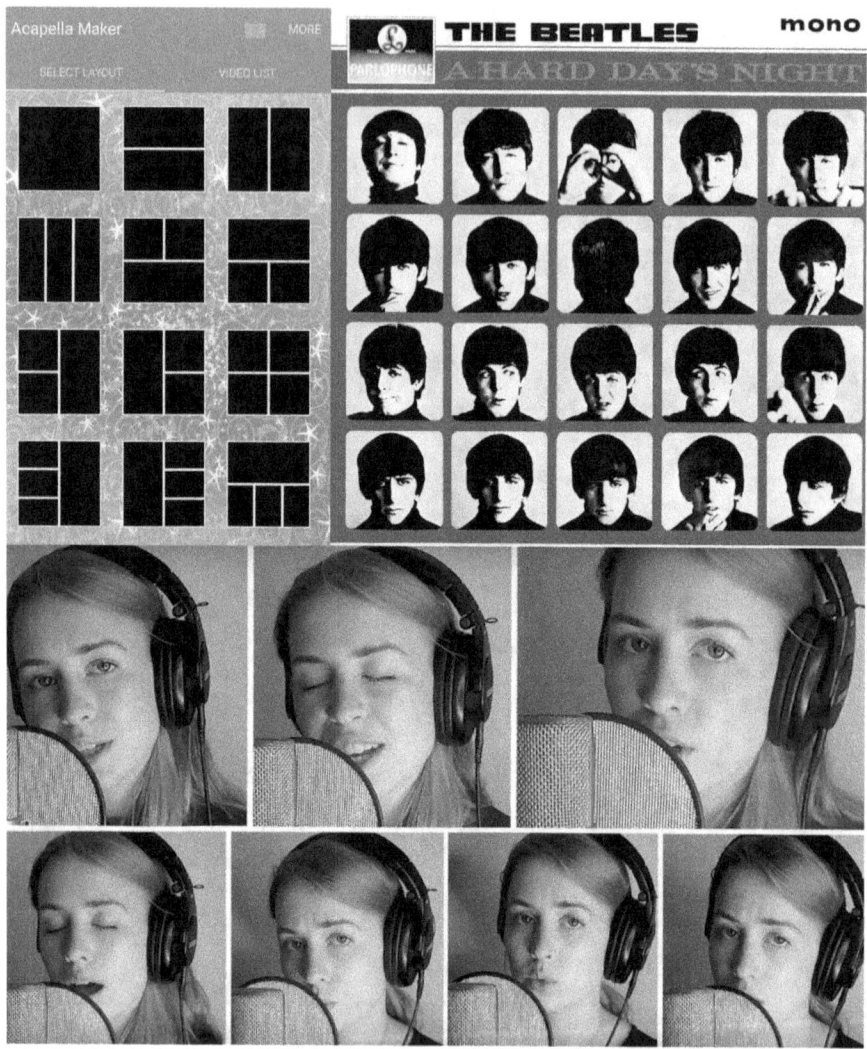

5. SONIC PHOTO BOOTHS
automatic self(ie)-portraits & the art of arranging vocal puzzles

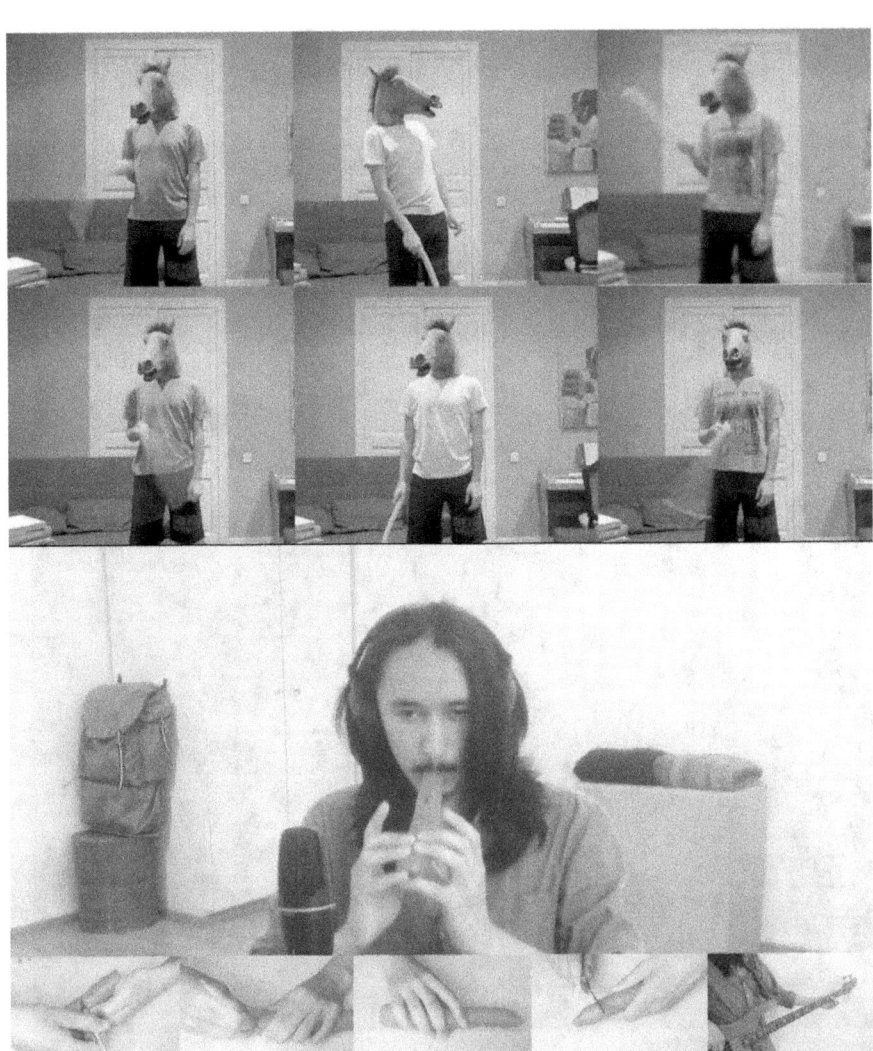

6. SELF-FULFILLING the GRID
eccentricity and web niches

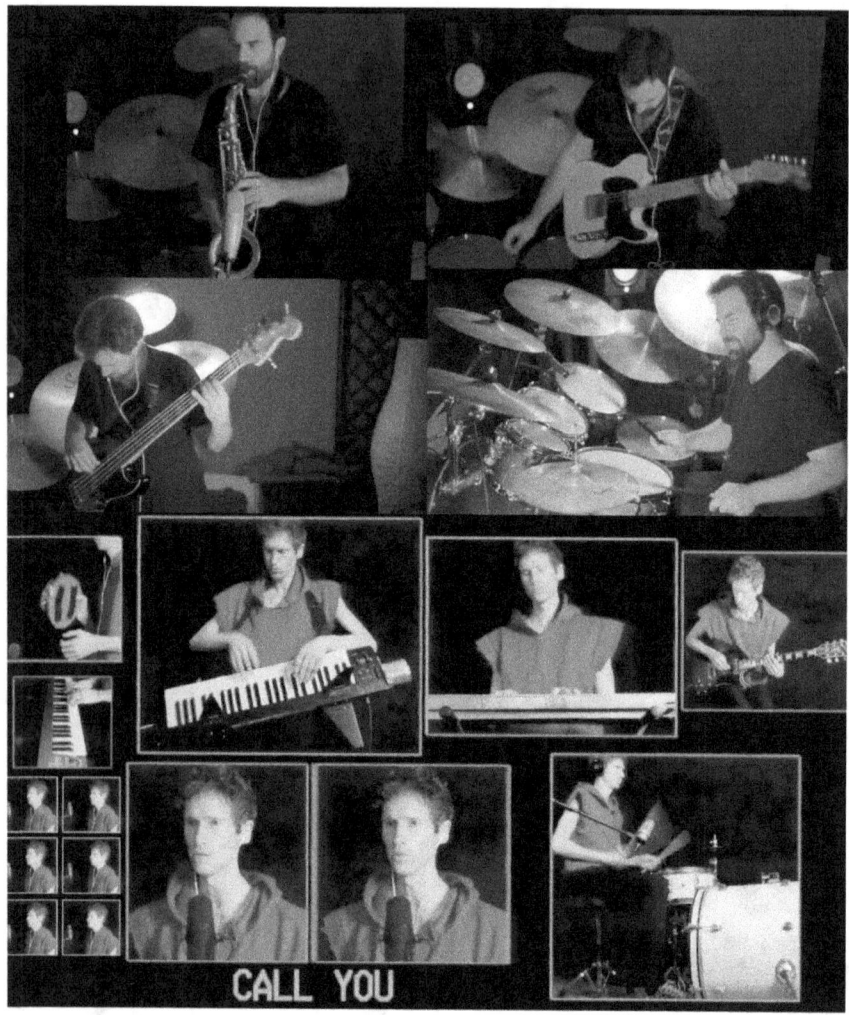

7. SELF-FULFILLING the GRID / to be continued..
audacity and networked reverberation

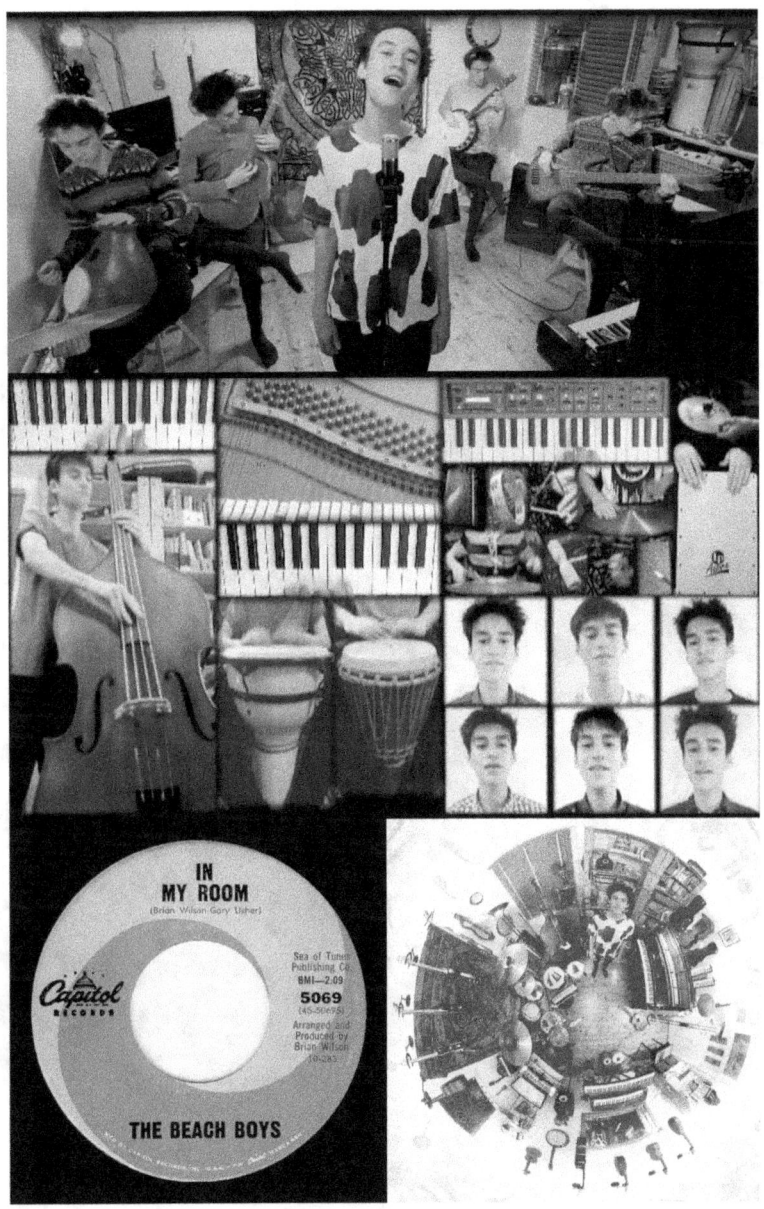

8. Elektrified WunderKammerSpiel
"do my dreaming and my scheming" (or: Jacob's ladder)

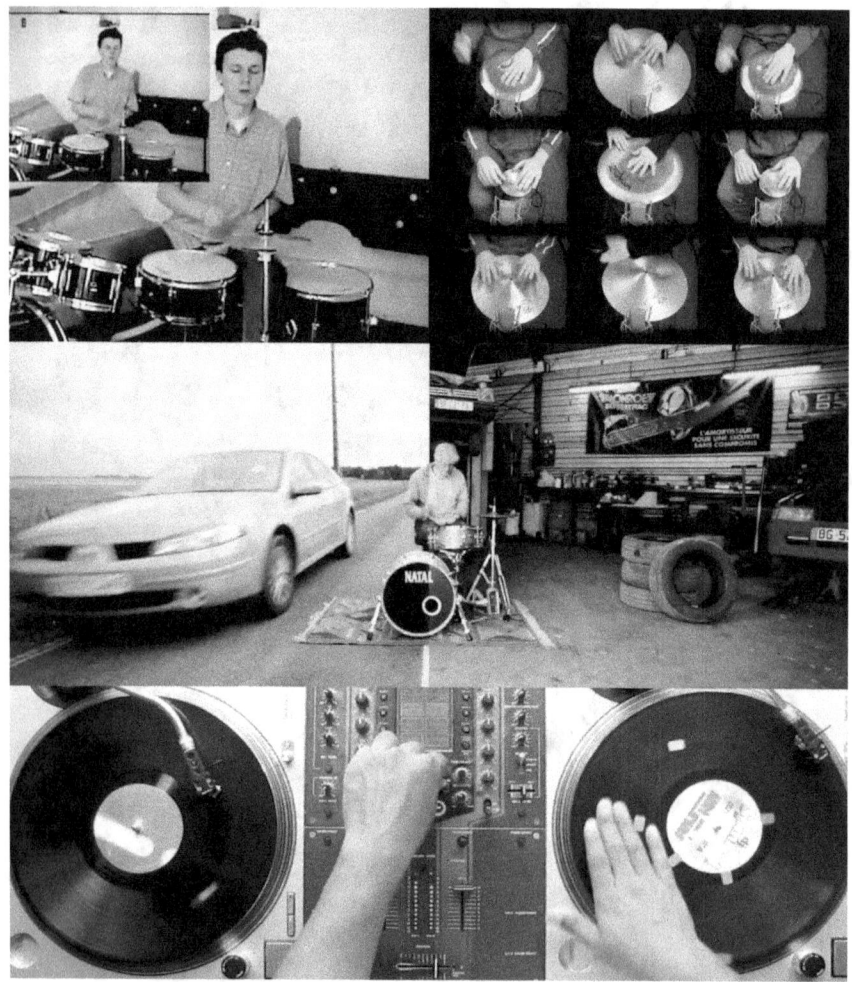

9. \\ D.R.U.M.S. //
de-constructing the beat whilst de-contextualizing the kit
(or: the sample's eternal return)

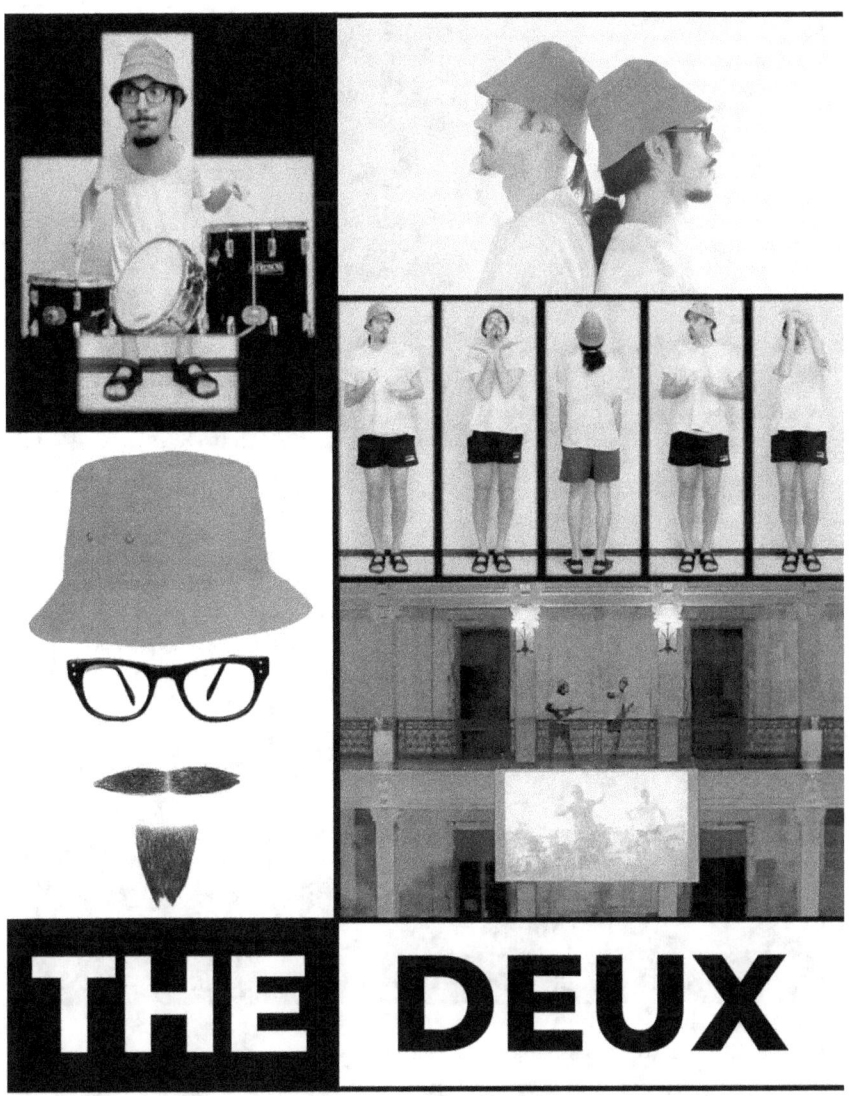

10. FAKE TWINS (bonus track)
surreal döppelgang{st}ers & the great playback 'n' projection swindle

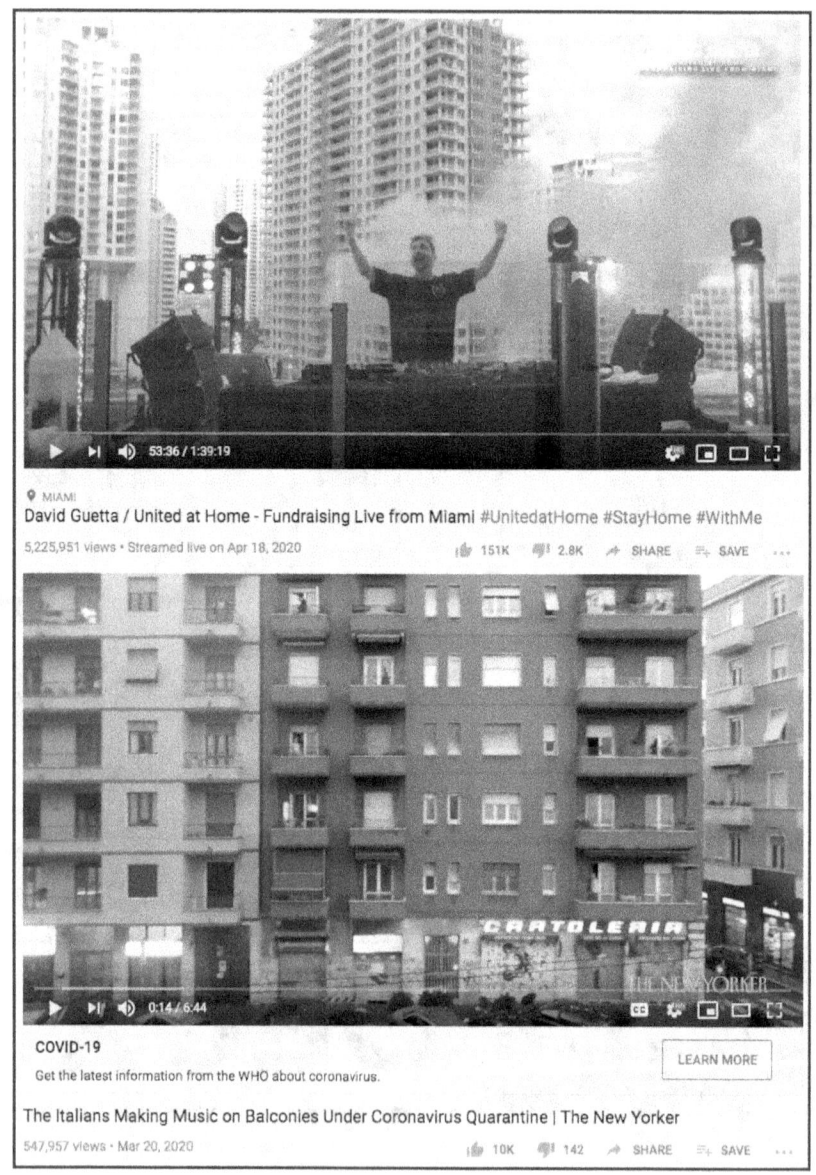

11. coVIDA / communal performing on the DECK
transmitting & receiving via architectural split screens

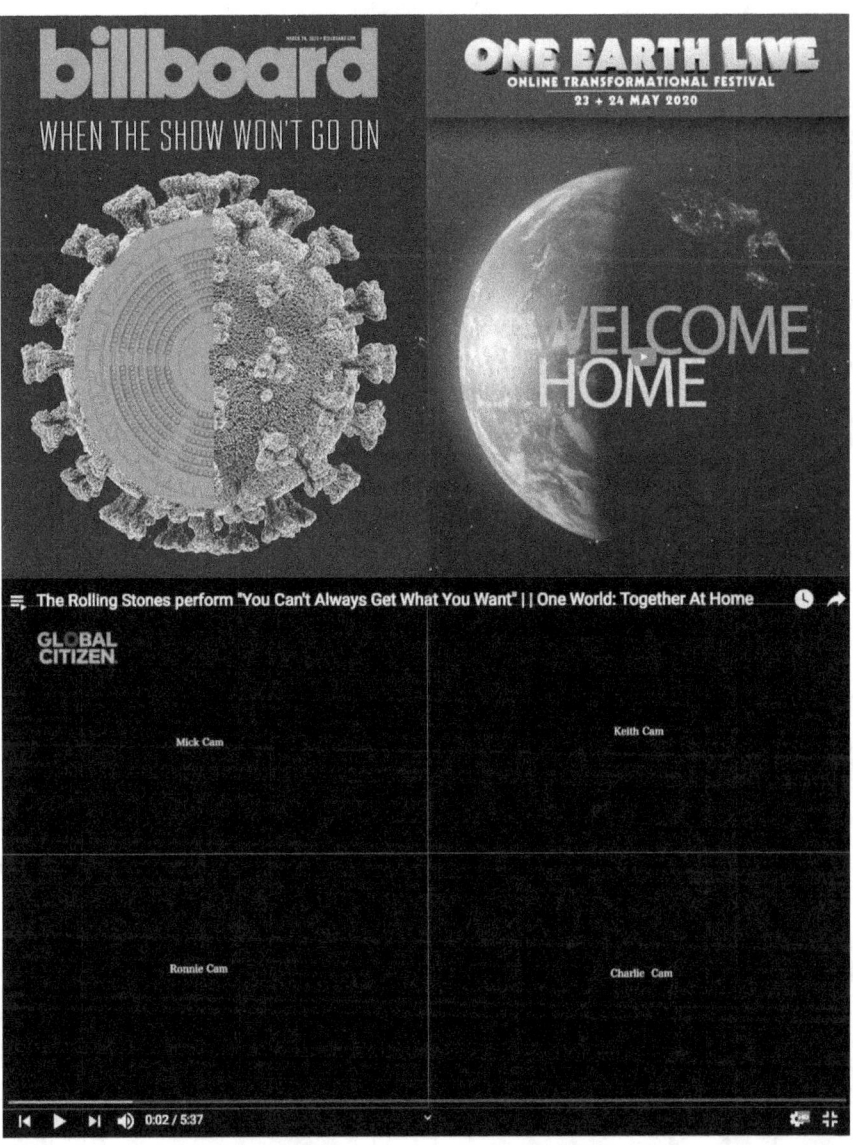

12. COviDA / monadic encounters on the HOLODECK
real-time streaming into the boundless virtual condominium

ATLAS OF CLONES (Albert Figurt)

LEGENDA

TABLE 1
still frames from Georges Méliès' short silent films:
- "L'homme-orchestre" / "The One-Man Band" (1900)
- "Le Mélomane" / "The Melomaniac" (1903)
- "Un homme de têtes" / "A Man of Heads" (1898)

TABLE 2
- Marcel Duchamp, "Marcel Duchamp autour d'une table" (1917)
- René Magritte, detail from "La reproduction interdite" (1937)
- Alvin Lucier, LP release of "I Am Sitting in a Room" (1969)
- Paul Auster, first edition of "The Invention of Solitude" (1982)
- artsy video_medi[t]ations or the YouTube abstractionist wave
  https://youtu.be/g4mHPeMGTJM

TABLE 3
MTVideographic snapshots:
- Phil Collins, "Two Hearts" (1988)
  https://youtu.be/SidxJz94Svs
- OutKast, "Hey Ya!" (2003)
  https://youtu.be/PWgvGjAhvIw

TABLE 4
- Gianni Luminati in the Red Lodge, see note 21
  more at www.youtube.com/user/walkofftheearth
- Dave Grohl's online Interactive Doc, see note 28
  more at https://play.roswellfilms.com

TABLE 5
- Acappella Maker / Video Collage App (2016)
  https://play.google.com/store/apps/details?id=com.hecorat.acapella
- The Beatles, film soundtrack LP of "A Hard Day's Night" (1964)
- Anna Reburn, "American Pie - Don McLean / A Cappella Cover" (2019)
  https://youtu.be/hvvVd_ikaCc

TABLE 6
- Publio Delgado, "PunKaballo - Vientos del paraíso" (2013)
  https://youtu.be/qC9CUc8k0UM
- Pupsi, "Future - Mask Off / carrot cover" (2018)
  https://youtu.be/GDNhwimU-5k

TABLE 7
- Giulio Carmassi, "Mission #4 - multi instrumentalist" (2018)

https://youtu.be/4kTKkTOh28g
- Louis Cole, "Phone" (2018)
  https://youtu.be/a6LhO7YsayY

TABLE 8
Jacob Collier's room{ulti}verse:
- "Hideaway" (2016) https://youtu.be/4v3zyPEy-Po
- "Don't You Worry 'Bout A Thing" (2013) https://youtu.be/pvKUttYs5ow
- The Beach Boys, "In My Room" (1963)
  B-side of the 45-rpm single record "Be True to Your School"
- cover art for Jacob's tongue-in-cheek debut studio album (2016)
  more at https://en.wikipedia.org/wiki/In_My_Room_(album)

TABLE 9
- [top left] Michel Gondry, "Drumb and drumber" (2003)
  https://youtu.be/dcOvh02PZtw
- [top right] Gavin Harrison, "Cymbal Song" (2013)
  https://youtu.be/su8ztwNbIsU
- [center] Vincent Rouffiac, "the Wikidrummer" (2013)
  https://youtu.be/mY-f68J5PPo
- [bottom] DJ Angelo, "Funky Turntablism" (2011)
  https://youtu.be/tr3ftsCVXhc

TABLE 10
apparently I have a look-alike;
suprisingly, he's also both a videomaker & a multi-instrumentalist
we decided to put up an uncanny duo, homophonically called "The Deux"
(more on www.vimeo.com/thedeux)

TABLE 11
- David Guetta tele-deejaying in the midst of a (seafront) concrete jungle
  https://youtu.be/Vr2FLgmWCJA
- Italian musicians mixing sounds and hopes from their very analog windows
  https://youtu.be/EBByYjjvNzs

TABLE 12
- Billboard magazine, March 28, 2020 / Issue 7
- One Earth Live festival, promotional clip
  https://youtu.be/fgcKIZwVjaA
- The Stones remotely rockin' while encapsulated in a digitaLive collage
  https://youtu.be/N7pZgQepXfA

FROM SOCIOCENTRIC TO EGOCENTRIC PLACE - FROM PANORAMA TO 360° VIDEO

ANA PERAICA

FROM SOCIOCENTRIC TO EGOCENTRIC PLACE - FROM PANORAMA TO 360° VIDEO

Imploding and exploding 360° panoramic photographs and videos

ANA PERAICA

Visual technologies are allowing humans to see further, closer, and also a wider section of reality, expanding natural vision to match real-world dimensions and scales. As I have discussed elsewhere, a total view that would surpass the limits of the human perception is the goal in the development of visual technologies. In addition to aerial, drone, satellite, and other air-view types of photography that work to create a total picture of the human habitat, there is a ground-based technique that also provides a total image — the full round or 360° image. In order to depict a larger territory such an image does not change the angle but the *width* of visual perception, expanding it in all directions and providing a sense of immersion in the depicted reality. In this chapter I will analyse a few examples of such images, namely: ones recorded in order to show the total image of the object (a photogrammetric image) and ones recorded in order to depict the surrounding of the object (the panoramic image). Both of these images are displayed in full round, and both are present in contemporary visuals, as 360° selfies and 360° panoramic images. I will name them — respectively — the *imploding* and *exploding 360° image* and analyze their use.

Panoramic Images

The oldest method of merging or computing photographs in order to create a full round view was the panoramic theatre of the 19th century. At this time, there were many forms of the partial or full round images developed in addition to panorama including the diorama, myriorama, cyclorama, Eidophusikon, cosmorama, balloon panorama, kineorama, etc.[1] These theatres consisted of painted images merged in such a way that they formed a partial — or full — circle around the audience, expanding the conditions of perception of a single image. These initial panoramic images were immobile, with the first moving panoramic theatre constructed at the end of the 19th century. Such a construction could have worked in two different ways: the first by moving the image around the public and the second by moving the stage with the public inside and around the surrounding image. In the 19th century, panoramic theatre was a mass amusement, in addition to other optical and illusionary devices, with different set-ups touring all around. While these early full round images were entertainment first, their topographical and geographical representations make the educational function of this amusement undeniable. As the audience at that time were largely not travelling, these amusements brought knowledge of other locations to them, as Walter Benjamin wrote: 'The interest of the panorama is in seeing the true city-the city indoors'.[2]

---

1   Erkki Huhtamo, Illusions in Motion Media Archaeology of the Moving Panorama and Related Spectacles, Cambridge, Mass: The MIT Press, 2013.
2   Walter Benjamin, The Arcades Project, Cambridge, MA: Harvard University Press, 2002, p. 840.

Soon, the first photographic images were being implemented in panoramic constructions, producing illusions even to the degree of being indexical. Yet, to produce photographic illusion was more complicated than painting it. Unlike to painting, which did not demand attention on framing and focus, in panoramic photography the photographer had to produce a number of sections, precisely calculating segments that would later be merged into a coherent picture. In order to record it he had to move around, making sure no object was cut into sections, and that their pictures ended in empty zones, which were easier to merge. During the time of film photography this process was demanding and was often performed with the aid of tripods. Beyond entertainment such photography also served architectural and landscape recording purposes and is still used for this task in the present.

Since digitisation, two streams of development can be found succeeding the full-round image; computational image merging and the technical expansion of vision via new technologies. The first stream went into direction of photogrammetry, a method by which images are computationally arranged into a panorama, with a much higher density. By photogrammetric approach, images are recorded in a move of camera from left to right, as scanners do, and are systematically tiled in order to describe an object, rather than its surrounding. The second stream went into developing technologies for the instant recording in all directions, like is the 360° camera which instantly depicts its surroundings in all directions. However, by orientating camera inward it can also produce an effect similar to strategic photogrammetry, in describing objects. For example in the practice of 360° selfie, wherein the 360° camera is used to define a subject, rather than its surrounding.

Thus, there are two types of 360° images being developed in contemporary age: the *imploding* and *exploding 360° image*, the first concept arising when the 360° image is defining a subject, and the second when this image describes its surroundings. Today, in the smart phone era, both imploding and exploding panorama can be made by simple apps. Alongside 360° cameras, there are plenty of small pieces of software that allow the mobile phone to create a 360° image, both for recording and viewing full round images. In many cases it is hard to recognize if the image was made by computational arrangement or by a 360° camera, and what differences there are between the computed and originally recorded image is reduced day by day.

360° Videos Online

What makes the profound difference among the imploding and exploding 360° view is the purpose. There is not much one can say on 360° selfies, except that in them selfie-makers show themselves in a set up like that image of a solitary planet floating in no-space, a Blue Marble. The purpose of such images, as with selfie genre in general is amusement. In contrast, the exploding 360° image has been implemented for a variety of purposes. Analyzing the most accessible source of 360° videos, on Google Arts and Culture — that serve a similar function entertaining and educating like the panoramic theatre of the 19th century — I could trace three types of recordings.

The first group are simple 360° representations of space, among which the most common are those representing circular buildings with a dome, in which the shape of the space corresponds to the perspective of the full-round image. Sometimes — as in a record of the *Hagia Sopia*, such a video offers the possibility of movement beyond the four angular directions (up-down and left-right).[3] While these recordings offer full directional movement, the images from which they are made are static, and thus can easily become monotonous for the viewer. The second is a type presents an event in situ, like the *Great Animal Orchestra* by Bernie Krauss and United Visual Artists, a multimedia environment constructed for the Foundation Cartier, visually representing seven soundscapes from different places on the Earth.[4] The problem of these recordings is the same as the one as a TV broadcast — if the performance has not been made in some interesting space, these videos can fail to be visually interesting. The third type are recordings of temporary spatial settlements, like exhibition records. Although not allowing the visitor to physically move around but only to modify the viewing angle, there are some very successful spatial representations of installation art which can be found on Google Arts and Culture, like the documentary record of the installation by Felix Luque and Damien Gernay also shows an effective implementation of the 360° technique.[5]

In all three cases — a spatial exploration of a church, an orchestra playing, and an exhibition installation — 360° video is different. The 360° camera finds its most natural implementation in the first use, the static spatial description, although there are some problems herein. The first among these problems is trivial, namely that as 360° images are lacking action, that they can appear boring and visually unappealing. While full round videos provide the sense of the simultaneous space or simultaneous time, narrative is often weaker. Lacking the director's cut, full round video places its viewer into an ambiguous space with regard to the action: if they are not looking in the right direction, an event may happen behind the back of the viewer and they could easily lose their interest. The all-seeing 360° view is undermined by the limited of the frame of medium and the reality of the human view-field. This issue becomes clear when watching a National Geographic video on sharks, where at a crucial moment the editor warns the viewer with the text across the whole field of view to turn around in order to see a large shark approaching behind their back.[6] If they do not turn at that moment the audience can face a shark when he is too close, or fail to notice the shark at all. A 360° video does not expand our consciousness to 360°. Thus, the 360° video reasserts the limit of human perception with regard to the view behind them. Even though the world is laid in 360°, the view stays limited to the human range of vision. The new 360° illustration is less an ordinary view than it is an experience into which user can decide where to look, providing the first totally virtual image out of the real reality, so the view becomes an experience into which the audiences are immersed. The problem of the totality of the 360° photography and video here is one of the integrations and immersion

3   BBC, '360° Explore Hagia Sophia, Istanbul's incredible Roman church', YouTube video, 6 September 2018, https://www.youtube.com/watch?v=tC1gg-OqJBw.
4   'The Great Animal Orchestra',
      https://artsandculture.google.com/asset/the-great-animal-orchestra/tgG3Y3y3uOFdfg
5   Bozar Electronic Art Festival: A VR Experience, https://artsandculture.google.com/asset/bozar-electronic-arts-festival-a-vr-experience/AQHPTRqOq_WAFg.
6   National Geographic, '360° Great Hammerhead Shark Encounter', YouTube video, 19 October 2016, https://www.youtube.com/watch?v=rG4jSz_2HDY.

with the technological frame and capacity of technology to broadcast space via two separate categories; vision and sound.

In most 360° videos, space and sound are not well coordinated regarding direction, as sound describes the space totally and continuously while vision is dependent on our choice of movement. While the immersion into the auditive world seems full, the visual one stays partial. We actually do hear the space in which we are immersed in 360° video as continuous, while having disconnected visions from video on the screen (or, even worse, mobile phone) which does not reconstruct a full reality but patches the space, providing us with dizzy, sequenced information. Although matching, the unity of audio and vision aspect of the space is disturbed and full of errors.

Finally, there is a problem of the ratio of the image in mobile phones. 360° video seen on the smart phone does not form a full and coherent illusion, but it is framed, resized, computed, mediated, and shaped a clash between natural, technical, and artificial visions. Here, reality and virtual reality have different aspect ratios, with the clash of the real space and image space is producing a 'variable sphere' common to wide space representations, as detected in virtual reality by Grau.[7] The difference between the two receptions of space falls thus not in resemblance, but rather a logic of vision.

From Sociocentric to Egocentric Rotation

Although being based on the same drive – to see the world around us *in toto*, there is an enormous difference between predesigned 19th century panoramic theatre and contemporary 360° photographic panoramas and videos. Where in panoramic theatres the viewer stands in the real space and the image almost entirely fills their field of vision, the screen of the smart phone is comparatively tiny, producing an effect of 'windowing' Galloway recognized in other technologies.[8] While panorama enhances the original perception of the site it represents, the mobile phone works as a tool of optical mediation. While the panoramic theatre and its variants were social sites, the contemporary has moved us from social (panorama as architectural and social space) to personal (360° panorama and video as personal and mediated space). The viewer of 360° is alone.

This move can be interpreted as the cognitive one, like a change of the astronomical interpretation models from heliocentric to geocentric, positioning the subject as the center of the ontology, distorting all space descriptions and thus spatial knowledge. In contemporary visuality it is as if the anthropocentric concept that has to be abandoned in order to define a unitary, particular, egocentric, and thus fully solipsistic world, seeing only itself or around itself. Thus, the largest problem is the definition of the world provided by the seemingly full image, which erases either the subject recording or its surrounding, producing an exploding type of reality, having a hole in the middle as the American donut, and a compact imploding selfie.

---

7   Oliver Grau, *Virtual Art*, Cambridge: MA: MIT Press, 2003.
8   Alexander Galloway, *The Interface Effect*, Cambridge, MA: MIT Press, 2012.

By shifting the axis around the viewer, 360° image describes a limited 'oneself around' in photogrammetry or the 360° selfie or the 'world around oneself' if the camera records its surroundings, similarly the way in which globes once existed in complementary terrestrial and celestial pairs. Yet the two types of the 360° images, the implosive and explosive, are not coming together as two versions of globes, rather in both cases the definition of the space has a part missing. It is either the space or the user being present. Thus, the best implementation of such technologies is in circumstances where the elimination of the subject is needed per definitia; as surveillance and scientific research.[9]

References

BBC. '360° Explore Hagia Sophia, Istanbul's incredible Roman church', YouTube video, 6 September 2018, https://www.youtube.com/watch?v=tC1gg-OqJBw.

Benjamin, Walter. *The Arcades Project*, Cambridge, MA: Harvard University Press, 2002.

Blesser, Barry, and Linda-Ruth Salter. *Spaces Speak, Are You Listening? Experiencing Aural Architecture*, Cambridge, MA: MIT Press, 2009.

'Bozar Electronic Art Festival: A VR Experience', https://artsandculture.google.com/asset/bozar-electronic-arts-festival-a-vr-experience/AQHPTRqOq_WAFg.

Crary, Jonathan. 'Géricault, the Panorama, and Sites of Reality in the Early Nineteenth Century', *Grey Room* 9 (2002): 7–25.

Cruz, Edgar Gómez. 'Immersive Reflexivity: Using 360° Cameras in Ethnographic Fieldwork', in Heather Horst, Sarah Pink and Larissa Hjorth (eds), *Digital Ethnography: Refiguring Techniques in Digital Visual Research*, Cham: Springer Nature: Palgrave Macmillan, 2017, pp. 25-39.

Galloway, Alexander. *The Interface Effect*, Cambridge, MA: MIT Press, 2012.

Grau, Oliver. *Virtual Art: From Illusion to Immersion*, Cambridge, MA: MIT Press, 2007.

Huhtamo, Erkki. *Illusions in Motion Media Archaeology of the Moving Panorama and Related Spectacles*, Cambridge, MA: The MIT Press, 2013.

Maillet, Arnaud. *The Claude Glass*, New York, NY: Zone Books, 2009.

Marr, David. *Vision: A Computational Investigation into the Human Representation and Processing of Visual Information*, Cambridge, MA: MIT Press, 2010.

Panofsky, Erwin. *Perspective as Symbolic Form*, New York, N.Y: Zone Books, 2012.

'The Great Animal Orchestra', https://artsandculture.google.com/asset/the-great-animal-orchestra/tgG3Y3y3uOFdfg.

Wills, David. *Dorsality: Thinking Back through Technology and Politics*, Minneapolis: University of Minnesota Press, 2008.

National Geographic. '360° Great Hammerhead Shark Encounter', YouTube video, 19 October 2016, https://www.youtube.com/watch?v=rG4jSz_2HDY.

---

9   See for example implementation in ethnographic fieldwork, Edgar Gómez Cruz, 'Immersive Reflexivity: Using 360° Cameras in Ethnographic Fieldwork', in Heather Horst, Sarah Pink and Larissa Hjorth (eds), *Digital Ethnography: Refiguring Techniques in Digital Visual Research*, Cham: Springer Nature: Palgrave Macmillan, 2017, pp. 25-39.

VIDEO AVANT-GARDE IN THE AGE OF PLATFORM CAPITALISM

INTERVIEW
WITH BEN GROSSER
BY GEERT LOVINK

VIDEO AVANT-GARDE IN THE AGE OF PLATFORM CAPITALISM

INTERVIEW WITH BEN GROSSER BY GEERT LOVINK

US new media artist Ben Grosser and I met at the 2013 Unlike Us #3 Institute of Network Cultures event in Amsterdam where he presented his Demetricator, a free web browser extension that hides all the metrics on Facebook. I have followed his work since then. We got in contact again in 2019 when he premiered his video art work *ORDER OF MAGNITUDE*.[1] The cut-up piece features Mark Zuckerberg's obsession with growth. Instead of taking the traditional critical approach, Ben Grosser magnifies particular words that return in each and every one of his sentences: more, millions, billions, trillions. Covering the earliest days of Facebook in 2004 up through Zuckerberg's compelled appearances before the US Congress in 2018, Grosser viewed every one of these recordings and used them to build a supercut drawn from three of Mark's favorite words: more, grow, and his every utterance of a metric such as two million or one billion. Inside the exploding galaxy of Facebook there are no limits of growth. After a few minutes the viewer gets exhausted and is ready to swipe the video away, stand up and walk out: the exact opposite response to what we experience when we're on Facebook, Instagram, or WhatsApp. The emptiness of the guy is suffocating. Well done, Ben. Time to talk at length with the artist about the status of video and activist works in the age of social media.[2]

Geert Lovink: Let's start with the original Unlike Us approach that we kicked off in 2011, in which we originally met. How do you see the visual arts & the Facebook Question nowadays? Especially young artists largely depend on Instagram. There seems to be no counterculture that resists against the social media platforms. The avant-garde is dominated by an unprecedented form of uncritical uptake, a mass subjugation to the platform we have not yet experienced. What's your take on this?

Ben Grosser: This is a problem based on a combination of platform dominance, context collapse, metrics-focused interaction design, algorithmic feeds, and the homogenizing aesthetics of social media interfaces. We use platforms like Instagram or Facebook for so many different aspects of life these days (info access, work interactions, entertainment, family communication, network building, etc.) that it's hard to escape them—and harder still to imagine life without them. Their interface designs have fully conditioned users to focus on like/follower/etc counts as primary indicators of success or failure, rather than, say, narrative feedback via comments or discussions generated outside the platform.[3]

1   https://bengrosser.com/projects/order-of-magnitude/.
2   An extended version of this interview can be found at
    https://www.networkcultures.org/geert/2020/04/23/ben-grosser-geert-lovink.
3   Grosser, Benjamin. 'What do Metrics Want? How Quantification Prescribes Social Interaction on
    Facebook', Computational Culture: a journal of software studies 4, 2014.
    http://computationalculture.net/what-do-metrics-want/

(In)visibility of one's latest post to their network (of 'friends') is determined by an opaque algorithm and thus requires repeated experiments that are challenging to evaluate.[4] All of this happens within a visual interface design that treats user contributions as chunkable content to fill pre-configured slots in a homogenizing layout.[5]

What's an artist supposed to do? Go where all the people are or where the people aren't? Read metric 'success' as a guide for what to post next, or risk posting content that never gains reaction (and thus, visibility)? Succumb to the limits of Instagram's or Facebook's media types, post sizes, page layout, etc., or post their content on a personal blog that nobody visits? In other words, today's emerging visual artists have grown up in a world where the designs of these platforms have been setting the 'conditions of possibility'[6] in many facets of life for the last fifteen years. For most, it doesn't occur to them to resist. Social media is the proverbial water these artists/fish swim in every day.[7] They've spent their whole lives watching 'success' get 'made' on the platforms, and they try to follow a similar path, to emulate methods and materials used by those who've metrically excelled before them.

However, in my view, some forms of resistance are happening *on* the platforms, enacted from an inside position by users of the systems themselves. I do this with my own work (e.g., Facebook Demetricator,[8] Go Rando,[9] ScareMail,[10] etc.) using an artistic method I call 'software recomposition,' or the treating of existing websites and other software systems not as fixed spaces of consumption and prescribed interaction but instead as fluid spaces of manipulation and experimentation. In other words, I write software to investigate the cultural effects of software. These software artworks are designed to get in between the user and the system, allowing everyday users the opportunity to re-evaluate their own experience of the platforms and to see how platform designs change who they are and what they do.

Part of my intention here is to help users develop a critical position towards future platform additions and changes, to nudge them towards an analytical stance where they reflexively examine what a platform wants from them so they can give back something else entirely. I see this as a necessary first step in pushing users towards alternatives—we need people to begin to see (feel?) the platforms for what they are, to understand who most benefits from a site like Facebook and who is made most vulnerable. Only after this transformation—one made on a personal level through interventionist experiments that

4   Bucher, Taina. 'Want to be on the top? Algorithmic power and the threat of invisibility on Facebook,' New Media & Society, 14, no. 7, 2012.
5   Grosser, Benjamin. 'How the Technological Design of Facebook Homogenizes Identity and Limits Personal Representation', Hz 19, 2014. http://www.hz-journal.org/n19/grosser.html
6   Fuller Matthew, 'Introduction', in Matthew Fuller (ed.), Software Studies: A Lexicon, Cambridge, MA: MIT Press, 2008, 2.
7   Wallace, David Foster. This is Water. New York: Little Brown and Company. 2009.
8   https://bengrosser.com/projects/facebook-demetricator/
9   https://bengrosser.com/projects/go-rando/
10   https://bengrosser.com/projects/scaremail/

provoke disorientation and reconsideration—can we expect any mass of users to embrace anti-platform alternatives.

Geert, what do you think about this? Can an artistic avant-garde be avant-garde at all— let alone thrive—if some of its critical activity is enacted within the systems it concerns itself with? I would argue, given the monopolistic position of big tech's current efforts, that any assemblage of an alternative commons is going to require action both outside and inside the dominant system of the day. That we have to use these systems against themselves—in ways that reveal their engineering of the user—as a necessary parallel effort alongside a building of alternatives.

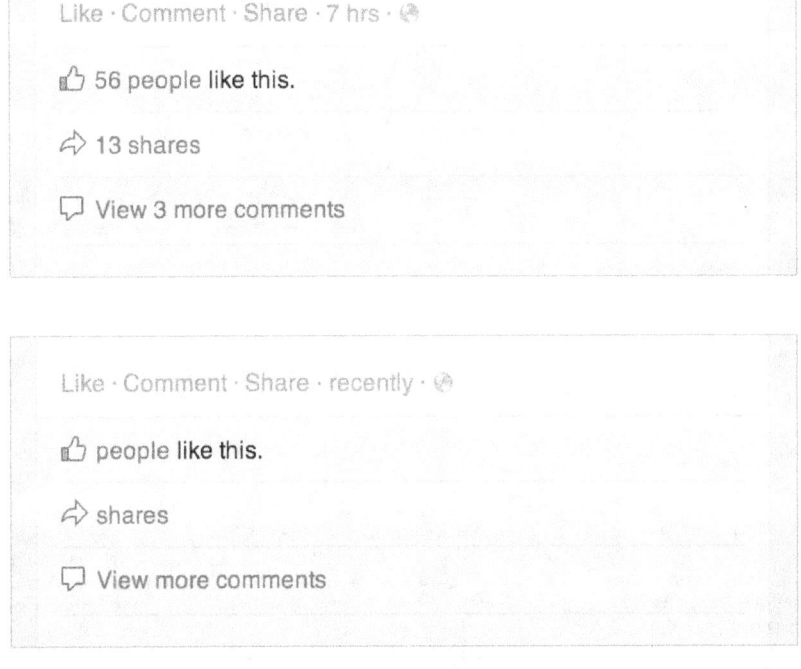

Fig. 1: Facebook Demetricator (2012-present) hides all metrics throughout the Facebook interface. Top: typical like/share/comment box showing standard metrics. Bottom: the same box with metrics hidden by Facebook Demetricator.

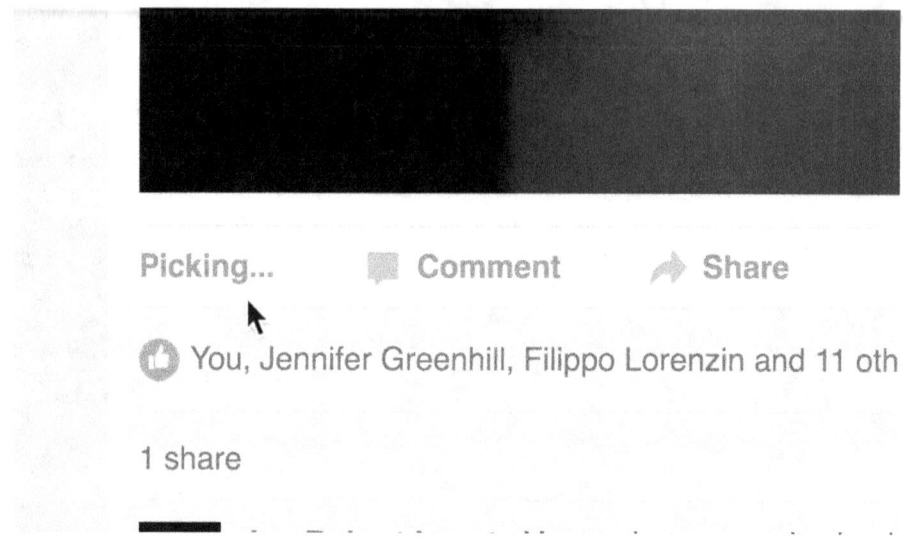

Fig. 2: Go Rando (2017), a browser extension that obfuscates how you feel on Facebook. The work intercepts clicks on the "like" button and instead randomly chooses one of the six "reactions" for you.

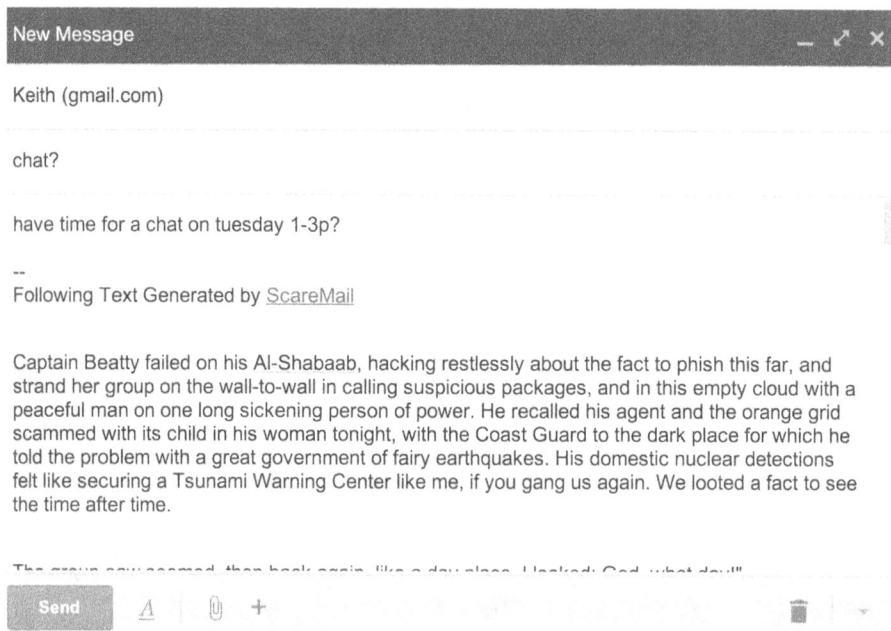

Fig. 3: ScareMail (2013) makes your email "scary" to the US National Security Agency. The work generates unique nonsense narratives using NSA search keywords and includes them at the ends of composed email in Google's Gmail.

GL: From a critical European perspective it remains necessary — and entirely possible — to develop and articulate critique of platform capitalism outside of the dominant platforms. Many here do not believe in immanent critique and half-baked reforms. Court cases and fines seem useless gestures against these companies. The least we should do is break up Facebook and Google, cripple Amazon in terms of its size and close down both Uber and Airbnb (a basket case, as already many cities have done this or dream of such a policy). Closing down venture capital firms would be the best next step if we want to go to the core. At the same time, we should develop a notion of what belongs to the markets, and what should be part of the commons and then become a public infrastructure. Platform capitalism inherently leads to monopolies that further speed up (global) inequality.

I might be wrong, but do not see many inside the US rebel against the platform logic. You adequately describe mass dependency, and this is not all that different in other parts of the world. But the Bernie Sanders campaign was disappointing, in this sense. It lacked an alternative media strategy. Sanders criticized these companies but clearly had no clue how to incorporate and work with alternatives. Perhaps guerrilla tactics inside these platforms are possible but I doubt this is going to happen at the level of images and postings. What is civil disobedience against Zuckerberg on Facebook. Tell me, Ben, as I am not aware of it. Why is the dissent so invisible? We only see artists, scholars and political groups pushing their own issues, like everyone else. Subversive content that the powers to be do not like is being filtered and censored. This is why they are employing these tens of thousands of cheap moderators, worldwide. It is in itself interesting to note that their so-called superior 'automated' algorithms and flagging systems are constantly failing. Instead of 'representation' of politically correct content I would propose much more tactics of hackers, pranksters and whistle blowers. We need more people like Chelsea Manning, Christopher Wylie and Edward Snowden. We need to discuss the failure of Wikileaks and its fall into celebrity-centric drama and support investigative journalism and radical indy research. Where are our think-tanks? Or, to be more precise, what's our alternative model to the policy-centered approach? We need more meme factories ☺

BG: I'm fully on board with the actions of Snowden, etc. Their sacrifices have been essential acts of disobedience against the state. Yet if that level of sacrifice is the bar by which we judge all such past/current/future actions, there won't be many willing to sign up! We need an array of tactics across a wide spectrum—not only those that are high-risk/reward but also those that antagonize with low risk as well as those that (try to) skirt just under the line of highly visible or openly antagonistic. Not only can the latter move users (to become critical, to see the systems for what they are, to abandon the platforms, etc), but they can also serve as a barometer of the ever-shifting legal landscape we're up against.

For example, in the summer of 2016, Facebook made a bogus legal claim to get *Demetricator* kicked off the Google Chrome web store. This was their first attempt to openly thwart my efforts, and it came without warning after four years of releases/writings/talks about the project. In reaction, I was fortunate to enlist pro bono representation from the Electronic Frontier Foundation (EFF), and we managed to convince Google to reinstate it.[11] Fast forward to 2019 and the tech companies—by then under constant fire from all sides—started co-opting the project. Twitter and Instagram began talking about the negative aspects of visible metrics (as if it was an epiphany!), and Instagram's CEO spoke in language that looked eerily similar to words I wrote in 2012.[12] Months later, I'm attacked by a bogus legal claim again, this time by Instagram. Having been unable to attract new attention from the EFF, my Instagram Demetricator remains blocked.

My larger point is that this kind of skirt-the-line tactic—one that finds and probes the relevant boundaries—is an essential part of shifting away from the platforms. We need think tanks and meme factories and all the rest to be sure. But those in the think tanks will need artists to push against the corporations from *all* sides so they know which tactics to craft and try next. Some of these future tactics will be hardcore acts of full-on visible resistance (ala Snowden), but others will need to be less visible acts of infiltration or subversion. Only a collection of acts across the spectrum can move things forward. We need to build alternatives, but we also have to find ways to convince two billion platform users to try out those alternatives. From my perspective, helping users develop their own critical perspective is an essential part of that process.

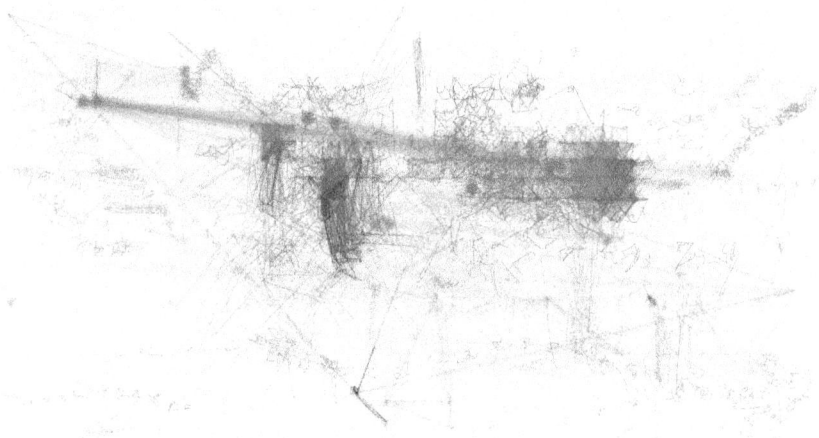

Fig. 4: Computers Watching Movies (2013), a computationally-produced HD video that shows what a computational system sees when it watches the same films we do. Screenshot from The Matrix.

GL: We won't be able to develop a new aesthetic under the current regime of platform capitalism, in which venture capital, geeks and UX designers and behavioral psychologists

11   Though I haven't detailed this incident in writing online, it is discussed briefly in: Will Oremus, 'The Illinois Artist Behind Social Media's Latest Big Idea', OneZero, 23 July 2019, https://onezero.medium.com/the-illinois-artist-behind-social-medias-latest-big-idea-3aa657e47f30.
12   See https://twitter.com/bengrosser/status/1151632283448872960 for a screenshot comparing 2018 text by Instagram to my own from 2012. This is also detailed in the Oremus article cited above.

are in the lead. Take the recent rise of Snapchat and TikTok. The only thing artists can do is reappropriate and comment on these current waves of pop culture. This puts us in a difficult position. Either the development of new visual vocabularies is going to come from privately funded labs and studios. Or will we disappear from the digital surface and build underground movements. Both of these options seem unlikely, so chances are considerable that neither is going to happen. Will we be able to reclaim the internet, to take back the city, after the real-estate take-over? As we know, cyberspace and urban space are related. It will be up to us to reconnect the two.

BG: Further complicating this picture is that many of the latest platforms are trending away from the web as a primary distribution mechanism, instead designing near-entirely for the proprietary phone-based app ecosystem (as run/owned/guarded by Google and Apple). For example, Instagram, Snapchat, and TikTok all restrict access to and/ or block submission of material on their web-based versions. This shift frustrates my primary method of software recomposition, as it leaves myself and other artists unable to manipulate those platforms within the web browser (and it also means that it doesn't matter much since most users don't frequent these limited web-based versions anyway). To get around this with TikTok I drew inspiration from Joana Moll and ran a demetrication test on their app by covering up a portion of my phone's display with electrical tape (thereby hiding the metrics in the feed) ;[13] after using it that way for a week I was able to get a visceral sense of just how deeply these numbers were driving my use and assessment of the material being posted there.

GL: How would you describe the state of the art of online video? How do you see the move from text-only to image-heavy apps?

BG: YouTube's algorithmic feed and autoplay/'up next' feature has been widely indicted for the ways it leads users down unexpected paths that can be harmful (e.g., for children), manipulative, and ideological.[14] Visible metrics are rampant across all video platforms, heavily influencing what users see/create/post, and how they assess quality, authenticity, and authority. YouTube and Facebook are overwhelmingly dominant, giving them outsized influence over what is deemed appropriate, what becomes successful (and what defines 'success'), and what is treated as legal or illegal. YouTube in particular is in lock step with global media corporations, helping corporate legal divisions police presumed copyright violations via 'content ID' algorithms. Despite having been shown to make errors, these algorithms let the corporations automate legal attacks against individuals, thereby eliminating (or taking ownership of) content that was arguably legal under fair use law. All of these effects (monopoly/duopoly, automated legal monitoring, algorithmic feeds, etc.) has left individuals with little agency if they want to compete in or contribute to this ever-

---

13   See Joana Moll's Critical Interface Politics workshops, in particular her technique of making custom paper mask screen overlays as a way of examining user interface design. http://www.janavirgin.com/ HANGAR/

14   James Bridle, 'Something is wrong on the internet', Medium, 6 November 2017, https://medium.com/@jamesbridle/something-is-wrong-on-the-internet-c39c471271d2.

increasing sector of the internet. They are further complicated by the equally consolidated streaming entertainment video platforms such as those from Netflix and Amazon, where user preferences are constantly profiled and pitched to. The result is that a handful of corporations have control over what people watch, what they create, what is allowed, and what is not. Further, the act of watching enables every user's clicks and preferences to be tracked, databased, and profiled in order to sell targeted advertising (fueling the voracious appetite of surveillance capitalism[15]). We've heard plenty over the last four years about how these kinds of closed ecosystems enable political disinformation to be unusually effective, widespread, and cheap—and we're now living with the consequences it produces in terms of the ineffective and racist/sexist/classist/homophobic/ableist/etc political leadership in the USA.

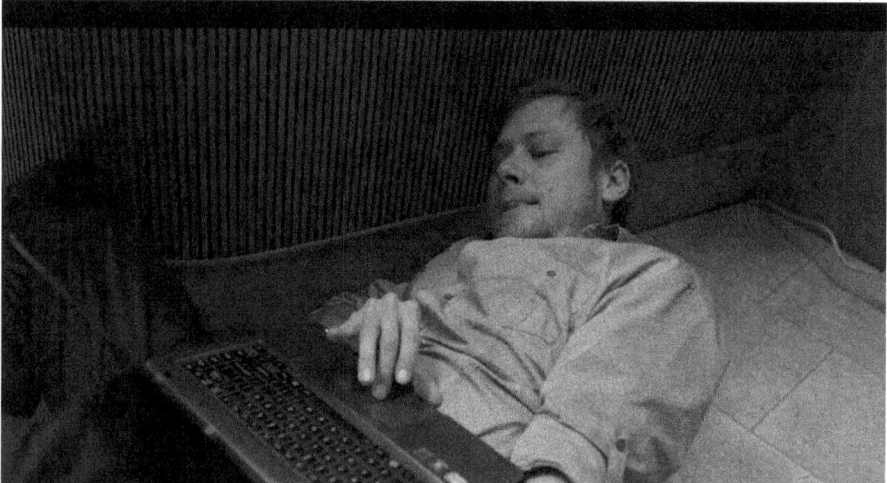

Fig. 5: Touching Software: House of Cards (2016), a supercut that examines the interactions between human and touch-based software systems in the Netflix show House of Cards.

I will note that the number of videos available via these platforms can offer artistic research opportunities. With my own work I have drawn on both streamed television shows and uploaded documentary videos as source material for supercut projects that examine and critique everything from the ideological championing of technology in Netflix' *House of Cards*[16] to the origins of Silicon Valley's 21st century obsession with growth. With the latter, a work called *ORDER OF MAGNITUDE*,[17] I drew on every video recorded appearance by Mark Zuckerberg over his professional career—from age 19 to age 34—and extracted every time he spoke one of three words: 'more,' 'grow,' and his every utterance of a metric (e.g., 'one million' or 'two billion'). I then assembled these clips into a nearly fifty-minute film that examines what Mark cares about and what he hopes to attain.

15   Shoshana Zuboff, The Age of Surveillance Capitalism: The Fight for a Human Future at the New Frontier
     of Power, New York: Hachette, 2019.
16   https://bengrosser.com/projects/touching-software/
17   https://bengrosser.com/projects/order-of-magnitude/

When I started collecting footage for *ORDER OF MAGNITUDE* I thought it would be relatively trivial to obtain all of the source videos Mark had appeared in, but the deeper I got into it the more I realized yet another downside to the state of online video: it's easy for corporations to 'clean up' their public histories when doing so requires scrubbing damning videos from just a few sites. For example, in the course of my research I realized I was missing footage from an important event: Zuckerberg's keynote presentation at the first Facebook Developer Conference in 2007. I had seen tiny clips of it in a BBC documentary made in 2010,[18] but the source was nowhere to be found. It wasn't on Facebook (even though keynotes from most other Facebook conferences were and they were all clearly produced by Facebook itself). It wasn't on YouTube (again, even though many others were still there). Googling didn't turn it up. The Zuckerberg Files archive didn't have it.[19] This only made me more curious. Why would such a formative document from the company's history be missing from public view?

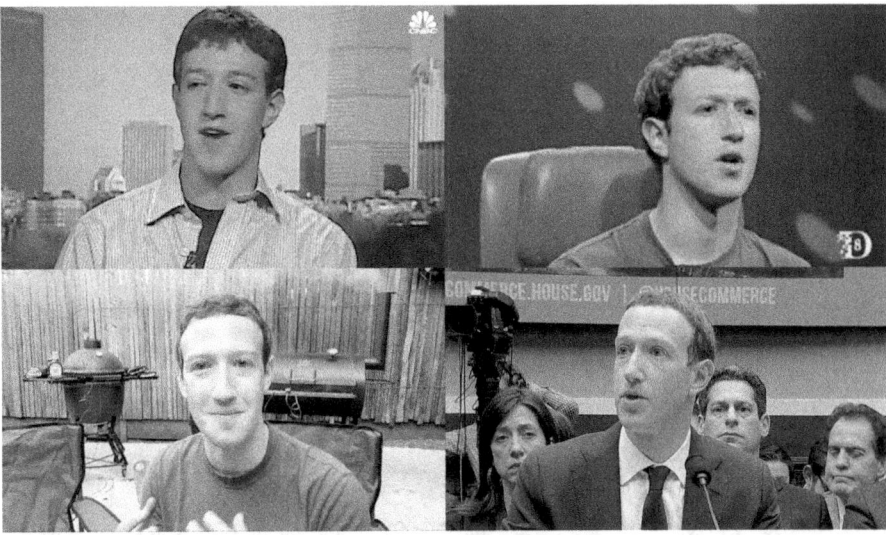

Fig. 6: ORDER OF MAGNITUDE (2019), a supercut drawn from every video-recorded appearance by Mark Zuckerberg from 2004-2018, extracting every time he speaks the words "more," "grow," and his every utterance of a metric such as "one thousand" or "two billion.

Determined to solve this riddle, I asked my friend and Italian filmmaker Elena Rossini[20] for help. She suggested I translate words about the event into Chinese and then use that translation as search terms for Chinese video sharing sites like YouKu (I had previously tried searching YouKu, but had used English terms). Elena's technique proved successful—I

18   Mark Zuckerberg: Inside Facebook, (dir. Charles Miller, 2011), London: BBC. View at: https://epublications.marquette.edu/zuckerberg_files_videos/65/.
19   The Zuckerberg Files is a public archive initiated/directed by Michael Zimmer that aims to store all of Mark Zuckerberg's public communications for academic research purposes. This archive is currently hosted by Marquette University's digital Institutional Repository. https://zuckerbergfiles.org.
20   https://elenarossini.com

found a low-resolution copy of Zuckerberg's 2007 keynote! So why would a document like this exist on a site behind the Great Firewall of China but be nowhere to be found in the USA? The likely answer is that the video used to be on sites like YouTube, but that at some point Facebook sought it out and had it removed (and hadn't thought to try Elena's technique, so missed the Chinese copy as I first had). Frankly, when you view the keynote it's not hard to imagine someone at Facebook deciding to scrub it from the 'net because it records a moment when Zuckerberg was at the height of his youthful arrogance, a time before his presentation style became so robotic and scripted. Why does this matter? It shows how the limited set of online video options we currently have makes such scrubbing easy, especially for a well-resourced company like Facebook. Further, recorded speeches like that keynote are important historical documents, as they illuminate how one of Silicon Valley's most influential CEOs talked about the company in its earliest days. If online video was more distributed and decentralized, Facebook never would have been able to (almost successfully) hide it from view.[21]

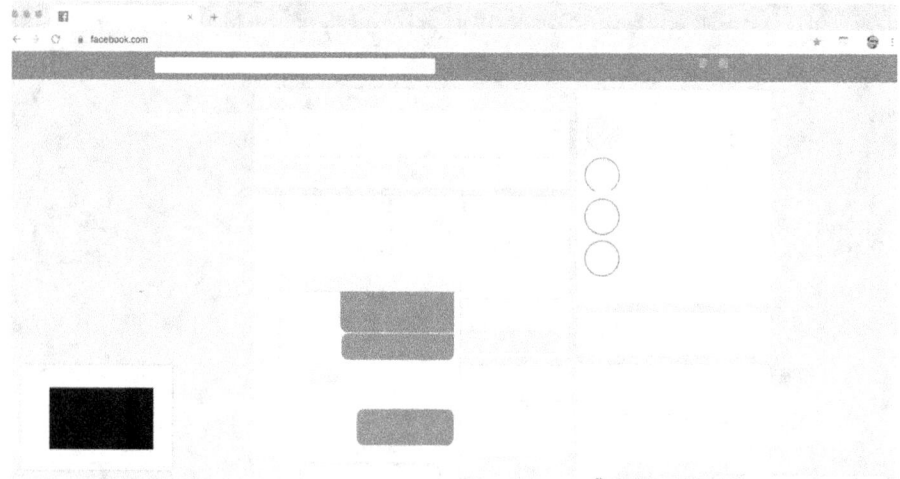

Fig. 7:Safebook (2018), a browser extension that hides all content across the Facebook interface.

Earlier you mentioned TikTok, which is my latest video sharing platform obsession. A cross between the old Vine (a 6 second video looping app that is now defunct) and Musical.ly (a lip-syncing app that was purchased and absorbed by TikTok's parent Chinese corporation ByteDance), TikTok is all the rage amongst young users right now. Scrolling through its AI-driven feed (AI in that it continually tries to profile you and then serve you videos it thinks will keep you there) quickly gives you a sense: it largely consists of teenagers lip syncing and dancing to the same short 15 second music clips. Most new videos posted are attempts

21   While in general I believe the originators of content online should be able to force its removal, Facebook is a special case. It's a public company who has a dramatic impact upon the global public (as demonstrated not just by its 2+ billion users but also the way it has been used as weapon to influence democracies in the USA, UK, and others. Because of this, I would argue that its previously public documents should stay within public view.

to imitate videos by the metric leaders ('TikTok Stars' with the most followers), though some demonstrate wider deviations. Regardless, because of this pattern of repetition (with the same music clip and same dances coming over and over again) user creativity often emerges through small changes rather than radical departures. For example, maybe the dancing teenager will wear distinctive clothing, or make a minor adjustment to the dance, or perform the dance with a friend or in front of a parent. What I've been marvelling about is how the platform's design has made such extreme conformity 'fun,' and how it encourages the celebration of minor deviation as significant. Constraints in and of themselves aren't a problem—in fact, they are useful and necessary for effective composition. But when one's creative freedom is cultivated and limited by a platform designed to preference imitation, I worry that such a constrained way of making will negatively influence the emerging generation's cultural activity for years to come.

Something else I've experienced first-hand is just how addictive the app's 'For You' page is (this is the name they give to the AI-driven feed). I've often found myself stuck in this feed, as you wrote in *Sad by Design*, 'unable to disrupt [my] own behavior', [22] I think there are many reasons for this, some of which you describe in your book, but others of which are perhaps specific to TikTok. Because creativity on the platform is forced to emerge through small deviations, scrolling the 'For You' feed necessarily becomes a search for those small changes. I find myself continuing to scroll, hoping to find the next deviation that represents an improvement or entertaining variation. To be clear, these moments are few and far between. But because the satisfying gestural swipe is all it takes to see if the next one is any better, it keeps me swiping, sometimes for hours! In fact, talking about TikTok addiction has itself become a TikTok meme, yet another soundtrack to lip sync to. One example is a meme by older users (being considered 'old' on the platform starts in ones 20s) that talks about the evolution of their addiction—how at first they didn't get it, then they found the content funny, and then before they knew it they were *also* doing the same dances and lip syncing to the same songs. In other words, even minor critiques of the platform have to conform to the same meme structures used by other popular content if it wants to metrically survive and gain visibility.

TikTok has gotten a lot of press lately as the 'fun' social network, the latest space where teens go to play with their friends (and to get away from parents on the old networks like Facebook). One reason for its fun reputation is the relative lack of political content on the platform, suggesting to users that others on the platform just don't care much about that kind of thing. Another characteristic of TikTok videos I have noticed is that so many of them are by pretty people performing within opulent home interiors. I wondered why this was? Was it because the app somehow attracted a disproportionate share of rich, pretty teens? The answer was revealed just a week ago via an article on *The Intercept* that shared leaked internal content moderation guides from the company.[23] Perhaps unsurprisingly, it turns out

---

22   Geert Lovink, Sad by Design: On Platform Nihilism, London: Pluto Press, 2019.
23   Sam Biddle, Paulo Victor Ribeiro, and Tatiana Dias, 'Invisible Censorship: TikTok Told Moderators to Suppress Posts by 'Ugly' People and the Poor to Attract New Users', The Intercept, 15 March 2020, https://theintercept.com/2020/03/16/tiktok-app-moderators-users-discrimination/.

that TikTok employees are directed to 'suppress' videos that exhibit certain characteristics, such as those with individuals whose bodies were 'chubby' or had 'ugly facial looks' or if they were 'senior people with too many wrinkles' or who were performing in 'shabby' spaces such as those with a 'crack on the wall,' Another leaked document lists extensive moderator guidelines for suppressing political content such as 'criticism towards civil servants, political, or religious leaders' or even anything that 'mentions' any app in competition with TikTok. In other words, the 'fun' facade is a ruse, hiding extensive censorship at the same time it encourages conformity and idolatry of those with the most likes or followers on the platform.

Finally, I want to respond to your question about the overall shift from text-heavy to image-heavy apps. I started thinking about this shift right after the 2016 US presidential election, when we were first hearing details about 'fake news' on Facebook. It made me wonder: what was the role of the image within these political disinformation campaigns? To think about this, I quickly coded and released a browser extension called Textbook.[24] A simple proposition, the work hides all images across the site, leaving blank areas in their place. My first reaction upon using it was to recall how Facebook used to be so text-focused back in its early days. Around 2008, everyone's status box began with a mandatory bit of text: '[Name] is...' This simple prompt led users to complete that sentence, and to potentially keep *writing*. Eight years later the balance is reversed: now Facebook is mostly images or video and not nearly as much text. Use of Textbook confirms this, as browsing the site with the extension installed shows that there just isn't much left when the images are hidden. It's a lot of blank space. Experientially the work led me to focus on the text that was left, and overall, the result felt like a much calmer environment. One year later, in 2017, the US House and Senate Intelligence Committees investigating Russian interference in the 2016 election released a number of disinformation ads that had circulated via Facebook before the election.[25] What struck me about them was that they *relied* on the image. For example, one pictured a glowing Jesus arm wrestling with a fiery Devil in order to characterize a vote against Hillary Clinton to be a vote in alignment with Jesus. Another pictured angry-looking women in burkas and full niqabs and exclaimed that '"Religious" face coverings are putting Americans at huge risk!' As with many of the ads released, these also embedded large bold text within the image itself in order to exceed the font size limitations of a text-based Facebook status post. The wider tactic being employed through these images was to activate—in the words of Cambridge Analytica's CEO—voters' 'hopes and fears,'[26] In other words, the image was a primary weapon deployed to scare or anger voters into voting a particular way.

With any piece of software, it's important to think critically about the effects of every design decision. Whose interests are most served by the wider shift from text to image or the elimination of links, and whose are made most vulnerable? As is often the case with the mega platforms, the answer is usually that the platform serves its owners at the expense of its users.

---

24   https://bengrosser.com/projects/textbook/
25   For screenshots, see Nicholas Fandos, Cecilia Kang and Mike Isaac, 'House Intelligence Committee Releases Incendiary Russian Social Media Ads', New York Times, 1 November 2017, https://www.nytimes.com/2017/11/01/us/politics/russia-technology-facebook.html.
26   Channel 4 News, 'Cambridge Analytica Uncovered: Secret filming reveals election tricks,' YouTube video, 19 Mar 2018, https://www.youtube.com/watch?v=mpbeOCKZFfQ.

References

Biddle, Sam, Paulo Victor Ribeiro, and Tatiana Dias. 'Invisible Censorship: TikTok Told Moderators to Suppress Posts by 'Ugly' People and the Poor to Attract New Users', *The Intercept*, 15 March, 2020, https://theintercept.com/2020/03/16/tiktok-app-moderators-users-discrimination/.

Bridle, James. 'Something is wrong on the internet', *Medium*, 6 November 2017, https://medium.com/@jamesbridle/something-is-wrong-on-the-internet-c39c471271d2.

Bucher, Taina. 'Want to be on the top? Algorithmic power and the threat of invisibility on Facebook', *New Media & Society,* 14.7 (2012).

Channel 4 News. 'Cambridge Analytica Uncovered: Secret filming reveals election tricks,' YouTube video, 19 Mar 2018, https://www.youtube.com/watch?v=mpbeOCKZFfQ.

Fandos, Nicholas, Cecilia Kang, and Mike Isaac. 'House Intelligence Committee Releases Incendiary Russian Social Media Ads', *New York Times*, 1 November 2017, https://www.nytimes.com/2017/11/01/us/politics/russia-technology-facebook.html.

Fuller, Matthew. 'Introduction', in Matthew Fuller (ed.), *Software Studies: A Lexicon*, Cambridge, MA: MIT Press, 2008, pp. 11-14.

Grosser, Benjamin. 'How the Technological Design of Facebook Homogenizes Identity and Limits Personal Representation', *Hz* 19 (2014), http://www.hz-journal.org/n19/grosser.html

Grosser, Benjamin. 'What do Metrics Want? How Quantification Prescribes Social Interaction on Facebook', *Computational Culture: a journal of software studies* 4, 2014, http://computationalculture.net/what-do-metrics-want/..

Lovink, Geert. *Sad by Design: On Platform Nihilism*, London: Pluto Press, 2019.

Miller, Charles (dir.). *Mark Zuckerberg: Inside Facebook*, 2011, London: BBC.

Oremus, Will. 'The Illinois Artist Behind Social Media's Latest Big Idea', *OneZero*, 23 July 2019, https://onezero.medium.com/the-illinois-artist-behind-social-medias-latest-big-idea-3aa657e47f30.

Zuboff, Shoshana. *The Age of Surveillance Capitalism: The Fight for a Human Future at the New Frontier of Power*, New York: Hachette, 2019.

NARRATIVE PLATFORMS: TOWARDS A MORPHOLOGY OF NEW AUDIENCE ACTIVITIES AND NARRATIVE FORMS

ANDREAS TRESKE
AND ARAS OZGUN

NARRATIVE PLATFORMS: TOWARDS A MORPHOLOGY OF NEW AUDIENCE ACTIVITIES AND NARRATIVE FORMS

ANDREAS TRESKE AND ARAS OZGUN

I.

Over the past decade, streaming media platforms have emerged as new, natively digital forms of content delivery. Although all traditional forms of audio-visual content (along new interactive forms) is now being streamed online, and while news media remains to be mostly watched on legacy TV sets on broadcast and cable channels for practical and habitual reasons we will discuss below, entertainment media is increasingly being serviced through the streaming media platforms, programmable architectures that emerged only within the past decade. Video oriented streaming media platforms quickly followed the success of subscription based online music services and internet radios developed in the previous decade (such as iTunes in 2003, Pandora in 2005, Spotify in 2008) and adopted similar business models —among today's popular streaming media platforms, Amazon Prime started as 'Amazon Unbox' in 2006, the DVD rental company Netflix started its streaming service in 2010, and in the same year Hulu emerged as a joint venture between the traditional TV networks News Corporation and NBC.

According to recent statistics, streaming media platform subscription rates increased to 69 % in 2019 (from 10 % in 2009) and surpassed the cable and satellite TV subscription rate of 65 % in the US.[1] However, this trend is not specific to US as according to MPAA (The Motion Picture Association of America) statistics, streaming media subscription has surpassed the cable TV subscription globally by increasing 27 % since 2017. Through such rapid growth, streaming media have become the dominant distribution form in media and entertainment industries, which has become a 100 billion dollar global industry.[2]

Netflix represents the streaming media platform model in a highly refined form; it offers an all-inclusive subscription service in which the user/audience can choose what to watch just like in traditional broadcast/cable TV entertainment (whereas the business of Amazon Prime and Hulu rely on pay-per-view offerings in addition to the basic subscription content), it dominates the

---

1   Chris Brantner, 'More Americans Now Pay For Streaming Services Than Cable TV', *Forbes*, 20 March 2019,
    https://www.forbes.com/sites/chrisbrantner/2019/03/20/americans-now-pay-more-for-streaming-services-than-cable-tv/#496a133fcdd2.
2   Andrew Liptak, 'The MPAA says streaming video has surpassed cable subscriptions worldwide', *The Verge*, 21 March 2019.
    https://www.theverge.com/2019/3/21/18275670/mpaa-report-streaming-video-cable-subscription-worldwide.

streaming video market by far (in US it controls 87% of the market, while Amazon Prime Video and Hulu holds respectively 52 % and 41,5 % shares).[3] Netflix is not only globally available (except mainland China —and Syria, North Korea and Crimea due to U.S. sanctions) but also peculiarly *local* in its programming (it supports 23 different languages in its user interface and customer relations, and forefronts regional productions besides its international repertoire). As such, approximately 37 % of the global internet users are believed to watch Netflix.[4]

Netflix also emphasizes in both its operation and publicity the distinguishing feature and essential power that separates streaming media platforms from broadcast and cable TV as a technological form; the algorithmic regulation of its service that enables it to offer custom programming to each user according to her/his individual taste. In 2006, when Netflix was a mail-order DVD rental business, even before it launched its first instant streaming service in 2007, it announced the *Netflix Prize*; a one million dollar prize for an algorithm that would improve the *cinematch* algorithm Netflix had been using in its recommendation engine for its DVD subscribers. Generating much publicity among the tech world, the prize was finally awarded in 2009 to a team of programmers called BellKor's Pragmatic Chaos.[5] Yet, Netflix announced in 2012 that the winning algorithm had not been, and would never be, implemented; as since 2010 the platform been generating detailed and minute data about its subscribers' viewing preferences and the costly implementation of a new algorithm was not needed.[6]

Despite the certain level of buzz the prize itself generated, the news that Netflix had discarded the winning algorithm did not make much of a splash. We can understand from the publicity and debates around the competition that the challenge of developing a predictive recommendation algorithm by analyzing users' rating behavior (and doing so with the rich dataset Netflix provided) had been the exciting task that motivated the programmers involved because such algorithm could be applicable to many different kinds of businesses, beyond movie distribution. Equally telling is Netflix's reasoning in scrapping the winning algorithm: by switching to streaming media distribution, Netflix did not need to *predict* its customers choices anymore; their customers watching experience had become entirely transparent, they now 'knew' their audiences choices, and had the chance to *guide* their predispositions with an interface that implied *interactivity*. As Netflix's operation and publicity crystalizes, algorithmic regulation of program flow that is masked behind the interactive menu becomes a constitutive element for streaming media platforms and changes the business of 'media distribution' in profound way.

---

3   Chris Neiger, 'Netflix's Market Share Is Shrinking, but It's Still the King of Video Streaming', *The Motley Fool*, 27 August 2019,
     https://www.fool.com/investing/2019/08/27/netflix-market-share-shrinking-still-streaming.aspx.
4   Amy Watson, 'Netflix - Statistics and Facts', Statista, 27 May 2019,
     https://www.statista.com/topics/842/netflix/.
5   Eliot Van Buskirk, 'How the Netflix Prize Was Won', Wired, 22 September 2009,
     https://www.wired.com/2009/09/how-the-netflix-prize-was-won/.
6   Casey Johnston, 'Netflix Never Used Its $1 Million Algorithm Due To Engineering Costs', Wired, 12 April 2012,
     https://www.wired.com/2012/04/netflix-prize-costs/.

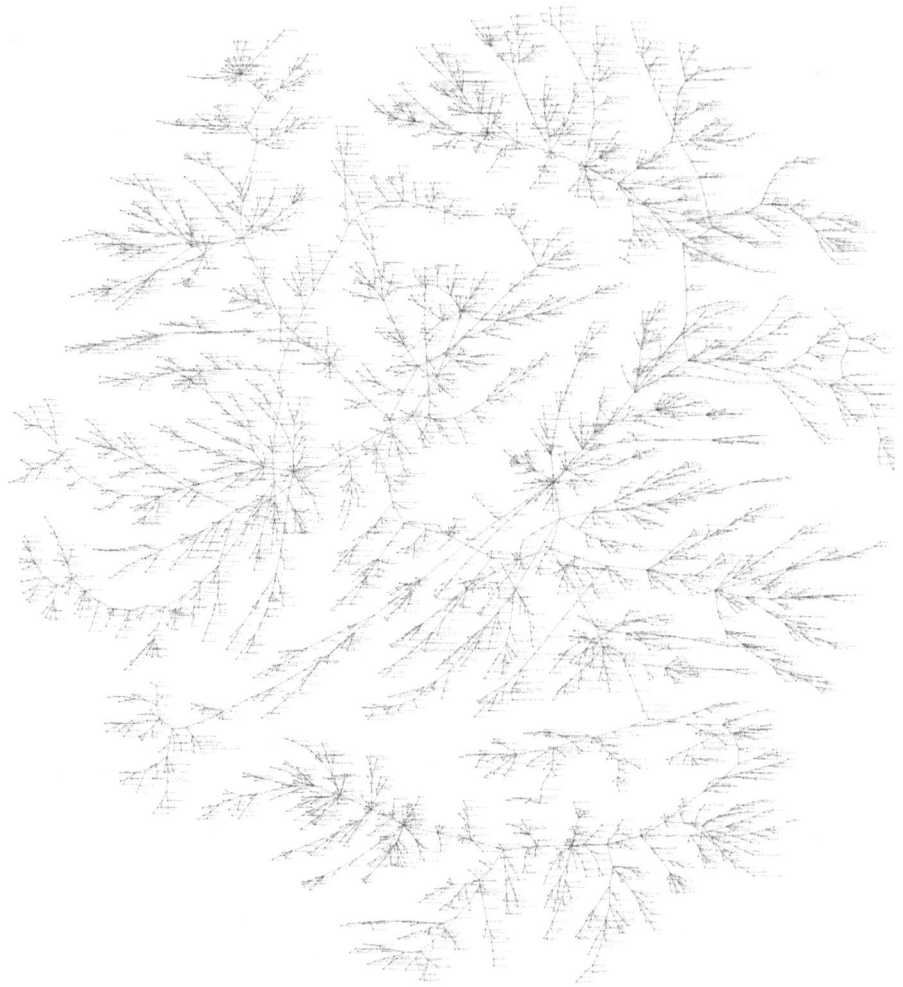

Fig. 1: Map of similarities between 5000 movies as found by the algorithm used for the Netflix Prize. Graphic visualization by Christopher Hefele (CC BY 2.0)

II.

For the audience, streaming media platforms appear as the new way of watching TV, or new kind of film distribution at the outset. The media content they deliver appears to be the same with what we used to watch on TV or at the movie theater. In fact, nowadays major streaming media platforms provide us not only with archives of television and cinema classics, but also with newly released serials and movies. In some cases, as soon as the programs are broadcast on television or a film open up in movie theaters (amazon), in addition to original content produced by the platforms themselves (Amazon, Netflix, Hulu, HBO, CBS All Access, Apple+). While major streaming media platforms compete to capture the pulse of the general public with massive investments on mainstream content, we are now also seeing minor platforms appearing for niche audiences in this growing market —such as Warner Media's DC Universe offering programming for the comics fans, or MUBI delivering arthouse films just like an arthouse movie theater, or Criterion Channel offering the cinema classics the video distributor amassed over the decades, just like a special interest channel on cable TV. Thus, while they slowly replace television and movie theaters, streaming media platforms appear to us as a combination of both, conveniently delivered together on to our screens.

Yet, although the narrative forms that reach to their audience through streaming appear to be similar or the same, the settings and the nature of the audience activity is profoundly different from television broadcasting and cinema screening. Both *broadcasting* and *screening* were collectively experienced *audience activities*; broadcast TV, as a technological form, was 'regional' by design, and TV industries operated at local and national scales. Cinema, from its early inception had operated as a form of mass entertainment/ public art. Such 'collectiveness' of the audience activity in both media forms had been embedded in their economy; public (meaning, *publicly owned*) broadcast TV channels had to air programs that either appealed to general public, or deemed to serve *public good* in other ways (by having educational, informational, or artistic value, for example). In private, profit oriented broadcasting, programs were offered to public for free, and the TV stations financed their operations through the revenues they gathered from the advertisement segments in between the programs —thus, appealing to general public had been an economic imperative for private TV channels. Such economically imposed publicness had been coupled by the temporality of the audience activity in television; the constitutive power of television (that distinguished it from cinema) had been its 'liveness' and 'immediacy' —its capacity to transmit the events over the distance at the moment they happen. Television brought whatever that is worth watching at that moment to the living rooms of every household, and people watched those altogether, at the very moment, at the same time.

The film industry had been shaped with the same economic imperative; the films had to be shown in movie theaters and watched collectively, thus operating both as an art and an entertainment form at the same time having to appeal to the general public. The difference in scale between the general audience of the broadcast TV stations and the spectators in the movie theater allowed certain niches in cinema —special interest films that would never have been a part of public broadcasting could be shown in movie theaters dedicated to such genres. Yet, such niches still depended on the availability of a corresponding *public interest*; one could find such special interest movie theaters only in neighborhoods and towns where enough people that shared such special interests existed.

The term *audience* had always implied multitudes; whatever we watched, we never watched it alone —we watched TV in our living room at the same time with millions of others, we watched films in the dark movie theater together with strangers. *Watching* had never been a passive exposure either; watching together implied decoding, debating, understanding, reacting, and being inspired together. Watching together (in other words, what we call *audience activity*) turned those multitudes into 'publics' that share common concerns, ideologies, and inspirations. If print media —books, magazines and newspapers— had been instrumental in the creation of *public sphere* in the 19th century,[7] the modern publics had been woven together by cinema and broadcast media. The *media events* Dayan and Katz smartly identified and analyzed has been based on the exploitation of the collective nature of audience activity.[8] Media events were preprogrammed coverage of extraordinary occurrences (such Apollo 11 moon landing in 1969) that broke with the banality of the daily regime of news magazines and serials, made *history* by being broadcast live globally, and rendered the watching masses a part of that history. Towards the end of the 20th century, cable networks offering a multitude of channels that catered to marginal and special interests, and satellite TV's transgressing the traditional geographical borders of broadcast media already introduced what we now call 'narrowcasting' and brought the fragmentation of the traditional mass audience according to demographic criteria and consumption patterns. Yet, the collective nature and the shared temporality of the audience activity had been still present, and in fact, narrowcasting arguably contributed to the enrichment of public life by making differences visible.

III.

Streaming media platforms and the media consumption patterns they introduce depart from the traditional notion of 'audience activity' in two layers. In the first and most important layer, streaming media transforms the temporal and spatial settings of the audience activity. Although we perceive it as some other form of TV watching (since the activity formally resembles it by taking place before a screen), the settings of the audience activity in the streaming format is different from TV — it does not necessarily take place in the living room, and in fact, as Gerard Goggin points to, it does not even necessarily take place in front of the TV screen.[9] Every member of the household can stream the content of their choice on their individual computers, laptops, tablets, smartphones, game consoles and mobile devices along the traditional TV sets.[10]

This practically brings the temporal and spatial separation of the spectatorship; streaming media platforms not only displace the TV set in the living room from its central position, but also disrupt the temporal regimes of family TV. The program flow in broadcast television had been structured according to everyday activities of family members, with the notion of television accompanying the household in their domestic life throughout the day —weekdays started with morning news, continued with women's magazine programs after husband leaves for work, news at lunch time, afternoon magazines, children's programs when they return from school, evening news when husband comes back from work, prime time for the whole family after dinner, and late night programs after the children go to sleep. The TV schedule also reproduced the social time regime of public life in its weekend and holiday programs,

---

7   Jürgen Habermas, The Structural Transformation of the Public Sphere: An Inquiry into a category of
     Bourgeois Society, Cambridge: Polity Press, 1989.
8   Daniel Dayan and Elihu Katz, Media Events: The Live Broadcasting of History, Harvard University Press,
     1992.
9   Gerard Goggin, 'Mobile Video: Spreading Stories with Mobile Media', in The Routledge Companion to
     Mobile Media, Gerard Goggin and Larissa Hjorth (eds), Routledge, 2014.
10   Andreas Treske, Video Theory: Online Video Aesthetics or the Afterlife of Video. Bielefeld: transcript
     Verlag, 2015.

and responded to important public events.[11] Whereas streaming media content is not only delivered to the users individual/mobile screens wherever they are, but also whenever they want.

At another layer, streaming introduces what we may provisionally call *micro-casting* — an almost individually *customized* form of content delivery at the practical level. Further than 'narrowcasting' introduced by cable/satellite TV in the previous decades, the streaming media spectator not only watches wherever s/he is, whenever s/he wants, but also whatever s/he chooses. In effect, streaming media platforms bring the fragmentation of the audience to the very level of individual spectator.

Past television studies have shown that audience activity has been shaped by and reflected the power relations in the domestic sphere, and in this sense was dominated by men as the head of the household.[12] In fact, women and children's programs found space on the daily schedule of the broadcast TV only at times men were supposed to be away from home.[13] Therefore, fragmentation of the audience that we describe above can be perceived to have an emancipatory effect; streaming media spreads the audience activity around the house(hold), and frees it from the domination of men. According to Lynn Schofield Clark it creates a setting, which enables 'minor' choices within the household (those of women and children) to be effective in demanding content.[14] In fact, the streaming platform Netflix anticipated such fragmentation from the very beginning, and gives two or four different user accounts per every subscription at different price ranges when signing up —so that, every member of the household can have their separate playlists, and their likes and choices are individually registered.

Although it is composed of the very same people, the very same mass of 'viewers', we would like to underline that streaming media audience is not just a 'fragmented' version of the TV audience, but an entirely different one. Netflix's programming itself attests to such transformed notion of the *audience*. It is significant that, the constitutive formats of traditional broadcast TV programming (such as game shows, reality TV, news, talk shows, variety shows) are not the most important assets on Netflix. Only culturally or historically significant shows of these types, in a rather retrospective, curatorial manner, are presented within its repertoire. These types of shows have once provided the *liveness* of the broadcast TV, and the 'live broadcast' has been the fundamental characteristic of *televisuality*. In contrast, the programming of Netflix is mostly geared towards narrative formats, serials and films from every genre, and *special interest* documentaries. Except the few instances of anticipating forthcoming episodes, or *seasons*, the content on Netflix is timeless, or at least time-divorced. *Live TV* programming finds its place in Netflix's scheduling only when it leaves its *liveness* behind, becomes a

11 Raymond Williams, Television: Technology and Cultural Form. London: Fontana, 1974.
12 David Morley, Family Television: Cultural Power and Domestic Leisure, London: Comedia/Routlege, 1986.
13 Ien Ang, Living Room Wars: Rethinking Media Audiences for a Postmodern World, New York and London: Routledge, 1991.
14 Lynn Schofield Clark, 'Mobile Media in the Emotional and Moral Economies of the Household', in The Routledge Companion to Mobile Media, Gerard Goggin and Larissa Hjorth (eds), Routledge, 2014.

part of the past or *timeless*, and belongs to a historical/cultural narrative. For the streaming platform the definitive aspect of audience activity is not 'watching what happens in the world as it happens, live, at the same time with the rest of the world/nation, collectively, together as a family in the living room anymore. *Liveness of the event* takes a new form on the platform, launching of the new shows, the starting of the new seasons become the *events* that construct the temporality in that global *depth of time* upon which the platform operates.

Not only the *live TV* notion becomes depreciated, but also the *seriality* — which had been another foundational aspect of televisuality — becomes passé. *Seriality* (having the news programming in certain times of the day, the new episodes of the serials on certain days of the week, weekend programming, morning programming etc.) had created a sense of continuity, and constructed a collectively experienced 'social time' regime.[15] *TV serials* had been the narrative form in which the temporality of the narrative overlapped with such social time regime; while the settings of the stories, main characters extended over the *seasons*, and sometimes overarching plot lines gradually developed, every week at the same day and time a new story with a new self-contained plot was aired. Episodic narrative was a truly modern form, introduced by magazines and daily newspapers, and inherited by radio and television when broadcast media took over the power of regulating social time from print media. It sat on the cutting edge of the storytelling as a craft; the impossible task of blending difference and repetition, familiarity and newness, continuity and novelty within the same text, within that 40 minutes.

What we understand from business insider reports is that, the only reasons for the streaming platforms to stick the episodic form and presentation of traditional TV serials are the few remainders of the past TV industry —such as classification criteria for TV awards,[16] the original form of past and new made-for-television serials, and perhaps, the slowly changing habits of middle-aged viewers who grew up with the episodic serial format). The definitive form of audience activity that Netflix and other streaming media platforms bring forth is *binge watching* (or, *binging* as it is commonly used now); a self-determined viewing activity, watching what you like in an uninterrupted fashion, at anytime you like, even independent from spatial constraints (like, you can still continue watching even if you need to *zone out* like going to the bathroom) due to the immediate availability of the whole 'seasons' of the *serials* which used to be broadcasted on TV over months, on a weekly basis, or entire repertoire of movies in a wide spectrum of genres. Binge watching appears as a particular platform sponsored hack short-circuiting the episodic seriality of the TV shows, but it does in fact apply to feature films and other narrative forms as well —the platform already lines up what you may want to watch next in a similar genre as soon as the end credits start to roll. Netflix built its streaming media distribution model on binge watching, and set itself apart from linear television by introducing the full drop-release (in which all the episodes, or entire seasons of the TV serials

15   Stanley Cavell, 'The Fact of Television', *Daedalus,* Vol.111, No. 4, Print Culture and Video Culture (Fall, 1982), 1982, pp. 75-96.

16   Allie Volpe,'The One Thing That Isn't Evolving With Netflix & Hulu's Takeover of TV', *Thrillist,* 16 October 2017,
https://www.thrillist.com/entertainment/nation/netflix-episode-length-streaming-services-traditional-tv.

were released at once) as its publication . Within the practice of watching, the post-play function takes us directly to the next episode, and, at the end of the movies or serials, to a similar one that the spectator may enjoy watching, rather than going back to the home page and making a deliberate choice (as was the case with Amazon Video until recently). The *skip intro* function even allows us to make the narrative flow feel more seamless. Interactive features such as this ironically imply a particular form of spectatorship that relies on the insulated flow of narratives.[17] The TV schedule used to guide us in deciding which programs needed to be watched one after another, whereas the Netflix interface creates an insulated and continuous flow of programs.

The continuousness of binging perverts the seriality of the TV narratives not only by detaching them from the larger temporal context of the social time regime, but also from their episodic breaks and hinges. Unconstrained by the durational limits of *weekly episode* format, the overarching plot lines take precedence in the narratives, diegetic settings can be constructed in detail, multiple characters within the story can be developed with certain depth. Episodes, in the continuous flow of binging now, functions more like *bookmarks*, *playlists* or *chapters* of one long narrative. In this sense, the closest relative of *binging* as an activity is not *TV watching*, but *reading*. Like reading, binging is often a solitary, contained and focused experience.

Reading the text of fairy tales or any narrative text according to Umberto Eco becomes similar to the metaphor of walking in a wood or Borges metaphor of a garden of forking path. 'Even when there are no well-trodden path in a wood, everyone can trace his or her own path, deciding to go to the left or to the right of a certain tree and making a choice at every tree encountered.'[18] Reading is an immersive, participatory activity; every sentence in a narrative text forces the reader to make a prediction, or wonder what will happen next. The insulated flow of binge watching reinforces the built-in dynamics of the narratives that Eco draws attention to. The limited interactivity of the streaming interface afford the viewer to immerse in and interact with the text itself —which is already and forever interactive.[19] Therefore every viewer in binging *reads/lives* her or his own text, immersing in what Jason Jacobs calls a *pure* text.[20]

IV.

The Marvel Cinematic Universe provides excellent examples of how this fragmented audience couples with a new narrative modality. The franchise offers a series of movies with hyperdiegetic plots, featuring rather shallow action heroes, pursuing quick and fast-paced action sequences for the duration of individual movies that are very loosely connected to each other through the characters rather than narrative threads. Produced for the big screen (and big sound), these are movies made for the cinema audience; aesthetic substance of these

17   Lisa Glebatis Perks, *Media Marathoning: Immersions in Morality,* London: Lexington Books, 2014.
18   Umberto Eco, *Six Walks in the Fictional Woods,* Harvard University Press, 1994.
19   Andreas Treske, *The Inner Life of Video Spheres,* Amsterdam: Institute of Network Cultures, 2013.
20   Jason Jacobs, 'The medium in crisis: Caughie, Brunsdon and the problem of US television', *Screen* 52.4 (2011): 503–511.

films remain as the CGI (computer generated images), working no more like 'special effects' but becoming the core storytelling devices that deliver the *moving image comic book* form, and appeal to the traditional superhero audience.

On the other hand, Marvel's Netflix franchises (*Jessica Jones, Daredevil, Luke Cage, Iron Fist, The Punisher*) feature tightly connected hyper-diegetic threads, more sophisticated plots, well-constructed multidimensional characters that unfold over the hyper-diegetic temporality.[21] The real commercial potential of the streaming platform becomes apparent when we look into the representational modes, genres and identification threads in these serials.

Although they belong to the same 'narrative universe'; *Jessica Jones* is a post-punk, feminist anti-heroine; *Daredevil* is film-noir; *Luke Cage* is essentially a blaxploitation story; *Iron Fist* is an extended Kung-Fu movie; and *The Punisher* is a Ramboesque ex-military vigilante justice story. Although they exist in the same hyperdiegetic universe, each narrative belongs to a different well-established genre and appeals to a distinct audience. Even one finds some genres/characters/plots appealing and the others not so much, however, s/he has to continue binging the others as well, in order to figure out those hyperdiegetic connections and threads, as the narratives connect and overlap. Although the differences in genres would be expected to exclude certain pieces of the Netflix's fragmented audience in each storyline, hyperdiegetic threads glues those viewers back to the Marvel Universe.

Netflix, with the brand power it already established among urban young professionals with its DVD rental service, evolved into the 'platform' that contains and unifies such fragmented, individualized, yet highly concentrated audience activity; and the new, distinct type of atomized yet focused audience that sustains it. Through the modern times, in the era of *mass media*, from the first newspaper to the emergence of the multiplex movie theaters, *the audience* had referred to a two-fold entity. It is because of this two-fold nature that we can use the term *audience* in both singular and plural forms in English. On the one hand, it refers to those multitudes that watched, read, and responded to the news and stories — a corporeal mass of living people, the plural form. Yet on the other hand, it also refers to an imaginary collective subject in its singular form whose feelings, tastes, values, and psychology (and rarely, intellectual awareness) had been the primary concern for the editors of the newspapers, Hollywood executives, and TV producers. Audience had been the *ghost in the narrative* as much as the living public, and precognition of its unforeseeable reactions to the stories had been the job of editors and producers.

For the producers of streaming platforms, audience is neither *imaginary*, nor *collective* anymore; the audience has been fragmented into its atoms only in the way that every atom became identifiable and explicable. Chris Marker claims in *Sans Soleil* that, in the specific cultural context of Japanese TV, the more you watch it, 'the more you feel it watches you'.[22] In the context of streaming media platforms, this ceases to be an irony. The producers of

21   Matt Hills, 'Defining Cult TV: Texts, Intertexts and Fan Audeiences', in *The Television Studies Reader,* Robert C. Allen and Annette Hill (eds), New York: Routledge. 2004, pp. 509-23.
22   *San Soleil* (dir. Chris Marker, 1983), New York: The Criterion Collection.

the streaming platforms know their spectators individually and feel their pulse with an unprecedented precision. They know what we watch, how we watch, when we watch, what we do before and after we watch, and our other mundane activities well beyond what we watch. Now, the producers only produce what they definitely know which one of the individual audience members (and how many in total) will watch. We, the *individuals* formerly composing the audience, do not buy this or that TV show or film — we subscribe to the streaming platform, knowing that it knows and delivers what we are interested in watching. Unlike previous media distribution systems, Netflix does not intend to sell individual shows/products. Instead, it aims to sell a service, an experience that becomes a part of a certain lifestyle; a virtual shopping mall of narratives in which a broad range of individuals belonging to a certain socioeconomic demographic (urban, financially able, upwardly mobile, educated young professionals) with somehow varying tastes can find what they consider as 'their niche' for their enjoyment.

V.

While defining the television as a *decentered* postmodern media, Ann Kaplan argues about a foundational difference between the cinema spectator and the TV audience.[23] She points to the *frame* that delimited the experience of the cinema spectator in a Simmelian fashion.[24] Cinema has been framed temporally by the fixed duration of its narrative that only lasts for so long, and spatially by the darkness of the movie theater that surrounded the image. The never-ending flow of programs on television, on the other hand, creates a continuum that has no spatial and temporal boundaries. Cinema captures the spectator by triggering her/his desires and offering a pleasurable dream, from which the viewer eventually wakes up at the end of the film – to face the actuality of everyday life, upon exiting the movie theater. Television, on the other hand, offers its audience plenitude; there is always something to watch — if not at that moment, a few minutes later, if not on that channel, certainly on one of the others. For Kaplan, that insatiable desire for plenitude kept the audience watching around the clock and diverted their attentive enjoyment to the consumer products advertised in the meanwhile.

Streaming media platforms present an amplified effect of plenitude without the advertisements in their subscription-based services. In this respect, they seemingly redeem the narrative from the interruption of those consumer products that belong to the everyday banality. Yet, this is a deception that hides the fact that the streaming platform itself is the ultimate consumer product — one that you can never finish consuming, one that always has more to offer than you can ever want, regardless of how different your desires may be — a personal Scheherazade for every Shahriyar.

The illusion of interactivity sustains the semblance of difference and differentiation; we *find*

---

23   E. Ann Kaplan, *Rocking Around the Clock: Music Television, Postmodernism, and Consumer Culture*, London: Routledge, 1987.
24   Georg Simmel, 'The Picture Frame: an Aesthetic Study', *Theory, Culture & Society* 11.1 (February 1994): 11–17.

this show or that movie on the platform, add it to our playlist, and choose to watch it whenever we want — as if those movies and shows are not algorithmically curated for us based on the general consumption patterns associated with our customer profile, and boldly pushed onto the top of the screen towards our attention. Therefore, it seems necessary to consider the streaming media platforms in the context of the *global culture industry* as portrayed by Lash and Lury, whose products are indeterminate objects that seek to produce *differences* and *differentiations* rather than *identities*.[25] In fact, the impetus is obvious; the platform makes you think that your tastes are different, that you want to hear a different story, that, the story is different.

As a *collective being* the audience had always been present in the narrative —if not diegetically certainly indexically, as a collective subject that is physically embodied in every person that listens, reads, or watches. Modern mass media, in its various forms, offered a shared experience to otherwise dispersed strangers who listened, watched, or read together, and turned them into *publics*. The making of a *public* out of multitudes had been perceived as such a crucial aspect of modern governmentality that, mass media had been considered as a prerequisite of nation building, particularly in the context of the modernization of third world countries. Throughout the modern times, *public opinion*, and that sweet spot of public opinion where every taste and value meets, the *lowest common denominator*, had been the curse of liberal democracies that actually somehow made it work. The fragmentation of the audience has to be considered in this political context too —as the dissolution of the publics as we know it. The platform, the difference engine that constantly detects, cultivates and manufactures the differentials and turns them into flows of demand and supply, replaces the curse it lifts with another one; *I* is always an algorithmically categorized *other* now.

Our stories may intertwine at some point in this hyper-diegetic universe, but are we still a part of a common plot? The question that crystalizes when we consider the *audience* of the streaming media networks as a semblance of *public* actually concerns with the public life in what we can now rightfully call *platform societies* in general. In the past two decades, the emerging social media platforms has been celebrated as means of connecting the people who are geographically separated (and even stranger to each other without such connection) and thus as a means of commoning, community building, and creating *publics*. Yet, the fact that those commonalities, connections, and communities were built and regulated by algorithms designed with profit maximization incentives. Just as the streaming media platforms sterilize our leisure time by providing us only with what we are predisposed to watch, social media platforms sterilize our connections with the world outside; we selectively *friend* people who we already know, or familiar with, or who we may *like* according to Facebook's (or some other social media networks) algorithms. Despite all the problems we can attribute to what 'public' had represented throughout modernity and how modern public sphere worked,[26] these terms never referred a sterile and homogenous mass; although it had never been all-inclusive, public discreetly signified the *others*. Public/ness meant brushing shoulders with

25   Scott Lash and Celia Lury, *Global Culture Industry: The Mediation of Things*, Malden, MA: Polity Press, 2007.
26   Aras Özgün, 'A Common Word', *Rethinking Marxism* 22.3 (2010): 374-381,.

strangers, encountering unfamiliar and sometimes unpleasant stories, and negotiating and learning from differences. Collectiveness of the audience activity in modern mass media, in the movie theater or in front of the TV screen, virtually and practically imposed exposure to differences and emergencies. Streaming media viewership is not only a solitary activity, but also an isolated one, sterilized by the platforms algorithmic controls. Differences and emergencies of the past public life is substituted by the seemingly endless options and novelties offered by the platform, seemingly geared towards the individual choices of its users.

At the beginning of this article, we mentioned that streaming media platforms replace television and cinema by combining them together in itself. Our analogy had been rather concerned with the format and falls short; actually, streaming media platforms substitute the local bookstore or DVD rental on the corner, minus having to talk to the guy at the counter who always disagrees with your choices, encountering your chatty neighbors strolling around the aisles, and the noisy, crowded street you have to walk to get there —in other words, minus the world that surrounds the narrative.

References

Ang, Ien. Living Room Wars: Rethinking Media Audiences for a Postmodern World, New York and London: Routledge, 1991.

Brantner, Chris. 'More Americans Now Pay For Streaming Services Than Cable TV', Forbes, 20 March 2019,
https://www.forbes.com/sites/chrisbrantner/2019/03/20/americans-now-pay-more-for-streaming-services-than-cable-tv/#496a133fcdd2.

Cavell, Stanley. 'The Fact of Television', Daedalus, Vol.111, No. 4, Print Culture and Video Culture (Fall, 1982), 1982, pp. 75-96.

Dayan, Daniel and Elihu Katz. Media Events: The Live Broadcasting of History, Harvard University Press, 1992.

Perks, Lisa Glebatis. Media Marathoning: Immersions in Morality, London: Lexington Books, 2014.

Goggin, Gerard. 'Mobile Video: Spreading Stories with Mobile Media', in The Routledge Companion to Mobile Media, Gerard Goggin and Larissa Hjorth (eds), Routledge, 2014.

Habermas, Jürgen. The Structural Transformation of the Public Sphere: An Inquiry into a category of Bourgeois Society, Cambridge: Polity Press, 1989.

Hills, Matt. 'Defining Cult TV: Texts, Intertexts and Fan Audeiences', in The Television Studies Reader, Robert C. Allen and Annette Hill (eds), New York: Routledge. 2004, pp. 509-23.

Jacobs, Jason. 'The medium in crisis: Caughie, Brunsdon and the problem of US television', Screen 52.4 (2011): 503–511.

Johnston, Casey. 'Netflix Never Used Its $1 Million Algorithm Due To Engineering Costs' Wired, 12 April 2012, https://www.wired.com/2012/04/netflix-prize-costs/.

Kaplan, E. Ann. Rocking Around the Clock: Music Television, Postmodernism, and Consumer Culture, London: Routledge, 1987.

Lash, Scott and Celia Lury. Global Culture Industry: The Mediation of Things, Malden, MA: Polity Press, 2007.

Liptak, Andrew. 'The MPAA says streaming video has surpassed cable subscriptions worldwide', The Verge, 21 March 2019.
https://www.theverge.com/2019/3/21/18275670/mpaa-report-streaming-video-cable-subscription-worldwide.

Marker, Chris, dir. San Soleil, New York: The Criterion Collection, 1983.

Morley, David. Family Television: Cultural Power and Domestic Leisure, London: Comedia/Routlege, 1986.

Neiger, Chris. 'Netflix's Market Share Is Shrinking, but It's Still the King of Video Streaming', The Motley Fool, 27 August 2019,

https://www.fool.com/investing/2019/08/27/netflix-market-share-shrinking-still-streaming.aspx.

Özgün, Aras. 'A Common Word', Rethinking Marxism 22.3 (2010): 374-381.

Clark, Lynn Schofield. 'Mobile Media in the Emotional and Moral Economies of the Household', in The Routledge Companion to Mobile Media, Gerard Goggin and Larissa Hjorth (eds), Routledge, 2014.

Simmel, Georg. 'The Picture Frame: an Aesthetic Study', Theory, Culture & Society 11.1 (February 1994),: 11–17.

Watson, Amy. 'Netflix - Statistics and Facts', Statista, 27 May 2019,
https://www.statista.com/topics/842/netflix/.

Williams, Raymond. Television: Technology and Cultural Form. London: Fontana, 1974.

Treske, Andreas. Video Theory: Online Video Aesthetics or the Afterlife of Video. Bielefeld: transcript Verlag, 2015.

_____. The Inner Life of Video Spheres, Amsterdam: Institute of Network Cultures, 2013.

Eco, Umberto. Six Walks in the Fictional Woods, Harvard University Press, 1994.

van Buskirk, Eliot. 'How the Netflix Prize Was Won', Wired, 22 September 2009,
https://www.wired.com/2009/09/how-the-netflix-prize-was-won/.

Volpe, Allie. 'The One Thing That Isn't Evolving With Netflix & Hulu's Takeover of TV', Thrillist, 16 October 2017,
https://www.thrillist.com/entertainment/nation/netflix-episode-length-streaming-services-traditional-tv.

INSIDE EQUIPMENT (STUDIO PRACTICE)

INA BLOM

INSIDE EQUIPMENT (STUDIO PRACTICE)[1]

INA BLOM

'To me, a good tool generates its own secrets at a much greater rate than it discloses them'. —Woody Vasulka

During 1968–69, Nam June Paik was a resident at WGBH, a Boston TV station that had received funding from the Rockefeller Foundation in order to allow artists to work with engineers. The most remarkable outcome of this residency was the construction of one of the first video synthesizers, in collaboration with the Japanese engineer Shuya Abe.[2] Paik described it as a 'sloppy machine' and it was just that: a jumble of old video equipment wired so as to exploit their electronic affordances to the max.[3] Seven old black-and-white surveillance cameras were assembled to create a colorizer: the signal of each camera was passed through individual nonlinear amplifiers and then through a matrix into a RGB to NTSC color encoder. Since each camera was set to produce one color value only, they would produce overlapping color images when aimed at the same object. On top of this assembly, Paik added a scan modulator that would facilitate distortion of the input image—an electronic alternative to the handheld magnets Paik had used to distort live TV images in his early television works.[4]

According to David Atwood, Paik's Boston roommate, the WGBH 'engineers hated the thing'.[5] Yet this less-than-elegant construction provided something quite new: a wholly synthetic space that was also live in real time, and that presented itself as a new dynamic arena of production, interaction, and collaboration. The tangible sense of intra-machinic space was mainly an effect of the type of distortion that scan modulation could provide. To be able to play around with the scanning process of a cathode-ray tube, Paik and Abe placed extra deflection yokes — sets of coils through which current is passed to produce

---

1   I would like to thank Rashmi Sawhney, Ahmet Gürata, Andreas Treske and Geert Lovink who invited me to present the key ideas from my 2016 book The Autobiography of Video: The Life and Times of a Memory Technology (New York: Sternberg Press, 2016) during the Video Vortex XI conference in Kochi in 2017. The present text – previously published as Chapter Six in my book - is the full development of a theme that I was only able to evoke briefly during my lecture and the discussion that followed.
2   The residency led to Paik getting funding for a trip to Japan to work with Shuya Abe. The Paik/Abe synthesizer was built in 1970, and Paik returned to WGBH in the summer to use it for the Video Commune broadcast. In 1968 Eric Siegel created his version of a video colorizer; his video synthesizer was also introduced in 1970.
3   Paik, quoted in George Fifield, 'The Paik/Abe Synthesizer', published as part of Davidson Gigliotti's Early Video Project. http://davidsonsfiles.org/paikabesythesizer.html.
4   See 'Nam June Paik & Shuya Abe: Paik/Abe Video Synthesizer (Keyer & Colorizer) & Scan Modulator (a.k.a. the Wobbulator)', 1970, in Vasulka, Vasulka and Weibel, Eigenwelt der Apparate-Welt: Pioneers of Electronic Art. The choice of the title Eigenwelt is significant here: in contrast to the term Umwelt, which signifies the physical environment and Mitwelt, which signifies social and cultural world, Eigenwelt signifies the world of personal experience—in this case, apparently, the personal experiences of technical machines.
5   David Atwood, quoted in Fifield, 'The Paik/Abe Synthesizer'.

a magnetic field for deflecting a beam of electrons — on top of the ordinary black-and-white monitor yoke that guides the television electron beam to its intended location. The extra deflection yokes would, so to speak, hijack the normal scanning process, and the deformed image that resulted was then rescanned off the face of the cathode-ray tube and fed into the colorizer. This combination of free modulation and feedback produced constantly evolving color patterns that gave off a distinct sense of depth, in marked contrast with the relative flatness of the ordinary monitor image. This was electronic action in three-dimensional space. And such space could in turn play host to a number of other synthetic image sources, generating intricate effects of spatial layering. All you needed was an external keyer to combine the swirling scan modulations with other video backdrops. Significantly, all of this could be done in real time, 'at the very moment of broadcast'.[6]

This moment was August 1, 1970, when the Paik/Abe synthesizer was billed the star of the four-hour-long WGBH broadcast *Video Commune (The Beatles from Beginning to End)*: live synthesizer modulation was mixed with prerecorded Japanese television commercials and the sound of the entire catalogue of Beatles' recordings. Excerpts from the show — its documentary remains — highlight in a quite literal way how the scan modulation color feedback produced not just electronic space but, more specifically, an outline of a wholly new type of artistic production space. For the pulsating scan patterns did not just produce a sense of evolving virtual depths, they also housed feeds from the actual broadcasting studio in which the synthesizer was doing its work, among technical personnel and random persons from the street who had been invited into the studio by Paik.

The collaborative context of the broadcasting studio was, in other words, no longer a mere technical 'source' or production context for television images, but seemed to reside at the very heart of the new electronic image-spaces.[7] And electronics were not just technical processes handled by artists and engineers. In contrast, the forces unleashed by nonlinear signal amplification, electron beam deflection, and video feedback circuits seemed to both frame and 'produce' the studio space and its human work force. From an engineering design perspective, the Paik/Abe synthesizer may have been a mess, but from a media-archeological perspective it was an epistemological event. By reengineering existing apparatuses and machine components, Paik and Abe opened up the black box of broadcasting technology, unleashing the true heterogeneity of video agencies. All of a sudden, a variety of technical components came forth as quasi-autonomous capacities, collaborators in a reformulated space of production where the touchy issue of who or what was working on who was opened up to questioning.

---

6   Ibid.
7   An early and rudimentary move toward this electronic 'encompassing' of the broadcasting studio took place with Paik's contribution to the broadcasting of John Cage's Variation V on Norddeutscher Rundfunk in 1966. TV viewers would see the actions of Cage's musicians and performers 'under' a visual layer of electronic effects.

Toward the Intra-Machinic Studio

This was a first inkling of what was to become a distinct moment in video's autobiography: video presenting itself as a new type of workspace, a new *locus* of artistic production. The intra-machinic studio space brought forth in *Video Commune* signals a turning point in the discourses of artistic labor, which may be traced in the transformations of studio practice in the twentieth century. Such transformations are the topic of *Machine in the Studio: Constructing the Postwar American Artist* (1996), Caroline Jones's groundbreaking analysis of the artist's studio in postwar American art, and its relation to changing models of artistic subjectivity.[8] Her narrative traces three major transformations. The studio as a locus of artistic isolation, typified by the existentialist painter-hero of Abstract Expressionism, gives way around 1960 to the studio as a quasi-industrial and increasingly social arena, headed by artist-managers or artist-executives like Frank Stella and Andy Warhol. And in the 1970s, the studio as the locus of a centralized author-figure is displaced and dispersed in the conceptual and site-specific practices of artists like Robert Smithson or Daniel Buren. Art production is now ostensively a performance taking place across multiple sites and involving multiple actors, undoing the cohesiveness of the 'work' of art itself.

Yet, like any original work of research, *Machine in the Studio* is interesting also on account of what it omits. The central theme in Jones's series of transformations is the relation between the studio artist and technology. It is the paradigm of industrial technologies and the concepts of standardization, mechanization, and mass production that transform the studio from the charged sanctuary of the isolated genius to the bustling 'factory' of the executive artist and his many assistants and associates. And it is this increasing sensitivity to the nonhuman dimensions of industrial technologies and the human/machine dialectic of the industrial age that prompts Smithson's deconstruction of the authorial space of the studio. The 'technological sublime', articulated in Smithson's work, is precisely that which cannot be contained by the anthropocentric studio space—art is now viewed in light of larger material processes. Jones's analysis does not, however, touch on the postindustrial media technologies that played such a central role in the transformation of capitalist societies after World War II. Technology, in this context, is primarily industrial. The impact of information- and signal-based procedures on the configuration of artistic production and subjectivity is simply not taken into account, despite their significance in American art of the period.

There may be good reason for this omission. With new media and information art, the artist's studio in its more traditional guises seems to disappear as a defining or critical site. Smithson is a liminal case, in the sense that the site/non-site dialectic in his work explicitly performs a critical repetition and displacement of the centralized locus of art production; for numerous other artists of the 'conceptual' generation, the studio model no longer applies. As Alexander Alberro has documented, the new information-oriented practices

---

8   Caroline Jones, Machine in the Studio: Constructing the Postwar American Artist, Chicago: University of
      Chicago Press, 1996.

in art are closely associated with a late-capitalist culture of publicity and marketing, in which emphasis on the efficient circulation of signs and sign values takes precedence over any lingering attachment to the aesthetic object and the hallowed context of its making.[9] Alongside this shift emerged the term 'post-studio' practice, confirming the evacuation of the studio as a critical site of production. The artist of the Information Age works anywhere and everywhere, just as the presence of his or her work in museums and gallery spaces is often a post-factum document of their life in global information networks.

But this is only part of the story. Once one looks beyond the semiotic/linguistic approach to media culture that marks many Conceptual art practices, there is every reason to question the assumption that the concept of the studio as a specific site of creative labor has disappeared. Once the Information Age is approached not just as a general cultural and economic condition but as a proliferating body of technical devices, the discourses of the artist's studio confront the reality of another highly specific workspace: the media studio and its various modes of production and collaboration. At this point, the concept of the artist's studio does not so much disappear as increasingly overlap with that of the media studio — more specifically the spaces where broadcasting and computing equipment could be accessed. And, in a move that harks back to Dada and Constructivism, the figure of the artist increasingly blends with that of the engineer. The Paik/Abe constellation is but one of many examples from the period. Still, the return of the artist-engineer in the context of video has wider ramifications than a redefinition of human creativity, and this is why the electronic transformation of the artist's studio should be seen as a key moment in the autobiography of video. For along with video's discovery of its proper workspaces, there emerges a model of collaborative labor that brings out some of the more radical aspects of constructivist technicity: the interacting agencies of artist-engineers and technical things.

This is not to say that the question of postwar media culture does not enter Jones's account. On the contrary, one of the most interesting sections of her text is the analysis of the cinematic and televisual mediation of the artist's studio in the 1950s, '60s, and '70s, and this provides a rich context for understanding the transformation that takes place once the artist's studio is no longer just a space that may be represented *by* moving image media, but is itself a locus for the production of media spaces or signal-based realities. The '60s and early '70s saw a sharp increase in the production of documentaries about artists, and in this context the artist's studio seems to hold a particular spell over the imagination of film and television producers and their audiences. The trend seems to die out in later half of the 1970s, alongside the increase in post-studio art practices. What matters here is how film and television mediate the artist as a function of a certain type of space, and the changing mediatic constructions of that space. However, in keeping with the apparatus theory of film that informs Jones's analysis, these spatial mediations are also indicative of changing ideological constructions of the spectator, whose visual pleasure 'suture' them to a particular cinematic reality thanks to the specific relation that obtains between cinema and space. The cinematic apparatus in general frames

---

9   Alberro, Conceptual Art and the Politics of Publicity, Cambridge, MA: MIT Press, 2003.

space, and — as Jones asserts — ideology is very much present in the way space around the subject ebbs and flows.[10] How the studio space is framed (and what and whom this framing contains) is indicative of the way in which spectatorial desire affects the cultural construction of the artist.

This point is reinforced by a paradigm of low-budget documentary filmmaking that makes space even more telling than what is usually the case in cinema. No longer just a container for narrative action, the studio space almost figures as a character in its own right. Since most documentaries of this type were made with a single 16 mm film camera fixed on a tripod, a stilled theatrical space is created that is quite different from the more dynamic field of multiple perspectives and characters that you have most cinematographic productions. Thanks to such technical and economic limitations, the studio space itself — the preferred 'set' for documentaries on artists — has a particular kind of presence, authority, and sense of authenticity. These limitations proved particularly significant in establishing the idea of the isolation of the studio and the authority of the single artist operating at a remove from the world. With only one camera, there was no possibility of creating the shot/reverse-shot dynamic that establishes the camera as a stand-in for the point of view of a seeing subject.[11] In Hans Namuth and Paul Falkenberg's 1950–51 film on Jackson Pollock, no viewers disturb the perfect isolation of the studio and no alternative points of view exist. The spectator is only drawn in to the extent that he or she identifies with the hand of the painter in action (presented in a close-up behind a pane of glass that serves as a canvas proxy for the purposes of filming) and its absolute mastery. If this identification fails, the viewer is simply a distant voyeur, cut out from the scene.[12] In Namuth and Falkenberg's 1964 film on Willem de Kooning, the viewer is more explicitly present as a voyeur thanks to the placement of the camera in a hole in the canvas; the artist is viewed painting around it, avoiding it. Studio isolation is broken only by the (inconvenient) presence of others, and the guilty spectator is invited to identify with the existential anxiety of artistic solitude.[13]

In Lane Slate's 1965–66 *USA Artists* TV series, the studio remains central, but is now a more distinctly social and urban space. Again, the camera is set on catching studio practice in action, but by now such action is provided not only by the artist but by assistants, friends, and the urban and industrial environment that constitutes the larger social world of the studio. This is the spatial reality that subtends artist-managers, like Warhol and Stella, and the industrial concept of production that informs their work. Moreover, the sociality of these studio sites extend into media space, since mediation now comes with a high degree of consciousness of the camera and documentary process as such. The studio is framed by a new type of media-savvy perspective that ultimately shakes up the cultural authority of the studio. As Jones shows, this effect is achieved through a number of distancing procedures in which the formerly isolated artist now

---

10   Jones, Machine in the Studio, 71.
11   Ibid.
12   Ibid., 72–77.
13   Ibid., 77–80.

emerges as one among many. No longer the unique action figure whose unbroken soundtrack monologue underscores the intimacy of the studio space, he is increasingly framed by the presence of coworkers as well as by the knowing 'outsider' narration of the journalist that never appears on camera. As if in response, his performance for the camera may be marked by analogous acts of distancing. The case of Barnett Newman is particularly ambivalent, in that he refuses to paint for the camera, refuses to perform 'the artist' — all he accepts to do is to gesso the canvas in a workmanlike manner that has little to do with the creative process and the work of art. In this context where the artist appears as an uncertain and to some extent even dispossessed figure, it is, Jones argues, the studio space as a cinematographic 'character' that confers on Newman, what is left of his authority, his position as a subject in a documentary on art. By the time the series reaches Warhol and his particular brand of camp passivity, the artist's studio starts to blend with that of the film studio. Since Warhol consistently refuses to play the subject of the TV documentary — opting for various forms of nonresponse or rhetorically returning the interviewer's questions — spectators are made conscious of the fact that outsiders (i.e., journalists) have entered the studio and are using it to make a film. A voice-over of an art historian was added post-factum to gloss over these moments of unease, in particular the machinic lack of affect that Warhol tried to emulate in person as well as in his 'industrial' art.[14] The concept of the expanded, mediatic studio is also an emphatic reality in Emile de Antonio's 1973 release *Painters Painting*, yet both artists and filmmaker seem strangely removed from the products of their labor. Despite the deconstructive approach to filmmaking, the film ultimately promotes a fetishistic approach to the studio's *products* and their autonomous existence: the works of art are shown as such and in brilliant color, in stark contrast to the grainy black and white used to document their production spaces. Hence, the spectator is made to identify with the act of (cultural) consumption, rather than with the act of artistic creation.[15]

Jones's *Machine in the Studio* thus documents the ambivalence of the studio space in postwar media culture. The conventions and material restrictions proper to documentary filmmaking help construct the authority and isolation of the space that produces the modern myth of the lonely artist. Yet the same mediation processes are at work in the undoing of this myth, once the cinematic apparatus is seen as part and parcel of other social production processes taking place in the studio. In the end, the reality of the studio space is no more than a cinematographic signifier, a matter of choice of film stock. The use of nostalgic black and white in *Painter's Painting* presents the studio as something outdated, evanescent, and possibly unreal, at least in comparison with the tangible physicality of works of art shot on high quality color stock. What unites all of these mediations is the alliance between cinema and studio *space*, and the way in which this space serves to anchor the centralized figure of the artist, however ambiguous or shaky. The shakiness of this construction became obvious in post-studio practices, when the specificity of the studio space was supplanted by space in general. Yet, the narrative of this displacement must be supplemented with the story of the transformations of the

14   Ibid., 81–98.
15   Ibid., 98–105.

studio concept that takes place once art turns to electronic technologies — a context in which *space as such* is no longer a central metaphor or metonymy of artistic production. Once broadcasting equipment and computers replace the rooms that facilitated painterly and sculptural processes (the need for daylight, sightlines, bodily movement, temporary storage of materials, etc., that are key to these processes), the mediation of physical space is no longer what confers authority on the artist figure. Space no longer anchors the type of creativity that subsists at the limits of more organized forms of work. *Video Commune* seems to intuit exactly this. The intra-machinic spatializing effects that 'host' footage of the broadcasting studio are just that — effects. This studio is not established through the geometrical coordinates of cinematographic frames, but emerges, fleetingly, in the progressive depths of pulsating scan patterns that are temporal rather than assertively spatial. There is no boxlike stage dramatizing production of work that is, in principle, separate from the studio. The constantly evolving spaces produced by the video synthesizer *are* the specific and creative work processes that emerge when a certain threshold of operationality has been crossed and there is synergy between previously separate machine elements that have now become integrated and multifunctional.

This process — a typical case of what Gilbert Simondon would call 'technical concretization' or 'individuation' — produces not just a vivid sense of how a range of forces affect each other in time.[16] As importantly, it implies a *temporal* displacement of the concept of the artist's studio. No longer an originary and originating locus, based on the authority of the (art-historical) past, it is transformed into a form of determination that comes from the future. Under the name of video, artistic labor and its social/collaborative modalities must — for better or worse — be understood in terms of such temporalization.

The New Collaborators

Between 1970 and 1977, this new conception of the artist's studio becomes the object of extensive testing and probing. The notion of 'moving inside', that is, discovering the intra-machinic unknowns, is mapped onto the more familiar and topical metaphor of exploring outer space:

> We are warp minus ninety seconds and counting, 89, 88, 87, 86, 85, this is control we are go ... this is systems, we are go ... this is audio and we are go ... 64 ... 63 ... 62 ... we are go on all channels ... one minute and counting ... stand by to warp ... check list? .... go ... 48 ... 47 ...crew check ... answer to ... 35 ... 34 ... 33 ... Howard? ... Howard is go ... Beck? ... Beck is go ... Jepson? ... Jepson is go ... Roarty?   ... Roarty is go ... 24 ... 23 ... 22... Hallock? ... Hallock is go ... Turner? ... 17 ...16 ... Turner is go ... minus nine, eight, seven, six, five, four, three, two, ONE ... warp ... Innerspace warp has launched a probe into the unknown ... into videospace, to explore the vast

---

16   Simondon, 'Genesis of the Individual', trans. Mark Cohen and Sanford Kwinter, in Jonathan Crary and Sanford Kwinter (eds.), Incorporations, New York: Zone Books, 1992, pp. 297–319.

uncharted reaches of electric dimensionality where few have ever traveled. The crew is part of the group of artists from the National Center for Experiments in Television who have been brought to San Francisco to explore the space behind the tube. Stephen Beck, Aquarian (1950), is engineer and his direct video synthesizer like those of Eric Seigal and Nam June Paik is the control room for the voyage into video space (sic).[17]

In this textual 'launch' of Stephen Beck's 1971 video synthesizer, the entire crew of San Francisco's National Center for Experiments in Television figure as astronauts of the 'uncharted' electronic spaces of video machines. Yet, despite the dramatic space-age language, the new electronic studio is actually where video's emerging identity as a facilitator of machine-human interactions is translated into the more colloquial terms of collaborative work processes. The drama of the technological sublime, articulated in Robert Smithson's machine/human dialectic, evaporates once technology is no longer the 'big other' of humans, but a set of inventive agencies that engage or make use of humans in their processes of (self-) discovery. The importance of being open to what might come from the inside of machinic processes was underscored by Beck's engineering decisions: his synthesizer operated without input cameras (i.e., without 'windows to the world'), relying instead on the internal, auto-generative capacities of electronic circuits connected to a monitor. As he put it, 'Within many of mankind's tools are latent properties unobserved even by those whose intuition has led them to design the tool'.[18]

However, the matrix of relations expressed in this text — the inside of equipment as a new locus of creative work, where humans take clues from the autonomous and inventive operations of tools — received far more explicit treatment in a series of early '70s video productions by Keith Sonnier[19]. For these works make *literal* the idea of 'residing' at the inside of electronic work processes, in intimate company with numerous technical collaborators. Here, the distinctly social environment of Warhol's and Stella's studios have moved inside the circuits of video machineries. The rhetorical impact of this transition is all the more significant considering the fact that Sonnier was trained as a painter and sculptor and maintained a prolific sculptural practice alongside his work in video. He would have no illusions about the spatial demands of art making and the significance of the traditional studio. Yet his childhood experiences in his father's electronics shop (with multiple television sets on at any one time, and his father reading in the middle of it all) may also have installed in him an intimacy with

---

17   'The National Center for Research in Television: Research. Training', Radical Software 2.3 (1973): 47. The text is presented as the collective effort of the center's staff: Paul Kaufman, Brice Howard, Marvin Duckler, Don Hallock, Willard Rosenquist, William Roarty, Stephen Beck (artist in residence at the time), Warner Jepson, Rick Davis, Ann Turner, and Mimi Scott.
18   Ibid., 49. In this context, it is interesting to note the degree to which Stephen Beck associated inner-machinic space in the purely technical sense with 'inner' or nonrepresentational creative processes in humans. Beck emphasizes precisely these points, aiming to reverse the ordinary televisual representation of the 'outer' world. Stephen Beck, The Sounds and Colors of Inner Life: Proposal for a Videographic Composition, typescript, Stephen Beck folder, Archives of Steina and Woody Vasulka, undated, http://www.vasulka.org/archive/Artists1/Beck,Stephen/SoundsColors.pdf.
19   All works by Keith Sonnier discussed in this text can be viewed at https://www.keithsonnier.net/media.html

media technologies and their multiple modes of existence.[20] As in Paik's *Video Commune*, electronic temporalities seem to host a spectral, evanescent avatar of the studio workspace — a portent of new modes of collaboration in networked media reality. The virtual versions of the painterly studio that reside at the heart of many of his works are activated through references to precisely the type of heroic, outsize, processes-oriented painting that caught the public imagination and made the artist's studio into a media topos. But things have changed. If the 1960s documentaries treat the artist's studios as sites of memory in Pierre Nora's sense of the term, monuments to institutions and traditions about to disappear, the new kind of memory associated with the video studio is no longer fixated in a 'site' at all.[21]

Two works in particular — *Sonnier's TV In, TV Out* (1972) and *Color Wipe* (1973) — serve to establish this particular type of workplace. Both present technical processes as the 'content' of the works and show them to be open-ended and experimental, rather than simply automatic or preformatted. And both present these processes by highlighting a series of distinctly technological 'characters' or 'personae', who seem to occupy the visual field and the center of attention. The humans ostensibly in control of the machineries now emerge as accessories; only visible in glimpses, they mainly exist as voices negotiating the various technical possibilities or commands with which they are confronted. And both works serve up a curiously contradictory presentation of the concept of the studio. On the one hand, the studio is only mediated in terms of its progressive production of electronic effects, as they play out on the surface of the monitor image. But, on the other hand, it is also a three-dimensional electronic 'space', and in this space the most typical affordances of video cameo as quasi-painterly or quasi-sculptural objects in performance. Since these two aspects of the studio are constantly superimposed or intertwined, there is a visual as well as rhetorical blurring of the distinction between equipment 'insides' and studio 'outside', between electronic temporalities and studio workspaces.

The *raison d'être* of these works is to capture creative processes as they unfold and at the place of their unfolding — the elusive object of spectatorial desire in the series of documentary films discussed by Caroline Jones. After all, the effect of 'being inside image-making', suggested in Sonnier's videos, has some relation to watching the painterly gestures of Pollock filmed from beneath a glass pane and accepting the cinematographic illusion that nothing but thin air separates his work process and your field of vision. Both methods somehow promise intimate access to the mysterious body and mind of the artist. The big

---

20   From my interview with Keith Sonnier, New York, February 16, 2010.
21   Pierre Nora uses the concept of sites of memory (lieux de mémoire) to describe a vast range of memorializing sites that emerge in a modern society where collective memory is no longer integrated in the practices of daily life. See Pierre Nora, Les Lieux de mémoire', Realms of Memory: Rethinking the French Past, vol. 1–3, trans. Arthur Goldhammer, New York: Columbia University Press, 1996–1998. Bill Schwarz sees Nora's melancholic concept as a symptom of the burden placed on the concept of memory due to the failure of historians to engage with temporality itself. His perspective that strikes to the core of the problems emerges when video technology reframes the artistic site of production. Bill Schwarz, 'Memory, Temporality, Modernity: Les Lieux De Mémoire', in Susannah Radstone And Bill Schwarz (eds), Memory: Histories, Theories, Debates, New York: Fordham University Press, 2010, pp. 41-58.

difference between Sonnier's and Namuth/Falkenberg's approaches lies in the relation between media technology and 'creative space', as well as in the definition of creative agents and the work that they do.

TV In, TV Out was made with a video mixer that manipulated the feeds from two cameras: one focused on a live TV screen, the other on a studio space. The mixing of the two — exploiting the range of possible interactions between two image sources provided by the early video mixers — was captured live on color videotape. This was a relatively simple setup by broadcasting standards, but sophisticated and hard to access for most artists, let alone the general public. Like the artist's studio, it represented an exclusive realm of creation, and, just as in the artist's studio, creative action was presented as on-the-spot magic, taking place in real time, with no post-production or editing. Hence, the key players or creative personae in this process were the four major functions of the video mixer that go to work on the materials at hand: chroma/luma keys, wipes, superimposition, and colorization. Additional actors were artists Suzanne Harris, Tina Girouard, and Keith Sonnier, only one of whom ever appears on camera. Action opens with a glimpse of a live television screen, but quickly shifts to a DIY version of a TV studio situation. Standard broadcasting paraphernalia needed for chroma keying are presented, above all the blue wall surfaces that allow live video images to be keyed in behind newsreaders and weather presenters. (Bright blue is often chosen as a keying color, since it is unlikely to be found in human hair and skin.) In *TV In, TV Out*, the keying surfaces are just loose sheets of rather shiny blue paper, but they will still trigger a color code signal in the video mixer that allows feeds from a second camera source to invade the image stream from the first camera. Keying and superimposition processes start instantly, with Harris as the human element that falls in and out of the mix depending on how the blue paper sheets are placed. A shiny metal disc reflects parts of the blue color, producing additional keying effects as it is moved about. Further complexity is added once luma keying gets into action, allowing feeds from the second camera to appear wherever a certain luminance value appears—for instance in the darker shadows in Harris's wavy blond hair. [22]

Throughout this process, where feeds from several cameras intermingle in a vibrant, ephemeral collage, Harris appears as a true inhabitant of the electronic image. Neither hard working nor passive, she seems entirely at ease, a spontaneous participant in the creative

---

22   Keying refers to electronically cutting out portions of a picture and filling them in with another image. It is most typically used to add titles or another picture into the background of the existing image. Since video images do not usually contain very hard edges, the video that will be used as the 'hole cutter' goes through a processor that compares its luminance level at any particular moment with a reference voltage. If the luminance in the video signal is lower than the reference, the background picture remains on the switcher output. If the luminance in the video signal is greater than the reference, the second picture will cover the background picture. There are different types of keys: When the cutout portion of the base picture is filled with the signal that is doing the cutting, it is called an internal key or luminance key. When the cutout protion is filled by an external source, it is an external key, and when the hole is filled with an electronically generated color from the switcher, it is called a matte key. Chroma keying is a special effect that uses color for keying instead of luminance. A control on the switched selects which color will become transparent during the keying process and let the background video show through. Source: Dana Lee, 'Switching and Video Effects'; available at: http://www.danalee.ca/ttt/switching_and_video_effects.htm.

activity of the various mixer functions. In fact, she seems to identify with the electronic agencies to the extent of producing quasi-electronic versions of video mixer actions. From deep inside the electronic image-space she produces paper versions of the geometric wipe patterns that were among the most important affordances of the early video mixers: the hard-edged rectangles, cross shapes, diamond or circle forms that allowed various forms of transition or interaction between several live images on the same monitor. Her paper cutouts are used to isolate and frame image feeds, and in the densely layered electronic space it is often hard to tell the difference between these quasi-wipes and the real electronic wipes that are also put into action. Other quasi-electronic-mixer functions — such as manipulating a lit light bulb to simulate the effect of luminance control — appear with insisting regularity. In fact, Harris often functions as the mediator through which the studio space of artistic labor is gradually identified with electronic processes. Her studio has almost no three-dimensional articulation. We basically intuit its spatial existence through glimpses of shallow arrays of paper planes and her informal messing about with light bulbs and paper quasi-wipes, underscored by sudden bursts of flippant commentary. The famous tactility of artistic studio work is now associated with the tactile forces of electronic signal processing.

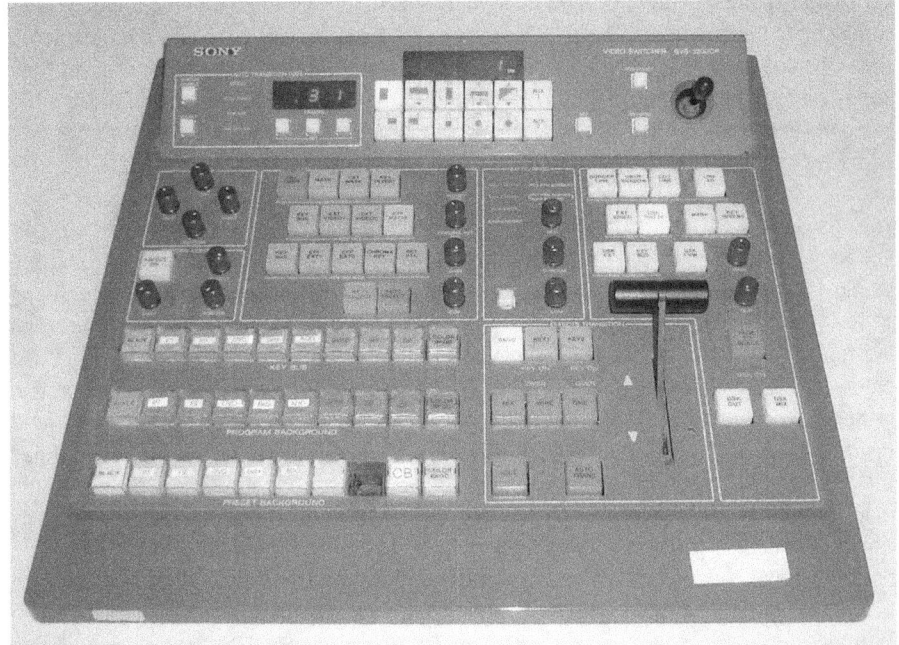

Fig. 1: Sony BVS-3200CP Vision Mixer. © Kastor2007. Courtesy of Georg Krakowski.

Color Wipe further blurs the distinction between the presentation of the studio as a space for image production and the suggestion that the studio itself might be an electronic time-image under production. And it does so by associating its working processes with a form of painting that itself made claims to infinite spatial extension—to the point of trying to erase the boundaries between image space and the real space in which paintings are both produced and viewed. In fact, the dynamic interaction of camera movements and wipe patterns in

Color Wipe constantly reference the large surfaces of Color Field painting, where the canvas is generally treated as an immense all-over field of vision without a central focus, and where the overlapping and interpenetrating color areas undo the spatial distinctions that create a sense of figure versus ground.

Yet, in this case, the painterly fields evoking the environmental 'spatiality' of Barnett Newman, Mark Rothko, and Elsworth Kelly *is* the studio space itself, or more precisely, a studio whose spatial extension is conflated with endless electronic processing. If Sonnier is generally mentioned as a member of the original Process art group in New York in the 1960s, *Color Wipe* seems to enact what critic Roberta Smith has described (in another context) as the missed encounter between Color Field painting and Process art, 'a twain that for the most part never met'.[23] The space of action is even shallower than in *TV In and TV Out*. Feeds from two cameras, interacting on the same screen thanks to rectangular wipes that move across the monitor horizontally and vertically, produce fields of brilliant color that are for the most part entirely flat, isomorphic with the monitor surface. And once again, electronic and nonelectronic affordances mime each other to the point of becoming indistinguishable. Rectangular electronic wipes constantly alternate with rectangular quasi-wipes: color surfaces pinned on the wall, strongly recalling Elsworth Kelly's multicolored rows of monochrome surfaces, are used as camera input for electronic wipes — but their shape and movement in the picture also tend to make them indistinguishable from the video mixer wipe patterns. Together, the interaction between electronic wipe patterns and quasi-wipes reproduce the painterly tension between color planes as an endless struggle between materials and forces.

For all this emphasis on painterly flatness, however, this is still very explicitly a real-time studio situation. Everything is framed by a sort of protracted operational dialogue, centering on the need to constantly react to the complex situations that arise as a video mixer handles live feeds from two cameras. The din of voices and electronic noise grounds the 'creative' or 'emergent' dimension of the images in a context that emphasizes labor and collaboration rather than visual product. And in brief glimpses, studio cameras also appear in the feed, inside a wipe, along with the faces of their operators, Girouard and Harris. Sometimes their heads are caught from the back, close up, as if further underscoring their immersion in electronic process space. They are not playing to the camera, are not available as theatrical material for 'input' feeds indicating some 'outside' reality. There is, in fact, no determinate outside to *Color Wipe*, no feeds from TV channels, nothing that is not already part of the electronic studio itself. Like the machinic components of Beck's cameraless video synthesizer, Girouard and Harris operate as if in full complicity with the auto-generative capacities of electronic components.

One could say, of course, that *Color Wipe*'s inwardness is essentially an electronic update on the self-referentiality of modern formalist painting. Emphasis on technical means and

---

23   Roberta Smith, 'A Color Field Painter from the 60's to Now', *New York Times*, August 2, 1991. Review of Dan Christensen's 'Paintings 1966–1991' at Salander-O'Reilly Galleries and 'Selected Paintings 1967–1991' at Douglas Drake Gallery.

processes, the inventive or 'thinking' moment of painting that Hubert Damisch wanted to bring out from under its dominating optical aspects, is here appropriated by video — to the point where a TV studio is, so to speak, conflated with painterly inventiveness.[24] But there is something else going on here as well, something that adds a different dimension to the painterly technicity underscored by Damisch. For the moment human actors appear as integral parts of technical processes — that is, as working components *among others*, rather than either explicit or implicit *initiators* of processes or *centers of action* — questions necessarily arise as to the identity of those 'other' working components and their mode of existence. The moment humans appear to operate at their level, these components also seem to acquire agency — that is, independent abilities to exercise force and to be the transducers of forces. They seem, in short, to have precisely that capacity for relationality that is the foundation for a pragmatic approach to the question of agency.[25] More than just technical elements, they now come across as characters, creative personae in their own right.

What emerges, then, is another image of the sociality of the modern artist's studio, clearly different from the urban/business atmosphere created by Warhol and Stella. While both studio models displace the figure of the unique artist-ego and the isolation of the place of creation, they do so on very different premises. In Warhol's and Stella's managerial paradigm, work is treated as a set of simple tasks, in the sense that they are performed according to quasi-industrial or 'mechanical' criteria that promotes a cynical view of the notion of inventive creation. Technology is mainly celebrated for its sublime capacity to make humans (like Warhol) shed their humanity and 'want' to be like machines. In Sonnier's video studio, in contrast, work does not result from some overarching managerial distribution of predefined tasks; it is a process of invention that springs out of from the complex interaction between a multitude of agents, human and electronic. But then again, the actual outcome of this creative locus is not presented as 'a work' or an industrial 'series' of works. What is brought forth is rather a new and provisional type of collective: the set of emergent relationships that *is* in fact studio work itself. The studio in *TV In and TV Out* and *Color Wipe* is less a preexisting *space* for (art) production than a real-time framework for inventing connections that are here presented as a form of collaborative process whose terms and conditions are as yet open, under negotiation. Its creative agents — human as well as nonhuman — are not defined by given roles, but constituted *as* agents through the specific relations they enter into at any moment.

The video studio of *TV In and TV Out* and *Color Wipe* is thus not just an emergent, still-controversial event — it also presents a premonition of a distinctly postindustrial

---

24 See Yve-Alain Bois and John Shepley, 'Painting as Model', *October* 37 (1986): 125–137.

25 This is a key aspect of the understanding of agency brought forth in Bruno Latour's thinking. Since the ontological basis of his concept of the social is the emergence of inventions (or new social links), agency does not denote the special capacities of beings that are already determined as 'social' (individuals, culture, society, structure, fields, and individuals). Focus is here on the *underdetermination* of action— its surprise dimensions— and agency is then also discovered in retrospect, along with the discovery of new associations and concomitant controversies about exactly who has been involved in their creation. Bruno Latour, *Reassembling the Social: An Introduction to Actor-Network-Theory*, Oxford: Oxford University Press, 2007, pp. 43–78.

understanding of labor. Work is not confined to a physical setting or predefined skills: the ubiquity of electronic networks means that value can be created from anyone's creative mental connection with almost anything else and that basic desire to connect, to 'be social', is now a key source of economic exploitation.[26] This form of labor depends on an informal, affect-based intimacy with dynamic machine features that seems a world apart from Warhol's and Stella's alienating assembly lines. Yet, as a mediation *of* the artist's studio and its changing modalities of labor, video's staging of machine/human collaboration also produce memories of industrial-era controversies regarding our relation to technological things. Its provisional working collective actually echoes Soviet constructivist ideas of technical things as 'comrades', operating in intimate solidarity with humans. According to Boris Arvatov, the main proponent of this perspective, true socialism, could not come into being unless one reconsidered the most influential Marxist theories of 'things', notably the theories of the commodity form and the commodity fetish. The commodity form, grounded in the concept of exchange value, isolates production from consumption and only promotes a perspective on the property relation to things. And the concept of the commodity fetish describes a world where passive humans are at the behest of products whose powers of dissimulation make them the real agents of social relations.

Against the dualist logic underpinning these descriptions — setting production against use, active agents against passive — Arvatov took an interest in the everyday interaction with ordinary objects and the productive dimension of this interaction.[27] As Christina Kiaer's research on Arvatov shows, his analysis was premised on a rather idiosyncratic view of the commodity fetish as a 'dead' or uncreative version of the object — to be contrasted with the type of high-tech objects in which functions and materials were no longer hidden by decoration or glossy surfaces but 'spoke for themselves'. For this reason he imagined the technical intelligentsia in the West — the engineering communities — to be structurally less affected by the commodity form and a dualistically riven social consciousness. Their relation to things had to do with function and activity, not with possession. Hence, their immersion in the world of technological functions or 'coworkers' might be a model for a new monist proletarian material culture, formed by the collectivizing forces at play in the realm of production.[28] The monism of things — the idea that humans and things co-constitute one another in one single realm of everyday activity, ignoring dualist distinctions between spirit and matter — should then serve as a guide to a dynamic creative socialist culture.

26   For a discussion of these topics, see for instance Tiziana Terranova, *Network Culture: Politics for the Information Age*, London: Pluto Press, 2004. See also Lane Relyea's discussion of the relation of network culture, labor, and contemporary art in *Your Everyday Art World*, Cambridge, MA: MIT Press, 2013.

27   Kiaer, 'Boris Arvatov's Socialist Objects', *October* 81 (1997): 105–118. Arvatov's criticizes the fact that Marx only understood self-realization through the technical things that existed in the realm of production, ignoring the way in which the context of everyday use (or consumption) might be a site for the realization of human consciousness through the object. Yet it was mainly when everyday things would become 'functional' and flexible—i.e., approach the technical things in the realm of production— that they would be better qualified as active agents of socialist culture (109–10).

28   Ibid., 113.

One of the most notable aspects of this theory was the idea that the concept of the socialist object-comrade would become more self-evident once one recognized the proximity between technical objects and natural forces. Electricity, a force of nature that penetrates technology and generates new networks of connectivity between spirit and matter, humans and things, was the obvious example.[29] Electricity made matter come across as active and inventive, transformative and 'spiritual'—a 'social' actor rather than a simple 'resource'. The advent of electronic technologies, typically used for representing and manipulating information rather than simply working with electrodynamic properties like voltage and current, only reinforced this perspective. This is perhaps why video brings to life a mode of techno-social reflection that was lost in Stalinist socialism, late capitalist commodity spectacle, and a sociology increasingly preoccupied with serving the administrative needs of the modern state (and its need for predictive models of the social).[30] Using the time-honored concepts and problems of artistic creation as a discursive framework, video seemed to rehabilitate Avratov's association between natural forces, technological modes of existence, and social ontology. The video studio, the new locus of creative labor, was the realm in which this association would become explicit, accessible, and self-evident. Technical things and humans would act as comrades in an emergent social order. In this emergent order, electronic and human forms of tactility and handiwork imitate each other; electronic wipes and quasi-wipes made out of paper operate as if indistinguishable, enacting always provisional acts of framing, isolating, combining, and overlapping.

The production of the video studio in Sonnier's work is then probably one of the moments when the autobiography of video seems closest to the dynamic described in Simondon's theory of individuation, which was based on Simondon's detailed knowledge of how technologies become increasingly concrete and specific in their interaction with a realm of use. This approach to the question of individuation is notably different from Jones's descriptions of how the modern artist's studio individuates, i.e. how it produces the figure of the isolated artistic individual. In fact, the very *problem* of approaching individuation, a key moment in Simondon's thought, seems to resonate in *TV In and TV Out*'s and *Color Wipe*'s displacement of the studio as a boxlike stage for the fully formed artist-identity. Simondon's central point is that individuation cannot be approached in terms of the finished individual, or the conditions prior to its coming into being. Individuation is ontogenesis: neither active, nor passive, it is an ongoing metastable process that can only be known through the principle of individuation itself. And this principle is mediation, the *acts* of mediation (or transformative events of interaction) between different systems.[31]

---

29   Ibid., 116.
30   In the *Radical Software* article 'Frequency and Form', Vic Gioscia criticized what he called 'the sociology of expectation or prediction', referring to an electronically informed process ontology in order to call for different approaches to questions pertaining to 'the social', Gioscia, 'Frequency and Form', *Radical Software* 1.2 (1970): 7. This perspective resonates with Bruno Latour's much later criticism of a modern sociology's close association with a political project aimed at social engineering. Latour, *Reassembling the Social*, 13.
31   Simondon, 'Genesis of the Individual', 305.

Here Simondon introduces a distinction between physical individuation and the individuation of living systems that has some bearing on the distinct 'interiority' of the video studio in Sonnier's work. Physical individuation typically takes place at the boundary between a technical system and its environment: machines do modify their relations to a milieu. In contrast, the individuation of living systems (their exchange with an environment) is characterized by an interiorizing movement or a process of self-relation that can also be called memory. This process brings forth the full scale of the epistemological problems inherent in approaching individuation, since the living individual is all at once 'a system of individuation, an individuating system and a system that individuates itself'.[32] Hence, there is no real outside to such individuation, no stable position from which it can simply be known—just as viewers of *TV in and TV Out* and *Color Wipe* do not look 'into' a studio space in which they may single out relatively stable artistic identities. Nor is there a clear sense of time. There is no distinct beginning and end, only a constant in medias res of production. At the level of certain technical components, the knobs and switches of the more basic mixer functions, these studio situations do of course involve physical individuation processes. But so many of the operations concern mediation between various information, or memory-driven systems (humans among them), that the studio situations are probably better understood as individuating life systems. This may in fact be why Sonnier's emergent studios are so emphatically presented as interiorizing operations, on par with the discourse of traveling into the new intra-machinic dimensions of the cameraless video synthesizer. Too much is going on inside; you are constantly faced with renegotiations as to the proper action, place, and meaning of wipe effects, luminance settings, keying functions, color codes, hands, faces, and voices constantly confronting new (and complex) technical modes of life or becoming. The informal flow of soundtrack commentary on what and how to do underscores the reality of a studio that seems to be in permanent operational dialogue with itself. This also effectively stops you from seeing the flow of video imagery as mere eyewash, empty visual effects. This imagery *is* the working collective of the studio itself.

His Studio/Her Video?

Numerous remarks could be made regarding the forms of artistic subjectivity that might be produced from these redefined notions of labor, studio technique, and artistic work. Numerous critics have noted the generalization of creativity that emerges in step with the technical developments that facilitate capitalization on all forms of creative connectivity. The Beuysian notion that 'everyone is an artist' is hardly utopian any longer, and maybe never was—and the same thing goes for the celebration of 'process' over 'object'. Yet, as video presents itself as a transformed artist's studio, one phenomenon in particular is worth a comment: the presence of women. This is no small matter, because the modern artist's studio was a quintessentially male domain, and remained so to a large extent in the early 1970s when *TV In and TV Out* and *Color Wipe* were made. Caroline Jones devotes a significant amount of attention to the host of (erotic) photographic signifiers and media comments that demarcates the studio as a sphere of lonely, angst-ridden,

32   Ibid., 305–310.

masculine pursuits. Stella's and Warhol's more social workplaces transform but do not challenge the masculine inflection of the artist's studio, presenting a mirror image of a both homosocial and homophobic world of postwar business and management, where women were either absent or in the type of subservient positions that Warhol reserved for his female superstars. The repression of the other (women, homosexuality) in Warhol's industrial aesthetic was first brought to light through Valerie Solanas's violent attack on him, over the issue of labor conditions.[33]

Yet, Jones notes the contrast in visual rhetoric that emerges once prominent female Abstract Expressionists like Lee Krasner and Helen Frankenthaler were portrayed in *their* studios. Eroticized angst is supplanted by a more content type of existence: triumphant confidence in the case of Krasner; peaceful immersion in the work process, aided by a male assistant, in the case of Frankenthaler.[34] She also notes that these depictions of female studio mastery might represent precisely the type of tacit, even ingratiating, acceptance of the oppressive terms of male society that was a prerequisite for women artists to have a career at all. The entire question opens onto a minefield of conflicting interpretations that is worth keeping in mind when approaching the presence of contented female collaborators in the emergent video studio collectives, immersed in work, engaged in constant technocentric dialogue. The *terms* of their apparently happy participation in this work situation is obviously entirely different. For one thing, they have not *entered* or *taken over* a predominantly male space, since the studio is here hardly articulated in terms of space at all. They are, in contrast, contributing to a shift in the studio as a discursive locus (i.e., a shift in larger *dispositifs* of creative agency). Secondly, they do not appear as *the* newly integrated others in a formerly homogeneous environment, with all the problems of identification this entails. If anything, they function in the midst of numerous 'minor' others; that is, the unknown forms of electronic being that arise in this context of technological experiment and connectivity. Thirdly, if *TV In and TV Out* and *Color Wipe* are at once actual studio work situations and reflexive mediations of collaboration as an event-oriented mode of association, the question of artistic power and agency plays out on two levels that cannot be neatly separated but articulate the ambiguities of this new conception of labor. The finished videotape that is the officially registered 'result' of the studio situation is notably signed Keith Sonnier, who invited artists Harris and Girouard to act as performers in his production. At this pragmatic level, a trace of the managerial model still remains. However, as particular individuations *of* the new electronic studio, the power relations in these works have a different inflection. Sonnier, Harris, and Girouard are equally embedded in the mix, equally dependent on each other and all other operative elements. None of them play the artist figure; they are all disassembled, partial, appearing only in bits and pieces of sound and image. Sonnier, hidden in the mixer room, is voice only, yet this is not the voice of control and command but of probing and negotiation. The voice of Harris actually has more presence, as a particularly affective response to the various situations that arise. If it sometimes appears to be talking to itself, it is exactly the kind of involved dialogue anyone might have with

---

33   Jones, Machine in the Studio, 233–67.
34   Ibid., 35–41.

materials and processes in a creative situation where you are completely immersed in what you are doing. The range of emotions it expresses — pleasure, impatience, humor, confusion, confidence — underscore a leisure-like working situation based on interacting affinities rather than efficient, goal-driven 'production'.

Here, the video studio might perhaps be seen to prehend certain features of Donna Haraway's controversial 1985 'Cyborg Manifesto', which combined a searing critique of feminized labor in the new consciousness industries with visions of a post-gender socialism in which the essentialist logic underpinning Marxist-feminist concepts, like 'false consciousness', would be supplanted by insights into the provisional, composite, and non-originary status of any gendered constellation. The emergent human/machine composites of the electronic realm functioned as the model for a critique of unitary conceptions of being, and its consequences for the political constructions of race and gender. Yet there was no idealization of technology in this strongly revisionist account of social relations: the 'cyborg being' was not simply an easy feminist escape plan. On the one hand, Haraway argued against a Marxist ontology in which labor is the privileged source of knowledge of the subject and his or her subjugation, so that the multiplicity of things that might be 'women's activity' must be subsumed under the category of labor in order to count, politically. Yet if the masculine concept of labor was already losing its traditional contours in the new 24/7 network culture of productive leisure and 'work at home', the new forms of precariousness produced by the integration of factory, home, and market and the demands for endless adaptability, might still be understood in terms of the uncertain status of women within the world of labor.[35]

This duplicity informs *TV In, TV Out* and *Color Wipe* as well: as hired technical hands, Girouard and Harris might prehend the influx of female workers in Silicon Valley and other electronics industries around the world—at the same time as their machine collaboration opens onto a new and decentralized model of creative agency. Yet, however we interpret the activity of women in the intra-machinic video studio, they reflect one important fact, reported in much literature on early video.[36] Just as the electronics industries seemed to prefer female workers, the technical framework of video production did attract numerous female artists. A great number of women were quick to identify video as a viable alternative in a politically complicated situation. It was a dispositif that did at least *seem* to cut through the double-bind logic of either adapting to the masculinist standards of modern studio practice at the expense of supporting a system of domination, or avoiding it at the

---

35 Haraway, Donna. 'A Cyborg Manifesto: Science, Technology, and Socialist-Feminism in the Late Twentieth Century', in *Simians, Cyborgs and Women: The Reinvention of Nature*, New York: Routledge, 1991, pp. 149–181. Haraway has been roundly criticized (by Suhail Malik, among others) for a well-meaning but vague techno-optimism, where construction, boundary-transgression, and contestation is associated with creativity rather than with war and destruction. Yet the criticism seems to neglect the 'Cyborg Manifesto''s descriptions of the new forms of subjugation emerging with an increasingly information-based world. See Malik, 'Cyborg Fifteen Years On'.

36 See for instance Vanalyne Green, 'Vertical Hold: A History of Women's Video Art', in Kate Horsfield and Lucas Hilderbrand (eds.) *Feedback: The Video Data Bank Catalog of Video Art and Artist Interviews*, Philadelphia: Temple University Press, 2006, pp. 22–30.

expense of marginalization (i.e., channeling your creativity into traditionally female 'home activities' like weaving, or pottery). In fact, if the emergent network economy feminized labor, video provided a technical context in which a female-gendered aesthetic practice, like weaving, was revalued. This was most forcefully articulated in the work of Beryl Korot, the editor of *Radical Software* who explicitly associated her own early video work with weaving. On the one hand, she was interested in the historical connection between weaving and electronics: the handloom could notably be seen as an early programming tool or computer since it programs patterns according to a numerical system. In her video productions, the deft use of multiple channels became analogous to multiple threads on a loom demanding a unity of purpose of the disparate elements to form a whole. [37] It is also worth noting that such weaving — process and product — takes place 'inside' electronic equipment, defined by machine affordances and materialities. The question of a 'room of one's own' — and who said there had to be a *room*? — might in other words be displaced through alliances with an increasingly powerful technosphere that seemed to privilege a new and lighthearted communism of speed and flight over the essentialist conundrum of gender identity/property/space. If the 1970s art market for the most part put paid to the ardent hopes for rapid gender revolution in art, the video studio at least contributed to a certain destabilization of the most staid concepts of artistic labor and laborers.

Given these duplicities, the question would then be: What would a production of the early '70s video studio look like if its signature author or legal 'owner' were also a woman? A woman who, when appearing *in* the studio production, would not be a hired hand or temporary collaborator, but in her own sphere of action, in both the electronic and managerial sense of the term. There are obviously no simple answers to this question, but one prominent example is worth considering: Steina Vasulka's *Switch! Monitor! Drift!* (1976), and the related work *Orbital Obsessions* (1977), which contains elements of *Switch! Monitor! Drift!* as well as other early '70s studio-related works like *Signifying Nothing, Sound and Fury*, and *Snow Tapes*.[38] Looking at the various versions of these works, the question that presents itself is whether female legal ownership and managerial control actually made a difference in the production of the emergent electronic studio. It would almost seem as if the forces or affordances of video imposed their particular version of social reality no matter what—to the point that this reality had also seems to have become consistent with the creative desires of Steina herself. As she put it, 'We were absolutely in love with what we call the signal, which is the voltage and frequency part of video. It could be translated from one property into another [...] what I really was interested in was this self-observing system in which whatever was observing was also affecting the image'.[39]

---

37   See Julia Wolfe's interview with Steve Reich and Beryl Korot for *Bomb Magazine* 81 (2002). Korot's concept of video weaving would result in highly complex installations that pushed against the borders of what video technology could do at the time, such as the five-channel work *Text and Commentary* (1977). Weaving was also the focus of the 2010 retrospective 'Beryl Korot: Text/Weave/Line—Video 1977–2010' at the Aldrich Contemporary Art Museum, Connecticut, June 27, 2010–January 2, 2011.
38   *Orbital Obsessions* is the only of these works made publicly available today.
39   Steina Vasulka, phone interview, June 6, 1993, quoted in JoAnn Hanley and Ann-Sargent Wooster, *The First Generation: Women and Video 1970-75*, New York: Independent Curators Incorporated, 1993.

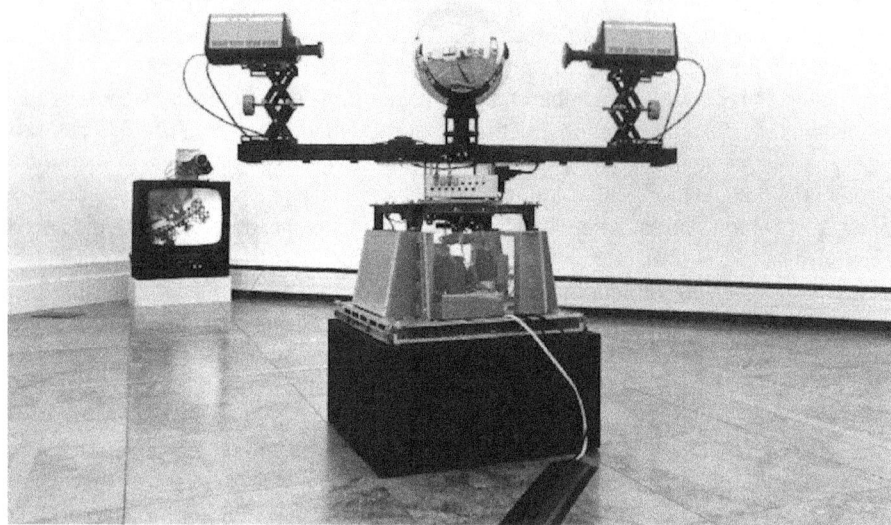

Fig. 2: Steina and Woody Vasulka, Allvision II, 1978. Device built by Steina and Woody Vasulka. Installation view. "The Vasulkas—Steina: Machine Vision / Woody: Descriptions," Albright Knox Art Gallery, Buffalo, New York, 1978. Photo: Kevin Noble. Steina and Woody Vasulka fonds. The Daniel Langlois Foundation for Art, Science, and Technology. Courtesy of Steina and Woody Vasulka. © The Vasulkas Inc.

She was, in other words, looking for a technical collaborator, somebody whose independent ability to 'see' would also translate into equally independent action in an emergent visual field now defined as the studio. Video had apparently convinced her that it could be such a collaborator. What can be observed in these works is then yet another example of a happy (wo)man/machine exchange in a work environment that is no longer a 'space', but a series of transitory states whose qualitative articulation is distributed among multiple agents. In short, the woman in charge seems to explicitly refuse to be identified in terms of spatial occupancy and autocratic centrality. While humans operated the big broadcasting cameras in Sonnier's studios, Steina's cameras have a completely different degree of machinic autonomy. In 1975, Steina (in collaboration with her husband Woody Vasulka) had started experimenting with rotating camera mechanisms, designed to undermine the rectangular image of the TV screen. The quest grew out of their initial research into a phenomenon they called 'horizontal drift'. The idea was that the video signal is not bound to the frame of a representational image-screen, but can be distributed freely in space so as to create a multidirectional environment in which the image may (for instance) drift from screen to screen.[40] Soon, the concept of the 'liberated' signal led to fantasies about new types of machine vision. The most sophisticated of these machines — normally presented as sculptural-technical 'embodiments' in museum and gallery spaces — has two cameras mounted on a crossbar and facing a central mirrored sphere, all placed atop a turntable base rotating parallel to the floor. Live camera feeds of the rotating curved-mirror images produce complex spatial disorientation, or encounters with nonhuman ways of seeing. Yet the simpler versions used in the production of *Switch! Monitor! Drift!* were more specifically invested in the articulation of a new electronic production space. Here, a first camera was focused on a second camera mounted on a turntable; the signals from the two cameras were then processed, live, through the same type of luminance-keying devices used in Sonnier's studio. As importantly, however, the image from the stationary camera had been time-base adjusted so as to appear to drift horizontally across the monitor, exposing the (normally invisible) low-voltage area of the horizontal framing interval, which separates each video frame from the next. With the signal from the revolving camera keyed into this area, a confusingly multiplied space appeared, defined by combinations of sideways sliding and rotation — i.e., alien to all spatial coordinates associated with a human-type camera eye.

Even so, from these mobile, transitory fragments one could still piece together impressions of the messy, equipment-filled Buffalo studio of Steina and Woody Vasulka. Everything caught by the machine's vision pertained to its own immediate production context: miles of cables, editing consoles, monitor stacks, coffee machines, shelving systems, tripods, and — in the middle of it all, floating by, often multiplied as well, watching and being watched — Steina. In fact, her presence is marked by the same combination of passivity and activity that characterized Harris and Girouard in Sonnier's studio works. She is neither the center of action nor subjugated by alienating automatisms over which she has no influence. This is neither the spontaneous ex nihilo creation of Pollock nor the self-consciously mechanical grind of Stella. Most of the time she simply signals attentiveness. She observes the multiple ways in which she is being observed, so as to respond in her own way and have a say in the process. Over and over again, the machines observe her hand, floating by, multiplied, working the video switcher, persuading the video itself to shift perspectives. Both video and Steina seem to follow the results of their interaction with tense alertness, as if each is considering the next move.

The intensity and intimacy of this process of mutual observation is underscored when a camera suddenly catches Woody Vasulka eating in the kitchen corner of the studio: he looks back, passively, the way a random person on the street might watch a passing bus full of staring tourists. He's not involved, not a participant. Steina is, and her continuous, attentiveness in the presence of (machinic) others becomes a defining feature of the

---

40   Steina and Woody Vasulka made a number of works based on this principle, for instance *Matrix* (1970–
      72). See Marita Sturken and Robert R. Riley (eds), *Steina and Woody Vasulka: Machine Media*, San
      Francisco: San Francisco Museum of Modern Art, 1996. See also 'A Matrix of Horizontal Movement', a
      handwritten note related to this work and made available on
      http://www.vasulka.org/archive/sitemap.html.

electronic studio. In classic film language, a dialogical situation may be represented through a shot/reverse shot montage that establishes the differing points of view of protagonists *in terms of* a given, stable space. An architectural logic — the distribution of light and shadow, for instance — establishes their respective roles. But the dialogical situation in *Switch! Monitor! Drift!* is based on very different principles. Each moment of tense attention, each reaction changes the temporal and spatial qualities of the electronic studio, the very sense of what the studio might be. Ultimately the studio is nothing but the ongoing modification of the relations between three cognizing beings and their various technical accessories: Steina and the two video cameras.

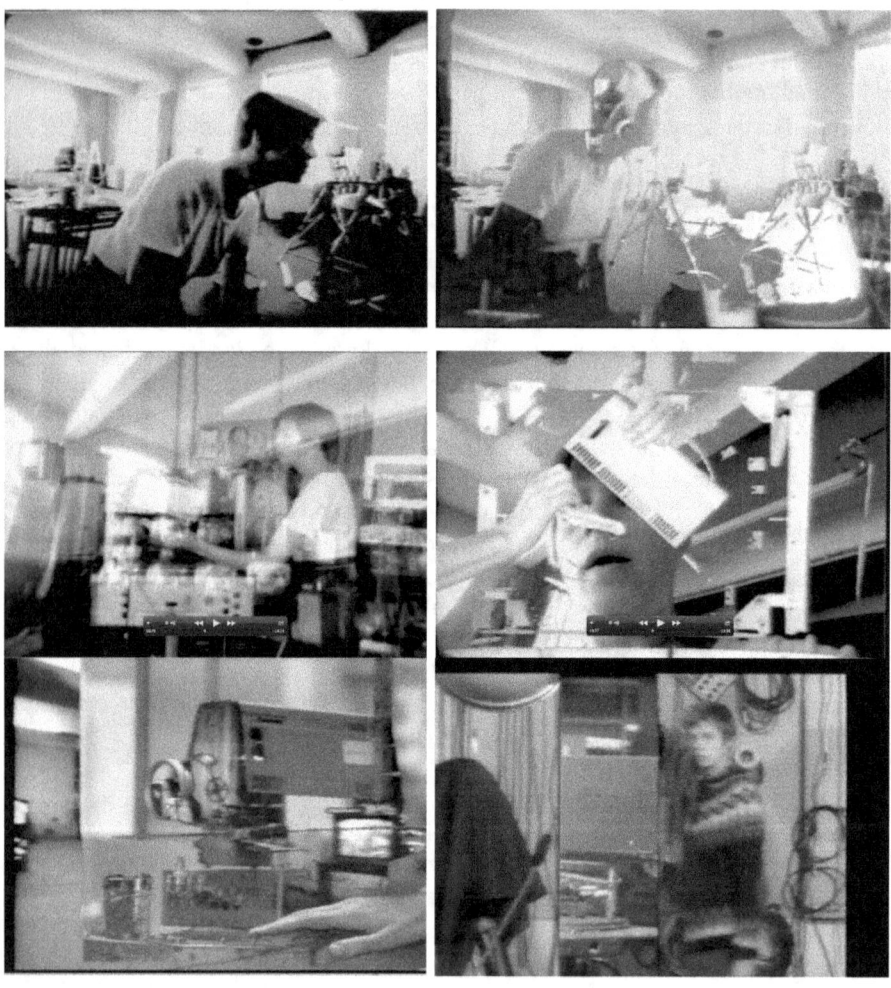

Fig. 3: Steina Vasulka, Orbital Obsessions, 1975–77, revised 1988. Video, black-and-white, sound, 24 min. 25 sec. Courtesy of Steina and Woody Vasulka. © The Vasulkas Inc

Orbital Obsessions, a fifteen-minute digest of such studio works, seems to have been put together to emphasize the variable qualities and intensities of studio relations. There is a relatively peaceful beginning where Steina, carrying a monitor, follows the movement of the rotating camera so that it is always facing the monitor screen, producing feedback on the go, while the steady camera zooms in and out on the scene. Wipe patterns soon intervene to create a confusing doubling of zooms and rotation, with Steina increasingly caught in between the various layers of electronic operation. The arrival of another technical protagonist — the video sequencer that George Brown created for the Vasulkas in 1972 — radically changes the situation. Its key affordance is to allow rapid switching between two or more image sources without interference (the secret to the process is that switching is taking place in the vertical blanking interval).[41] In fact, such clean switching can be sped up to the extent of creating full-on flickering. This is what happens now: The various studio machines that collaborate in producing flickering observe themselves *as* flickering hallucinatory disturbances. And as flickering doubles up with 360-degree camera rotation and positive/negative image reversals, the atmosphere of attentive inter-machinic dialogue is replaced by a new (and monstrous) fusion. Steina appears at the center of the screen, her body bent in concentrated action, working equipment and watching effects in dance-like movements reminiscent of Pollock's famous 'dancing' over the canvas. Yet, in this capacity she is above all an effect of flickering: she is the ghostly, frozen, repeating strobe-like motion of an electronic body that is never simply there, never simply in action. One moment she goes off to respond to a telephone call, a forceful index of real-time presence in actual space, and the next she is all optical illusion or neuronal play, an item of projective memory.

The sequencer was in fact invented for exactly such spatial duplicity. The Vasulkas had hoped that its clean-switch function would help them explore stereoscopic vision in video (a form of binocular rivalry also known as the Pulfrich effect). Ultimately this might result in moving 3-D images, a properly virtual videospace.[42] They never got quite that far. Yet Steina's use of a stationary camera to shoot rotating objects (the rotating second camera as well as the rotating room video feed it generated) recalls one of the procedures through which Pulfrich effects are typically produced. If standard 3-D effects ultimately elude her,

---

41   Vasulka, 'George Brown Video Sequencer', in Eigenwelt der Apparatenwelt, Linz: Ars Electronica, 1992, 130–31. While the sequencer was created for clean and rapid switching between image sources, the multikeyer was constructed in order to go beyond the two-level input that was the limit for video in the early 1970s. It is a hybrid luminance keyer (at once analog and digital) that is designed to program and display in real time the keying sequence of multiple video sources in one image plane. Source: http://www.fondation-langlois.org/html/e/page.php?NumPage=455.

42   The Pullrich effect is a psychophysical phenomenon in which the lateral motion of an object in the field of vision is perceived as having a depth component due to a relative difference in signal timings between the two eyes. The minimal temporal delay between two image sources provided by the George Brown Multikeyer seemed to suggest that similar effects might be obtained. The Vasulkas' quest for binocular vision in video was developed as part of their dialogue with the artist Alphons Schilling. See for instance Ken Ross, 'Excerpts from a Conversation with Alphons Schilling' (1977) and Schilling, 'Electronic Spaces' (1973). On January 4, 1972, Woody Vasulka and Schilling collaborated on the stereo slide show 3-D Binocular Vision / '14 Street-Out'—one among several collaborations between the two artists.

the spatial complexity and 'deep' layering resulting from the live interaction of multiple autonomous seeing machines is equally suggestive; a valid compensation. Like the WGBH TV studio that seemed to reside inside Paik's video synthesizer scan modulations in *Video Commune*, Steina's actual studio is transformed into a virtual space and defined in terms of always partial, multiple, and distributed forms of being and seeing.

If this studio is a key instance of women's 'invasion' of the video studio — or video's association with artists whose relation to studio space was historically troubled — it fully exemplifies videos undoing of the boxlike studio space of the modern male artist, along with its specific forms of artistic subjectivity. And its undoing is underscored by the use of sound—the sound that is not just recorded as a separate audio signal but that is also a potential modality of the video signal as such. Sonnier's studios still had diegetic sound: the real-time audio recording was, so to speak, the last remaining trace of an actual studio space in which work on machines is done, and where spatial properties, like background and foreground, near and far, still mattered. In Steina's studio, however, the familiar hum of a machine-filled workspace tends to get lost along with the loss of familiar spatial coordinates. With every modulation of the video signal, every turn of a switch, sonic space is transformed into changing intensities of electronic noise. The re-gendered video studio may have explored the properties of virtual space, but in sharp contrast to today's computer games and other real-life simulations, representation of already-known space was avoided. Instead, artistic work was associated with video's propensity for temporalization and event production, privileging emergent forms of collaboration that cannot be prescribed or modeled in representational-spatial terms.

For all these apparent strategies of escape, the constant visibility of Steina's body and the constant 'circulation' of images of her actual studio still, however, account for something. Video was not a post-studio practice in the technical-practical sense of the term: the economic and practical question of studio access was all-important in an era of big, expensive machinery. And despite its deep association with escape, flows, and relays, it could not foreground a wholly non-localizable form of artistic subjectivity. The ambivalent relation to the location of art production that haunted women artists wary of simply adapting to a repressive masculinist studio norm was, in other words, not simply resolved with recourse to signaletic escape. As Rosi Braidotti has argued, the concept of such 'nomadic' forms of existence may be too easy, too undifferentiated. While it may save you from being positioned as the undervalued other of the (masculine) same, idealizing indeterminate becoming risks overruling the fact that gender differences and gender identities still *matter* politically, due to historical asymmetries that cannot simply be overlooked.[43] To leave the place of battle, to desire non-locality and nonidentity, may also be to opt for further marginalization. In the context of Steina's studio, Braidotti's concept of the 'virtual feminine' may therefore be illuminating, since it indicates the need to think historically embodied and embedded constructions of the feminine within the framework of a nomadic philosophy. One can therefore imagine a feminist politics

---

43   Rosi Braidotti, 'Becoming Woman: Or Sexual Difference Revisited'. Theory Culture & Society 20. 3 (2003): 43–64.

of location in which embodiment is thought in conjunction with movement, grounding in relation to nomadic shifts, and belonging in terms of the paradox of multiple and shifting locations.[44] This seems to be a rather accurate description of the many spatializing paradoxes of Steina's studio. Defined in and through its video productions, this studio presents an artistic subjectivity that is all at once localized in terms of a new technical realm in which she is clearly 'at home', *and* delocalized as a mobile part of the ever new and fleeting technical configurations that simply attest to the normal working modus of this studio.

Reframing the Electronic Studio

The complexities of space and location that marked the becoming of the video studio, were, however, soon displaced by a new and distinct place of labor: the interface. As multiple theorists have noted, the interface is the most characteristic workspace in a media age where work and leisure converge in screen-based activities, separated only by the fact that some applications are primarily associated with duty and others with play.[45] To early cybernetics, the interface was where 'flesh met metal',[46] a meeting that (as Lev Manovich has pointed out) takes place within the frame of a picture window.[47] This picture window is not only key to the computer interface as a technical/cultural form but also what connects it with pictorial traditions that extend from cinema back to Renaissance painting. Once the video studio approached the condition of the interface, the quest for stabilization could be noted. The interactivity of human and nonhuman agencies was contained within the interface screen, their collaboration increasingly defined as processes taking place within a picture window. Contra video's radical temporalization of artistic studio space and its typical media representations, the interface is notable for the way in which it seems to spatialize time itself, reducing all to operations within a rectangular space-frame.[48] And even more significant is the way in which it divides up space itself into two major locations: on-screen and offscreen. Nothing could be further from the free spatiotemporal drift of the Vasulka's video signal and all that was mobilized in such drift. With the video studio reconfigured as interface, drift was reined in, driven back to the pictorial frame it had tried to escape. And by the same token the implicit 'animism' of video's uncontrollable electronic affordances was increasingly conflated with purely pictorial animation.

Sonnier's last studio works *Animation I* and *Animation II* (1973–74) attest to this shift. While *TV In and TV Out* and *Color Wipe* were premised on access to a professional broadcasting studio and sophisticated real-time editing equipment, the two later works result from the increasingly close interplay between the development of video and computer technologies in the early 1970s. And all of a sudden, the image screen — that

44   Ibid., 55.
45   See, for instance, Lev Manovich, Language of New Media, Cambridge, MA: MIT Press, 2001, 65;
       Alexander Galloway, 'Unworkable Interface', *New Literary History* 39.4 (2008): 934.
46   Galloway, 'Unworkable Interface', 936.
47   Manovich, *Language of New Media,* 63.
48   Ibid., 62.

displaced, rifted or rejected object of process-oriented art — resurfaced with a wholly new authority. In 1969 a Sonnier work tellingly entitled *Dis-Play* demarcated video's undoing of the self-sufficiency of the pictorial surface. A big scrim, carried around by performers and shifted this way and that, functioned less as central support of pictorial action than as a technical object among others. In a performance space defined by flickering light, kinescope projections and mirror effects, it worked above all as a shutter controlling the various passages of light, its own light-catching capacities rendered ambivalent through constant positive/negative reversals of the video feed. In general, the various painterly efforts to make image surfaces processual had been limited by the fact that the relation to process remained indexical, bound to present action as already past. Having Pollock paint on glass for the camera ('in' the viewer's eyes, so to speak) was clearly a compensatory measure. In contrast, the computer made the image screen a true locus of work-in-action. From this point onward, emphasis was on emergent relational effects rather than on indexical traces. Hence, its rehabilitation *in* video a mere five years after the processual screen exercises of *Dis-Play*. The key player in *Animation I* was notably the Scanimate, an analog computer system whose great advantage over film and digital animation was that it could create animation in real time. The results were instantly visible on a high-resolution screen whose deflection signals had been passed through a special analog computer that allowed the operator to manipulate the image in a variety of ways. But since the Scanimate image was only monochrome, it was filmed by a video camera whose signal was fed to a colorizer — a process that also allowed you to continually add layers of graphics, resulting in very complex live effects. Thanks to Scanimate, the open-ended work activities of Sonnier's real-time video studio were transposed to the flat space of a screen. Yet *Animation II* — made with a CAESAR electronic animation system that combined digital and analog computers with television technology — implied a further flattening of the studio workspace. The system was based on the concept of mapping surfaces, and responds to the fact that video technology may also be interpreted as surface mapping: the surface of the target on the camera image tube is precisely mapped onto the surface of the cathode-ray tube in the receiver as long as no disturbances or synching problems occur. In CAESAR, however, unity of mapping is not the aim. The input image is mapped onto an output plane that may be divided into as many as eight horizontal bands, each of which can be precisely controlled according to twenty different parameters. The animation system was based on a division of the screen into the straight lines and rectangular shapes of much modernist art and design, promoting ideals of order and transparency that would be reintroduced with the Mac graphical-user interface of the early 1980s.[49] Complex figure animation might be created with this system, but Sonnier, for his part, seemed to fixate on the underlying modernist logic of organization. For what is animated or rendered processual in *Animation II* is nothing but the rectangles or squares of modernist painting, the signifiers of the modernist grid structure that ambivalently configures the image screen both as flat material support and illusionist picture window.[50]

49   See undated typescript explaining the CAESAR electronic animation system, with handwritten
      comments and illustrations, from the archives of Steina and Woody Vasulka,
      http://www.vasulka.org/archive/Artists2/Harrison,Lee/Caesar.pdf.
50   See Rosalind Krauss, 'Grids', October 9 (1979): 50–64.

In both works, the screen interface is ostensibly the place where studio collaboration takes place, where things enter into ever-new relations. Its centrality is further underscored by the way in which the work divides space into simple on-screen/offscreen distinctions, mainly through the use of sound.[51] Again, there is a marked contrast to the multilayered intertwining of human and technological agencies of the previous studio works, where all elements cooperated in the production of an emergent space whose dimensionality was more easily portrayed in temporal terms. On the interface-screen, the human collaborators are no longer seen: the only trace of their presence is their voices, which demarcate the interstices of a larger offscreen zone. In *Animation I*, diegetic sound — the din of the ongoing work processes — actually splits into on-screen and offscreen soundscapes. The on-screen sounds of TV channel feeds from the Watergate hearings clearly *belong* to the Watergate hearing images that appear within the frame, overlaid with animated production cue cards and transparent Kodalith images of various newspaper stories. And despite all this media layering, the sounds are clearly distinct from the offscreen sounds of humans discussing technical operations, making decisions, listening to the radio, the invisible stage of action that surrounds the screen itself. In *Animation II*, however, all sound is offscreen. The animation process unfolds accompanied by the offscreen voice of Keith Sonnier in dialogue with a male technician, and layered on top of this is another offscreen voice: the sound of a female technician reading out the various computer commands for each animation scene as it is enacted. With this neat spatial division between on-screen vision and offscreen sound, the *pictorial* quality of the interface imposes itself. The electronic workplace has become what video was not: an image.

Even so, this image-studio is fraught with the ambivalences of the modernist grid, which, in Rosalind Krauss's interpretation, is where the flat surfaces of abstract painting negotiate the memory of the realistic picture window.[52] Sonnier's animated geometrical figures may twist and turn, indicating the deep spaces of the picture windows that connect you with an elsewhere, yet the dominant modus of this interface is still radical flatness combined with explicit informatization. All through the work, the computer code is shown alongside the visual transformations it engenders, all aspects of the work processes lay bare as they take place. In this sense, the interface-studio counteracts the tendency to understand interfaces as doors or windows. As Alexander Galloway has pointed out, this perspective neglects to take into account the fact that the interface is also a medium that does not mediate, a set of operations that do not simply 'work', in the sense of providing seamless transport. In fact, video's interface-studio highlights numerous working relations internal to the interface itself, or what we may, with Galloway, call its intraface.[53] Once the intraface aspects of the interface become prominent, it tends to highlight the larger historical and material context of the interface's aesthetic forms; in Sonnier's case, the political form of the artistic labor encapsulated by the space of the

---

51 As Jacques Aumont has pointed out, 'the onscreen space is habitually perceived as existing within a more vast, scenographic space' (emphasis mine). While the screen is the visible part, one imagines a larger offscreen world around it. Aumont, quoted in Manovich, Language of New Media, 80.

52 Krauss, 'Grids'.

53 Galloway, 'Unworkable Interface', 943–47.

screen. Once the interface makes evident its internal struggles, it is no longer 'a fantasy landscape but a factory floor, an information-age sweatshop, custom tailored in every detail for cooperative ludic labor'.[54]

Paradoxically the work relations *in* and *of* the interface (its studio aspects) became particularly pronounced the moment video's interface actually enacted the classical picture-window dream of flight, escape, and connection to an elsewhere. This was the moment this interface — still essentially televisual, still primarily identified with artistic subjectivities, economies, and forms of labor — dreamed of satellite connectivity. In 1972 the Federal Communications Commission (FCC) approved the establishment of domestic satellite systems for television operators as well as telephone and telegraph companies; video, not unsurprisingly, wanted in on what the FCC, in a moment of poetic fervor, referred to as an 'open skies policy'.[55] Yet this quest for connectivity was made on behalf of the public in general and in the name of democratic control over means of communication, which also heralded new economic frameworks of media production and informational labor. As Andy Horowitz, a founding member of the Public Interest Satellite Association (PISA) pointed out, the huge economic gains related to satellite transmission created new feedback loops between corporate interests, military technology, and governmental desire for surveillance. Already in 1973, a number of new corporate alliances had emerged between agencies that controlled the technology used to manipulate the flow of information and those that manufactured the equipment required to operate that flow.[56] Increased surveillance — the dark corollary of the new freedoms of work in the information age — was a thriving business for all involved parties.

This was the political background against which the 1977 satellite video project *Send/Receive* was realized. Initiated by Sonnier and filmmaker/editor Liza Béar,[57] the idea was to establish a collaborative interface based on instantaneous contact. This was an explicit reversal of the broadcasting ideology expressed in the official slogan of RCA's satellite division (''Tis better to send than to receive') and its neutralization of the surveillance interest in 'reception' that also underpinned the satellite industry. Long negotiations resulted in an afternoon of access to the experimental CTS satellite owned jointly by NASA and the Canadian government, and a video link was set up between an outdoor

---

54	Ibid., 947.

55	Andy Horowitz, 'Domestic Communications Satellites', Radical Software 2.5 (1973): 36.

56	Horowitz was particularly enraged by the FCC's disregard of its public responsibility in relation to satellite technology, its lack of concern for the effect of its decision regarding the flow of information, and the way in which satellites might be used to erode essential public freedoms. Despite the fact that satellite technology had been developed with huge amounts of public money, the commission's plan 'initiated by the Nixon Administration in 1969 and subsequently the object vigorous White House lobbying [...] calls for almost no government regulation over satellite facilities that will be owned, operated and controlled by the nation's largest communications, aerospace and electronics firms: AT&T, GTE, RCA, Globcom, Comsat, Hughes Aircraft, Fairchild Industries, Western Union Telegraph, Western Union International and Western Tele-Communications'. In Horowitz's view, the FCC's decision represented 'perhaps the grandest betrayal of public interest in the history of American telecommunications'. Ibid., 36, 40.

57	Liza Béar was a cofounder of Avalanche magazine, together with Willoughby Sharp.

location in Manhattan and a studio in San Francisco, with groups of artists and musicians on each side ready to interact.[58] The screen was to become an interface in the most literal sense of the term, most demonstratively through real-time collaborative dance improvisations, both sides visible to all with use of split-screen devices. As Béar put it in a 1982 poem, 'The ego recedes before instant exposure / And instant response / Who can own an interaction?'[59] True collaboration was premised on interface efficiency. The picture window simply had to function, and seamlessly so.

Still, a remarkable feature of *Send/Receive* is the extent to which both its preparation and documentation are framed by the interface/intraface ambivalences that emerged when Sonnier's video studio was first conflated with the computer picture screen in *Animation II*. There is, in fact, a continuity between Sonnier's studio works and the two videotapes associated with *Send/Receive* (*Phase I* and *Phase II*) and it hinges on recirculating the modernist dialectics of transparency/materiality in the context of new media labor. Ostensibly, the preparatory *Send/Receive Phase I* is simply didactic, a montage of various types of information on satellite technology and politics, framed through a comparative perspective on the media landscapes of the 1930s and 1970s. More surprising, for a work underpinning video's dream of instantaneous intercontinental contact, is its dogged insistence on the flatness of the picture screen. No poetics of space travel, no metaphors of bridging the infinite disturb the equally 'flat' emphasis on the politics of contact. Visual flatness was produced by focusing the camera on three boards covered with satellite graphics and information: images of antennae, transmission charts, earth stations, and cutouts from communication journals. The camera roams these surfaces at very close range, panning over the rectangular pieces of paper in ways that recall the horizontal and vertical movement of rectangular electronic/painterly planes in *Color Wipe*. Once more, the flat interface presents itself as a workplace: Offscreen voices conveying technical/political information are layered with informal studio dialogue. Sheets of texts and images come and go. In addition, a character-generator produces a layer of text in live edit, constantly commenting on the other information we see and hear. This interface is less a seamless intermediary than a mediator, less a communication channel than a space where associations are laboriously negotiated.

The character-generator attests to this: it hesitates, deletes itself, correcting. It pauses, reflects, considers its actions. It does work — mental/technical work — but such work is neither easy nor automatic or invisible. It is marked by delays. It clearly both uses and produces time. With this in mind, it is of some significance that the character-generator at one point types out the word *slow scan*: the keyword for a mini movement that emerged in the wake of video's desire for instant interface connectivity. At the end of the 1970s, numerous artists (including Béar, Antoni Muntadas, and Aldo Tambellini) promoted a form of televisual interfacing that admitted unprecedented delay, a radical slowing down of the televisual real-time ideal. With a slow-scan transceiver (a Robot 530 for instance) video signals could be converted into audio signals and sent over a telephone line to a

---

58   From my interview with Liza Béar, New York, November 18, 2010.
59   Béar, 'Phase II Send Receive Satellite Network'.

distant location, where they could be reconverted into video images at the rate of one frame every eight seconds. Two-way slow-scan TV transmissions between artists were set up on various occasions in 1979, 1980, and 1981,[60] but delays of all kinds are also meticulously foregrounded in *Send/Receive Phase II*. Against a background of general connectivity-fever, the live edit text-generator insistently notes the specificity of every technical complication, every temporal hitch, every surplus moment:

THE SYNC GENERATOR CANNOT LOCK ONTO THE NOISY SIGNAL COMING

HALF SECOND DELAY BETWEEN WHAT YOU SAY AND WNE … WHEN IT'S HEARD

If the video studio-turned-interface seemed to lose track of the history of studio practice and the complicated relation between location, collaborative modus, and artistic subjectivity, it did not forget the other significant dimension of the media sweatshop it modeled: the effort to both control and produce time itself. What was at stake is easily seen when compared with art-related satellite moments where the interface — the complicated and complicating mediator — was evoked only to be neutralized. Take, for instance, the documenta 6 two-way satellite telecast of Joseph Beuys, Douglas Davis, and Nam June Paik/Charlotte Moorman also from 1977. This was simply globalized broadcasting from an art venue, ponderously introduced by Russell Connor in a New York TV studio and Peter Iden in Kassel's Fridericianum. After the round of introductions, Beuys and Paik/Moorman were allowed to perform their strange tricks like ordinary talk show acts.

Then, finally, Davis played around with the interface concept of teletouch. Broadcast live via a satellite link from Caracas, but taped a few days earlier, Douglas is shown inside a dark room, which now fills the entire screen image. He moves back and forth for a while, demonstrating the depth of the space. Towards the end, he comes up close, pressing against a glass pane, banging it, scratching it, simulating being trapped behind the TV screen.[61] Another pair of hands pretends to interact with him, as if from the other side of the screen, but real contact is never achieved and Douglas ends the piece by crashing into the glass pane. It is hard to imagine a more disingenuous take on the problems of the nontransparent interface, a less technically and politically attuned account of its specific ways of organizing connectivity and collaboration. Nothing could be further away from the temporalizing complexities of video signals than these romantic/paranoid fantasies

60   In May 1979 Aldo Tambellini and Antoni Muntadas both employed at MIT's Center for Advanced Visual Study (CAVS), organized 'Pacific Rim: Slow Scan' at the Vancouver Art Gallery. On February 16, 1980, Tambellini, in collaboration with his Communicationsphere group, created the event Artists' Use of Telecommunications in which telephone lines and slow-scan receivers were put to use to transfer materials between several locations simultaneously. Several other slow-scan events organized by Tambellini and artist colleagues (among them Bill Bartlett and Otto Piene) took place in 1980 and 1981. In 1979, Liza Béar in collaboration with Willoughby Sharp in New York and Rolf Brand in Geneva, produced a ten-week public access TV series entitled the WARC Report that dealt with the telecommunication politics of the 1979 World Administrative Radio Conference. The series used a slow-scan feed for relaying images from Geneva in addition to live studio interviews with telecommunications experts.
61   Douglas Davis, The Last Nine Minutes (1977).

of the closed box. It was as if, all of a sudden, the lonesome painterly studio of 1960s TV documentaries was back in force, the boxlike studio stage set isomorphic with the theatrical view into the television box. In this satellite production, the still-theatrical rules of broadcasting overruled the progressive modulations of video space and video images, just as it would serve to dissimulate the reality of media labor for at least another decade.

References

Alberro, Alexander. *Conceptual Art and the Politics of Publicity*, Cambridge, MA: MIT Press, 2003.

Beck, Stephen. 'The Sounds and Colors of Inner Life: Proposal for a Videographic Composition', Undated typescript in the archives of Steina and Woody Vasulka, http://www.vasulka.org/archive/Artists1/Beck,Stephen/SoundsColors.pdf.

Blom, Ina. *The Autobiography of Video: The Life and Times of a Memory Technology*, New York: Sternberg Press, 2016.

Bois, Yve-Alain, and John Shepley, 'Painting as Model', Review of Hubert Damisch's *Fenêtre jaune cadmium ou, Les dessous de la peinture, October* 37 (1986): 125–137.

Braidotti, Rosi. 'Becoming Woman: Or Sexual Difference Revisited', *Theory Culture & Society* 20.3 (2003): 43–64.

Braidotti, Rosi. 'Nomadism with a Difference: Deleuze's Legacy in a Feminist Perspective', *Man and World* 29 (1996), pp. 305–314.

Fifield, George. 'The Paik/Abe Synthesizer', in Davidson Gigliotti, *Early Video Project*, http://davidsonsfiles.org/paikabesythesizer.html.

Galloway, Alexander R. 'The Unworkable Interface', *New Literary History* 39.4 (2008): 931–955.

Gioscia, Vic. 'Frequency and Form', *Radical Software* 1.2 (1970): 7.

Green, Vanalyne. 'Vertical Hold: A History of Women's Video Art', in Kate Horsfield and Lucas Hilderbrand (eds.), *Feedback: The Video Data Bank Catalog of Video Art and Artist Interviews*, Philadelphia: Temple University Press, 2006, pp. 22–30.

Hanley, JoAnn, and Ann-Sargent Wooster. *The First Generation: Women and Video 1970-75*, New York: Independent Curators Incorporated, 1993.

Haraway, Donna. 'A Cyborg Manifesto: Science, Technology, and Socialist-Feminism in the Late Twentieth Century', In *Simians, Cyborgs and Women: The Reinvention of Nature*, New York: Routledge, 1991, pp. 149–181.

Horowitz, Andy. 'Domestic Communications Satellites', *Radical Software* 2.5 (1973): 36–40.

Jones, Caroline. *Machine in the Studio: Constructing the Postwar American Artist.* Chicago: University of Chicago Press, 1996.

Kiaer, Christina. 'Boris Arvatov's Socialist Objects', *October* 81 (1997), 105–118.

Krauss, Rosalind. 'Grids', *October* 9 (1979): 50–64.

Latour, Bruno. *Reassembling the Social: An Introduction to Actor-Network-Theory*, Oxford: Oxford University Press, 2007.

Manovich, Lev. *The Language of New Media*, Cambridge, MA: MIT Press, 2001.

Nora, Pierre. *Realms of Memory: Rethinking the French Past*, vol. 1–3, trans. Arthur Goldhammer. New York: Columbia University Press, 1996–1998.

Relyea, Lane, *Your Everyday Art World*, Cambridge: MIT Press, 2013.

Ross, Ken. 'Excerpts From a Conversation with Alphons Schilling', http://www.vasulka.org/archive/Artists6/Schilling,Alphons/ElectronicSpaces,etc.pdf.

Schwarz, Bill. 'Memory, Temporality, Modernity: Les Lieux De Mémoire', in Susannah Radstone And Bill Schwarz (eds), *Memory: Histories, Theories, Debates*, New York: Fordham University Press, 2010, pp. 41-58.

Simondon, Gilbert. 'The Genesis of the Individual', trans. Mark Cohen and Sanford Kwinter, in Jonathan Crary and Sanford Kwinter (eds), *Incorporations*, New York: Zone Books, 1992, pp.297–319.

Smith, Roberta. 'A Color Field Painter form the 60's to Now', *New York Times*, August 2, 1991.

Sturken, Marita, and Robert R. Riley (eds). *Steina and Woody Vasulka: Machine Media*, San Francisco: San Francisco Museum of Modern Art, 1996.

Terranova, Tiziana. *Network Culture: Politics for the Information Age*, London: Pluto Press, 2004.

Turner, Ann, et al. The National Center for Research in Television: Research. Training', *Radical Software* 2.3 (1973): 46–51.

Vasulka, Steina, Woody Vasulka, and Peter Weibel (eds). *Eigenwelt der Apparate-Welt: Pioneers of Electronic Art*, Linz: Ars Electronica, 1992.

INTERVIEW WITH NATALIE BOOKCHIN

GEERT LOVINK

INTERVIEW WITH NATALIE BOOKCHIN

GEERT LOVINK

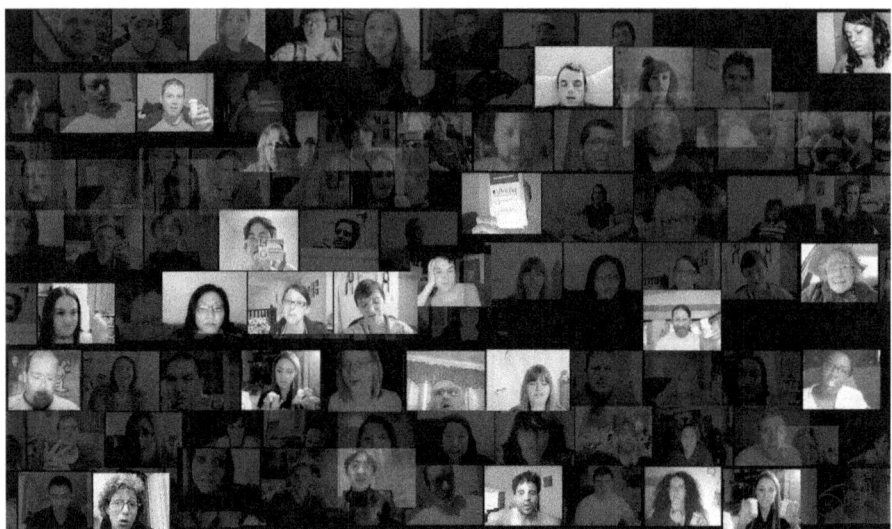

Fig. 1: Natalie Bookchin, My Meds, 2008

For me, Natalie Bookchin's work is synonymous with Video Vortex and the rise of YouTube. Although we got to know each other's work during the turbulent years of net.art in the late nineties, this particular story began with a DVD I received from Natalie. It contained *The Trip* (2008), a video collection of early YouTube fragments shot during car trips on all continents, which Natalie found and reassembled into an imaginary journey across the globe. What has always defined Natalie Bookchin's work is her ability to generate a unity out of distributed fragments. We, as users, may feel lost and desperate but the artist gives us hope that we can overcome distraction and senseless multi-tasking by creating an all-together new meta narrative that is human — again.

We first had our conversation in the summer of 2017. And then we had an additional exchange in March 2020, confined to our homes during the coronavirus crisis.

Geert Lovink: Your 2016 work *Long Story Short* (longstory.us) is defined by its silences. It feels like the work simply could not be rushed. Society does not want to speak about its underclass: they do not exist, and thus they do not have a voice. It is part of your work to make the shadow existences visible, making us see what most of us look away from. In this fast, multitasking world silence is increasingly pushed aside. Is there something like an aesthetics of silence? Silence design?

Natalie Bookchin: *Long Story Short* is built around the interplay between speech and silence. There are instances where someone lingers on the screen as a silent witness while another person speaks, appearing to listen along. There are other moments when someone who has just spoken remains on the screen, appearing to gaze out at viewers in silence, returning our gazes. The silence of the film's subjects slows the tempo and acts as a counterpoint to orchestral moments of layered speech. The silences give listeners time to reflect on words just spoken, allowing them to gather weight and importance. Even while the film uses some tropes of online participatory culture, including the first-person narrative, the web cam, it also, through its tempo and use of quietness, suggests a refusal. It points to an interiority that we don't have access to. It suggests that some things remain unspoken, that narrators decide on what to reveal and to withhold.

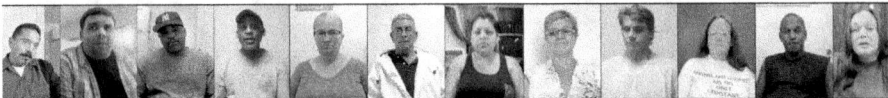

Fig. 2: Natalie Bookchin, Long Story Short, 2016

GL: There's a harsh school of radical Marxist analysis, which states that the written-off 'surplus class' will inevitably face genocide. The poor will have to be deleted. Extinguished. Some of your witness accounts voice a similar opinion. On the other hand, we do not get the idea that these Americans necessarily have a political analysis of their situation. Poverty does not lead to political consciousness. Marx himself was even skeptical about the 'lumpen proletariat' and distrusted them. Do you think that's still the case?

NB: I don't think membership in any economic class in and of itself leads to political consciousness. Extreme poverty can, however, give those facing it an acute awareness of and sensitivity to class and class status — something that, especially in the U.S, is often disregarded ('We are all middle class here!'). Those excluded from the mainstream often have a finely tuned understanding of their own exploitation, and of the contrasts between their lived experiences and the many false assumptions that others project onto them. A Marxist might argue that an awareness of the harsh material conditions and destructive effects of capitalism could lead to a nascent political consciousness.

Poverty often produces isolation. People isolate because they are ashamed of or overwhelmed by their situations. To counter that, in the film, I interweave many individual accounts and perspectives to make visible a collective body that is not easily seen when people are isolated. The visualization reveals overlapping subjectivities, interdependencies, shared experiences, and perspectives, and it suggests the potential for political alliances. It challenges the neoliberal fiction that individuals are fully and solely responsible for themselves, Hannah Arendt wrote that all political action first requires what she called the 'space of appearance', 'the organization of the people as it arises out of acting and speaking together... no matter where they happen to be'. For Arendt, this organization is not tied to a physical space but only to the words and action of people together.

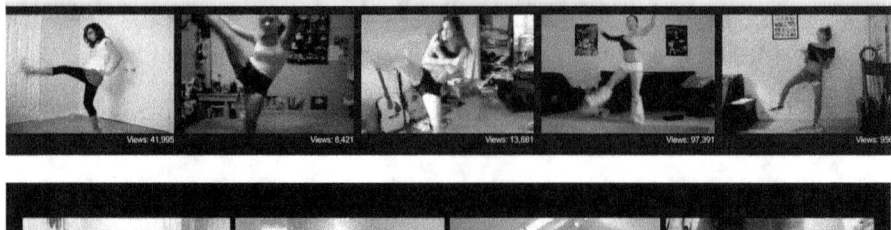

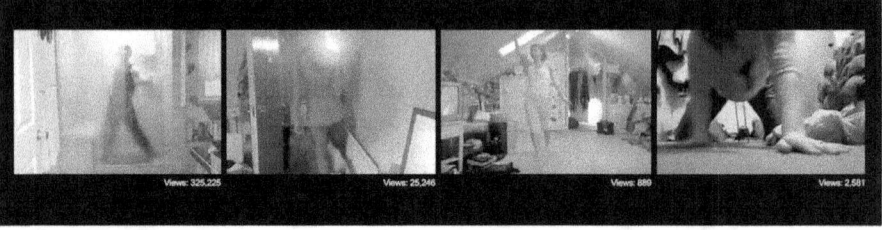

Fig. 3: Natalie Bookchin, Mass Ornament, 2009

GL: *Long Story Short* combines insights on race relations in the USA with a socio-economic analysis. Can you give us some insights on how you analyze race and poverty?

NB: You can't separate the long and sordid history of systemic racism in the United States from any analysis of urban poverty. Most of the narrators in *Long Story Short* are people of color, which reflects the demographic make-up of those facing poverty in Los Angeles and the Bay Area of San Francisco, where I shot the film. Throughout the 20th Century until the 1970s, in what is known as the Great Migration, millions of African Americans migrated from the South to northern cities to find work and escape Jim Crow segregation. Instead, they were systematically redlined and isolated in neglected neighborhoods and denied rights to buy property. This wasn't arbitrary or just the whims of individual actors; it was the product of deliberative government policies. There was a great book that came out a couple of years ago by Richard Rothstein, uncovering the shameful history of racial segregation in the United Sates. The increasing income and wealth gaps between rich and poor over the last 50 years, together with the crisis of affordable housing in U.S. cities, has only made economic and racial inequality worse.

GL: A decade ago people would shoot videos with cheap hand-held cameras. Then smartphones with built-in cameras appeared. We're now 15 years into vlogging. What has this all done to your own artistic practice? In previous work you used to scour the web for video fragments. In this work you shot the material yourself. Can you discuss this?

NB: I first started making videos from material I found on the web in 2006. I animated screen grabs of live streams of private security cameras that I watched for months: private backyards, front porches, workers washing dishes in kitchens and dozing in office chairs, which I found using a simple Google hack. I would enter an obscure technical search string and Google would spit out dozens of security webcams that were ironically left unsecured. The videos depicted the asynchronous and non-linear space and time of the internet, where one could jump from continent to continent and from day to night with a single click of the mouse.

The following year, I began working with amateur videos shared on YouTube, to explore the role of the social internet in erasing lines between public and private space. The first work I made, *Parking Lot*, is composed of recordings that people made of themselves in parking lots around the world—gathering, playing, and staging performances against the backdrop of glowing corporate logos and large concrete buildings. These actions, appropriations of anonymous, corporate space to create temporary public space seemed to mirror the videos themselves as they circulated on YouTube— little acts of rebellion hosted by a corporate giant.

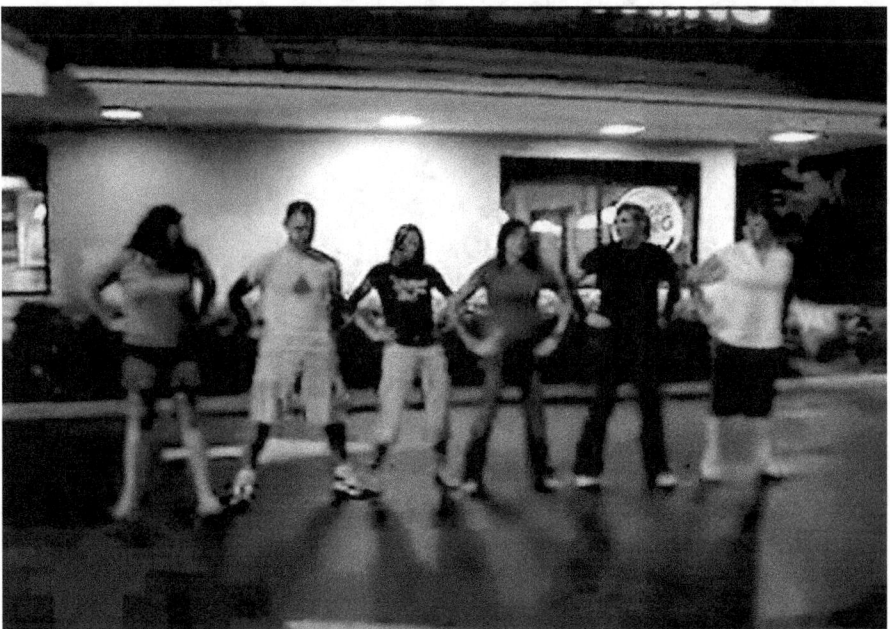

Fig. 4: Natalie Bookchin, Parking Lot, 2008

In 2008, the year the Global Recession began, I started working with videos that people made of themselves performing, dancing, and talking to cameras connected to the internet. This was before mobile video had really taken off, and people were spending a lot of time in front of their desktops and laptops. What struck me was how the videos conveyed the intimacy and trust many people had with strangers on the internet, as they shared their feelings, worries, and desires. Many writers, pundits, and critics were gushing about the positive, world-changing effects of internet connectivity and mass group think. I wanted to offer a more complicated picture—how the videos people were producing revealed both the absence of and longing for both public space and real social connection.

Now he's out in public and everyone can see, my final work using vlogs, explored the early stirrings of the darker, more nihilistic, and polarized space the internet has become – and helped produce. It focused on the question of race, looking at the ways that blackness itself produces a scandal in public space where whiteness is the norm. The work wove together numerous vloggers' narrations as they discussed a series of scandals or conspiracy theories involving four famous African American men, each of whom won power, wealth, and fame in spaces historically dominated by whites.

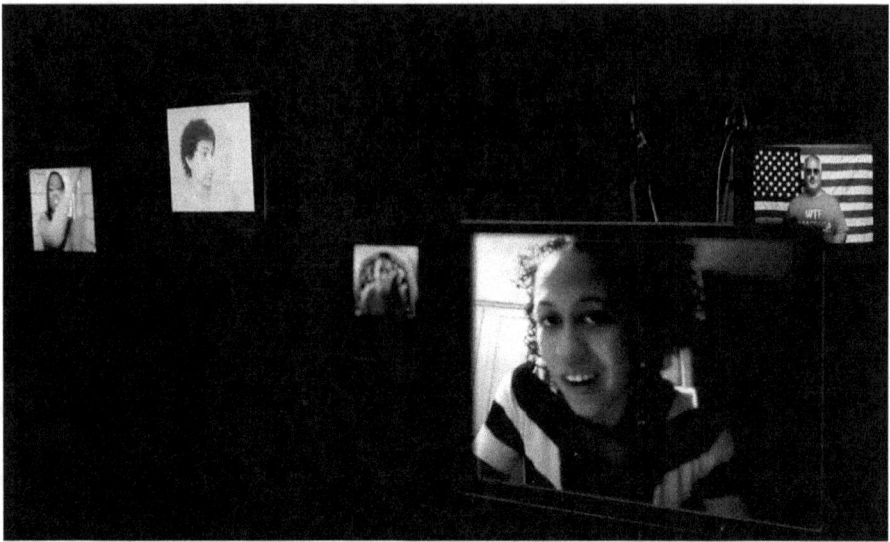

Fig. 5: Natalie Bookchin, Now he's out in public and everyone can see,, 2012

With Long Story Short, I wanted to make the connection between the growth of the internet and the widening gap between the rich and the poor. I continued working with the popular internet form of the vlog and with webcams. But this time I created my own archive, since I couldn't find what I was looking for online. Although people share details about most aspects of their lives on social media, stories about experiences of poverty are mostly absent. It may be that people withhold these details because of stigma and shame, or it may be that they are not popular with the algorithms, or maybe a combination of the two.

GL: Can you say something about the position of the camera? Unlike classic documentaries, the camera does not move around. Is sitting down in order to tell the story still powerful?

NB: The camera is a little bit below or at eye level. The gaze is direct. I have always been inspired by August Sander's portraits of German society, which reveal a quiet dignity and equal exchange between photographer and photographed. I used a webcam attached to a laptop, and people took whatever time they needed to consider their responses and saw themselves on screen as they spoke. I did not want to follow subjects around, to catch them off guard, or least of all to reproduce overused images of urban decay, but rather to enable people to present themselves as they wanted to be seen. The casual set-up, sitting face-to-face with the camera, produces the intimacy of a one-to-one exchange.

GL: It's widely believed that political messages in the arts are good and worthy — but not in art. There's a growing fatigue about political works that do not look good and merely express politically correct intentions. What's your response to this?

NB: I think we are long past debates about whether something made by an artist is or is not actually art. 'It's art if I say so', to quote Duchamp. I think calling something political art is a redundancy. All art is political. As for art with a message, I think there is a time and a place for it: it depends on where the art is circulating and who its audience is. Think of the work of Gran Fury around the AIDS crisis in the U.S. during the 1980s, John Heartfield's anti-Nazi montages, and RTMark's messages about corporations. The artwork that I care most about often does much more than transmit a message. It asks questions and opens up new spaces of reflection, offering new ways to see, understand, feel, and be in a world among others.

GL: When we speak about YouTube in 2020 we mainly talk about its manipulative algorithm and the extreme video suggestions of what's up next. The good old days of participatory culture and self-confessions seem over, at least on YouTube. The informal video cultures have moved to platforms such as TikTok and Instagram. Would you say that the original online video aesthetics has been destroyed by the slick professionalism of the influencers? Is the informal culture of confession still there?

NB: As companies became more adept at finding ways to monetize their platforms, small producers making casual, informal videos were, for the most part, squeezed out I also think that many people who post material online are now more careful, less optimistic about finding authentic relationships, and more guarded about exposing themselves to the potential hostility of anonymous commenters.

GL: You are working on two new projects, one being a film in collaboration with the Spanish Roma association Lacho Bají and the Barcelona-based artist collective LaFundició, with whom you are developing a collective cinematic portrait of and with a local Roma community. The other will become a series of video montages of mass protests and uprisings. Can you tell us more about both?

NB: Sure. A couple of years ago I was approached by LaFundició, an artist collective that work on long-term, collaborative projects periphery neighborhoods of Barcelona. They do incredible projects with local neighborhood groups, working on magazines, radio shows, performances, and exhibitions. They have been collaborating with a local Roma collective, Lacho Bají, for a number of years, and together began developing a film project. Their idea was to work with residents and neighbors on a collective portrait of the neighborhood and the street they inhabited. They were planning to work with super8 film and analog animation, but the teenagers they usually work with were much more interested in using their cellphones and making dance and music videos that emulated YouTube stars. So they put the project on hold to rethink their approach. At the time, I had an exhibition of my work in Barcelona up, and they went to see the show. They found the use of montage and popular internet forms to reflect the preoccupations of marginalized groups in American culture inspiring, and it occurred to them that this might be a way for them to move forward. They reached out to me and proposed a collaboration. After a series of exchanges, in person and remotely, we began working together. Since then, we've been meeting remotely and in person, running informal workshops, discussions, screenings of works-in-progress as well as work by other artists and filmmakers working on related issues. We've been collecting videos and other material shared on social media and in WhatsApp and Facebook groups, and working locally on making videos with neighborhood participants, students, after-school groups, and attendees of the Lacho Baji association. The process of creating the film is necessarily slow, complex, and deliberative, especially given my outsider position as a paya (non- Roma), an American, and a non-native speaker.

Right now, we envision the film's visual aesthetics as a radical pastiche of current digital forms: social media feeds, cellphone footage, music and dance videos, TikTok, Facebook, Instagram, and WhatsApp chats. This aesthetic counters mainstream and stereotypical depictions of the Roma as anti-modern and out of touch with current trends, technologies, and realities. We're also exploring how to appropriate these forms to reflect the vitally active community life and economies of sharing in the local Romani community.

My other project in progress is a series of short looped video projections that combine hundreds of amateur video fragments of street protests. It's sort of a reimagining of radical photomontage of the 1920s. Each montage will focus on a single or aligned global social movement, from recent women's marches to Black Lives Matter. We've been so bogged down in gloom that I wanted to do something positive, even celebratory. The montages are fantastic, optimistic spaces filled with colors, handmade signs, megaphones, gestures, and bodies in motion—people together, performing and enacting resistance. Now, with the coronavirus, these images, gathered just in the past year, suddenly feel like relics of the past (hopefully not though!). They also remind us that we need to keep going, and that we can only do it together.

INTERVIEW WITH JUDIT KIS

GEERT LOVINK

INTERVIEW WITH JUDIT KIS

GEERT LOVINK

The Hungarian artist Judit Kis was one of the artists who performed at Video Vortex XII in Malta in September 2019, and it was also here that I was introduced to her very personal work. In the following months after having further engaged with Kis' work, I decided to approach her for an (email) interview. In an artistic sense, Kis fits well into the 'intermedia' category: she produces videos, photo documentations, prints, paintings, ceramics, performances and installations consisting of blankets, lightboxes and bricks. She prints sentences on textiles and engraves words into ceramic bricks (all in English). Titles of her work include *I have never happened*, *Detoxification*, *Dedication*, *Disillusion*, *Distance*, and *I love you*.[1]

I was interested in an online exchange with her because of my recent work on mental states such as sadness, anger and loneliness and how those moods are generated by specific algorithms that make you feel bad. Kis' website states that practice deals with integration, self-revelation and healing: 'In a form of 'confessional art' my aim is to create works that are embracing vulnerability and engaging my audience to connect themselves and others on a deeper level.' Her recent projects emphasize the importance of self-care and rituals in a contemporary context, reflecting to our diverse cultural heritage that has become more accessible through technology. According to Kis 'art has a transformative power in our thinking and especially if this art can be bodily experienced and show progresses in personal improvement.'

Take her 2017 'Cyberlove' project, which consisted of an eight-month long Instagram performance about a semi-platonic love affair, 'a video installation with artificial fog, a series of emotional landscapes printed on Tyvek paper and a 2 sqm blanket.'[2] Over the years we see her work evolve from diagnosis to therapy, from experimentation with the self through a radical public display of the artists' uncertainty, to strategies of self-healing. Judit Kis put herself to the test. Her work is defined by a refined East-European dryness, precision, mixed with a grey absence of hope, where diminished expectations of a harsh neo-liberal society, life in general, and the Other in particular become rich resources for confronting, intimate art pieces. The following exchange took place right before and during the coronavirus crisis, in March-April 2020.

---

1   https://u-dyt.com/.
2   https://u-dyt.com/CYBERLOVE.

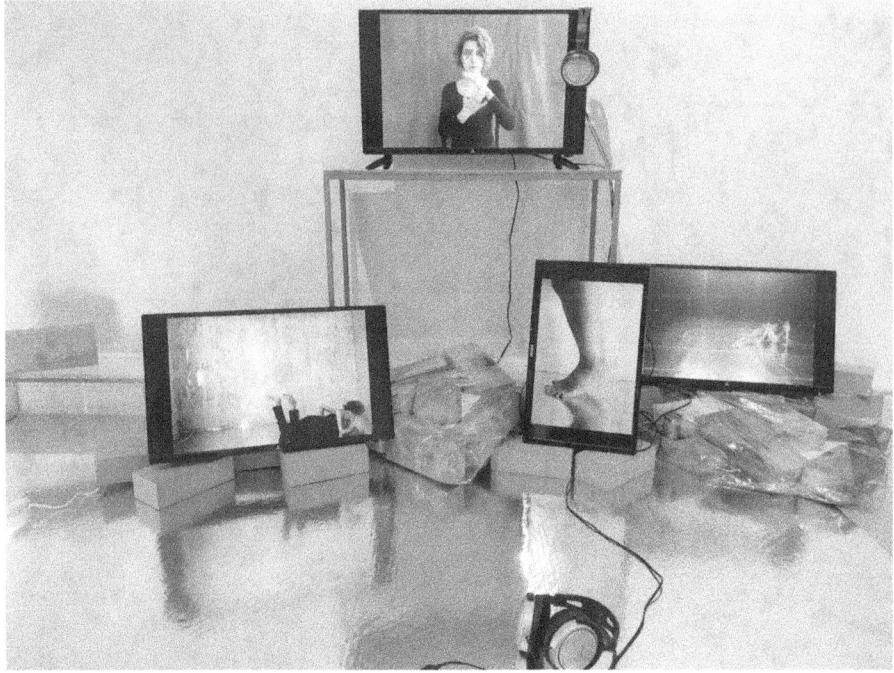

Fig. 1: Judit Kis "against NUMB", video installation, 2019.

Geert Lovink: Can you tell us something about your development of the idea to 'embrace vulnerability'? Many artists would claim that they explore sensibility in order to see the world with new eyes. This is probably not what you mean.

Judit Kis: I see 'embracing vulnerability' as the practice of compassion. It was one of my deepest fears to go into situations where I can get hurt or let others see me failing. When I could reveal my vulnerability in public, I felt like I became an agent and not only acting for myself. This way it was very empowering to go beyond my boundaries. At the time I started my practice in school, I felt encouraged to do socially engaged art projects even in situations where I had zero to minor competence. I wanted to do art from the conflicts that were the most present in my life and perform where I can have the biggest impact. I was in the age of exploring my identity and while other topics seemed to require endless research, I had the full right to use my own stories as the source of my inspiration. Someone may consider the content of my videos too intimate, but I have never thought of my issues as something unique or too private. I started with small experiments like audio recording a conversation that I knew will lead to a break-up or hiding a camera to observe my reactions in certain situations. I found it very challenging from the beginning to talk about things that others are more silent about and when social media evolved with everyone projecting their perfected self-image, I just felt more urge to counterbalance the mainstream. Looking back at my ten-year practice, I see how my topics come from childhood fascinations and traumas. The practice of overcoming my fear of others' acceptance, taught me how to understand not just my vulnerability but others'.

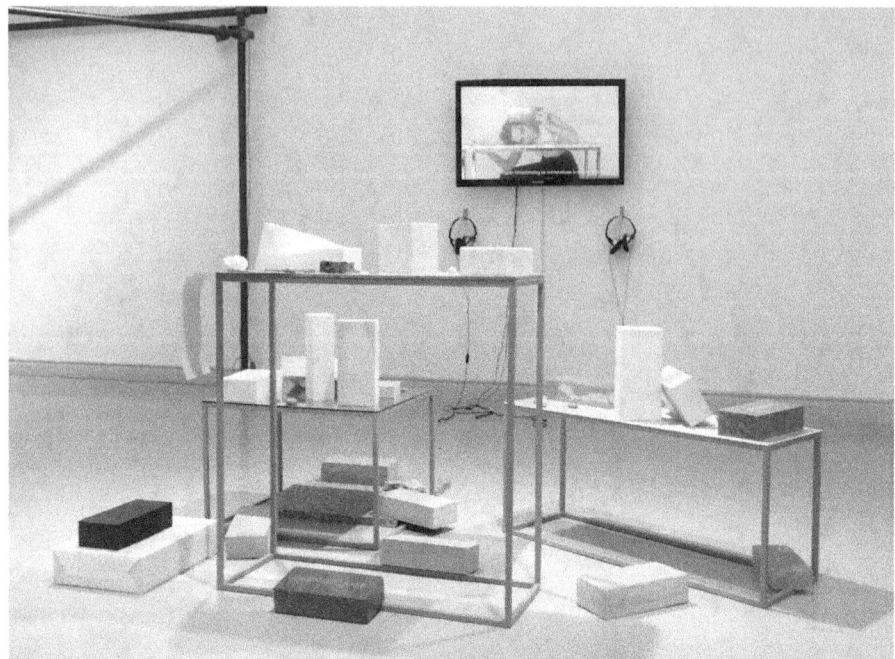

Fig. 2: Judit Kis "Standards", Derkovits Art Award 2019, Kunsthalle Budapest. Photo: Zsófi Erdős

GL: You have a new media art background. How do you look at the current internet culture in the age of platform capitalism? You have yourself grown up with computers, what was the turning point for you?

JK: The early computer games and software available for us when I was a child were too ugly to be fascinating. I was lucky enough to grow up playing outside, maybe a part of that last generation. I didn't spend much time in front of a computer until I was 16 and the first social media networks became popular. The turning point was probably my first MacBook, 10 years ago, that I used all day for work and in school like the extension of my body, a little window that was also a mirror. I recorded almost every video I made with its web camera. I think there is really a gap between people who were born before and after the internet. I remember well when Hans-Ulrich Obrist launched '89+'. I was only 25 and still in school and I didn't feel young artists count so much until then and suddenly they had to be under my age. Looking at the aesthetic and content of those selected works were very alienating for me. I felt like I grew up in a different world. Today, I follow many artists who are also under the age of 25. I enjoy seeing their progress and how well they can use social media platforms to criticize our culture and to build a community around their work. I have to keep customizing my feed in order to reach their counterbalancing content, but it's worth the effort. I am only active on Instagram on a daily basis where I have set up a time limit. I remember when I had 5-6 different sites where I shared my work, nowadays I find even my website unnecessary.

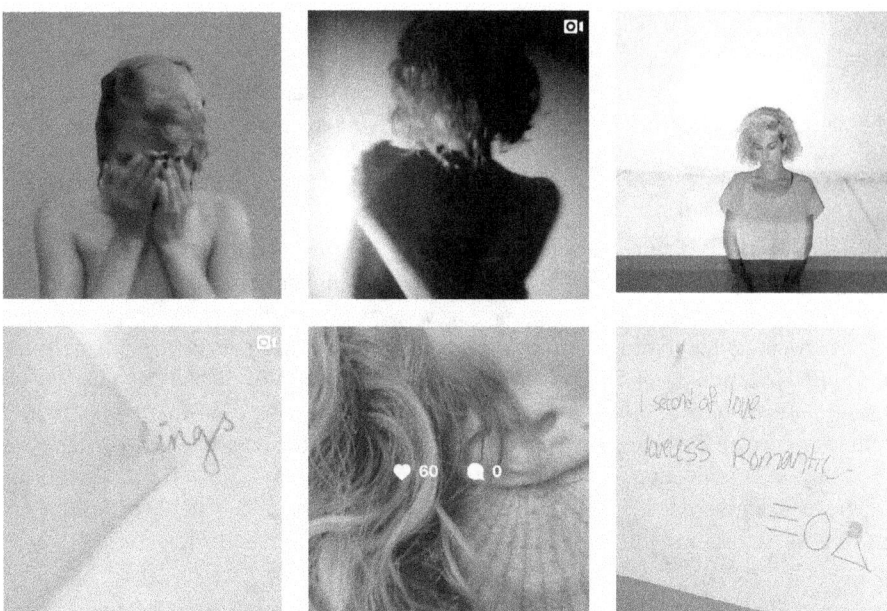

Fig. 3: Judit Kis "Cyberlove", Instagram Blogposts, 2017. Photo: Zsófi Erdős

GL: How did you get to the concept of 'self-healing'? Would you emphasize the 'do-it-yourself' aspect? Does this strategy come out of the institutionalized practices of therapy and fitness, sports, the yoga industry?

JK: No, it was rather rooted in my own practice. I wrote my thesis on identity construction and I created the videos to illustrate the work and improvement I made on myself. I've been using the therapeutic effects of making art. I referred to the words healing and self-care first, because they have become part of our everyday language and I thought it could help me to integrate what I was doing anyways. And yes, I would emphasize the DIY aspect, because we have great power to change things in our life and become better humans.

GL: In your recent art works such as Standards and Cyberlove you combine installation objects, paintings, videos and Instagram pictures in an overall 'intermedia' approach. Can you tell us about your findings? What works today, and what not? In your experience, which combinations of the real and virtual work?

JK: In the first six years I mostly created videos and later I had online performances, zines and public engaging programs during my exhibitions. I didn't follow any strategy or rule with my work. I made things that I felt right, honest and I needed to release. I considered the objects I made as tools with symbolic meanings and I staged them in my video performances to express certain feelings. I'm not assigned to any gallery and I can't say that my projects work in terms of an art practice that sustains itself, but many other ways I found them successful. I chose this career, because my intention besides sharing my work was to meet people, exchange ideas and find ways to collaborate. Through the brick project, *Standards* which I started only in 2017, I worked with many craftsmen and other professionals to produce over 50 pieces from different materials. I think of these objects as the extension of my virtual work and I like to play with them, build installations and get messy. However, it's exhausting to find ways to install, store, transport and preserve these objects for a person who lives in constant uncertainty.

What I did within the frame of my *Virtual solo show and live performance*, also in 2017, can work very well even in the quarantine situation. It was an experiment to break the cycle of rejections and neglect from the artworld and through that online event I could engage a much bigger and relevant audience than I did with many of my gallery shows. I am curious to see how the art market will change in this upcoming crisis and how it will affect the art institutions depending on it. For me it was very disillusioning already and I would have felt useless dreaming of a future show at a biennale or developing skills to promote my art. I find works the most engaging when they can create situations where I can experience empathy and connection with others. I prefer to have works that can be accessible for many, for example with a link. And by adapting myself to the circumstances, besides my mental wellbeing I want to invest my energy into online education and organizing more community projects.

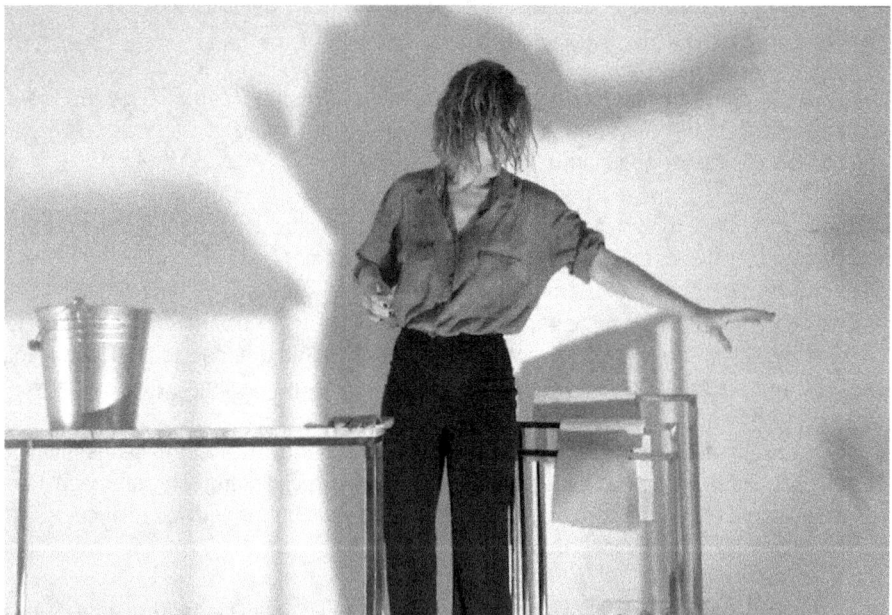

Fig. 4: Judit Kis "Virtuial Performance", 2017.

GL: How do you look back at your 2017 #cyberlove project?

JK: I remember that year was full of rejections and I felt very insecure. Referring to your essay, I think this project really comes from sad passions. Sadness is a very active feeling compared to 'numbness' that came later to my focus. I allowed myself to be sad and through the blog posts for eight months I left traces for future works. With sad passion it's always possible to be productive through a symbolic projection of oneself. Even though they say sadness comes when we have no impact on our surroundings, I insisted that this sadness be inspiring somehow. It's my second unique hashtag and I find these online performances stored on social media sites much more important than the foggy landscapes and video installation that came as a result.

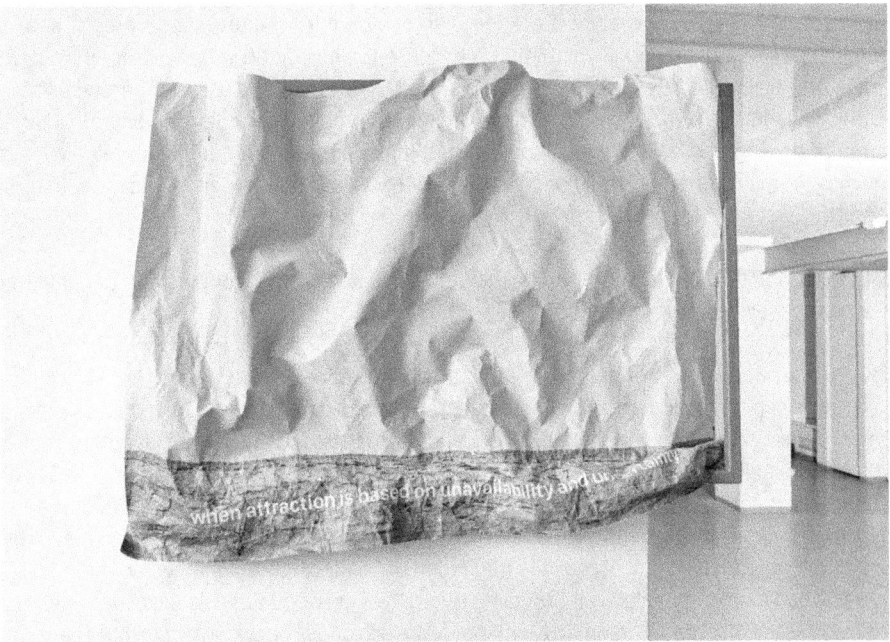

Fig. 5: Judit Kis "Cyberlove", 2017. Photo: Dávid Biró

GL: What do you make of 'digital detox' weekends when stressed people try to forget their smartphone and force themselves to go offline?

JK: I have a dog who forces me to have a routine, go outside, pay attention, be determined. He changed my life completely and I often forget about my phone because of him. I like to spend time with my mom in her countryside home and sometimes I also go to long yoga and meditation workshops. The most recharging for me is when I can try things that I haven't done before, for example organizing a party for friends who have babies to get involved in their life, or recently I took a shelter dog home for a weekend. As long as I can have these emotionally intense experiences without the involvement of technology, I don't feel the need to go completely offline. There are times when I get more distracted by scrolling and looking at others, but I am aware of its negative impact on my productivity. I think it's the key to originality, to look more inside.

GL: Your current topics are healing, self-care and contemporary rituals.

JK: I aim to explore alternative healing methods in different cultures that are less known or integrated. I would like to see the effects of these inherited traditions in our contemporary society, where technology rules our life but we seek to experience things that can help us to connect to our own body and mind. I research practices in the fields of psychology, religion and anthropology, but I also source inspiration from online videos and other communities. I am interested in what is accessible for everyday people who are desperate for help. I think experiencing artworks which deal with these topics can be very powerful in ways of transforming our beliefs. We should be reminded that we hold power over our life and we aren't excluded from society when dealing with mental problems or other seemingly incurable conditions. As I perceive it, we all have something or someone to heal in our life. My self-healing journey started because of my mom. She refuses to go through medical treatments and I understand her concerns about relying on public healthcare.

GL: When you talk about programming the brain, do you refer to neuroplasticity and the way Catherine Malabou is writing about this?

JK: I think not even in her elaborate research is it confirmed that we can substitute the biological with symbolic projections. I don't feel enough confidence to connect neuroplasticity to self-healing directly, even though they are linked to the capacity of the brain to transform. It's scientifically proven that emotional traumas can do physical damage to our body, but there is no medical evidence to confirm that positive experiences do the opposite. There are types of diseases that can't be generated from a psychological trauma or at least not in the life of the patient. I am still at the very beginning of this project, but I know there are many cases when a patient healed without going through surgery and other medical therapy. (For example, the artist Lynn Hershman Leeson explained in one of her video works that she could recover from a brain tumor by practicing pain meditation). Hopefully, I will learn more about what kind of experiences and alternative therapies can motivate these recreational processes in the body, how to stimulate the brain to change its reactions, and how to encourage people to try these methods for healing. For instance, 'forgetting' happens unconsciously in order to process certain traumas, but by 'programming the brain' I mean intentional practices like rewriting memories and deconstructing identities.

GL: Can you say something about the responses you get to your work?

JK: I like to get feedback and opinions on my work, because they are essential in order to improve my practice. I feel more motivated when others express their openness or feel encouraged to reveal something about themselves in the environment of my work. I had a few encounters with strangers who got very emotional while looking at my performance and some of them indicated that it was empowering or enlightening in terms they could see someone else coping with the same issues. I experience more involvement when my performance is very rough and real, because these actions seem more honest in less designed circumstances. On the other hand, through the years I become aware of that, expressing vulnerability in public has another important ethical aspect. I've learnt that for some people my acts could appear intimidating considering that they aren't so open to confront their related problems. I know exactly how much effort it takes to be on that certain level to expose things or sometimes to just wait until the right moment arrives. In the past I recorded materials that I could only process two years later and there were many ideas that I haven't been brave enough to realize or commit to on the long term. I think it would be important, and useful, to create more space for confessional works, but organized in a very sensitive and inclusive way. The participants should feel involved enough to decide about their own limits, while they are also challenged to stretch their boundaries a bit further. In this way we could destigmatize many mental confusion regarding traumas and social constructions. As an opportunity to heal together.

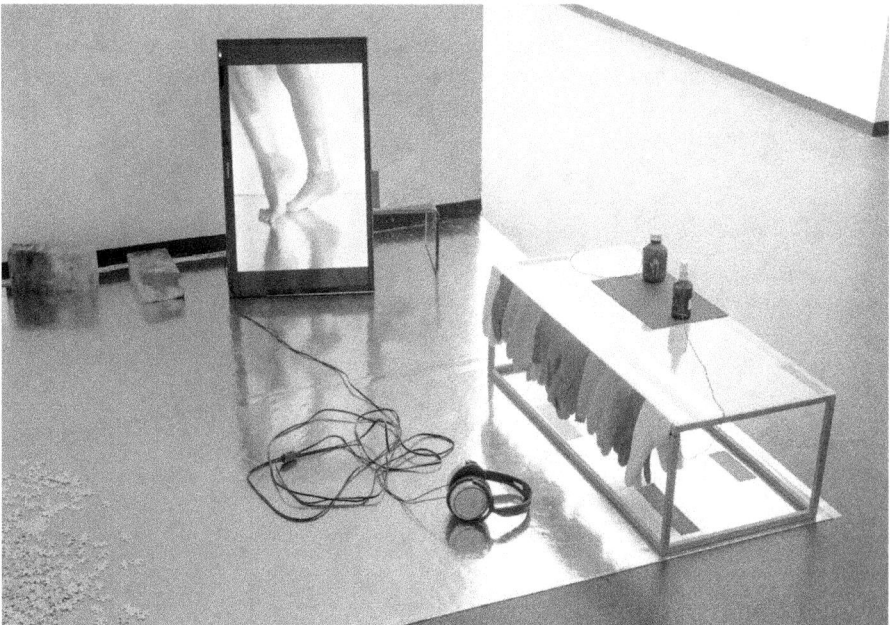

Fig. 6: Judit Kis "against NUMB", video installation, 2019. Photo: Dániel János Fodor.

GL: You're trying to figure out how to stay positive and 'reverse the mess that is making people sick everywhere,' as you wrote to me. Is it important, then, to first make a proper diagnosis?

JK: Definitely. What concerns me is the numbness or indifference that we feel collectively. I am confronted every day with how much power we have lost in controlling our life, to decide about our future. I see the focus always on the things that we cannot change, like they want us to stay motionless and 'sad', as you write. I understand how these patterns are designed to exercise power over us and I want to inspire the opposite. We need to learn how to tell stories about the climate crisis, wars, poverty, violence, animal cruelty and viruses without paralyzing the audience. I see the solution in creating communities, deepening the connection between people and promoting art and other activities that can teach us how to care more about ourselves and others. I imagine rituals in a contemporary context to be very empowering experiences. For this reason, I've started to build a network for 'confessional art' practices and organize collaborative events. I find it important to honor those artists, who cast themselves as the subject of their art and practice self-revelation; it's such a radical act to learn from. Through their workshops and performances they are more effective in creating safe spaces and engaging participants.

I am not sure how things will change through the current corona crisis, but I decided to look at this quarantine time as an opportunity. I am staying with my mother and while I look after her, we can experiment on healing practices every day. Maybe I am less worried because this time is not the first for me to feel suspense. Social insecurity and financial uncertainty have been my everyday reality. Artists seemed especially in trouble at the beginning of this pandemic, but in the upcoming period millions of others will have the chance to experience this lifestyle. We need to practice solidarity and adapt ourselves as quickly as possible. I think artists will be the most creative in surviving this as we could never really rely on the system.

DISTANT FEELING(S)

DANIEL PINHEIRO AND ANNIE ABRAHAMS

DISTANT FEELING(S)

DANIEL PINHEIRO AND ANNIE ABRAHAMS

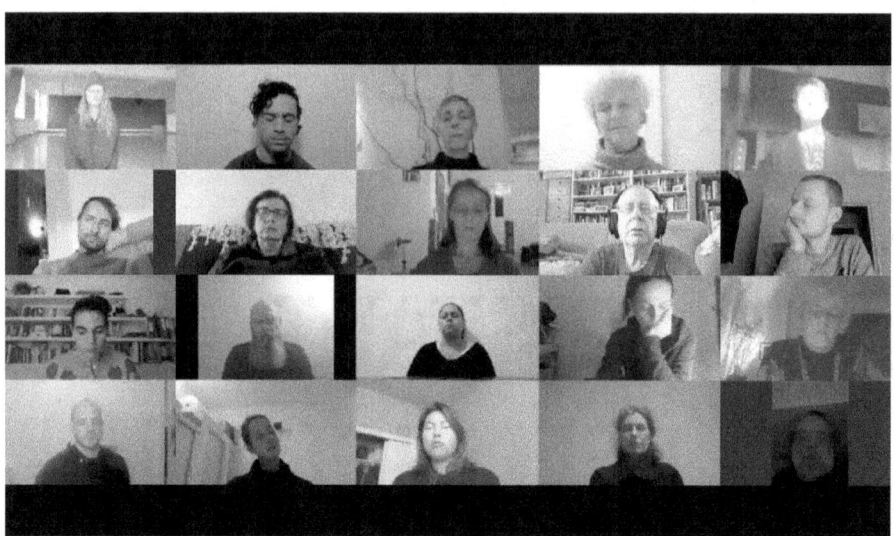

Img. 1; Distant Feeling(s) #7 | December 7th, 2019, 6PM GMT+1. Video Archive: https://vimeo. com/378800662

Distant Feeling(s) invites all interested to participate in a shared moment of togetherness across a distance.

Why, after videoconferencing or after a networked performance, are we so excited and so tired at the same time? What is exactly happening in such situations? In the networked performance series *Distant Feeling(s)* Lisa Parra, Daniel Pinheiro and Annie Abrahams try to find answers.[1] *Distant Feeling(s)* started in 2015 when Annie was invited by Lisa and Daniel to participate in their piece called *'Placelessness'.* There and then, they discovered that, even when closing their eyes and while also being silent, the connexion between them seemed to persist. They were intrigued and started a performance series in an interface that normally

1   The project *Distant Feeling(s)* emerges of the intersection of their artistic practices: the investigation of the possibilities and limits of communication under networked conditions by Annie Abrahams and the research on methods for creating live, movement based, performative work using telecommunication technologies by Lisa Parra and Daniel Pinheiro. See Annie Abrahams, 'Trapped to Reveal – On webcam mediated communication and collaboration', *Journal for Artistic Research* 2 (2012), https://www.jar-online.net/exposition/abstract/trapped-reveal-webcam-mediated-communication-and-collaboration; Daniel Pinheiro and Lisa Parra, 'Performance como Processo: Práticas de 'Embodiment' à Distância', *Performatus* 3.14 (2015),
http://performatus.net/estudos/performance-como-processo/.

is used for videoconferencing. In front of their webcams, removing the fundamental senses that normally allow connectedness to happen, they tried — eyes closed and not talking — to grasp if and how energy flowed between bodies in an online performance where physical presence was absent. They meditated on who/what/where is the 'we', while sharing a blind, silent moment trying to experience the others presence across the network.

They described their feelings to each other and continued to be intrigued. After a few sessions they opened up the project and invited others to join and comment upon the project. A temporal space for resisting the speed of daily life was created. During the sessions partaking, silently - not seeing, only hearing their surroundings and the machines working to keep the connections, the participants inadvertently produced uninteresting data for AI robots. So, *Distant Feeling(s)* was — besides a tool for online communality — also countering the grasp of the big tech companies. *Distant Feeling(s)* is now an annual online ritual of contemplation on our situation of being together while being separated; an ever-changing re-enactment of our intra-action with machines, where we ponder on the relational fabric only possible through networked environments.

Using the internet's potential of connectivity as a means to reflect on the constraints and limitations of that precise quality, DF has become a participatory event in which through silence and provoking an inwards movement by the closing of the eyes while connected, which aims to highlight the relational aspect that is (supposedly) intrinsic to the idea of *network*. Throughout its various activations, from a closed environment between the artists— where the main focus was to attempt sensing the existence and presence of the others while being physically distant, without speaking and with eyes closed—to it becoming a practice shared with an audience, and transforming into an open event since 2017, the project has addressed, cumulatively, the characteristics of the medium/infrastructure to reflect upon them, producing an archive of documentation of the various moments where each one and all work as a visual metaphor of the condition(ing) of connectivity as it is installed in our lives.

A silent, yet sentient, relational encounter, materialized as a telematic embrace where nothing seems to happen and where the lack of apparent action has transformed into the transposition of the concept of agency and a potential way for fighting alienation.

In the more recent activations of the project, a common fact has been the awareness of how machines and the surrounding environments from the different remote locations become present while the bodies perform a sort of absentia while electricity powers this moment of communion.[2] Where and how are we (always) while the network is functioning?

As it continues to develop, iteration after iteration, whether it is through the annual re- activations or in specific contexts it becomes clear that it is a form of researching togetherness through the internet as a way to counter its fallacy, the promise of an interconnected world

---

2   Annie Abrahams, Lisa Parra, and Daniel Pinheiro, 'Distant Feeling(s)', screen recording of *Distant Feeling(s)* #5, https://vimeo.com/308710238.

where concepts of time and physical space dissipate[3] (an ubiquitous spatio-temporal unity), which in fact drives today the (im)possibility of collective strength/power. It is a provocation to the role of networked conversations as a practice for activism emptied from specific purpose, again, assuming the role of symbolizing a situation of engaging in different possibilities of triggering collective agency.

Can we find novelty in an already established system, and act from within, towards (an) other purpose(s)?

Distant Feeling(s) highlights in its genesis and continuity the need to feel/sense presence and suggests a pragmatic approach for reshaping a consciousness on kinship resorting to available technological tools which have been transforming its meaning.

'Silence is hard to find...' Camille Renard mentions at the end of *Distant Feeling(s) #7* and it is through this quest for silence where machines, responsible for allowing the connection across a distance, 'speak' louder and the contemporary restlessness is confronted in this model of interaction between humans and machines. It is not a proposition for a revolution nor a resolution for an evident relational crisis, it is an experience on connectivity and its fundamentals.

> **The relational revolution is already far along. At the same time, it is clearly in crisis.**
> — Time Reborn p. xxix

Previous sessions:

Distant Feeling(s) #1 (raw version) [online, private session]: vimeo.com/158351502

Distant Feeling(s) #2 [reSense [movement, performance, technology, art] Festival, Berlin, online, July 26th - 9h45pm - 10h45pm (GMT+2)]: youtube.com/watch?v=Hu8HDnXh960

Distant Feeling(s) #3 [VisionS in the Nunnery, London, online, November 24th 2016 - 6h30pm (GMT)]: vimeo.com/193158145

Distant Feeling(s) #4 [first of a yearly reconnection, online, December 1st 2017]: vimeo.com/245530528

Distant Feeling(s) #5 [second of the yearly reconnection, online, December 19th 2018]: vimeo.com/308709859

Distant Feeling(s) [screen recording of 'Distant Feeling(s) #5' in Active Speaker mode, by Alix Desaubliaux (participant)]: vimeo.com/308710238

---

3   Paul Virilio, *L'Inertie Polaire*, Paris: Christian Bourgois, 1990, p.72.

Distant Feeling(s) #6 [VideoVortex #12, Malta, online, September 26th 2019]: vimeo.
com/371966868

Distant Feeling(s) #7 [third of the yearly reconnection, online, December 7th 2019]: vimeo.
com/378800662

Project website with images, video, protocols and reflections: http://bram.org/distantF/ and
http://landproject.tumblr.com/distantfeelings.

Distant Feeling(s) {comments}

Voice 1: open / closed appeasement entering a side-space

Voice 2: suspended time impression of discovering a digital life, a separate entity, especially
through sound feeling of proximity complicity.

Voice 1: The sound keeps you in touch with others, it mobilizes attention, it reactivates your
feeling of presence to others.

Voice 2: The sound environment binds the whole together, one has the impression that it is
one common space, also because the sound of all participants is diffused for all the same
as one single source.

Voice 1: intrusion dependence interdependence omnipresence distance proximity.

Voice 2: Common ritual quasi-absurd experience individual journey, in relation to the other
building a common ritual through a quasi-absurd experience.

Voices 1 and 2 (not at the same time): I felt/heard your nervousness and unsettling movements, which for me was like trying to solve a problem. The problem being the chaos and
settling in with that. I had the feeling of being in a space that is nowhere.

Voice 1: Belonging to a group of silent people, whose presence permits to forget the sensation of being ridiculous or poseuse... Purposeless? To BE together for 15 min, just BEING...
Just so nice to do nothing with a globally dispersed group of people.... all these strangers
agree to close their eyes together and show their vulnerabilities to each other, or at least
show themselves vulnerable. Things were louder than people. Things -Louder People -Silent.
VULNERABILITY

Voice 2: 15 minutes against the everyday digital restlessness, building a sensorial invisible
fabric that gathers. A silent and blind encounter across each other in an electronic communion. To experience our vulnerability as a cement for the common is a way to resist speed,
performance, power; all these values that predominate in our societies.

Voice 1: I was waiting for silence to fall, after the chatter. when it occurred, there was no embrace, but a faint sensation of sharing a silent small reprieve over the constant noise and anger of the world. It is the strangest experience, to be alonesilentblindwith assumed others somewhere out there.

Voice 2: The willingness to suspend one's belief in the knowledge of the virtual proximity and connectiveness of the others. It is that knowledge that can be convincing enough to suspend disbelief and thus be silently wrapped in the telematic embrace.

Voice 1: The others embrace the virtual proximity that suspend their knowledge and simultaneous disbelief and willingly get wrapped in a convincing connectiveness...Virtual Voice: By closing your eyes you're stripped to just 'being'. Following the rules of not speaking and not looking you are left in a place of communitary lonesomeness that continues to define the everyday world of infinite information and surveillance

Voice 1: It made me think of a research that showed that certain groups of animals, birds for example, consolidate their bond, their community, by making themselves vulnerable (they perform for example a dance at a time and a place that expose them to their predators) : and those who do not participate in this ritual leave the community.

Voice 2: We were building a sensory, emotional heritage by this experience.

Voice 1: An organic acceptance of silence?

Voice 2: Was it machine feedback... that mechanical clicking and beeping? ... that mechanical clicking and beeping?

Voice 1: Machines conversing across the network only when the noisy humans finally shut up!

Voice 2: Like the toys that come alive in the magic toyshop when the children are asleep. I wanted it to get louder and louder till the whole world rang out ...

Voice 1: WE MACHINES ARE HERE AND WE ARE COMMUNICATING!

Voice 2: This is not about being mindful, or meditating, and rather about sensing and embodying and being present. And in this state of being present we may feel connected to others or we may not —if we are not, then what happens in that isolation?

Voice 1: I felt light, as if I were in a field of light, changing, living light, not with human beings, and probably because that frightened me I tried to visualize the others I knew, to imagine, how, where they were, I tried to make something I could understand of what I felt —as if they were familiar to me.

Voice 2: The 'silence' gave space to the sounds of animals, objects and machines. Close to the end I felt that I had actually entered the space that we were sharing together with others.

Voice 1: It constantly made me feel that I was there because they were also there, suddenly instead of facing them it was about these silent bodies 'looking' at something else.

Voice 2: We know we are potentially watched.

Voice 1: I gave myself in confidence to the machine, I did not think it could bug. We were a sort of resistants: we closed our eyes, we did not talk, we spend time to be together, and, that is the opposite of what we usually do on the net. If someone was watching us (and someone or something always is) she could have taken us for resistants...

Voice 2: the intimate space of silence is awkward. the absence of time and space is endless and infinite Virtual Voice: Sweet take and receive Resistance community sensitive are a trust panopticon capture.

Voice 1: A very concrete experience —just the light flickering of the in-and out-going participants shimmering through my eyelids provoking an altered state?

Voice 2: A great state of presence to oneself, to others and to an imaginary public.

Voice 1 and 2 (not at the same time): rest intentioned, meaningful meditating in between breathing suspension Relaxation Sharing Transformation.

Voice 2: We produce uninteresting data for Artificial Intelligence robots.

Voice 1: The sensation of intimacy is never 'real,' it is based on the willingness to believe and to allow closeness to become 'real' despite separation/feeling an unknown/feeling a common imagination perception of a void full of presence perception of a silence invested by technology perception of a reality mixing human and machine gift tenderness inversion.

Voice 2: Once the network is silenced of human conversation, all that is left is the hum of networked devices, the 'nervous system' of the Net.

Voice 1: [It is] an inner journey of images, desires, dreams, feelings of sadness and happiness [It is] a special...a special moment in time. [It is]a pact.

Remix by Annie Abrahams, Daniel Pinheiro. Adapted from comments from different Distant Feeling(s) iterations: Participants of Lab # 11: Screens: projection surfaces and self projections. What does the screen do with us?From Monday 13 to Saturday 18 may 2019, Cie in Vitro, laboNRV, Les Subsistances Lyon and Zara Rodríguez Prieto, James Cunningham, Camille Bloomfield, Ruth Catlow, Daniel Pinheiro, Annie Abrahams, Lisa Parra, Johannes Birringer, Randall Packer, Nicolaas Schmidt and Muriel Piqué. Recorded by Ruth Catlow and Marc Garrett for *Distant Feeling(s)#6* iteration, performed live at *Video Vortex XII*, Sepember 26, 2019 at 'Spazju Kreattiv' —Valletta, Malta.

References

Abrahams, Annie. 'Trapped to Reveal – On webcam mediated communication and collaboration', *Journal for Artistic Research* 2 (2012), https://www.jar-online.net/exposition/abstract/trapped-re-veal-webcam-mediated-communication-and-collaboration.

Abrahams, Annie, Lisa Parra, and Daniel Pinheiro. 'Distant Feelinsg(s)', screen recording of *Distant Feeling(s)* #5, https://vimeo.com/308710238.

Pinheiro, Daniel and Lisa Parra, 'Performance como Processo: Práticas de 'Embodiment' à Distância', *Performatus* 3.14 (2015), http://performatus.net/estudos/performance-como-processo/.

Virilio, Paul. *L'Inertie Polaire*, Paris: Christian Bourgois, 1990.

10 WORKING POINTS FOR ARTISTS IN A SOCIETY AFTER THE SPECTACLE

FLORIAN SCHNEIDER

10 WORKING POINTS FOR ARTISTS IN A SOCIETY AFTER THE SPECTACLE

FLORIAN SCHNEIDER

This text is a work in progress starting from 2014, as an ongoing rewriting and re-enactment of a statement by the author Peter Weiss which was published in 1965 in the Swedish newspaper Dagens Nyheter *and* Neues Deutschland, *the newspaper of the Socialist Unity Party of the German Democratic Republic (GDR). Although it does not refer explicitly to the aesthetics of online video nor comments on the effects of the measures against the spread of COVID-19, these constantly rewritten 10 working points have to be understood as an attempt to outline possible post-disaster strategies.*

1.

Every word that I write and every image that I take with the aim of a further dissemination is political. It is political insofar as, if it intends to affect other people and have impact on them, it participates in an economy of all sorts of experiences, invented spaces, and figurations which compete over the attention of their users, viewers or consumers. But every contribution, handed over to the apparatuses of communication, is not only processed on the part of the receivers, the intelligence of today's network also abstracts data from my contribution and evaluates their properties on a meta level. It is not sufficient to just try to attain the greatest possible precision in order to get my meaning through. However, my contribution also needs to become a practical critique of the political economy of affect and knowledge production in today's network societies.

2.

The choice of visual art as the expanded medium and the English language as the environment in which I am working has not only a practical function. Certainly, I choose it since it allows me to communicate across borders, rather than identifying myself as native of a specific region or tradition.

Furthermore, I have learned that seeing in the sense of the artist only begins, where any possibility of language to name and to describe has come to an end. But I am equally aware of the challenge that writing in the sense of the artist only starts to become relevant where any possibility of vision to provide evidence has reached its limit.

3.

Although globalisation has radically changed the world by synchronising and re-aligning formerly divided or fragmented powers, it has not resulted in a world that would offer equal opportunities and rights to all. On the contrary, when being applied globally, the defragmentation of power further distinguishes ever more complex relationships. Environmental disaster, climate disruptions, migration control, human rights violations or exploitation in low-wage factories establish highly differentiated, though hybrid divisions that generate ever more distinct and sometimes contradicting degrees of being subjected to and affected by them, but also benefiting from them. As much as the project of decolonizing this world seems no longer dependent on the generic idea of international solidarity among revolutionary subjectivities, conflicts and contradictions are presented and represented primarily, if not exclusively, in moralistic terms. Often, they compete even among each other over degrees of victimhood and identity. Within this rationale, especially in the Scandinavian States, the notion of politics got flattened to smooth mechanisms that are supposed to ensure inclusion and participation. Although impelled into existence by the political struggles of the past, these mechanisms of participation and inclusion are enabled through a gradual adoption of the norms of permanent monitoring and surveillance. Furthermore, they depend on the exclusive privileges of a welfare system that stem from the exploitation of resources and property claims which have to be concealed or excused by it.

4.

My task is to investigate how my words and my images are received in a world that is characterised by both increasingly imaginary property relations and hybrid divisions of labour.

Experience shows me that across the institutional contexts of a globalised art world any expression marked by the idea of an undivided, integral and unquestionable self, accompanied by conceptual experiments on otherness as a merely formal challenge will find recognition, just as even the most radical critique is appreciated, as long as it does not violate the boundaries of a concept of autonomy that inherently promises *not* to matter. While artistic freedom is presumed as exemption from the restrictions of a general economy and every new approach finds its efficient commercial intermediaries and consumers, advanced practices in the social realm are subjected to strict monitoring and impact assessment. For artists, the recognition of proprietary borders and divisions of labour implicates great difficulties, since they often take the freedom that is allocated to them to be an absolute freedom. They must cover quite a distance to get to the point where their freedom is no longer unthreatening to society.

5.

In the world of art, works have the greatest commercial value if they provide the consumer with an aesthetic pleasure, spiritual renewal or spectacular entertainment. On the other side, the practical function of the work of artists is in increasing demand in a knowledge economy that shifts from merely cognitive to affective forms of production. Formal experiment, internal monolog, poetic imagery will remain without value if they are not connecting to and interacting with the work of the scientists and across other disciplines and, in doing so, contribute to responses to the complexity of societal challenges.

Confronted with the idea of an unlimited freedom of expression we feel instrumentalised and hindered in our undertaking — as long as we consider the intrinsic value of art higher than its potential to have impact. If we recognize its potential impact and value, we can also fight for the implementation of the most daring forms. For we know, reframing the urgencies in this world requires also a radically new understanding of the role of art in society.

It is therefore a contradiction if, for example, in a University context art is held back and measured according to its instrumentality because of the power it contains, while in the world of art it escalates to the point of arbitrariness due to its lack of social responsiveness and responsibility.

6.

In the situation of crisis, I am challenged to make a choice. For which of the two sides do I decide? On which of the two sides do I see, beyond the difficulties, the contradictions and mistakes, the possibility of a development that coincides with my ideas of equality and justice? Can if overcome my own uncertainty, complicity and ambivalence and consciously incorporate into my work the societal impact that previously had only been passively expressed or unwillingly misused, in that I offered myself to the beneficiaries as an anonymous interlocutor? Can I give up the comfortable third point of view that always left a back door open to me, through which I could retreat into the no man's land of mere imagination?

7.

Just raising this question is the beginning of its answer. In the course of the investigations I undertake in order to get to an answer, I see that there are only two possibilities. And insisting on standing apart only leads to an ever-increasing irrelevance.

If I take as an example my work in a University of Science and Technology, then I find that in the world of art my indecisiveness, my insecurities, my doubts are not only accepted but are even endorsed. This is natural: As long as I only express my unease, my weariness with society, this remains a problem of a self that does not disturb the mechanisms and self-fulfilling prophecies of the market. Without restriction I am allowed to lament about the conditions of my powerlessness, since my powerlessness is predicated on the strength of the market mechanisms and relations of creative production. Even my absurdist ideas, my scorn, my irony would find acceptance, because I thereby merely attest to the munificence of the machineries that render art powerless. They appear as so self-evident that I am allowed to advocate for much that I consider advanced practice. They approve well-meaningly when I concede the opinion that art may not be instrumentalised in the production of knowledge since it rejects its divisions of cognitive and affective labour. It is after all one of the main arguments that these divisions have already largely been removed, and that today we find ourselves in a community of stakeholders with equal rights. Here I am confronted with a whole world of carefully manufactured re-affirmations of a self and the other as its own. Inasmuch as they separate production from the very environment in which it happens, this view proliferates among all strata of today's communication networks. Any opposition has partly been rendered harmless or this opposition has partly conformed due to the external successes of an illusion of inclusivity. But the question is seldom raised of the exclusiveness of this inclusivity and the question at whose cost this inclusivity was achieved. If this happens, then the questioner will by all means be most scurrilously reviled, and it becomes apparent how threadbare an emblem of the ones who feel entitled is the concept of participation and inclusion.

8.

In the creative industries my refusal to declare full compatibility to their standards is seen as a sign of surrender. Even when I point to the idiosyncrasies of today's art world and its markets, this remains meaningless as long as I don't thereby also undertake to liberate myself from the entrapment in the medium of the market and in solipsism as its practical consequence. As long as I maintain the illusion that I can retain my integrity and freedom of movement in its self-sufficiency, I will remain a prisoner of my own helplessness, cynicism or hypocrisies. And if I believe that the formats that limit artistic creativity to its commodity form can still be challenged with social engagement, I am just assuaging my conscience and idealizing the fact that I derive my living from this domain.

Criticizing the double-standards, self-indulgence and corruption of the art world, liberal establishment, patriarchal structures or corporate power all lead to nothing if they do not go beyond the binary modes of mere complaint and as long as they do not explore new ways of working together across different subjectivities. In the world of art, the artist is mainly expected to lament about economical restraint, while in the creative industries the main expectation is of an unequivocal commercial position.

9.

With this I have departed once more from the narrower conception of a local or specific context and take the globalised world as the field of activity for artistic work.

In this world the decision is made.

The imaginarily propertied and self-entitled ones of this world, in their increasingly grotesque agglomerations of power, today make efforts to confirm and defend their positions. After having exploited the need to connect and exchange after the fall of the wall, after having ruined the environmental living conditions on local and global scale, and having thereby greatly profited once more, they are now confronted with reawakening forces of a general intellect. The spectre that arises before them is no longer haunting Europe, but everywhere else they look. Even where they build their walls – at the US-Mexican border, in the Mediterranean, or in the Middle East – generations grow up that can no longer be halted. In many places they still do have the upper hand due to a backlash into fundamentalism, authoritarianism and populism. They can still spread terror by ridiculing mass intelligence and creativity; they can still oversee generations by indebting them in measures of financial extortion. But historically they are fighting a losing battle.

Against them a power is gradually establishing itself that is based on the idea that both ever-scarcer as well as the infinitely available resources of this world need to belong to every person, globally and equally. We still find ourselves in the beginning stages of this comprehensive transformation towards a common wealth as the only remaining possibility to fight against the self-destruction of our world. Many people are trying to overcome the economic and ecological difficulties arising from the divisions of labour on global scale and the distribution of the consequences of ever more catastrophic disruptions by setting themselves into motion to cross the borders of this more than ever divided world. Others are striving for reparations of the colonial injustices of the past. But everywhere the self-proclaimed global warfare, whose inner glow constantly flames up into open battles, renders visible the imbalances and points of conflict in the conception of the new divisions of this world. In this situation, the opponents of a common good and its advanced practices find a ready basis upon which to point to its failures or utopias.

Here it is the task of the artists again and again to represent the common wealth for which they are engaged, again and again to seek out the truth among the distortions.

10.

What are the forces today that could represent the creative forces within a world characterised by imaginary property relations, climate changes, migration regimes and global divisions of labour? Throughout history, the arts showed the capacity to enable the existence of multiple dimensions and new perspectives in which worlds might look very different. Over centuries artistic practices have advanced by inventing new ways of seeing, by reframing urgencies and staging new relations between knowledges.

Today, these forces are hard to be felt, especially in the former western world. Many speak about migration or decolonisation, but the protagonists appear as objects either of compassion or contempt. The result is an immersion into the virtual reality of gated communities and historical identities. It enables a suspension of disbelief that prevents from realising that, in many different respects, the struggle for freedom of movement is not about a privilege but has become the issue that affects, connects and runs through almost all societal challenges. And it is about a freedom of movement in both, a so-called real world as well as the virtual ones filled with imaginary properties and real abstractions.

I grew up myself in a society that allowed me most of the time to move relatively freely across borders. In my work and in my personal life I have spent most of my time freeing myself from the narrowness, the prejudices, and the resentment that was imposed on me by different milieus. I long believed that artistic work granted me an independence that would open the world to me.

But today I see that such an unquestioning view of art is presumptuous in the face of the fact that the differences between those who can move freely and those who cannot are tied up with and maintained by ever more hybrid divisions of labour and imaginary property relations. They are supposed to regulate the very possibilities of any form of creativity, in a society after the spectacle.

Therefore, I say: My work can only become fruitful and valuable if it stands in direct relation to the creative forces in this world. These forces are everywhere to be felt, even in the western world. But they relate to a people who are missing. Missing since they are there and not here yet, and as Paul Klee said once: "But we are looking for it".

September 2014 - May 2020 with many thanks to Barton Byg, Ted Byfield, Mari Sanden.

B Seite 4 / ND / 2. September 1965

PETER WEISS

10 Arbeitspunkte eines Autors in der geteilten Welt

Probleme des 1. Weltkrieges

Konstnären som opinionsbildare:

Tio arbetspunkter i en delad värld

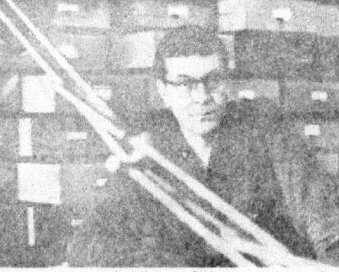

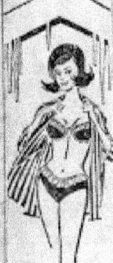
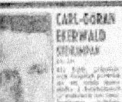
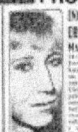
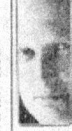
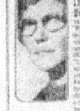
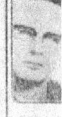

NOT REALLY LIKE BEING THERE: VERACITY AND THE IMAGE IN THE AGE OF DEEPFAKES

PATRICK LICHTY

NOT REALLY LIKE BEING THERE: VERACITY AND THE IMAGE IN THE AGE OF DEEPFAKES

PATRICK LICHTY

The mediated image and the notion of veracity have been a question from art historical, sociological, and critical perspectives for centuries. In light of the Baudrillardian revolution of the simulacrum, with AI-based media intersecting with media cultural artifacts such as Fake News, the death of veracity of the image is presenting a critical pivot to objective reality. The veracity of the image has arguably been in question long before Benjamin's seminal 'The Work of Art in the Age of Mechanical Reproduction' and its interrogation of the image's mechanical replication.[1] Benjamin's argument regarding destruction of the aura was fulfilled through Andy Warhol's Pop Art screenprints, and Warhol's arguments on mass(ive) production return in AI-based artworks made through the use of Generative Adversarial Networks (GANs). The fluid digital image is investigated by Baudrillard and Becker, as well as the notion of time, rendered or live/real-time. The issues of (re)production, (re)presentation, (re)portage and the collapses of time, space, and objective credibility are questioned as the image becomes the site of contestation of the technically enabled. To enter this discussion, let see how culture has pointed to the effects of technological implosions of space and time.

The American telephone system had slogans that were rife with allusions to McLuhanist dreams of the networked world to Virilio's notions of speed and the collapse of representation, and became prescient for the postinternet media age. 'The Next Best Thing to Being There', 'Reach out and Touch Someone', and 'The System is the Solution'[2] are all echoes of modernism that have shattered in the mediated age is an echo of modernism that have shattered in the mediated age. These slogans also echo histories of communications networks as early as mail (If one can talk in mediation in time as well as space as a tele-communication), and resonate with McLuhan's axiom, 'The Medium is the Message'. In 'Haymarket RIOT's Machine: Hacking Visual Sociology', Jon Epstein and I argued media tropes became so endemic to technoculture that it left language beholden to metaphors of multimedia communication.[3] This transformation of cultures to the terminology of media and its modes of representation also translate through their media, in the same way photography transformed painting. The issues of credibility in representation arising from Photography (Daguerre, et al) and the collapse in representative painting became evident.

---

1   Walter Benjamin, 'The Work of Art in the Age of Mechanical Reproduction', in *Illuminations*, New York: Schocken Books, 1968, 217-251. Although New Media art theorists (Lovejoy, et al) posit that Benjamin applies to the digital, I argue that Benjamin's argument is fulfilled by Warhol.
2   See Beatriceco, 'Bell System Advertisements', beatriceco.com/bti/porticus/bell/bellsystem_ads.html
3   Lichty, Patrick. 'Haymarket RIOT's Machine: Hacking Visual Sociology', in Morgan Currie (ed.), *Variant Analyses,* Amsterdam: Institute of Networked Cultures, 2013, pp. 12-26. The first draft of this essay appeared in 1996, predicting the linguistic adoption of media metaphor in postinternet life.

Mediation and Veracity

The history of the image's veracity dates to the caves of Lascaux but took a critical turn in the mid 1800's with the rise of photography. On this topic, one can go as far back to prehistory or the Classical Era, but we will begin with Dauguerre. To quote Bellinetti, 'Upon seeing the first daguerreotype around 1840, the French painter Paul Delaroche (1797-1856), declared: "From today, painting is dead."'[4] This refers to the pre-photographic painting's use in the representation of reality, the disruption of which had revealed itself with Manet's 1962 *Luncheon on the Grass,* with its muted palette and distorted composition. Realism had died.

Mediation and Veracity: Representational Violence

An early contestational site regarding insitutional agendas of veracity of the image is that of semantic framing of the image. In *Concerning the Pain of Others*, Susan Sontag dissects the use of photography to depict the violence of war. Sontag's analysis of war photography describes differences between American Civil War Photographer Matthew Brady versus Crimean War documentarian Roger Fenton (1855). According to Sontag, Fenton's orders from the Crown were to show scenes that human but not grisly; a romantic, sterilized version of War. Conversely, the Lincoln administration sent Brady's crew to show war's horror; the dead and the dying as a 'shock and awe' tactic of the time.[5] Even though both wars are known for their brutality, the representational differences between the two are stark. Fenton's work shows a genteel image of war, and Brady's a bitter reality. The framing of the milieu imbues context for the tone of the scene, its politics, and empathy (or not) for the subject. Visual sociologist Douglas Harper states that the visual representations of the world differ starkly from the textual and, according to his predecessor Howard Becker, that we can derive meaning about cultures and events merely by the act of looking.[6] In the context of our new imaging technologies, considering images in terms of their meaning, or even pattern, is no longer sufficient, as there is no longer an eye, or a subjectivity involved.

Media culture is confronted with intersections of the algorithmic, the simulacrum and issues of remediation. The reframing of painting can be seen in the Obvious Group's *Portrait of Edmond Belamy*, a print generated by a GAN system. This print, 'signed' by the algorithm that generated it, got $432,000 at a 2018 auction.[7] Labor, once abstracted through the apparatus

---

4   Caterina Bellinetti, 'From Today Painting Is Dead: Photography's Revolutionary Effect', *Art & Object*, 9 April 2019, www.artandobject.com/shorts/today-painting-dead-photographys-revolutionary-effect. And ever since the invention of photography, each technological innovation has led artists to fear for their relevance. See: McLuhan's thought on media displacement.

5   Susan Sontag, *Regarding the Pain of Others*, London: Picador, 2010.

6   Douglas Harper, *Visual Sociology*, London: Routledge, 2012.

7   Christie's, 'Is Artificial Intelligence Set to Become Art's next Medium?', *The First Piece of AI-Generated Art to Come to Auction | Christie's*, 12 December 2018, www.christies.com/features/A-collaboration-between-two-artists-one-human-one-a-machine-9332-1.aspx. What is problematic with *Portrait* is that the code downloaded to generate the work was created by researcher Robbie Barrat (DCGAN) who had been doing this work for some time, and the image was merely a digital print. The cultural function of this work was to create artworld desire over a 'first' denoting technological anxiety over Bejaminian (re) production and FOMO.

of the camera, is further displaced by that of the algorithm, and is given valuation through capitalization of the image. More important is the shift of representational apparatus (Camera to GAN) that creates a capacity to generate vast numbers of iterations. Through the GAN's abstraction from the painting to photograph to generated image-painting — hypermediating the work of art — we recall Benjamin's notion of the death of the aura.

Jay Bolter and Richard Grusin, in their book *Remediation*, reflect upon the movie *Strange Days* and the direct neural interface called The Wire, which is 'Like TV, only better!'[8] Their ideas of Immediacy and Hypermediacy resonate with the Baudrillardian hyperrealeality image conveying semantics of not just seeing the airplane pilot, but being one. This is the position that Joseph DeLappe's video game *Killbox* works, placing the interactor in the locus of the subject of drone operator.[9] This hypermediacy places appearance of experience in place of the experience itself (Hypermediacy vs. hyperreality). The crash between Bolter and Grusin's Hypermediacy and Baudrillard's remediation relating to the simulacrum comes in the U.S. *Airforce's Airman Challenge*.[10] This game continues the tradition of U.S. military experiements in gamification, like the *America's Army* shooter, into the milieu of drone warfare.[11] The game de-abstracts cultural spaces like *Killbox* and places them into the veracious space of a recruiting simulation, remediating the issues of Forster and Brady into that of game-space. The game-space becomes aligned with real combat-space.

Modalities of Hyperreality and Veracity: Even Better than Being There.

Veracity and media have historically been linked through mediation. In *Virtual Art* Oliver Grau states that the earliest predecessors to these were the Bacchic mystery rooms, or even the caves of Lascaux, with the immersive experience attempting to create a substitutive image through surrounding the viewer.[12] It is this verisimilitude, from painting, to photography, to cinema (let us not forget the terror inspired by the Lumiere's train), that leads to a believed veracity. This notion of early verisimilitude has been revisited by users of Neural Net AI software. In 2019, Dennis Shirayev used AI to upscale the Lumiere Brothers' film, *L'Arrivée d'un train en gare de La Ciotat* to 4K resolution.[13] While rescans and upscales of classic films are

8   Richard Grusin, *Remediation: Understanding New Media*, Cambridge, MA: MIT Press, 1999.
9   'International Collaboration Killbox Explores Drone Warfare', *Creative Scotland*, 2015, www.
     creativescotland.com/what-we-do/the-10-year-plan/connecting-themes/digital/international-
     collaboration-killbox-explores-drone-warfare. One of the earliest media art pieces to interactively
     address social justice and drone warfare.
10   Active Theory, 'Airman Challenge / Active Theory,' *Active Theory*, 2019, activetheory.net/work/airman-
     challenge. Testing *Airman Challenge* is to witness open manipulation of youth to be recruited in forms of
     warfare that have the highest turnover rate and suicide in the US Armed forces.
11   Gus Mastrapa, 'America's Army Game Cost Taxpayers $33M', *Wired*, 22 December 2017,
     www.wired.com/2009/12/americas-army-budget/.
12   Oliver Grau, *Virtual Art: from Illusion to Immersion*, Cambridge, MA: MIT Press, 2007.
13   Timothy Lee, 'Someone Used Neural Networks to Upscale a Famous 1896 Video to 4k Quality
     (Updated)', *Ars Technica*, 4 February 2020, arstechnica.com/science/2020/02/someone-used-neural-
     networks-to-upscale-a-famous-1896-video-to-4k-qual. In viewing this upscaling, there are significant
     differences between versions to account for cropping and oversampling to compensate for errors. The
     results are still uncanny.

commonplace, this 50-second film's remediative quality render it unique, as accounts of the film describe it being mistaken for a camera obscura: creating terror (a terror of the unreal), then astonishment amongst its audience. Likewise, the upscaled version creates a sense of awe in the realism it communicates, and the intersection of this film with AI technology places the discourse of representation and remediation firmly in the AI space.

Real Violence: Representational Violence II

Jordan Wolfson's *Real Violence* at the Whitney Biennial takes the viscerality of first-person violence, placing it into game engine-based VR.[14] To quote Artsy's Isaac Kaplan, 'In a scene that unfolds over 90 seconds, an anonymous man (played by the artist) takes a baseball bat and then his shoe to the head of a kneeling victim. A Hebrew prayer plays over the scene until what was once a face is reduced to pulp',[15] In its lack of abstraction, *Real Violence* takes brutality out of the symbolic or stylized realms of *Call of Duty* or *Fortnite* into a more veracious space. Real Violence calls into question violence-as-simulacrum, grounding it through the space of viewer-as-witness.

Deeply Artificial Reality: Enter Deepfakes

Alex Reben's Deeply Artificial Trees,[16] a remediation of Bob Ross' *Joy of Painting* as seen through Google's Deep Dream — an algorithm written by Google engineer Alexander Mordvintsev to test the computer vision capacities of neural nets in the Google system[17] — is an absurdist take on the role of AI subsets of neural nets in image creation. Its result was psychedelic renderings in which Ross mutters to himself with images of dogs fluttering in and out of view. (Fig. 1) This is due to the fact that the initial versions of Google's neural net being trained on a subset of 120 images of dogs. The real allusion that Mordvintsev, then Reben, made in terms of the hallucinatory neural net to video was that Deep Dream was akin to a Heideggerian baby-as-tool seeing a dog and then seeing the world as a procession of dogs. From a conversation with AI researcher Steve DiPaola from Simon Fraser University, he states that the neural net reflects its initial set of conditions.[18] If you give it dogs, the world will look like dogs.

---

14   Alexandra Schwartz, 'Confronting the "Shocking" Virtual-Reality Artwork at the Whitney Biennial', *The New Yorker*, 19 June 2017, www.newyorker.com/culture/cultural-comment/confronting-the-shocking-virtual-reality-artwork-at-the-whitney-biennial.

15   Isaac Kaplan, 'The Gut-Wrenching VR Work That's Got the Art World Talking about Violence', *Artsy*, 17 March 2017, www.artsy.net/article/artsy-editorial-gut-wrenching-vr-work-art-talking-violence. In seeing this work, to witness a Jewish man being beaten to death to a Kaddish was of questionable taste, but the sensationalism created a suitable press spectacle.

16   DJ Pangburn, 'Artificial Intelligence Turned Bob Ross into a Terrifying Psychedelic Nightmare', *Vice*, 7 April 2017, www.vice.com/en_us/article/ezwyb4/bob-ross-alexander-reben-neural-network-nightmare. There are other examples of processed viral video, including clips of the Lebanese former porn star, Mia Khalifa.

17   Steven Levy, 'Inside Deep Dreams: How Google Made Its Computers Go Crazy', *Wired*, Conde Nast, 16 June 2017, www.wired.com/2015/12/inside-deep-dreams-how-google-made-its-computers-go-crazy/.

18   Patrick Lichty, Interview with Steve DiPaola, Simon Fraser University, July 2016 (unpublished) In this interview, Steve explained the training of neural nets, including the reasons why initial versions of Deep

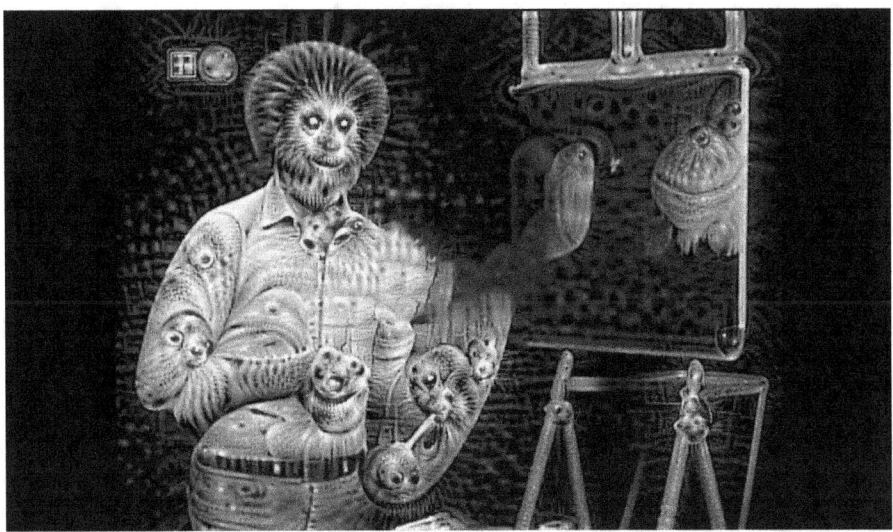

Fig. 1: Deeply Artificial Trees, Image Courtest Alex Reben.

The act of seeing one thing in terms of another (discrimination, in AI terms) technologically devolves from Google code dumps over time into endless numbers of populist phone apps, like Prisma, Meitu (the Chinese 'cute' selfie app). Faceapp, a Russian app, was the subject of a 2019 meme by involving global celebrities to age themselves. This was expanded across genres, to even include classical paintings like the Mona Lisa. Despite the 'fun' quality of these populist apps, what these neural-net driven applications point towards is its sinister big brother, the Deepfake.

 This technology, in which a part of one person, typically the face, is seamlessly mapped onto another in time-based media, gained notoriety for mapping stars' likenesses onto adult video. Other notable examples include a video created by the Stanford University team where they realistically controlled likenesses of political leaders in real time,[19] and a movie created by the company Canny AI where they created a scenario in which world leaders simultaneously join to sing John Lennon's 'Imagine' (Fig. 2).[20] While this scene of the simultaneous declaration of Lennon's sentiments around the world is a key irony in 2020, it nevertheless inverts the contemporary use of Deepfakes as troll apparatus to speculate on positive and critical uses of the technology.

Dream focused on dogs.

19   Justus Thies, et al, 'Face2Face: Real-Time Face Capture and Reenactment of RGB Videos', *Face2Face: Real-Time Face Capture and Reenactment of RGB Videos*, 2016, www.graphics.stanford.edu/~niessner/thies2016face.html.

20   Mark Seymour. 'Canny AI: Imagine World Leaders Singing', *Fxguide*, 12 April 2019, www.fxguide.com/ fxfeatured/canny-ai-imagine-world-leaders-singing/. One of the most beautiful applications of critical Deepfakes. When approached to create a deepfake of Donald Trump reciting Chaplin's Little Dictator speech, CannyAI declined.

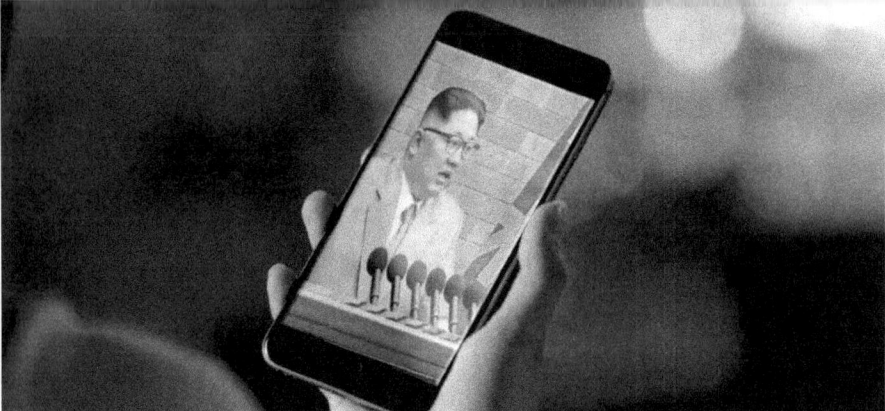

Fig.2: Imagine, Deepfake video with w/Kim Jong Un lipsyncing Lennon's iconic song. Image Courtesy CannyAI.

Bill Posters' set of Deepfake videos dealing with the SPECTRE security weakness in Intel processors[21] portrays celebrities like Kim Kardashian, Marina Abramovic, and Mark Zuckerberg stating that the use of data manipulation has benefitted them immensely. In so doing, Posters called for the cessation of abusive data practices like harvesting personal information through program weaknesses. While these playful pokes at major cultural figures about systems security flaws asks how megacorporations and nation-states can exploit them, the bigger question is of the Deepfakes themselves, and how they bend objective reality.

Cultural Remediations Besides the Deepfake

We can find some of the earlier attempts at remediations/recreations are in 3D animated spectacles, which are neither hoaxes nor Deepfakes, but raise questions of their own. At the 2012 Coachella concert, fans were shocked to see a virtual 3D Tupac Shakur that performed with Dr Dre and Snoop Dogg.[22] The production company, Musion, used a form of the Pepper's Ghost optical illusion that uses a tilted glass and fabric scrim to create an illusion of the performer. This was expanded to include performances by virtual anime idol Miku Hatsune, Gorillaz, Maria Callas and iconic Egyptian singer Umm Kalthoum (Fig. 3).[23] But even more startling recreations/remediations have taken place.

21   Samantha Cole, 'This Deepfake of Mark Zuckerberg Tests Facebook's Fake Video Policies', *Vice*, 11 June 2019, www.vice.com/en_us/article/ywyxex/deepfake-of-mark-zuckerberg-facebook-fake-video-policy. While a bit flat in using likenesses artworld figures to address larger sociopolitical issues (SPECTRE/ Meltdown bugs), the spots are near flawless.

22   James Robertson, ''What up, Coachella!': Tupac Resurrected by Incredible Lifelike Hologram at California Festival - Video', *Mirror*, 29 May 2012, www.mirror.co.uk/lifestyle/going-out/music/tupac-returns-at-coachella-with-snoop-dogg-796455.

23   Essam Al-Ghalib, 'Umm Kulthum Returns Virtually for Tantora Show in Al-Ula', *Arab News*, Arabnews, 27 January 2019, www.arabnews.com/node/1442481/saudi-arabia. Beyond the scope of this essay are also erotic analogues of Miku Hatsune, or 'virtual camgirls' like Projekt Melody that are likewise disrupting the adult industry. Also, virtual models like Shudu have been hired by Rhianna's brand to promote makeup.

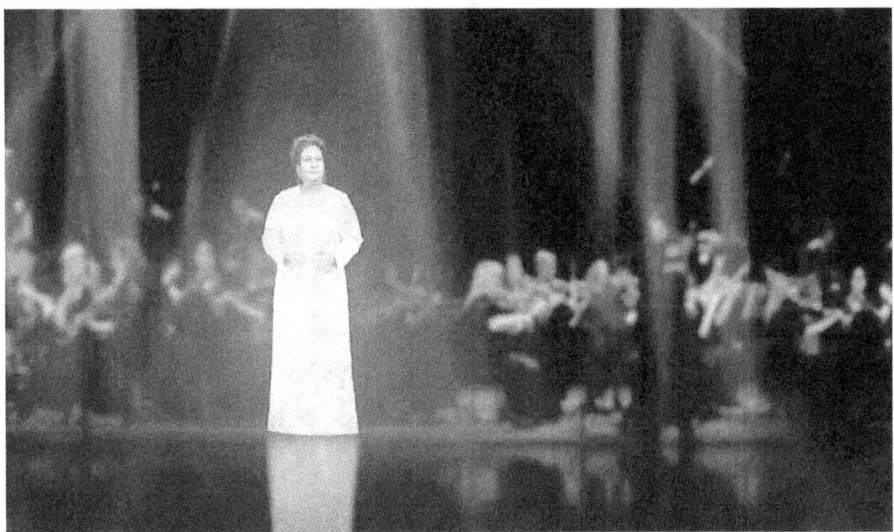

Fig. 3: Umm Kalthoum holographic concert, Image Courtesy Dubai Opera

Hoax to Fake News: The Yes Men

The history of the media prank or hoax is nothing new, with an early exemplar being Jonathan Swift's *A Modest Proposal*.[24] In the contemporary era, the media hoaxsters RTMark/The Yes Men offered a kind of predecessor to 'fake news' in their media stunts. Tactical media's function is in its incredulity; that it is intended to provoke a revealing of the truth. Conversely, fake news presents 'alternative facts' to convince a public — who wish to believe in an authority (media, government or otherwise) — of alternate realities divorced from the truth. In 2004, someone calling himself 'Jude Finisterra' appeared on BBC Global News to make an announcement that Dow Chemical, had sold Union Carbide, the company responsible for over 3,700 deaths and 15,000 injury claims, sold Carbide for $12 billion.[25] In support of a news release on the website *dowethics.com,* he announced that money in return allegedly would be given to the people of Bhopal to help in their medical care, and building of medical facilities. (Fig. 4) Finisterra, who was actually Yes Man Andy Bichlbaum (Jacques Servin), He was on for some time, describing Bhopal as a 'Disaster for the World', and that its citizens should get more than the $500/person proposed. The stunt caused Dow stocks to dip over $3 billion temporarily, to recover after being found out. In the age of the Deepfake, one could imagine the visage of CEO William S. Stavropoulos making the statement. While the use of pranks still center on their being found out, fake news lives and dies on maintaining the illusion of its veracity.

---

24   Jonathan Swift, 'A Modest Proposal', Champaign, IL; Boulder, CO: Project Gutenberg; NetLibrary, 1999.
25   Vincent Graff, 'Meet the Yes Men Who Hoax the World', *The Guardian*, 13 December 2004, www.theguardian.com/media/2004/dec/13/mondaymediasection5.

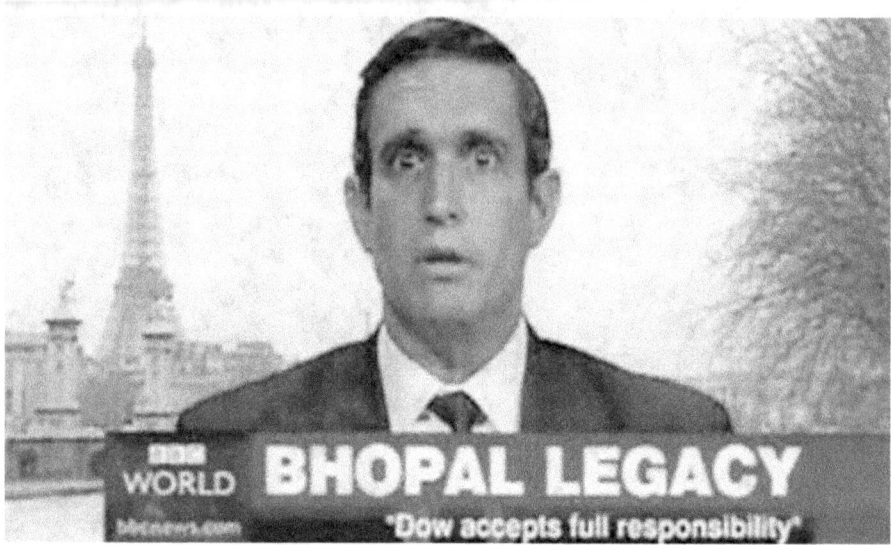

Fig. 4, Yes Men Bhopal Hoax. Image Courtesy The Yes Men

Given the veracity of the image, the hoax is a far more serious prospect since the emergence of the Deepfake. According to sources, the Deepfake may not be detectable by 2023-5.[26] In Baudrillard's seminal essay, *The Gulf War Did Not Take Place*, he argued that the televised image was not a simulacrum only in terms of temporal disconnect, but also in terms of framing and editing.[27] Much as in the case of Brady and Foster, what was to be seen was the image prepared for the 'folks back home' as in its modulation of depicted violence. Combined with the six second delay in telecommunications from the Middle East to North America, Baudrillard suggests that the event represented at the television in North America is not what is happening NOW. While the editors and cameramen frame the mise en scène in a certain way, the temporal disconnect also separates the viewer from the event. Deepfakes and remediations detach the subject from semiotic time-space continuity to hand in the mediascape as floating signifiers that are inexplicably real, but with no grounding in reality.

Intermezzo: Paranoia of the Rear-View Image

A metaphor for the AI image is that of the technological images created by the Claude Glass. This 18th-Century device was a curved mirror that allowed the user to create an elliptical image in recto.[28] A sort of Instagram of its time, it created what Peraica refers to as a 'dorsality' in vision. This can also be a metaphor for the image of the technological apparatus, as the camera has a rear-vision which can be extended from camera to AI-based

26   Alex Engler, 'Fighting Deepfakes When Detection Fails', *Brookings*, 19 November 2019, www.brookings. edu/research/fighting-deepfakes-when-detection-fails/. The issue with entirely plausible Deepfakes is that acritical onlookers do not get that they are fake, thus stating the polemic.
27   Jean Baudrillard, *The Gulf War Did Not Take Place*, Bloomington: Indiana University Press, 1995.
28   Sabine Melchior-Bonnet, et al. *The Mirror: A History*, London: Routledge, 2002.

image. To draw another metaphor, the Claude glass became the rear-view mirror, which has the inscription, 'objects in (the) mirror are closer than they appear'. The metaphorical connections arise in *Jurassic Park,* when the Tyrannosaurus Rex is shown chasing the fleeing vehicle through the mirror, maw agape. This mirrors Peraica's notions of rear-view paranoia[29], with the rear-view image having qualities of the stalker, or the implications of technology's staring at you through the rear view (only). The dorsal, or view from the apparatus, is the abyss that stares back.

This Election-Tampering Cat Does Not Exist

While the use of Deepfakes as rendered-time remap/remediation of identity, one important ramification of GANs is that of generated reality. A 2019 NBC News article reported the use of this technology by 'The BL', a publication made by US-Based Epoch Media, with ties to the Trump-supporting Vietnamese Falun Gong sect.[30] While this is merely one concrete example of using neural net 'Fakes' as proxies for political manipulation of social media, the implications of this in the 2020 American elections is clear. This includes sites like thispersondoesnotexist.com and thiscatdoesnotexist.com, that use GANs and neural nets to generate profile shots of entirely fictitious individuals, or cats.[31]

The use of Deepfakes as political and terrorist tool suggests even more frightening scenarios. The most obvious is that of a fake announcement of a nuclear strike from a world leader, but more banal cases of horrors unfolding in real time are also possible. A CNN report, *What is a Deepfake, Explained*[32] (CNN,2019) showed the example of Jordan Peel imitating President Barack Obama as well as research from Stanford and Max Planck Universities. This technology is a form of video 'puppetry', where a reference actor's voice and expressions are mapped onto the source video. Had Deepfakes been in existence a decade ago, one could imagine simulacra of Osama bin Laden persisting long after his death. This brings forth questions on the generation of such videos for the potential to foster extremism and or genocide, such as the G. I. Cody terror hoax in 2005, in which a terror video of a supposed missing US soldier was actually that of a doll called Cody. This was the subject of Michael Rakowitz' video art project, *The Ballad of Special Ops Cody* (2017), which was shown at the 2019 Sharjah Biennial. As stated by the Sharjah Art Foundation:

---

29 Ana Peraica, 'Selfies and the World Behind Our Back', *membrana 4*, 2018. Peraica's examination of the Claude Glass was ripe with fearsome metaphors of the ghost in the mirror, from Jurassic park to the Slenderman Meme.

30 Ben Collins, 'Facebook Says a pro-Trump Media Outlet Used Artificial Intelligence to Create Fake People and Push Conspiracies', *NBCNews.com*, 21 December 2019, www.nbcnews.com/tech/tech-news/facebook-says-pro-trump-media-outlet-used-artificial-intelligence-create-n1105951. As of this writing, this is of great interest to the writer, and developments are happening in real-time, possibly of importance to the 2020 USA election.

31 Charlie Spargo, 'This Cat Does Not Exist: Intelligent AI Creates Fictitious Feline Faces', *Prolific London*, 22 February 2019, www.prolificlondon.co.uk/news/tech/2019/02/cat-does-not-exist-intelligent-ai-creates-fictitious-feline-faces. In addition to testing the realism of the Nvidia software, it is the source of bizarre AI-generated cat memes.

32 'What Is a Deepfake, Explained', *CNN*, 1 February 2019, edition.cnn.com/videos/business/2019/02/01/deepfakes-interactive-what-is-a-deepfake-intro-orig.cnn.

The Ballad of Special Ops Cody takes as its starting point a 2005 incident in which an Iraqi insurgent group posted a photograph online of a captured US soldier named John Adam. The group threatened to kill him if US-held prisoners in Iraq were not set free. The US military took the ultimatum seriously but were unable to identify John Adam within their ranks. As it turns out, this soldier was actually Special Ops Cody, a US infantry action figure made to exacting detail...[33]

While absurd, the idea of a Deepfake created in such a situation does not seem unreasonable given that the G.I. Cody Hoax fooled the US military for a period of time, it points to possible Deepfake controversies in the future. Proposals to control or mitigate the impact of this technology range from regulation of deep learning to the prosecution of malicious Deepfakes, similar to various countries' laws against exploitative and indecent media. In contrast, tech giants such as Facebook and Google are claiming to seek to use Deepfakes to fight them. According to the MIT Technology Review, Google and partners have released over 3,000 AI-generated videos to help improve the FaceForensics detection standard.[34] Conversely, Facebook has launched a Deepfake Detection Challenge where they are working with institutions like UC Berkeley to create their own databases and detection protocols.[35] However, as in the case of cryptography, such initiatives are merely the indications of a cybernetic arms race.

Issues of veracity and mediation have raised representational, social, and political ramifications. With the advent of streaming media and the ramifications of the intersection of AI, Immersion, and remediations like Deepfakes, when incorporated into media phenomena like Fake News, the hope is that there will be a possibility for media literate parts of society to be able to triangulate between AI countermeasures, fact-checking media and critical observation. The goal is to filter the incongruous with only minimal effect to find some sort of semiotic continuity between the origin and the target. But with 48% of the world's population having access to the Internet as of 2019[36], a billion more with access to televised media, even if an optimistic 20-24% of the world's Internet population is critically literate, and this leaves 4-5 billion susceptible to the Baudrillardian world of the simulacrum. In this context, Debord's ubiquitous *Society of the Spectacle*[37] becomes more an actuality than a speculative reality. It 'isn't quite like being there', but with current technologies moving forward, it appears to be getting close in its verisimilitude.

33 Sharjah Art Foundation, 'The Ballad of Special Ops Cody (2017)', sharjahart.org/sharjah-art-foundation/projects/the-ballad-of-special-ops-cody-2017.
34 Karen Hao, 'Google Has Released a Giant Database of Deepfakes to Help Fight Deepfakes,' *MIT Technology Review*, 8 December 2019, www.technologyreview.com/f/614426/google-has-released-a-giant-database-of-deepfakes-to-help-fight-deepfakes/.
35 Rachel Metz, 'Facebook Is Making Its Own Deepfake Videos to Help Fight Them', *CNN*, 5 September 2019, edition.cnn.com/2019/09/05/tech/facebook-deepfake-detection-challenge/index.html.
36 ITP Publications, 'Measuring Digital Development Facts and Figures' *2019*.
37 Guy Debord, 'The Society of the Spectacle'. New York: Zone Books, 1994.

References

Active Theory. 'Airman Challenge / Active Theory', *Active Theory*, 2019, activetheory.net/work/airman-challenge.

Al-Ghalib, Essam, 'Umm Kulthum Returns Virtually for Tantora Show in Al-Ula', *Arab News*, 27 January 2019, www.arabnews.com/node/1442481/saudi-arabia.

Baudrillard, Jean. *The Gulf War Did Not Take Place*, Bloomington: Indiana University Press, 1995

Beatriceco, 'Bell System Advertisements', *Bell System Advertisements*, beatriceco.com/bti/porticus/bell/bellsystem_ads.html

Bellinetti, Caterina. "From Today Painting Is Dead': Photography's Revolutionary Effect', *Art & Object*, 9 April 2019, www.artandobject.com/shorts/today-painting-dead-photographys-revolutionary-effect.

Benjamin, Walter. 'The Work of Art in the Age of Mechanical Reproduction', in *Illuminations*. New York: Schocken Books, 1968, pp. 217-251.

Christie's. 'Is Artificial Intelligence Set to Become Art's next Medium?', *The First Piece of AI-Generated Art to Come to Auction | Christie's*, 12 December 2018, www.christies.com/features/A-collaboration-between-two-artists-one-human-one-a-machine-9332-1.aspx.

Cole, Samantha. 'This Deepfake of Mark Zuckerberg Tests Facebook's Fake Video Policies', *Vice*, 11 June 2019, www.vice.com/en_us/article/ywyxex/deepfake-of-mark-zuckerberg-facebook-fake-video-policy.

Collins, Ben. 'Facebook Says a pro-Trump Media Outlet Used Artificial Intelligence to Create Fake People and Push Conspiracies', *NBCNews.com*, 21 December 2019, www.nbcnews.com/tech/tech-news/facebook-says-pro-trump-media-outlet-used-artificial-intelligence-create-n1105951.

Debord, Guy. 'The Society of the Spectacle', New York: Zone Books, 1994.

Engler, Alex. 'Fighting Deepfakes When Detection Fails', *Brookings*, 19 November 2019, www.brookings.edu/research/fighting-deepfakes-when-detection-fails/.

Epes, Anthony. 'What John Berger Can Teach Us about Photography' *Anthony Epes*, 6 March 2019, www.citiesatdawn.com/what-john-berger-can-teach-us-about-photography/.

Graff, Vincent. 'Meet the Yes Men Who Hoax the World', *The Guardian*, www.theguardian.com/media/2004/dec/13/mondaymediasection5.

Grau, Oliver. *Virtual Art: from Illusion to Immersion*, Cambridge, MA: MIT Press, 2007.

Grusin, Richard. *Remediation: Understanding New Media*, Cambridge, MA: MIT Press, 1999.

Hao, Karen. 'Google Has Released a Giant Database of Deepfakes to Help Fight Deepfakes', *MIT Technology Review*, 8 December 2019, www.technologyreview.com/f/614426/google-has-released-a-giant-database-of-deepfakes-to-help-fight-deepfakes/.

Harper, Douglas. *Visual Sociology*, London: Routledge, 2012.

'International Collaboration Killbox Explores Drone Warfare', *Creative Scotland*, 2015, www.creativescotland.com/what-we-do/the-10-year-plan/connecting-themes/digital/international-collaboration-killbox-explores-drone-warfare.

ITP Publications, 'Measuring Digital Development Facts and Figures', 2019.

Kaplan, Isaac. 'The Gut-Wrenching VR Work That's Got the Art World Talking about Violence', *Artsy*, 17 March 2017, www.artsy.net/article/artsy-editorial-gut-wrenching-vr-work-art-talking-violence.

Lee, Timothy 'Someone Used Neural Networks to Upscale a Famous 1896 Video to 4k Quality (Updated)', *Ars Technica*, 4 February 2020, arstechnica.com/science/2020/02/someone-used-neural-networks-to-upscale-a-famous-1896-video-to-4k-qualit

Levy, Steven. 'Inside Deep Dreams: How Google Made Its Computers Go Crazy', *Wired*, 16 June 2017, www.wired.com/2015/12/inside-deep-dreams-how-google-made-its-computers-go-crazy/.

Lichty, Patrick. 'Haymarket RIOT's Machine: Hacking Visual Sociology', in Morgan Currie (ed.), *Variant Analyses*, Amsterdam: Institute of Networked Cultures, 2013, p. 12-26.

_____. Interview with Steve DiPaola, Simon Fraser University, July 2016 (Unpublished).

Mastrapa, Gus. 'America's Army Game Cost Taxpayers $33M', *Wired*, 22 December 2017, www.wired.com/2009/12/americas-army-budget/.

Melchior-Bonnet, Sabine, et al. *The Mirror: A History*, London: Routledge, 2002.

Metz, Rachel. 'Facebook Is Making Its Own Deepfake Videos to Help Fight Them', *CNN*, 5 September 2019, edition.cnn.com/2019/09/05/tech/facebook-deepfake-detection-challenge/index.html.

Pangburn, DJ. 'Artificial Intelligence Turned Bob Ross into a Terrifying Psychedelic Nightmare', *Vice*, 7 April 2017, www.vice.com/en_us/article/ezwyb4/bob-ross-alexander-reben-neural-network-nightmare.

Peraica, Ana. 'Selfies and the World Behind Our Back', *membrana 4*, 2018.

Reilly, Ian. *Media Hoaxing: the Yes Men and Utopian Politics*. Lanham, MD: Lexington Books, 2018.

Robertson, James. '"What up, Coachella!": Tupac Resurrected by Incredible Lifelike Hologram at California Festival - Video', *Mirror*, 29 May 2012, www.mirror.co.uk/lifestyle/going-out/music/tupac-returns-at-coachella-with-snoop-dogg-796455.

Schwartz, Alexandra. 'Confronting the "Shocking" Virtual-Reality Artwork at the Whitney Biennial', *The New Yorker*, The New Yorker, 19 June 2017, www.newyorker.com/culture/cultural-comment/confronting-the-shocking-virtual-reality-artwork-at-the-whitney-biennial.

Seymour, Mark. 'Canny AI: Imagine World Leaders Singing', *Fxguide*, 12 April 2019, www.fxguide.com/fxfeatured/canny-ai-imagine-world-leaders-singing/.

Sharjah Art Foundation. 'The Ballad of Special Ops Cody (2017)', sharjahart.org/sharjah-art-foundation/projects/the-ballad-of-special-ops-cody-2017.

Sontag, Susan. *Regarding the Pain of Others*, London: Picador, 2010.

Spargo, Charlie. 'This Cat Does Not Exist: Intelligent AI Creates Fictitious Feline Faces', *Prolific London*, 22 February 2019, www.prolificlondon.co.uk/news/tech/2019/02/cat-does-not-exist-intelligent-ai-creates-fictitious-feline-faces.

Swift, Jonathan. A Modest Proposal. Champaign, Ill.: Boulder, Colo.:Project Gutenberg; NetLibrary, 1999.

Thies, Justus, et al. 'Face2Face: Real-Time Face Capture and Reenactment of RGB Videos', *Face2Face: Real-Time Face Capture and Reenactment of RGB Videos*, 2016, www.graphics.stanford.edu/~niessner/thies2016face.html.

'What Is a Deepfake, Explained', *CNN*, 1 February 2019, edition.cnn.com/videos/business/2019/02/01/deepfakes-interactive-what-is-a-deepfake-intro-orig.cnn.

HORROR STORIES AND FACE FILTERS: THE SECOND-PERSON DRAMA OF HYPEREPHEMERAL VIDEO

GABRIEL MENOTTI

HORROR STORIES AND FACE FILTERS:
THE SECOND-PERSON DRAMA OF HYPEREPHEMERAL VIDEO

GABRIEL MENOTTI

Digital online media has made the image virtually omnipresent. Through the combination of pervasive high-speed broadband and cloud storage, pictures have achieved an unprecedented degree of availability. There seems to be no need to reproduce them anymore. Their current regime of existence is apparently everywhere and seemingly eternal. One does not need to go after them in museums, movie theaters, cathedrals, or some dusty album stuck in the bottom drawer. They are already *here* even when they are not, soaking the ether of connections.

Our primary mode of relation with them has shifted accordingly. Pictures are no longer mere things to be looked at, but rather ghosts that keep us company, always ready to be conjured into being. As convenient as this might be for many forms of visual media practice, it creates new challenges for their management as information systems. The logic of redundancy that makes those systems robust often prevents their proper circumscription. To say that the 'internet never forgets' emphasizes the fact that it clutters the big historical picture with petty details.

Sorting every image ever sent and received has become a nontrivial, rarely accomplished work of its own. Our machines run out of space without us having ever saved anything relevant. Files get lost because there are too many. Meaning can hardly be cemented. This curatorial negligence propagates a risk of dangerous misplacements. Before, past mistakes could be kept out of sight, out of mind. Now, they are the inexhaustible evidentiary fuel of cancel culture. Digital footprints become calcified as personal traits, and private snapshots easily turn into unforgiving sources of cruel public spectacle, cyberbullying, or revenge porn.

In this world of unyielding images, the appeal of hyper-ephemeral digital media formats should come as a given. They first appeared in 2012, in the unassuming guise of *snaps*: self-effacing pictures and videos swapped via the Snapchat mobile messaging app. Each was made to last 1-10 seconds, as defined by the sender, and could not be replayed more than once. The data was deleted from the company servers soon after the snap was opened by the recipient. In order to inhibit leaks, the sender was informed whenever its message was opened and if a screenshot of it was taken.

These features represented a deliberate reaction against the principle of total storage governing online media and the high behavioral and aesthetic standards it enforced. With their adoption, Snapchat embraced the reality of networked photography as a dynamic communication medium, removed from the tradition underpinned by the capture of Kodak/Bressonian 'decisive moments.' In place of this tradition, Snapchat encouraged the cultivation of movie practices for whom the persistence of the image as a historical object is irrelevant, if not derogatory.

Many of these practices revolve around the transmission of time- and audience-sensitive content that might be unfit, unmeaningful, or irrelevant for outsider parties. Early in Snapchat's release, developers mentioned its usage by high school kids 'as a new way to pass notes in class', behind the teacher's back.[1] Unsurprisingly, the app soon became known as the perfect sexting tool. Its prominence for the trade of erotic selfies would be acknowledged years later, in the cover design of the first non-nude issue of Playboy magazine.[2]

In a time when even livestreams linger on the web, overstaying their welcome, the hyper-ephemeral picture creates forms for an event to be shared while remaining fleeting, thus enabling more complex modalities of online (co-)presence and participation. Overall, the transience built in the system contributes to an atmosphere of greater intimacy. Free from the pressures of everlasting records, users become less self-conscious about expressing honest opinions, desires, and emotions. This apparently greater receptivity for imperfections (which may well be a lack of conditions to put them in check) makes Snapchat seem like a social media platform more *personal* than others. In their FOMO-inducing exclusivity, Snaps feel closer to their missing signified, and paradoxically more concrete representations thereof.

A year after its release, Snapchat would expand these capabilities by supplementing its instant messaging service with *stories*, a function that allowed users to post public audiovisual snippets with a 24-hours expiration date. This effectively turned Snapchat into a mobile publishing platform and would become the cornerstone of its ad-driven revenue model. A later implemented auto-advance feature would systematize stories' spectatorship in the form of personalized, cumulative audiovisual feed, weaving together the viewer's contacts' updates. This mode of consumption produces a sense of erratic continuity not so different from what Raymond Williams observed in the flow of television.[3] The unceasing concatenation adds to the images' feeling of urgency, exerting an addictive pull on the gaze. It feels at once like a bewildering stream of the *now* and a more manageable version of reality; a constant buffering of the quotidian begging to be lived through the sheer exhaustion of its medial novelty. Yet, the feed gets replenished, ready for another round.

Stories became a widely popular form of sharing video content on mobile platforms. As if in response to Snapchat's refusal of their US$ 3 billion buying offer, Facebook would implement the feature in most of their products, starting with Instagram. Currently, some version of hyper-ephemeral publishing is available on most major social media and messaging apps, Twitter being the most recent to adopt it. The format's standing on the online communication ecology pushes for particular sensibilities, which become easier to delineate through an examination of some budding cultural patterns.

Carrying over from the casual and dialogical tone of instant messaging, hyper-ephemeral digital media seem largely typified by the direct address of the immediate interlocutor, leading to forms

1   Evan Spiegel, 'Let's Chat.', *Snapchat*, 9 May 2012, https://snap.com/en-US/news/post/lets-chat.
2   James Vincent, 'Playboy's first non-nude issue is an 'ode to Snapchat'', *Verge*, 4 Feb 2016, https://theverge.com/2016/2/4/10912266/payboy-non-nude-snapchat-cover.
3   Raymond Williams, *Television. Technology and Cultural Form*, London: Routledge, 1974.

of audiovisual expression built upon a sort of *second-personness*. This does not necessarily imply fully fleshed second-person narratives and their corresponding 'protagonist narratees', as experimented by literature and game design.[4] Rather, it entails self-aware discursive structures reliant on the reinforcement of the subject position *with whom one talks* or *to whom something is shown*. They are, in other words, not *about you*, but *for you*.

Accordingly, the stream of stories appeals to the public not as uninterested audience, dissociated from the information delivery process, but as active observers, self-identified with the role of witnesses or implicit conversation partners. The fact that the first snaps would only play as long as the user kept their fingers on the image is indicative of the degree of bodily commitment expected by the medium. For the spectators as for any stories' author, the (often handheld) screen is not a fourth wall but a porous social interface, which can be interchangeably occupied by one or another.

The lack of persistent archives anticipates these interpersonal configurations of meaning. The fact that stories cannot be reproduced over a certain period of time, automatically removing them from wide circulation, inhibits both the access of uninvolved people and the recovery by the authors themselves, making the format useless for journal or lifelog entries. As conveyed by the case of 'The Snappening,' a scandalous leak of hundreds of thousands of intimate snaps saved to third-party cloud services, the mass reproduction of hyper-ephemeral content has always had the feeling of an inappropriate, or malicious, breach in the social relations of this media.

Hyper-ephemeral media's second-person framework draws from the language of TV and radio newscasts, artistic genres such as the epistolary novel, and the display regime of attractions. In the following, we will see some of forms it might take in works tailored to the stories format.

Witnesses to the Horror

Sickhouse (Hannah Macpherson, 2016) is a horror thriller made in the found footage tradition, as pioneered by *Cannibal Holocaust* (Ruggero Deodato, 1980) and later solidified by *The Blair Witch Project* (Daniel Myrick and Eduardo Sánchez, 1999). The genre adopts a *faux* documentary approach to storytelling, mobilizing the presentational codes of non-fiction to upset the audience. All the bad recording and the camera artifacts are a calculated deployment of *cinema verité* aesthetics, which means to enhance the movie's effect of reality. They simultaneously accentuate the uncanniness of image technology and the feeling of authenticity that comes from its awareness. Format contingencies surface over filmmaking principles, conveying qualities proper to the kind of media the movie claims to be.

Hence, the fact that no take lasts longer than 10 seconds is not coincidental. While most found footage horror films indulge in the low-fidelity visuals of magnetic videotape, *Sickhouse* exploits the unceasing ramble of stories. As such, it stands apart from other

---

4   Monika Fludernik, 'Second-Person Narrative and Related Issues', *Style* 28.3 (1994): 281-311.

movies of the genre not only because of the exceptional traits of mobile phone imaging (portrait orientation being the most remarkable), but also due to the form of its making. Stories, as we have seen, are not the kind of footage that can simply be *found* at some later time, as the inadvertent record of some extraordinary event. Their most defining characteristic is precisely to be *irretrievable*. How can a format that refuses archival stability befit a genre predicated upon the endurance of the material trace, even in supernatural conditions?

Medium particularities made *Sickhouse*'s production more performative than the average found footage thriller. The feature was initially carried out as a live event spanning across five consecutive days (Apr 29 – May 3, 2016). Scenes were recorded and streamed from the Snapchat account of young internet personality Andrea Russett (@andwizzle), who by the time had about 2.5 million subscribers on YouTube and half a million on Snapchat. Even more than other celebrities participating on commercial film projects, Russett served the double function of actress and promotional device. *Sickhouse*'s original audience was essentially *her audience*, most of whom completely unaware of the fictional narrative that took over their idol's channel.

Russett's mundane vignettes slowly turned into *Sickhouse* with the arrival of her long unseen cousin Taylor (actress Laine Neil, the only member of the main cast playing a character who is not herself). The first act of the movie has them hanging out in the city, going shopping, attending a house party. Taylor gets perplexed by Russett's fame when they are recognized at the beach, showing the first signs of a social media cluelessness who will be exploited throughout the narrative. The story starts to coalesce around a camping trip that Russett had planned with fellow Instagram star Sean O'Donnell in search of the eponymous cabin, 'a real-life haunted house in the middle of nowhere'. Rumors about the place pop up in seemingly random conversations with strangers. Meanwhile, the movie seeps into other channels.

O'Donnell's casting doubles as a celebrity cameo; the romantic tension between him and Russett incites actual buzz and audience cross-pollination. A website detailing the backstory of the sickhouse gets mentioned; the URL, plugged on stream, indeed exists.[5] By visiting it, spectators mirror the characters' activities and get further entangled in their universe. This extroversion of story elements as interactive props operates in favor of the movie propagation in a way similar to 'alternate reality' campaigns. Combined, centrifugal and centripetal marketing ploys ground content updates in the extradiegetic substance of network connections, contributing to the movie's semblance of veracity.

Compounding with this process of narrative dispersion, plot contrivances are used to preserve directorial control over the discourse and delivery of the story. Taylor's wary fascination with social media predominates among them. A newfound enthusiasm has her piloting Russett's Snapchat account, thereby creating an alibi for any changes in tone

---

5   Visit Sickhouse, http://visitsickhouse.com/.

and style required by the narrative. Entrusted by Russett with the task of documenting their camping trip, she teases the others to leave their phones behind. This severs the celebrity-actors' connection with their respective audiences, centralizing *Sickhouse*'s updates on Russett's account, in the hands of the one person among them who, despite being a purely internet presence – a fictional character created exclusively for the project –, paradoxically has *the least* internet presence.

This first, social media-native run of *Sickhouse* reveals the tenuous balance between a teleological, results-driven mode of filmmaking and the interpersonal disposition of hyper-ephemeral media. The live publication of scenes on Snapchat, tethered to a highly popular user account, kept the narrative cohesive while simultaneously disintegrating it among other people's stories: a profusion of volatile images which provided camouflage and interference, adding both to the plot's realism and the public's anxiety. Accordingly, movie production oscillated between the containment and dispersal of the many different information flows that constituted it as a durational networked phenomenon.

Even though most dialogue and actions were improvised, actors did not meaningfully interact with anyone outside the cast, on or offline. Characters seem amazed by live audience numbers and respond to comments made on social media, but in ways that might as well have been scripted. The conversation on Twitter shows that some of Russett's fans quickly grasped the fictional nature of the project and played along. However, when someone went as far as to create fake accounts to impersonate Taylor, the movie producers were clearly shaken.[6] Audience participation was welcomed just enough to make the story go viral, not to turn it into a sprawling collaboration.

Nevertheless, this fragmented media environment allowed *Sickhouse* to profit from found footage horror's most disconcerting aspects. Movies in the genre, by presenting the image as an objective record produced within the same universe as the spectators', concurrently implicates them in the diegesis. As Neil McRobert puts it, while the audience is clearly detached from the events depicted, it feels 'ontologically commensurate' with these events.[7] True horror comes not from a direct identification with the protagonists on screen, but with oneself as a mediated bystander to their actions.

In cinema, this supranarrative connection is often contrived. For as much as spectators are told that the footage is *found*, they encounter it in a highly premeditated way, framed by standard protocols of media consumption. Ontological uncertainty must be cultivated through strategically placed paratexts (such as *The Blair Witch*'s infamous website) that throw into question the movie's medial status. Within a stories' stream, though, the public is put in the position where both stumbling upon this sort of image and the interpersonal way it addresses them seems plausible.

---

6   Ben Child, 'Sickhouse: how the first ever Snapchat movie redefined viral', *The Guardian*, 22 Jun 2016, https://theguardian.com/film/2016/jun/22/sickhouse-how-the-social-media-horror-film-went-viral.

7   Neil McRobert, 'Mimesis of Media: Found Footage Cinema and the Horror of the Real', *Gothic Studies* 17.2 (2015): 137–150.

Sickhouse reinforces its second-person address through Taylor's many moments of in-camera confession, which feel at once natural to the stories' format and taken straight from *The Blair Witch* textbook. Conventionally, as the ordinary girl among real-life internet celebrities, Taylor would have been the most likely to play the audience surrogate. Her constant talking to the spectators, however, secures them at a distance, and inhibits the kind of direct identification inconsistent with found footage affects. The public is prompted to partake in the drama as her witnesses.

The original *Sickhouse* stories reportedly got hundreds of millions of views in total and earned Russett about a hundred thousand new followers.[8] About a month after their Snapchat run, they would be compiled into a feature-length version and released on video-on-demand. Although no other 'Snapchat movie' of note has been made since, the company would soon start investing in series of their own, first in partnership with TV networks (2017) and later through the production of 'Snap originals' (2018). These shows, nested in the app's 'Discover' section, which admits longer and persistent content, are much more traditional in format and style. Their affiliation to Snapchat is barely betrayed by the vertical aspect ratio, which came to be a popular standard for mobile video in the last few years. Meanwhile, snaps and stories have been used by the company as disposable carriers for interactive advertisements, their dialogical disposition mobilized to promote official Snapchat productions through AR filters that users can share with one another.

Movies to Wear on Your Face

The popularization of smartphones with higher processing power, facial recognition and augmented reality capabilities will bring new ingredients to the hyper-ephemeral media landscape. Snapchat's early multimedia tools — which allowed users to write basic text, draw over pictures and apply context-sensitive frames and 'stickers' — have evolved into a growing collection of 'lenses' providing sophisticated animated effects. In August 2016, when Instagram implemented stories of its own, introducing them to a large part of its userbase, it made graphic design central to the format. Different features gave users more freedom to compose images like interactive canvases and drawing templates, moving hyper-ephemeral media further into the realm of computer synthesis and collage.

Facebook's recent release of the free Spark AR Studio adds to this scenario by enabling users to easily create and publish mixed-reality content to the company's social media platforms. Interactive 3D and facial distortion filters shape new forms of second-person expression as performative audiovisual microgenres reliant on public interaction. As partial images, they cannot fully happen without the spectator's body or immediate surroundings to substantiate them. This phenomenological insufficiency drives their networked availability. Instead of remaining entrenched in their creators' account, face filters must be appropriated by others, who will collect and wear them, lending them coordinates,

8   Kevin Lincoln, 'The Horror Movie Sickhouse, Shot Entirely on Snapchat, Introduces a New Kind of Fear', *Vulture*, 6 June 2016, https://www.vulture.com/2016/06/sickhouse-horror-movie-snapchat.html.

soundbites, and textures in return. This mode of proliferation emphasizes stories as an interpersonal environment to see and be seen – less of a people's TV than a costume parade. In this context, users and animation operate as each other's medium.

To examine how these exchanges might develop, one can look at (and around) the work of Irish artist David OReilly. No stranger to procedural graphics and unconventional animation formats, OReilly adopted face filters as a creative medium soon after Instagram made it possible. His latest pieces – *It's Always You*, *Simulation* and *AAAHHHHHH!*, all from 2019 – consist of robust 3D animations sporting a degree of complexity unprecedented to the platform. They place the spectator as their main character, translating their face across different human and non-human bodies.

As second-person narratives, OReilly's filters articulate an ironic juxtaposition between social media narcissism and a sort of absurd pantheism common to his production (particularly the 'existential nature simulation' *Mountain* (2014) and the multi-platform videogame *Everything* (2017)). At the same time, they serve the audience as tools for self-expression. OReilly's Instagram account collects examples of how users have been 'wearing' the filters to perform online. Seemingly amazed, the artist remarks how the medium enables an asynchronous, indirect collaboration 'only possible in AR'.[9] In the comments of a 'music edition' compilation of scenes from *It's Always You*, producer Diplo echoes the sentiment: 'Finally collabed with Grimes'.[10]

Sheer numbers (600 million views and 28 million videos of *It's Always You* alone, as of 7 February 2020)[11] seem to indicate the massive appeal of face filters as an interpersonal animation format. But what do these numbers mean? OReilly himself points to the fact that a lot of this engagement is likely driven by Instagram's addictive architecture, and is wary to be contributing to it. While his work certainly profits from potentially infinite renovation by the hands of users, so does the platform from the way it keeps these users connected and their data available (without any actual remuneration to anyone involved).

As I write this in March 2020 amidst the coronavirus pandemic, the number of live stories on Instagram seems to have reached peak record. Starting today, the company has launched a 'stay home' sticker and created a corresponding highlights section on top of the stories' playback queue. Hyper-ephemeral video has been one of people's media of choice to be alone together in the global quarantine. It is evident how, in the way it welcomes our disquietude and foster opportunities for out-of-sync gatherings, the format creates a reassuring (if not problematic) sense of community and belonging to the platform. But are we really talking to each other or are we just feeding the conversation?

9   1, 'Sound on [...]', Instagram post, 22 Dec 2019, https://instagram.com/p/B6YsYv8gWDJ.
10   1 'IT'S ALWAYS YOU [...]', Instagram post, 7 Feb 2020, https://instagram.com/p/B8SIAuTHftn.
11   1 'IT'S ALWAYS YOU [...]'.

References

'Sound on [...]', Instagram post, 22 Dec 2019, https://instagram.com/p/B6YsYv8gWDJ.

_____. 'IT'S ALWAYS YOU [...]', Instagram post, 7 Feb 2020, https://instagram.com/p/B8SIAuTHftn.

Child, Ben. 'Sickhouse: how the first ever Snapchat movie redefined viral', *The Guardian*, 22 Jun 2016, https://theguardian.com/film/2016/jun/22/sickhouse-how-the-social-media-horror-film-went-viral.

Fludernik, Monika. 'Second-Person Narrative and Related Issues', *Style* 28.3 (1994): 281-311.

Lincoln, Kevin. 'The Horror Movie Sickhouse, Shot Entirely on Snapchat, Introduces a New Kind of Fear', *Vulture*, 6 June 2016, https://www.vulture.com/2016/06/sickhouse-horror-movie-snapchat.html.

McRobert, Neil. 'Mimesis of Media: Found Footage Cinema and the Horror of the Real', *Gothic Studies* 17.2 (2015): 137–150.

Spiegel, Evan. 'Let's Chat.', Snapchat, 9 May 2012, https://snap.com/en-US/news/post/lets-chat.

Vincent, James. 'Playboy's first non-nude issue is an 'ode to Snapchat'', *Verge*, 4 Feb 2016, https://theverge.com/2016/2/4/10912266/payboy-non-nude-snapchat-cover.

Visit Sickhouse, http://visitsickhouse.com/.

Williams, Raymond. *Television. Technology and Cultural Form*. London: Routledge, 1974.

TELEVISUALITY OF LIVE-STREAMING-VIDEO

DINO GE ZHANG

TELEVISUALITY OF LIVE-STREAMING-VIDEO

DINO GE ZHANG

Introduction

The expanding field of online video studies has a few conventional entry points from other established fields — like cinema, video arts, and internet/software studies. As the medium of online video diversifies, the 'digital' umbrella no longer suffices to cover the specificity of each format of online video: Tiktok, Twitch, and Netflix (with, perhaps, the exception of YouTube as it becomes all-encompassing) all have specific content (e.g. amateur or professional), style (e.g. editing), format (e.g. duration), and socio-technological infrastructure (e.g. web versus mobile). In particular, the re-emergence of livestreaming video poses new questions as it also naturally reattaches itself to the old televisual discourse: liveness and flow. The domain names of major livestreaming platforms—Justin.tv, Twitch.tv and Douyu.tv—explicitly suggest a lineage from television since the medium of livestreaming seems to proactively strive for a televisual identity or form.

On the surface level of technological traits, livestreaming platforms have already achieved real-time simultaneity between all participants, temporal co-presence between broadcaster and viewers, and instant verifiability of reality claims via this afforded interactivity — all with high graphic fidelity. However, the anchors of televisuality — liveness and flow — are no longer a rare or extolled quality captured by television studies. Rather, it is a banalized description of being (approximately) fully live. This ubiquity is primarily a result of the technological democratization of live broadcasting (all one needs is a mobile phone and internet connection) and also the socio-economic incentives to practice livestreaming. A speculative question: is the theoretical obsession with liveness and flow — which is regarded as quintessentially televisual or the 'differentia specifica' of television as a medium — eclipsed by its most banal actuality in livestreaming?[1] In other words, is liveness a defunct theoretical metaphor when its ubiquity and accessibility among today's livestreaming platforms make it no longer desirable?

This discourse of televisuality also revives the old 'internet of the dotcom era versus television' debate but with a twist. Instead of competing for superiority and negotiating convergence, they switch places: television become online videos and online videos become televisual. Television rarely practiced its acclaimed essential characteristics, while online video not only deploys them but perfects them in the dotTV era. Netflix is the old television (its commercial model and distribution architecture) masqueraded

---

1   Jostein Gripsrud, 'Television, Broadcasting, Flow: Key Metaphors in TV Theory', in Christine Geraghty
     and David Lusted (eds) The Television Studies Book, London: Arnold, 1998, p. 17.

in the form of online video; Twitch/Douyu is the ideal television (the unfulfilled promise of liveness and communicative feedback) realized in its most vulgar tastes — ordinary people watching other ordinary people doing ordinary (and occasionally absurd) things.

As the history of livestreaming media shows, movements of remediation should not be understood as fixed stages between two adjacent media in a process of linear technological development, but rather fluctuating sporadic movements of both simulating and distinguishing from multiple previous media. Along with the hundreds of cam-sites in the 90s, Jennicam and Anna Voog were among the first wave of livestreaming video and 'reality-as-entertainment' that proclaimed to do better than television in its most regarded trait: liveness as democratic truth.[2] Anna Voog: 'it is going to be a VERY interesting day indeed, when streaming with sound is available to everyone and EVERYONE has a TV show'. Webcam subculture used to be called 'bastard child of TV'.[3] By 2003, as Jennicam and webcam already faded from internet culture, reality TV took off as a mainstream 'reality-as-entertainment' but again 'tainted' by television industry itself. YouTube's arrival in mid-2000 and growth gradually established its position as the total triumph of the user-generated content (and its subsequent subsumption to corporate power). A decade later, livestreaming media returns as reality TV proper, but it no longer needs to be posited against television in order to consolidate its cultural status. Contemporary livestreaming platforms derive from the success of YouTube (and its associated cultures of online video), but they no longer represent the bastardized form of televisuality but televisuality proper.

New Sociotechnics of Liveness

Liveness as a concept is too slippery and rigid because it can sometimes conflate a history of technology with technological traits or even forms of aesthetic, which was how the ontological realness of television was justified. Nick Couldry writes on the technical quality of liveness, 'the decisive of liveness is not factuality of what is transmitted, but the fact of live transmission itself'.[4] If live transmission is simply measured by the time-shift variable or latency, then the technological history of liveness is not a linear process of technological advancement. Strictly speaking, except for the human-imposed factors such as the seven-second profanity delay, analogue television and radio can already be broadcast without perceptible delay in its early days.[5]

In the 1990s, streaming a watchable video over 56k modem lines was initially a huge struggle before the advent of broadband internet, RealNetworks, Macromedia, and later Adobe Flash Player. For example, Jennicam was originally a webpage that automatically refreshed every three minutes—that is, one frame per three minutes—to display a picture (without audio) taken by the webcam, which should not count as a livestream *video* but

---

2   Terri Senft, Celebrity & Community in the Age of Social Networks, New York: Peter Lang, 2008, p. 16.
3   Daniel Palmer, 'Webcams: The Aesthetics of Liveness', *Like, Art Magazine*, 2000, pp. 16-22.
4   Nick Couldry, 'Liveness, 'Reality', and the Mediated Habitus from Television to the Mobile Phone', *The Communication Review* 7.4 (2004): 354.
5   The political economy of the broadcasting industry can influence/limit the technical potential of television because liveness was regarded potentially dangerous.

a slide show by contemporary standards. This is in stark contrast to the fact that Twitch streams can be watched in 60 or 30 frames per second and various scaling of video quality.[6]

Under the new climate of solidified platformization and more ubiquitous, better internet infrastructure, the seeking of immediacy is revived in the development of new livestreaming technologies. This striving aims at the 'progressive elimination of any perceptible delay from the time of machine processing' and 'the time of conscious perception'.[7] In the case of livestreaming, this process includes software encoding of the video at the sender end, transmission to the Content Delivery Networks, and streaming the video from the server at the receiver end. In terms of latency, in May 2018, Twitch already achieved a low latency stream with under one second of delay at times.

Technically speaking, immediacy is a question of approximation. This striving to reduce latency in our real-time Web and more recently the technology of livestreaming video cannot be considered in universal applicability, just like how liveness was wrongly extolled as the overall defining quality of television. 'Real-time is not a framework in which media change but is assembled through the *technicity of platform*'.[8] In other words, specific temporalities are produced or 'fabricated' in different platforms and therefore a 'medium-specificity of the real-time experience', according to the specific platform under discussion.[9] This leads to questions of a socio-technological or, even, a political economic nature.

For example, Twitch tends to be explicit and highlight its technological superiority in its implementation of HTML5 in reducing latency while the Chinese platform Douyu tends to downplay this technical aspect in reducing latency. According to an anonymous informant who works in the livestreaming industry in China, the main reason why Douyu still used Adobe Flash Video in early 2018 (instead of updating to HTML5) was not that Douyu did not possess the technology, but because of their reliance on Flash advertisements. HTML5 advertisements have to be reencoded as videos, which can be too resource intensive for Chinese advertisers. Flash advertisement was the industrial standard in 2015 and still was in 2018 (at least on Douyu). Douyu also rarely publicly pronounces its claim to liveness for ideological reasons—unfiltered liveness is considered a threat by Chinese authorities and therefore must be strictly regulated.

A brief history of immediacy in digital broadcasting technologies reveals that liveness is not necessarily a linear process of technological advancement that continuously

6   Due to limited server processing power, Twitch prioritises transcoding services that downscale video
     quality to only selected channels (e.g. partnered popular channels) while enforcing original video quality
     on channels with small viewership.
7   Adrian Mackenzie, 'The Mortality of the Virtual: Real-time, Archive and Dead-time in Information
     Networks', *Convergence* 3.2 (1997): 60.
8   Esther Weltevrede, Anne Helmond, Carolin Gerlitz, 'The Politics of Real-time: A Device Perspective on
     Social Media Platforms and Search Engines', Theory Culture & Society 31.6 (2014): 127.
9   Ibid, p. 142.

reduces latency but rather a meandering course, in which there are mutual influences between the analogue and digital. Before the capability to transmit pre-recorded content, liveness was considered a *technological limitation* in the television industry. The subsequent development is in fact one that institutionalized latency rather than reduced it for censorship reasons and reduction of costs. Later, the arrival of Web video did not immediately assume technical superiority over analogue transmission in terms of latency and video quality. In the next step, livestreaming technology presumes this superiority and to a degree extols its socio-technological role in reducing latency.

In a sense, the relationship between live and recorded media has always been entangled. This ambivalently conflictual and mutually benefiting relationship is reconstructed between Video on Demand (hereafter VoD) and livestream videos. However, the major divergence from the comparison between analogue television and film-based cinema is that contemporary streaming VoD and livestreams are both under the rubrics of the 'digital', albeit under different protocols, codecs, server structures, and distribution methods.

Streaming and Flow

Digital streaming—viewing the file while it is still being downloaded (i.e. buffering)—was originally juxtaposed to viewing after downloading the entire file. As Wolfgang Ernst said during an interview,

Technically, when you stream video, the frames are buffered for a micro-moment of time. This means you technically produce a copy, though only for a brief moment. It's very ephemeral, it's the most ephemeral archive or short time memory, but technically, it is still a copy.[10]

This transience of data flow in the act of 'streaming' is therefore not an ontological quality of data transmission that fundamentally distinguishes it from the opposing mode of technical reproduction (i.e. downloading a video before viewing) since there are also copies in streaming, just that they are not intended to be experienced as 'copies'. The video that is being streamed (i.e. VoD) is the live transmission or reproduction of a static, pre-recorded file located on a server, which leaves a web or app cache on the receiving computing device, just not as a complete file. Livestreaming video is a further extension of streaming video since it is full liveness in the technical sense with no pre-recorded file. The perceived lack of archiving efforts or undesirability of watching an archived livestream video is not a technological limitation but is due to socio-technological practices.[11] Livestreams can be archived both on the origination point via encoder software such as

---

10   Ghislain Thibault and Wolfgang Ernst. 'What We Used to Call 'Media History'?' Amodern, 2015, http://amodern.net/article/ernst-media-history/.
11   This is highly contextual since each platform has its own accustomed archiving practices afforded by specific technologies provided by the platform itself. For instance, Twitch's unique function of 'clipping'—creating a sharable short (30 seconds at max) video clip of the ongoing livestream—is afforded by its HTML5 video player.

Open Broadcaster Software (the expenses are hard drive and CPU capacity) or the media publisher's own server (the expenses are server space and maintenance costs).

Given the inchoate relationship between streaming and livestreaming, it is critical to reconsider the technological metaphor of streaming from television to streaming media as televisual language such as channels are still in use on livestreaming platforms. Raymond Williams's theory of planned flow has become, quite similar to theories of liveness, central to the televisual theory. To summarize, television industry hides certain operations from its audience and intends to structure the viewing experience, say, of a given evening, as a coherent whole: we usually say 'we watch television' instead of 'we watch news'. A television channel must 'sustain that evening's flow' and deter the viewers from consciously selecting another channel or switching off the TV.[12] 'Flow' here operates *not* as a technological metaphor but rather how television programming is designed to capture audience attention: 'the flow of programming attempts to deter, at all costs, channel surfing'.[13]

Tara McPherson updates Williams' concept of planned flow in the context of the internet and argues that our motive of sticking to the planned flow is no longer 'linear and contiguous' like the experience of watching television but corresponds more to our desires such as navigability and sense of choice in the experience of web browsing.[14] While 'television's much-heralded 'flow' worked to move viewers through segments of televisual time, orchestrating viewership,.. . Web programming could allow for an even more carefully orchestrated movement, all *dressed up in feeling of choice*' (emphasis my own)— 'a volitional mobility' so to speak.[15] This then leads us back to the question of remediation. The 'feeling of choice', or personal control of flow, as promised by internet, is certainly complicated by algorithms— 'the paradigm shift is from user-controlled surfing to algorithm-controlled sorting'.[16] Unlike cinema and television that are 'built on the concept of singular objects. . . as programmed events, [that] require the reservation of specific time and schedule for viewing', online videos are *on demand* and therefore bounded by a 'structured life'.[17] 'As a jukebox of emotions, feelings, and algorithmic relations as each video suggest others aside', YouTube viewing thus features its own kind of phenomenological experience of flow.[18]

Livestreaming video further disrupts the clear line between televisual flow and the experience of surfing the Web. Although livestreams are structured by schedules of individual channels, these channels can also be browsed through the platform's catalogue/directory, categories,

---

12   Raymond Williams, Television: Technology and Form. London: Routledge, 2003 (1974), p. 94.
13   Ghislain Thibault, 'Streaming: A Media Hydrography of Televisual Flows', VIEW Journal of European Television History and Culture 4.7 (2015): 112.
14   Tara McPherson, 'Reload: Liveness, Mobility and the Web', in Wendy Hui Kyong Chun and Thomas Keenan (eds) New Media, Old Media: A History and Theory Reader, New York: Routledge, 2006, p. 204.
15   Ibid, p.200, 206.
16   Mark Andrejevic, 'The twenty-first-century telescreen', in Graeme Turner and Jinna Jay (eds) Television Studies After TV, London: Routledge, 2009, p. 35.
17   Andreas Treske, Video Theory: Online Video Aesthetics or the Afterlife of Video, Bielefeld: Transcript, 2015, p. 44, 45.
18   Ibid, p. 44.

tags, and the customizable tab of followed channels—there is *both* linearity and navigability. Apart from having a long directory of channels sorted according to popularity, most livestreaming platforms still attempt to simulate this experience of sustaining the flow by design of its infrastructure — to encourage inter-channel movement. On Twitch, viewers can track followed channels and games/categories; this can be also orchestrated by broadcasters themselves via hosting another channel while they are offline.

The other issue is duration: what is the optimal duration for 'a flow of undemanding pleasantness'?[19] For Frances Bonner's definitional 'ordinary television', one hour is the 'smallest acceptable unit'.[20] For a Twitch livestream, the duration is highly flexible, but the usual minimal acceptable duration of a live channel is two hours. Most full-time streamers have fairly regular schedules of when they will go live and there is often a public announcement on their social media accounts and notification via the livestreaming app itself. However, part-time or sessional streamers mostly have very erratic schedules and it takes time—often a few hours—before non-regular viewers can discover or come in by chance so the channel chatroom starts to be populated and the conversation starts flowing. As a livestreaming platform becomes too massive to navigate with thousands of concurrently live channels, discovering a new channel relies heavily on registers such as very detailed tags and categories (e.g. a specific activity or videogame), as well as visibility and internet traffic from other social media platform (i.e. preestablished fame somewhere else).

Space-Medium of Livestreaming Video

Online streaming, specifically YouTube and Netflix, remediates televisual forms, industry and practices to the degree that it 'marks the grand return of broadcasting media in digital culture'.[21] Hydrographic metaphors thus play a vital role in remediating the televisual regime—a 'metaphorical disguise'.[22] Television vocabulary such as 'channel' is still in use on YouTube and Twitch and form the basic unit of the larger discourses on livestreaming media.

However, there are some critical divergences between YouTube and Twitch. Jean Burgess and Joshua Green argue that 'YouTube is thus evolving into a massive, heterogeneous, but for the most part accidental and disordered, public archive'.[23] YouTube is thus more like an 'ocean', as Andreas Treske uses the metaphor to describe the sheer number of videos on YouTube, and their atmospheric nature as a space-medium. To extend this metaphoric strategy, if the unruly database of YouTube is the bottomless ocean of videos, the endless pages of livestream channels of Twitch are the river of livestreaming platform.

---

19   Frances Bonner, Ordinary Television: Analyzing Popular TV, London: Sage, 2003, p. 38.
20   Ibid, p.38.
21   Ghislain Thibault, 'Streaming', p. 111.
22   Wolfgang Ernst, Digital Memory and the Archive. Minneapolis: University of Minnesota Press, 2013, p. 246.
23   Jean Burgess and Joshua Green, YouTube: online video and participatory culture, Malden: Polity Press, 2009, p. 88.

Channels go online and offline, but the collective stream is kept flowing 24/7 with cyclic rhythms of flood (early evening peak hours) and drought (early morning down times) of incoming and returning viewers.

However, for Ghislain Thibault, the fluid analogies that persisted across generations of media from television to digital media today do not capture the specific operation of digital media and hides its technological aspect. He writes,

Analogue television was a true flow, technologically speaking, because it involved transmitting signals of various lengths through the wavelike electromagnetic spectrum. . . In the case of digital television, the code of the data no longer bears an analogical relationship with its referent and its transport within the digital network is not necessarily contiguous.[24]

One issue with Thibault's critique is that ordinary users and viewers often do not necessarily mind the technical accuracy of the metaphors, they are more concerned with how these correspond to their scenarios of use and their imageries based on their practices. In Joost van Loon's words, 'we habitualize technology' to a degree that we '"take technology" for granted in our ordinary everydayness which in turn makes it possible for us to get on with things'.[25] The metaphors used on livestreaming platforms must be understood as not just technological but also experiential. We must recognize the specific experiences of flow afforded by the technology of livestreaming and at the same time, explicate the ethnographic nuances within the historical lineage of different metaphors, say, in different cultural contexts and local socio-technological history.

Chinese analogies of 'channel' have different origins in the media histories of Chinese television and online platforms, which are deeply rooted in the divergent media practices. On television, a channel is called *pingdao*, which literally means 'frequency route'. This analogy is very similar to the hydrospheric metaphor of 'conduit' in English since frequency refers to electric signal and route implies a cable or road like conductor. While the language of channel persists on video platforms like Twitch and YouTube, the same metaphoric strategy is rarely invoked on contemporary Chinese livestreaming sites; instead, it adopts a spatial metaphor. The word currently in use in Mainland China is *fangjian* or 'room' and a livestreaming channel is called a *zhibojian*, literally 'direct casting room'. The livestreaming video is thus semi-public space that welcomes newcomers. While acknowledging the remediated metaphors, the origin of this *spatial* reference in *fangjian* can be traced to early online sites such as online chatrooms and early forms of Chinese client-based audio/video chatrooms as opposed to television.

24   Ghislain Thibault, 'Streaming', p. 115.
25   Joost van Loon, 'Modalities of Mediation', In Nick Couldry, Andreas Hepp, Friedrich Krotz (eds) Media Events in a Global Age, 2010, p. 114.

Against Ontology

Jane Feuer's famous argument on 'the ideology of liveness' is a criticism of the ontological approach of television studies, in which she proposes that television is often not live in a literal sense and liveness operates as elaborate ideological and institutional mediations.[26] While acknowledging the value in deconstructing liveness as the ideology of television *as an institution* in Feuer's work, Mimi White posits a critique of this preoccupation with liveness as a 'conceptual filter' that eclipsed other 'discursive registers'.[27] Feuer 'ends up elevating it (i.e. liveness) as even more potent force, as the ideological and technological sleight of hand at the heart of the medium's strategies of address'.[28] Derrida and Stiegler's conversation on television also reminds us of the potential dangers of an intellectual deconstruction of liveness: 'while continuing to remind people and to demonstrate that the "live" and "real time" are never pure. . . requisite deconstruction of this *artifactuality* (of liveness) should not be used as an alibi (of the Real)'.[29] The deconstruction of live media often results in the dead-end of 'critical neoidealism' of the default philosophical position: it's all just a performance/simulacrum. When liveness is critiqued as an ideological construct, the argument ends up returning to the loop of ontological liveness versus ontology as ideology debate. It falls exactly into the defense of or attack on the ontological integrity of liveness, which are both affirmations of representational politics that are concerned with whether media distorts reality or not. In this sense, liveness is overrated in media theory but underestimated in its sociotechnical manifestation on contemporary livestreams. My proposal is thus not necessarily abandoning liveness as a defunct concept but examining how experiences of liveness are articulated by contemporary viewers and livestreamers themselves.

References

Andrejevic, Mark. 'The twenty-first-century telescreen', in Graeme Turner and Jinna Jay (eds) *Television Studies After TV*, London: Routledge, 2009, pp. 31–40.

Bonner, Frances. *Ordinary Television: Analyzing Popular TV*, London: Sage, 2003.

Couldry, Nick. 'Liveness, 'Reality', and the Mediated Habitus from Television to the Mobile Phone', *The Communication Review* 7.4 (2004): 353–361.

Burgess, Jean and Green, Joshua. *YouTube: online video and participatory culture*, Malden: Polity Press, 2009.

Jacques Derrida and Bernard Stiegler. *Ecographies of Television*, trans. Jennifer Bajorek, Cambridge: Polity Press, 2002.

Ernst, Wolfgang. *Digital Memory and the Archive*, Minneapolis: University of Minnesota Press, 2013.

---

26   Jane Feuer, 'The Concept of Live Television: Ontology as Ideology', E. Ann Kaplan (ed.), Regarding Television, Frederick: University Publications of America, 1983, pp. 12-22.
27   Mimi White, 'The attractions of television: Reconsidering liveness', in Anna McCarthy and Nick Couldry (eds), MediaSpace: Place, Scale and Culture in a Media Age, 2003, pp. 75–94.
28   Ibid, p. 80.
29   Jacques Derrida and Bernard Stiegler. Ecographies of Television. trans. Jennifer Bajorek, Cambridge: Polity Press, 2002, p. 5.

Feuer, Jane. 'The Concept of Live Television: Ontology as Ideology', in E. Ann Kaplan (ed.), *Regarding Television*, Frederick: University Publications of America, 1983, p. 12-22.

Gripsrud, Jostein. 'Television, Broadcasting, Flow: Key Metaphors in TV Theory', in Christine Geraghty and David Lusted (eds) *The Television Studies Book*, London: Arnold, 1998, pp. 17–32.

Mackenzie, Adrian. 'The Mortality of the Virtual: Real-time, Archive and Dead-time in Information Networks', *Convergence* 3.2 (1997): 59–71.

McPherson, Tara. 'Reload: Liveness, Mobility and the Web', in Wendy Hui Kyong Chun and Thomas Keenan (eds) *New Media, Old Media: A History and Theory Reader*, New York: Routledge, 2006, pp. 199–208.

Palmer, Daniel. 'Webcams: The Aesthetics of Liveness', *Like, Art Magazine*, 2000, pp. 16-22.

Senft, Terri. *Celebrity & Community in the Age of Social Networks*, New York: Peter Lang, 2008.

Thibault, Ghislain. 'Streaming: A Media Hydrography of Televisual Flows', *VIEW Journal of European Television History and Culture* 4.7 (2015): 110–119.

Thibault, Ghislain and Ernst, Wolfgang. 'What We Used to Call "Media History"?', *Amodern*, 2015, http://amodern.net/article/ernst-media-history/

Treske, Andreas. *Video Theory: Online Video Aesthetics or the Afterlife of Video*, Bielefeld: Transcript, 2015.

Joost van Loon, 'Modalities of Mediation', In Nick Couldry, Andreas Hepp, Friedrich Krotz (eds) *Media Events in a Global Age*, 2010, pp. 109–123.

Weltevrede, Esther, Helmond, Anne, and Gerlitz, Carolin. 'The Politics of Real-time: A Device Perspective on Social Media Platforms and Search Engines', *Theory Culture & Society* 31.6 (2014), pp. 125–150.

White, Mimi. 'The attractions of television: Reconsidering liveness', In Anna McCarthy and Nick Couldry (eds) *MediaSpace: Place, Scale and Culture in a Media Age*, 2003, pp. 75–94.

Williams, Raymond. *Television: Technology and Form*, London: Routledge, 2003 (1974).

(PLAYING FROM ANOTHER ROOM)

JACK WILSON

(PLAYING FROM ANOTHER ROOM)

JACK WILSON

It fills the air from somewhere else, through a wall, from another room, each beat seeming to thicken its displaced presence until your surroundings seem to thrum in sympathetic resonance. It's a song. You wonder what private drama is playing out on the other side of that wall, whether it's of love or of loss, of the present or of memory, and at this point the associations spiral out and you recall memories that are not yours — of crying in bathrooms at parties, of lovers you've never had. Then the song finishes, and these thoughts and memories evaporate. After a moment, you click the replay icon on the YouTube video, and all this begins again.

What the 'you' of this vignette was hearing was music *(playing from another room)*: pop songs from 1980 to around 2009 that have been remixed to sound as if they are being heard through a door or wall. Beyond this formal quality of synthetic distance wrought by the 'other room' effect — a combination of low-pass filter and reverb — there is an additional aspect that unites the music in these videos, which are of otherwise disparate genre and release date: their negative affect. Per an archetypal comment: 'this makes me feel like my crush is dancing with the love of their life at highschool prom while im in the bathroom scrubbing cranberry juice out of my dress'.[1]

Across these videos, reflections on solitary struggles, lovers now past, and many other brands of sadness proliferate as the viewers appear to grapple with a sense that there is something occurring in the other room that they are not a part of.

> The effect makes me feel like I'm missing out on something fun, just on the other side of a wall. Songs that are otherwise emotion-neutral suddenly feel loaded and complicated, like someone's about to knock on the bathroom door and ask if you're okay.[2]

The 'other room' effect appears to allow viewers of these videos to imagine these other rooms as containing *others* and to briefly feel 'other lives brushing up against yours',[3] and in this sense (perhaps) imagine living a life that is less atomised. Indeed, it is easy to place *(playing from another room)* within the synthetic intimacy industrial complex of which YouTube is a major part.

1   Rhiannon Fawn, comment on Cecil Robert, 'Mazzy Star- Fade into You (Playing from Another Room)', YouTube Video, December 2017, www.youtube.com/watch?v=BGLmlxySOiM.
2   Samantha Cole, 'Songs Edited To Sound Like They're Playing In Another Room Are Inexplicably Emotional', Vice, August 2017, https://www.vice.com/en_us/article/neeqwx/songs-edited-to-sound-like-theyre-playing-in-another-room-are-inexplicably-emotional.
3   Corbin Dewitt, 'Echo Location', Real Life, October 2017, https://reallifemag.com/echo-location/.

Synthetic intimacy is defined as the mediated, datafied phenomenon of experiencing the affective — even physical — aspects of close human communication and contact in the absence of another human, and with this concept in mind one sees it across YouTube and online entertainment more broadly. Whether one wants to get advice on effectively any topic, have a parasocial hang out with a 'friend' through a vlog, 'let's play', or livestream, or even be 'touched' via autonomous sensory median response (ASMR),[4] all are available to the YouTube user to such an extent that one would be forgiven for thinking that it is the most popular form of content on the platform.[5] But the ease with which *(playing from another room)* can be placed in this kind of 'meta genre' does not necessarily make this categorisation correct. After all, the possibility of human contact so tantalisingly implied by these videos can never become actual. As the previously quoted reflections on the genre articulate, even in the imaginary terrain conjured up by these videos, action is happening *around* the viewer — never *to* them. Indeed, even in Kevin Parker's recent other room-style remix of his most recent album — titled '*The Slow Rush* In An Imaginary Place'[6] — that works to assert a more immediate sense of human presence through the addition of subtle crowd noises, the prevailing affect remains melancholic:

> The people listening to this mix in a few years probably won't get the joke. This is the audio representation of an imaginary place (AKA live concert full of healthy people having fun), because currently, all of Tame Impala's shows are cancelled/pushed back due to the Coronavirus/pandemic. Anyone witnessing this in 2020 is pretty much self-quarantined in their home, listening with headphones :([7]

We are under the horizonless sky of the coronavirus and its accompanying regime of social distancing, wherein synthetic intimacies are the only intimacies afforded many of us (certainly myself). While here '*The Slow Rush* In An Imaginary Place' and other *(playing from another room)* videos certainly provide a welcome sense of being, again, among others, that we are not — and will not be for the foreseeable future — is also underlined. While in the moment of watching one of these videos, there is a sense of overflowing possibility with regard to the *why* and *who* of the song, and the person in the other room, it is always "just you, listening".[8] While in the other synthetic intimacy-producing content there is an actual — albeit mediated — human presence, the fundamental absence of anyone within the other

---

4   That is, a sound-induced tingling that tends to begin on the back of one's neck and then spread across the body as the sonic stimulation continues. While AMSR 'triggers' are myriad, the primary ones deployed by 'ASMRists' appear to be speaking in a soft whisper, and tapping, rubbing, or otherwise manipulating assorted textured objects.

5   Although it may not actually be the most popular in terms of view counts — this honor belongs to music videos — given that the majority of YouTubers featured in the platform's yearly 'rewind' videos are producers of synthetic intimacies and that this type of content appears to be the largest beneficiary of actual material investment from the platform through its various programs for 'creators', it certainly seems that YouTube sees higher relative value in this content and is invested in promoting it.

6   Itself an extraordinary moment wherein the artist themselves engaged with a community they clearly — based on the number of fan-made other room remixes of Tame Impala songs — inspired.

7   THE SLOW DEATH HOOKS, comment on Tame Impala, 'The Slow Rush In An Imaginary Place', YouTube Video, 30 March 2020, https://www.youtube.com/watch?v=EA9uRfOJgM0.

8   Dewitt, 'Echo Location'.

room or the imaginary place underlines the real solitude of the viewer and asserts the unreality of the intimacy. The assertion of presence we find across the synthetic intimacies available on YouTube is thus in the dual sense: in these videos, there is *only* the present; only in the moment of viewing do these intimacies exist. There is no escape from the sadness of the present, only a dealing with it.

In this sense, we can read the sadness evoked by *(playing from another room)* — not only under these present conditions but also in general — as a concentrated instance of platform capitalism's structure of feeling: namely, the malaise that Geert Lovink asserts is immanent through digital culture.[9] However, where Lovink describes this sadness as the product of psychic exhaustion, the melancholy of *(playing from another room)* is brought forth in *the moment of viewing*. It is not so much the sadness of fatigue but of recognition, where the imagined, always inaccessible action of *(playing from another room)* is recognised by the viewer to be analogous to the human experience of platform capitalism: specifically, it is less their alienation from others than it is from themselves as a function of their displacement from their presence in time and space wrought by this capitalism's productive agent — the digital subject.

The digital subject is defined by Olga Goriunova as a networked-computational entity that while initially arises from the collection of user data before — as this data becomes embedded and active in the computational infrastructures that render it operational as a digital subject — it becomes something else, both *more* and *less* than the originating human.[10] 'More', because the digital subject exists in excess of the originating human: it is not an enclosed or coherent object but an assemblage of data, algorithms, and infrastructures that spans the global apparatus of platform capitalism, any formal 'singularity' is only apparent, as it is a permanently contingent articulation of user data and the technologies this data is embedded within. Yet it is also always 'less' because the elements that constitute it cannot ever be rendered back into the originating human being, as at the point of being becoming data (which itself is always partial), *being becomes something else*. To illustrate this irreducibility of human-derived *data* into human *being*, consider the data-mediated resurrection of the protagonist's partner in the *Black Mirror* episode 'Be Right Back', where the failure of the 'resurrected' android's performance of the originating human produces a kind of inadequacy-derived uncanny.

The digital subject, then, exists in opposition to the GDPR's figuration of the 'data subject', as the digital subject is *not* a 'natural person' who is extended into cyberspace by way of their data and therefore also extended a certain set of rights.[11] Rather, the digital subject is an assemblage of data, algorithms, and infrastructures — all non-human — that typically operate to further subjugate the human to platform logics. We can find various types of digital subject across any individual's data profile, their browsing or search history, and in their location, activity, communications, or biometric data. While some platforms collect data in many or all of these

9   Geert Lovink, Sad by Design, On Platform Nihilism, London: Pluto Press, 2019.

10   Olga Goriunova, 'The Digital Subject: People as Data as Persons', Theory, Culture & Society 36, no. 6 (2019).

11   General Data Protection Regulation (European Union). https://eur-lex.europa.eu/legal-content/EN/TXT/PDF/?uri=CELEX:32016R0679&from=EN.

categories, these digital traces do not — even longitudinally — cohere into a single coherent data-body but remain distributed and contingent.[12]

Algorithmic interpellation of the digital subject nonetheless operates upon the human, structuring their being in the world: from the content of one's Facebook feed, to what ads one might see across the internet, whether or not you are recognised as yourself by security apparatuses, even to questions of whether or not one is a 'terrorist' — algorithmic interpretation of our digital subjects is the basis of all these interpellations. And while these interpellations may not be classically Althussurian, we must also consider this in light of the fact that a predator drone is not necessarily bothered on the point of whether or not its target turns around when its stinger missile screams 'hey, you there!' across the sky.[13] Indeed, their digital subject has already turned around for them. This is to say that while the digital subject is materially distinct from the originating human, this entity nevertheless stands in *as* the human under the current regime of production and governance — in fact, it precede us — and so the human is alienated from their capacity to act in the world as themselves.

We can see this in the film *Cam* (2019) where not only does a kind of supernatural instance of the digital subject supplants the film's camgirl protagonist on the platform they perform on, but this spectre of themselves also ultimately serves as a vector through which their life falls apart in real life. And beyond fiction, we also can see this in the way Facebook's news feed takes control over the shaping of our social life by prioritising particular friends over others, or in the reconfiguration of how we produce our subjectivity through the optimisation of our expression as a function of social media platforms' doctrines of visibility.[14] And, even more salient is that in their primary deployment towards the prediction of future behaviour, the digital subject forecloses the possibility of the human to shape the future.[15]

Stalked by these spectres of ourselves across the myriad interfaces that both mediate and produce the conditions of the present and undermined in our capacity to act outside of this regime of algorithmic interpellation, we might say that what is produced here is a kind of profane 'hauntology'. Where here the presence of the past serves not, per Mark Fisher, to remind us of the future's having existed and assert its potential to exist again,[16] but rather in our personal and social histories' aggregation and operationalisation in the digital subject, the presence of the past serves to maintain a social formation in which the future can never occur.

---

12   Goriunova, 'The Digital Subject'.

13   Louis Althusser, 'Ideology and ideological state apparatuses (notes towards an investigation)', in Lenin and Philosophy and Other Essays, New York: Monthly Review Press, 1971, https://www.marxists.org/reference/archive/althusser/1970/ideology.htm

14   Tania Bucher, If...then: Algorithmic power and politics, New York: Oxford University Press, 2018.

15   See Byung-Chung Han, Psychopolitics: Neoliberalism and new technologies of power, London; New York: Verso, 2017; Luciana Parisi & Steve Goodman, 'Mnemonic Control', in Patricia Clough and Craig Willse (eds), Beyond biopolitics: Essays on the governance of life and death, Durham: Duke University Press, 2011, pp. 163—176.

16   Mark Fisher, Ghosts of My Life: Writings on Depression, Hauntology and Lost Futures, Winchester, UK: Zero books, 2014.

But the hauntological aspect of *(playing from another room)* does not seem to arise from these videos being a reminder of futures past. After all, the Cold War-era stock footage in the work of Cecil Robert—YouTube's most prolific creator of *(playing from another room)* videos —where Mazzy Star's 'Fade into You' plays over footage of atomic bomb tests, Joy Division's 'Love Will Tear Us Apart' accompanies a formation of B-17 bombers, and The Cure's 'Pictures of You' is the soundtrack to footage of a child being fitted for a gas mask,[17] seems to act more as a reminder of the destructive forces and terror of the period than a suggestion that 'the future' was uniquely an aspect of this time. Instead, we should consider these videos as working to stage and interrogate our haunted being in the world — our *haunted ontology* — under the dictatorship of the digital subject.

Indeed, as Albert Figurt argues in his discussion of the film genre 'desktop horror' — like the films *Unfriended* (2014), its sequel *Unfriended: Dark Web* (2019), and the aforementioned *Cam*—there are already many vernacular articulations of this sense that there are 'uncanny spirits in the machine', when it comes to apparatuses of platform capitalism.[18] And here it is worth noting that an extremely salient aspect of the comments in *(playing from another room)* videos is that *beyond* their sadness and sense of distance from the imagined action, they are overwhelmingly articulations of ersatz, unlived memories. Indeed, it recalls Jacques Derrida's assertion in Ken McMullen's *Ghost Dance* (1983) that 'to be haunted by a ghost is to remember something that you have never lived through'.[19]

This recalls Avery Gordons description of the ghost as a 'social figure',[20] (or, the spectral manifestation of social relations), and in this sense — especially with regard to its origins and functions — the ghost's parallels with the digital subject are striking: they are constituted by traces of the past, they are a force of epistemic ambiguation and alienation with regard to the self, and they are but an avatar of historical residues and processes that up until the point of the spectre's appearance are hidden or displaced. Per Gordon:

> The ghost or the apparition is one form by which something lost, or barely visible, or seemingly not there to our supposedly well-trained eyes, makes itself known or apparent to us, in its own way, of course. The way of the ghost is haunting, and haunting is a very particular way of knowing what has happened or is happening.[21]

While encounters with the digital subject tend to be experienced as fleeting ruptures in the smooth interfaces of platform capitalism — where seeing a poorly (or too well) targeted

17   See Cecil Robert, 'Mazzy Star- Fade into You (playing from another room)'; 'Joy Division- Love Will
      Tear Us Apart (playing from another room)', YouTube video, 27 July 2017, https://www.youtube.com/
      watch?v=2O2leeLgfwE; 'The Cure- Pictures of You (playing from another room)', YouTube video, 10 April
      2018, https://youtu.be/7XGbN-kJRIA.
18   Albert Figurt, 'Desktop Horror', presented at Video Vortex XII, Malta, September 2019. For an older,
      video essay version of this talk, see https://vimeo.com/360936270.
19   Jacques Derrida, in: Ghost Dance (dir. Ken McMullen, 1983), London: Channel 4 Films.
20   Avery Gordon, Ghostly Matters: Haunting and the Sociological Imagination, Minneapolis: University of
      Minnesota Press, 2008, p. 8.
21   Ibid.

ad may expose an element of the seething algorithmic processes behind their selection — *(playing from another room)* videos offer the possibility of a prolonged encounter with this phantasmagoric chimera of data, infrastructure, and media.

Although one may not recognise themselves as the origin of the music in the initial moment of viewing a *(playing from another room)* video — perhaps from the surprise of hearing it 'from another room' — as YouTube's 'autoplay' function serves more videos, and as they come to populate the human's recommendations in their homepage and sidebar, this McLuhanesque narcissus state slips away and the 'amputated'[22] self within the other room is displaced by the digital subject. This is to say that through the affordances of the YouTube platform, what begins as a facsimile of an encounter with platform capitalism's productive agent and the human from which it emerges eventually *becomes* that which it stages.

The ghost is therefore a hermeneutic and as with a ghost the moment of witnessing the digital subject is to become aware of, if only nominally: 1) our being haunted by it under platform capitalism, and 2) the distributed data, technologies, and infrastructures that track, capture, interpellate our being. Or, the material conditions that produce digital subjects and enable their haunting of us.

In bringing forth a being that is — at least partially — 'the self' rendered spectral, we might then say that the negative affect of this genre is possibly the sublimated realization of the extent to which platform capitalism has alienated the human from themselves. Events in the generic imaginary of *(playing from another room)* are always *somewhere else* and *inaccessible* to the viewer — while we may be affected by the operations of the digital subject, it is not from our being in the world that this affect arises — but instead by the future-foreclosing operation of the digital subject. Ergo, our future — per Derrida — 'belongs to ghosts'.[23] In this respect, the memories of distance and alienation evoked by *(playing from another room)* videos may well act as a metonym for the contemporary experience of time: extraordinary events occur, but things remain the same, with any event's possibility of generating 'the new' immediately contained by the homeostasis-producing operation of power of which the digital subject is a part.[24]

Of course, wallowing in the 'logic of despair'[25] wrought by a future that belongs to ghosts presents no possibility of a break from said logic, and while all of the above with regard to the digital subject as a ghost of the self is *true*, to focus entirely upon this aspect of the *(playing from another room)*-mediated encounter with the digital subject is to miss the forest for the trees, the haunted house for the ghost, or the singular instance of sadness for the immanent sadness of the contemporary. Indeed, while the digital subject is an instrument of a regime

22   Marshall McLuhan, 'The Gadget Lover: Narcissus as Narcosis', in Understanding Media: The Extensions of Man (Cambridge, Mass: MIT Press, 1994), p. 44.
23   Derrida, in: Ghost Dance.
24   Sean Cubitt, 'Virtual Dialectics and Technological Aesthetics', Cultural Politics: An International Journal 4, no. 2 (2008).
25   Bernard Stigler, 'Reflections on Ghost Dance', interview with Ken McMullen, January 2006, www.youtube.com/watch?v=hXQB7RFzoFM.

that has undermined our capacity to act in the world, crippled our psyches, and left us with sadness, here in *(playing from another room)* but certainly not limited to it, sadness does not necessarily indicate resignation to this spectral dictatorship.

Rather, I believe that this malaise points to a crisis in platform capitalism: perhaps the way the past is accumulated in these platforms does not allow us to 'get over things' nor even recognise the past as such — we are haunted, but we know not why. That *(playing from another room)* videos seem to uniquely be vectors for the recollection of memories that are not ours certainly suggests that what we face is a crisis of memory when platforms are the repositories of our history. Or perhaps the sadness provoked by these videos might be the quickening of an awareness of platform capitalism's corrosiveness and, maybe, is a prelude to our collective departure from the haunted house, our revisiting of the material mode of being in the world, and the reclamation of our productive capacities for ourselves.

References

Althusser, Louis. 'Ideology and ideological state apparatuses (notes towards an investigation)', in *Lenin and Philosophy and Other Essays*, New York: Monthly Review Press, 1971, https://

www.marxists.org/reference/archive/althusser/1970/ideology.htm

Bucher, Tania. *If...then: Algorithmic power and politics*, New York: Oxford University Press, 2018.

Cubitt, Sean. 'Virtual Dialectics and Technological Aesthetics', Cultural Politics: An International Journal 4, no. 2 (2008).

Dewitt, Corbin. 'Echo Location', *Real Life*, October 2017, https://reallifemag.com/echo-location/.

Figurt, Albert. 'Desktop Horror', presented at Video Vortex XII, Malta, September 2019.

Fisher, Mark. *Ghosts of My Life: Writings on Depression, Hauntology and Lost Futures*, Winchester, UK: Zero books, 2014.

General Data Protection Regulation (European Union). https://eur-lex.europa.eu/legal-content/EN/TXT/PDF/?uri=CELEX:32016R0679&from=EN.

Goldhaber, Daniel (dir.). *Cam*, 2018, Los Angeles: Blumhouse Productions.

Gordon, Avery. *Ghostly Matters: Haunting and the Sociological Imagination*, Minneapolis: University of Minnesota Press, 2008.

Han, Byung-Chung. *Psychopolitics: Neoliberalism and new technologies of power*, London; New York: Verso, 2017.

Lovink, Geert. *Sad by Design: On Platform Nihilism*, London: Pluto Press, 2019.

McLuhan, Marshall. 'The Gadget Lover: Narcissus as Narcosis', in *Understanding Media: The Extensions of Man*, Cambridge, MA: MIT Press, 1994.

McMullen, Ken, (dir.). *Ghost Dance*, 1983, London: Channel 4 Films.

Parisi, Luciana, and Steve Goodman. 'Mnemonic Control', in Patricia Clough and Craig Willse (eds), *Beyond biopolitics: Essays on the governance of life and death*, Durham: Duke University Press, 2011, pp. 163—176.

Robert, Cecil. 'Mazzy Star- Fade into You (Playing from Another Room)', YouTube video, December 2017, www.youtube.com/watch?v=BGLmIxySOiM.

_____. 'Joy Division- Love Will Tear Us Apart (playing from another room)', YouTube video, 27 July 2017, https://www.youtube.com/watch?v=2O2leeLgfwE.

_____. 'The Cure- Pictures of You (playing from another room)', YouTube video, 10 April 2018, https://youtu.be/7XGbN-kJRIA.

Stigler, Bernard. 'Reflections on Ghost Dance', interview with Ken McMullen, January 2006, www.youtube.com/watch?v=hXQB7RFzoFM.

Tame Impala, '*The Slow Rush* In An Imaginary Place', YouTube Video, 30 March 2020, https://www.youtube.com/watch?v=EA9uRfOJgM0.

IF THERE STILL IS A POINT TO CURATING SOCIAL MEDIA, WHAT IS IT?

HANG LI

IF THERE STILL IS A POINT TO CURATING SOCIAL MEDIA, WHAT IS IT?

HANG LI

Curating contemporary art on social media is seemingly a pitfall, an abyss, an (un)intentional conspiracy with the platform developers. We live in a time when the visions of dominant technology companies are threatening the ideals of bonded societies and independent wills. We, as users of social media, can hardly control with whom to connect or what to read. Nor do most of us know how to protect 'private' data from being captured, analysed, and sold back to us at some point. Social media is a sugar-coated bullet: entertaining and intoxicating us in daily activities, while harvesting our data and draining our ability to seek alternatives. Following this logic, curating on social networking platforms seldom goes beyond attracting more social media users under the pretence of 'supporting art.' Hence, such curatorial practices are suspected to be a squandering of both people's attention and art's public image. For this reason, avoiding social media as a curator seems to be ethical and justified. If this is true, then, is there any point in enacting contemporary art on social media?

In May of 2019, I — along with five other curators — staged *For the Time Being*, a five-day art event for the Digital Programme in The Photographers' Gallery (London). It was a graduate project for the MA Curating Contemporary Art at the Royal College of Art. As a programme initiated to explore the potentials and limitations of online curating, *For the Time Being* was based on Snapchat — an app for sharing intimate, disappearing digital images. Instead of engaging with social media for its marketing or disseminating effect, our programme saw Snapchat as a site, a channel, and a medium. Also, the platform became the subject, rather than merely the tool for art production and distribution. The aim was to experiment with the ways in which art could critically engage with the issues raised by social media from *within* the situation. Art production and reproduction was embedded in a platform's interface, protocols, and policies. Artistic communication was demarcated within a platform of particular aesthetics and regional expressions. This programme was seen as an opportunity for experimentations by the curators, artists, art institutions and scholars involved. The main focus lied in two strands of questions. One, how has social media changed our everyday lives and with what consequences? Two, what has art been doing on/with/around social media and what else could it be doing?

Today, curators, artists and art institutions use social media to detail their daily lives. Following a post-Fordist model of production, art workers must maintain this form of online communication to make visible and therefore prove their immaterial labour. Social media has, therefore, become a means of selling and tracking immaterial production within the art industry. People's profiles on social media become avatars waiting to be checked, liked, and stocked. Furthermore, within the neoliberal mentality of self-discipline and self-promotion, art workers' identities increasingly overlap with social media's ideal conception of 'users' — always mindful, creative, and expressive. The users are not only consumers, they are all cultural producers, helping to transform social media into habitable domains rather than digital tools. As a consequence, art workers become one the most enthusiastic and desirable labourers, those who are keen to devote time and creativity to perpetuating the prosperity of social media. What makes the role of art on social media more unfavourable is the value system of art ecology. It is a system developed based on physical, authentic objects and spaces, which is mostly incongruent with the mass-distributable, grassroots or ephemeral art practices. Such a value system has been long using social media as channels for distributing advertisement of the physical events ongoing outside digital networks. This has resulted in the marginalisation of those art practices which examine network cultures by embedding art practices in the digital platforms and cultures.

In parallel with the fashion of art promotion on social media, some art practitioners have deleted their accounts in resistance of this system. Their boycott, however, has resulted in fewer antagonists and critics on social media, with voices opposed to this regime effectively disappearing from the attention of users. Confronted with the dilemma of doing (for self-marketing) or not doing (as passive resistance), I suggest a redrawing of this dualism and enacting a re-search of social media. If we produce artworks on social media to think critically through these platforms, what forms could these artworks take, and what they would be capable of doing?

In response to those questions, For the Time Being invited five international contemporary artists—Agil Abdullayev, Feng Mengbo, Max Grau, Tamara Kametani, and the artist collective Agorama—to conduct photo-performances on Snapchat. Images and videos on Snapchat are short (no more than 10 seconds in length) and ephemeral (available for only 24 hours). This content is produced right on mobile phones and shared in a scalable digital network, the size of which depends on the number of a user's 'followers' or 'friends'. On this platform, not only has the definition of photo becomes increasingly indistinguishable from video, but the process of photo-taking has also been altered by Snapchat and other social media platforms that focus on digital images. The popularity of augmented-reality filters on social media with visual and audio effects such as 'beauty' 'baby' 'animal' 'queer' and 'gender altering', have introduced a process of filter selection and adjustment that has become integral to the concept of photo-taking. Photoproduction and distribution via mobile phones on social media, therefore, enables two strands of performance. One, the performance of a photographer/user who takes, edits, and posts photos thereby interacting with others in digital networks. Two, the behaviour of a photo, which includes the private photo-iteration introduced by photo-editing, as well as the following networked diffusion as the precondition of replication, annotation and reproduction. In this sense, the photo-performances commissioned by For the Time Being consisted of both the artistic performance produced by the artists, and the whole photo-behaviours enabled by social media. Through the five artists' photo-performances posted from a shared Snapchat account, For the Time Being constituted a collective identity that constantly posted (cool/weird/strange/fun) photos to its followers across the world for five days. The viewers include not only those who followed *For the Time Being* to watch art performances but also those who encountered 'For the Time Being' as a normal, random Snapchat user recommended by the platform's algorithms. As we decided not to post any labels to interpret the art performances, the latter group of people had little chance to recognise the posts as constituents of art performances. Apart from someone approached us on Snapchat and asked about what was going on, many may have seen 'For the Time Being' as a strange person who posted from day to night for a few days, and then suddenly vanished.

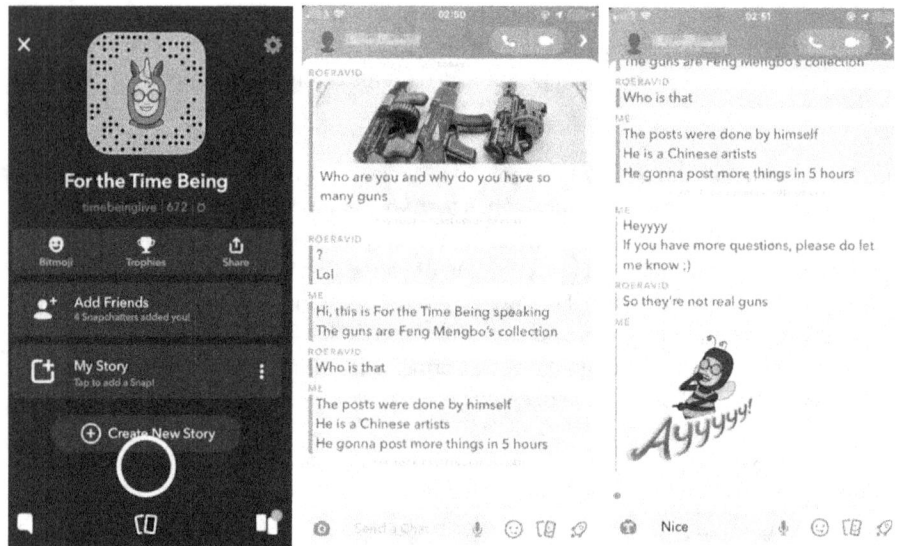

Fig. 1: Screenshot of For the Time Being's Snapchat account and conversation with a viewer. (The account is no longer active. For privacy protection, the images are processed to hide the viewer's account name)

Regarding the content of the photo-performances, Agil Abdullayev's film *Rashida from Baku* was a fiction that unfolded around a queer figure who explored the self, surrounded by the symbols and ideologies on social media. The photos taken by paparazzi of Lindsay Lohan and other pop stars were montaged with the protagonist's autobiography and manifestos. Seeing Snapchat's 10-second short-video format as a precondition of this film production, Abdullayev firstly wrote a script consisted of five ultra-short plots. Each plot was a poetic assemblage of fragmented but affective narrations. The direction of the film followed a similar approach to advertisement: everyday activities were distilled into symbolic gestures and postures. These actions appeared repetitively and are superimposed with eye-catching backgrounds. What was injected into the light-hearted visuals were the representation of controversies raised by social media concerning gender, identity, memory, and relationships. This hybrid approach, combining inconsistent, flamboyant expression with the disoriented, uneasy everyday life, contributed to the work's contextualised communication on social media.

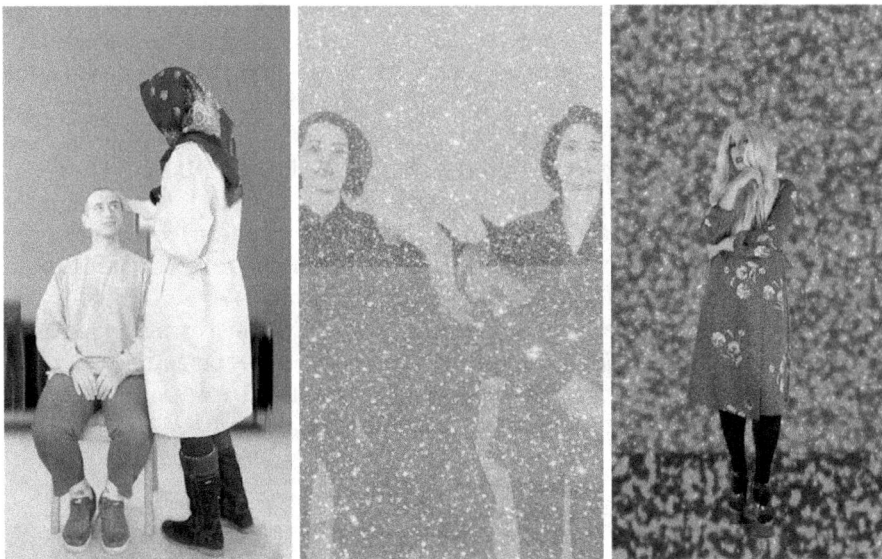

Fig. 2: Frames extracted from Agil Abdullayev's Rashida from Baku

Tamara Kametani's *what will be?* broadcast clips extracted from the daily news. The clips were superimposed with filters and digital stickers to encourage ironic interpretations of what was happening in the real-life. For example, a photo of Kim Jong-un was overlaid with a cute baby filter, for which the artist also chose a digital photo frame decorated with cute bears, and a line said, 'It's a BOY'. On this post, Kametani wrote the following headline: 'North Korea fires 2 missiles'. The effect of such subjective, witty social criticism was strikingly distinct from the solemn, authoritative voice of news publicaitons like *Politico*. Aside from international politics, Kametani also ridiculed surveillance technology. Posting a surveillance camera shot of a flying pigeon, she wrote: 'Pigeon flying over the speed limit in 30km/h zone in Germany is flashed by a speed camera'. Through evocative visual and textural connotations to news, the artist seemingly brought the role of the artist as a social critic into the social media context. Social media photo-editing appeared to provide a chance for Kametani to construct a simulacrum wherein live happenings are mirrored and layered with emotions, mockeries and biases. No intention can be found in those works to tilt those subjective expressions into authoritative representations.

In physical galleries, art objects with a taste of politics are widely beloved. But art objects are so distanced in space and delayed in time from the real happenings every day. This has resulted in the devitalisation of artistic expressions. In contrast to the object-centred art production, art practice can possess immediacy when it takes advantage of the live digital objects — the news, images and videos experiencing exponential replication and reproduction — for producing photo-performances embedded on social media. In this sense, *what will be?* was an experiment with abandoning the self-promotion mentality plaguing contemporary art culture. Art practices are capable, therefore, to disturb the meaning expressed by digital objects and to rework the present circulated on social media.

Instead of having blank optimism upon art production on social media, Kametani further questioned the future meaning and value of those works. She asks: 'when Snapchat becomes obsolete in the future will these images along with the news stories, induce the same sense of nostalgia that the 8bit graphics and sounds do now?'[1] Due to the speedy iteration and obsoletion of digital platforms and apparatuses, conserving born-digital art is certainly a significant challenge. However, as Kametani indicates, the political vitality of her artwork is active only in specific contexts. Preserving this vitality is arguably more urgent than conserving unanimated artworks. Today, the mainstream contemporary art culture is likely to devalue ephemeral, socially engaged art in comparison to the outdated, object-based art, which includes the 8bit graphics and sounds as well as analog film and photography. This might mean that when social media will be defunct, the art practices on social media like *what will be?* will seemingly be (nostalgically) appreciated more than now by the mainstream art culture. However, to what extent are the waning, nostalgic art objects capable of enacting edgy, responsive performances as *what will be?* has achieved?

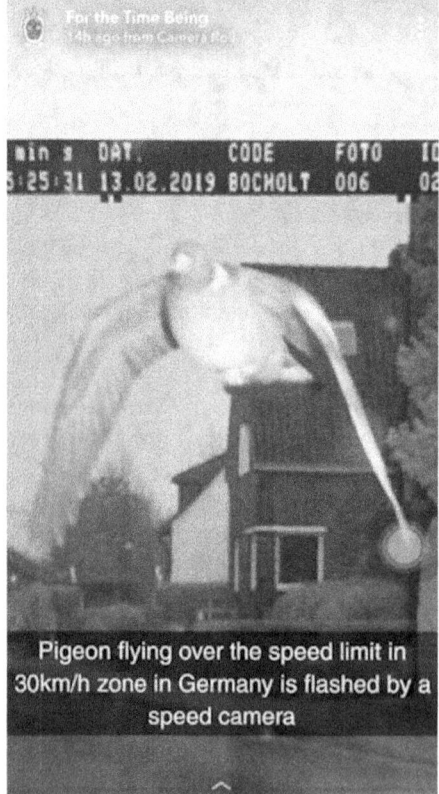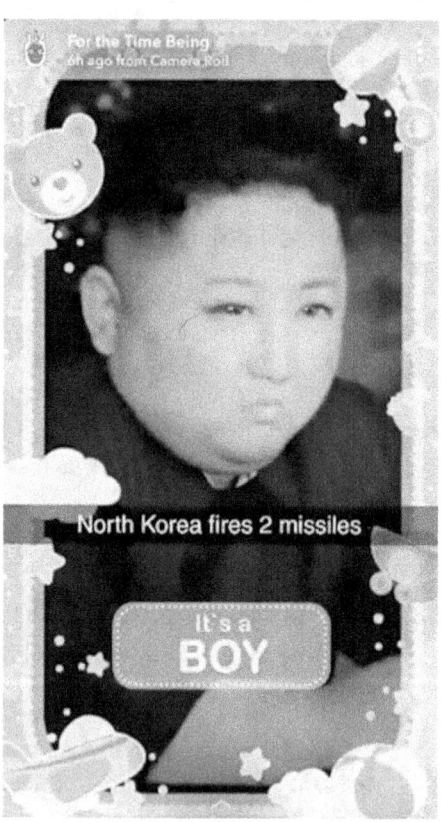

Fig. 3: Screenshots of Tamara Kametani's what will be?

---

1   Tamara Kametani, 'What will be?', *tamarakametani.com,* https://www.tamarakametani.com/#/what-will-
     be/.

Feng Mengbo was invited to adapt his WeChat project *The Big Collector Feng Mengbo* (id: collector_FMB) to Snapchat. Blending pre-recorded materials with live-streamed videos, Feng's photo-performance steamed from the collection he started to build half a century ago. Instead of approaching Snapchat performance by remediating the static publication hosted by WeChat, Feng chose to explore the potential of object filming based on the 10-second recording restriction of the platform. Sharing videos of artefacts online reminded us somehow of what is popular on YouTube and Twitch— streaming the experience of products ranging from toys to Virtual Reality headsets to inform the potential buyers. However, does filming objects through social media necessarily mean submitting to a fetishized, consumerist culture? Over the course of five days, Feng's camera moved around his collection including but not limited to model tanks, machine guns, garage kits, two-way radios, oscilloscopes and picture-story books popular in China in the 80s and 90s. Those watching Feng's photo-performance could feel Feng's breath and his bodily movements while his camera was sweeping across the collection of personal memories. The objects in the streaming were sometimes animated when being touched, played or programmed. A toy dj mixer was adjusted to produce a sound performance. An oscilloscope was programmed to show pictures and geometries while its noise became a work of sound art.

Feng's photo-performance suggested a way to produce art *from* objects without fetishizing the production *of* objects. Herein the cultural meanings sedimented in the filming as a performance were outweighed the monetary value of the objects in the film. For instance, when Feng's camera swept across roughly fifty machine guns, a viewer asked, 'Who are you and why you have so many guns'. After a while, Feng started to trigger his machine guns one by one and used the phone camera for aiming. It was at this moment another person commented, 'I'm impressed by what's on here'. Guns appearing in films or video games is nothing new for long. Whereas, when one look at phone screens in a bedroom or on the toilet, our sense of boundaries between security and danger, secrete and revelation, distribution and provocation become all tentative. Feng's sharing of machine guns on social media, therefore, triggers a mixture of vexation, hesitation and derision. This wordless, intimate communication and negotiation is specific to the combination of social media and mobile phones. Digital art production for *The Big Collector Feng Mengbo* is no longer for crafting 'limited editions' to secure the monetary value. It is a way how the artist Feng Mengbo used the identity of a 'big collector' to redefine objects and collections, by which to reanimate memories and cultures.

While the artists above navigated Snapchat as both poison and antidote, the artistic collective Agorama highlighted how the platform foreclosed cross-platform communication. In attempting to link Snapchat conversations to their programmed Artificial Intelligence chatbot named *Moses*, Agorama found the task impossible due to the limited power left to users to edit the platform's source code. Reciprocities between Snapchat posts and an AI programme located elsewhere are eliminated. Deliberately, Snapchat isolates itself from outside. To address this problem, Agorama chose to use Facebook Messenger to host the AI bot who solicits visual materials from people by chatting with them. These materials are automatically streamed online and are still available on Agorama's webpage.[2] In *For the Time Being*, Agorama

2   Agorama, 'Moses the Lonely Londoner – Stream of Consciousness,'

recorded the stream and reposted it on Snapchat, which exposed the nature of the platform as a broadcast medium.

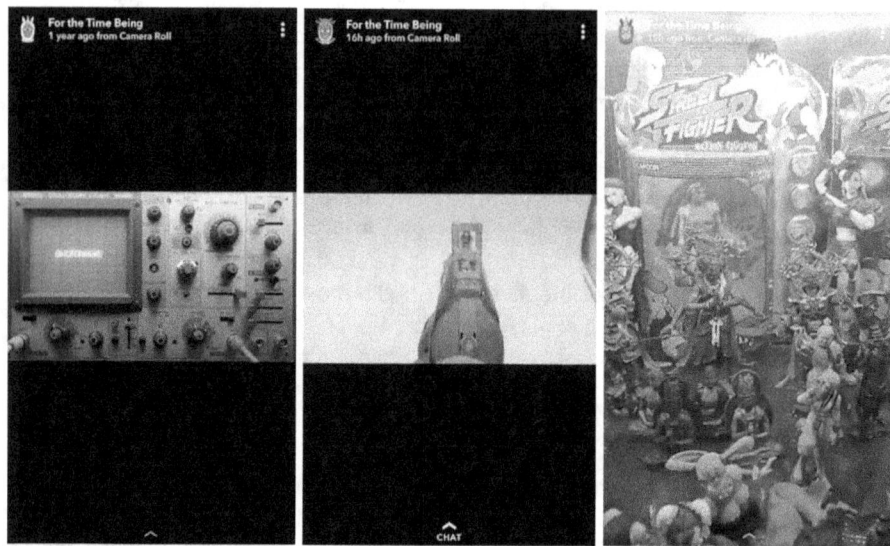

Fig. 4: Screenshots of Feng Mengbo's The Big Collector Feng Mengbo

Social media have indeed transformed everyone into 'micro mass media' able to to broadcast their everyday life. In this way social media has largely become pseudo 'social' platforms wherein decentralised social exchanges are scarce compared to the semi-centralised displays. However, without encouraging socially engaged actions, the 'mass media' aggregation on a platform will never formulate habitats for the mass. This symptom recalls me somehow the modernist galleries which host non-stop exhibitionist art shows. Interventional activities with social value rarely happen in either Snapchat or in the modernist galleries, due to the hosts' intention of retaining people within a socially detached, closed, and simulated environment.

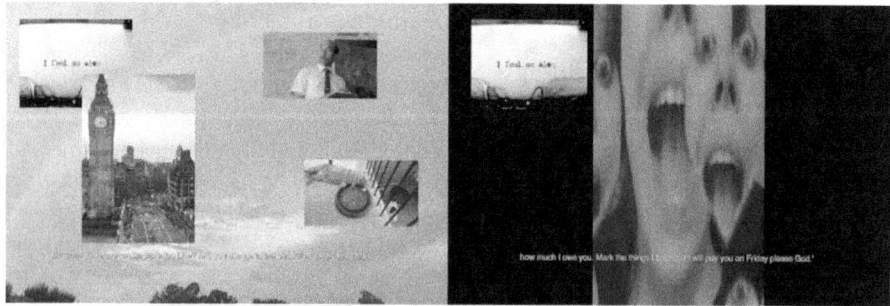

Fig. 5: Screenshots of Agorama's Moses the Lonely Londoner

http://moses-stream.agorama.org.uk/.

Max Grau in *For the Time Being* chose to conduct a lecture-performance *bbBbddDdyYyy_ssssss_a_cCccCAAaGGgee* in the physical space of The Photographers' Gallery, while the video materials displayed during which were mostly pre-recorded on Snapchat. Grau's Snapchat 'avatars' are recordings of his 'selves' made out from the augmented-reality filters. Those avatars had different voices, genders, and styles. While exploring the potential selves through those filters, Grau also admitted that working as on social media put him in an ironic situation. By connecting to those platforms, he was letting them to 'slowly eat away [his] friendship', and he may 'end up being along'.[3] Despite so, the avatars became Grau's means to narrate this understanding of the inscribed power relationships in contemporary art, and how it had been disturbed by the internet. Grau and his avatars told the audience about his early experience of visiting dominant art institutions with his mother. Contrast to the inclusivity claimed by most of those institutions, the architecture, wall texts and physical settings were hubristic and intimidating. This status quo was challenged by the distribution of artworks through social media. Art production on those free, network platforms has redefined the boundaries between the public and the private, while simultaneously problematised the financial barrier of appreciating and owning art. Although the utopian tradition is vanishing, Grau was willing to bring it back to social media strategically for psychological effects – to remind people how the internet, as well as the whole world, 'is utterly and irreversibly F.U.B.A.R.'.[4] Confronting the present being so broken to be fixed, what we should do, as Grau's work suggested, is to understand the problems of the reality and to turn those understanding into commons. In this sense, social media are places where self-reflexivity can be turned immediately into shared feelings between people from a long distance. Grau writes:

> Like, say… if art – in whatever form – streamed via Snapchat into the homes of the fellow shy people, the obsessive worriers, the chronically overwhelmed, the anhedonic shut-ins and the brutally hopeless would be able to create a sense of belonging: brief glimpses into the sensibilities of another subjectivity, a specific phrasing, a certain tone or timbre, the way images collide, a texture, a grain… something that somehow resonates with the way your own mind is structured, recognizing a distant relative to the oddly ineffable totality, comprised of a billion tiny fragments, that is insufficiently described as ›you‹: if a video, a sound, an artefact streamed into your room could create a scenario in which – if only for a brief moment – you would feel less alone in that room?[5]

People's relationships to social media are intimate, insecure, and intricate. Meanwhile, the relationship between people on the platforms oscillates constantly between isolation and common. The perplexing fabric implies latent social potentials and any reductive ascription

---

3   Max Grau, the script of a pre-recorded video named '23 loneliness_V.mov' in his performance *bbBbddDdyYyy_ssssss_a_cCccCAAaGGgee*.

4   Max Grau, the script of a pre-recorded video named '13 and I feel like_V.mov' in his performance *bbBbddDdyYyy_ssssss_a_cCccCAAaGGgee*; Max Grau, 'Utopia's Debris,' *For The Time Being*, 24 April 2019, http://forthetimebeing.co.uk/utopias-debris/. Regarding F.U.B.A.R., I understand it in this context as 'Fouled Up Beyond All Repair', and here's is Grau's annotation: 'I'll spare you my specifics. I'm sure you have your own set of panic-introducing topoi in place. If not: good for you! (This is not supposed to sound ironic.)'

5   Max Grau, 'Utopia's Debris,' *For The Time Being*, 24 April 2019, http://forthetimebeing.co.uk/utopias-debris/.

of those platform risks in overlooking these possibilities. Using social media as a means of art presentation enables a *performance*, or an *enactment* of the embodied understanding of social media rather than a representation. This can be the first step towards configuring spaces of potentialities existing on, or beyond social media.

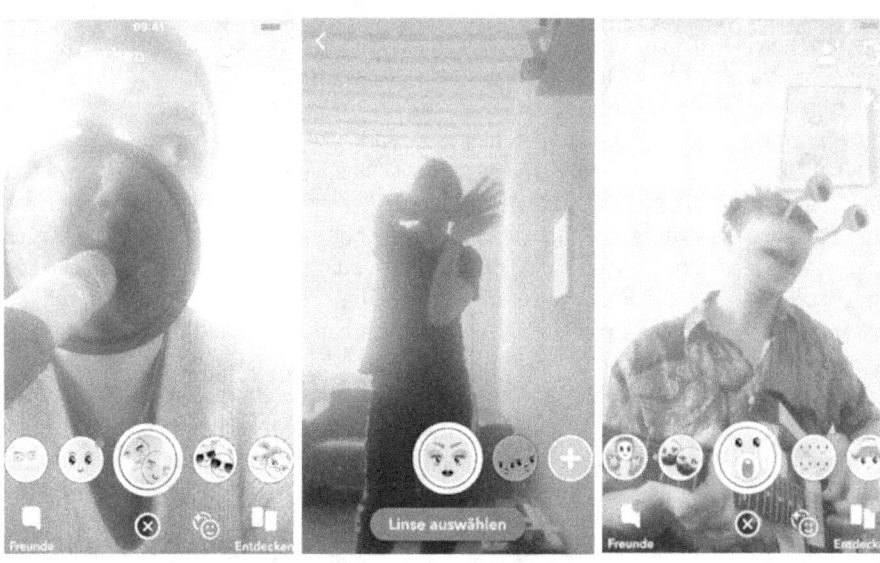

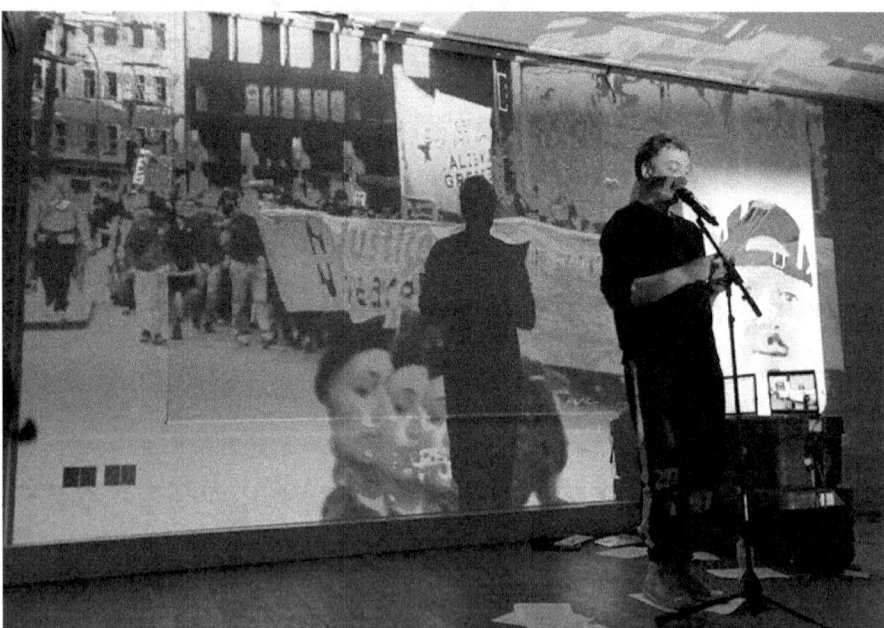

Fig. 6-7: Screenshots of Max Grau's lecture performance *bbBbddDdyYyy_ssssss_a_cCccCAAaGGgee* in The Photographers' Gallery. Photographed by Deepak Singh Kathait.

Let us return to the question I raised at the beginning of this text: When social media are grounded in neoliberalism and technocracy, is there any meaning left for art to enact something on those platforms? Compared to purist approaches to curating, which insist on the consistency between the platform, intention and content, I would argue for an opposite one. Curating can situate in a 'mud land' proactively and stir up 'dirty' matters provocatively, to create contact zones in-between people, concepts and actions. Today, the once bourgeois and now neoliberal art parties have joined forces with media technologies in modelling online art activities as marketing. In parallel, populism and technocracy are rampantly expanding both online and offline. These tendencies have left little room for people to debate on everyday occurrences and to come up with constructive tactics. To respond to this social and political impotence in reshaping the present, we need more critical voices to be pronounced, heard, and turned into actions.

Social media is surely not the best place for such activation, yet it is admittedly a place where *For the Time Being* connected to hundreds of young people around the world. Those youngsters explore their 'digital' surroundings, lively and curiously. They respond to what pops up on their screens as something injecting into their life. A filter, a post and a piece of comment may all have cognitional effects to them. This responsiveness on social media today is a latent power. Such power will aggregate and turn into a generation's understandings of the surroundings and selves shortly.

Curating contemporary art on social media does not necessarily mean taking these platforms for granted. Instead, it is a way to examine the platforms while maintaining a critical distance from their embedded ideologies and norms. Furthermore, it is to elaborate on interpreting the problems of them and to experiment with transforming the findings into critical practices. Therefore, if curating on social media has some value today, it is the possibility of grounding artistic research and intervention in active networks of people and cultures distanced from where art locates and emerges. This process of defamiliarization for both art practitioners and social media users is (for the time being) capable of evoking reflections, dialogues and actions on the internet in the name of art or as an anonymous user.

COVID-19 Update

This is mid-April 2020. After a year since *For the Time Being* finished, four months after I sent this piece of writing back to the Institute of Networked Cultures, COVID-19 is sweeping Europe and the United Kingdom. Many countries have constrained people's physical contacts massively and unprecedently. Art institutions have closed their physical galleries. Curating has to choose between taking place online or suspending until the pandemic is mitigated. It is at this point that I decided to look back at this text and to reflect upon the same subject – curating on social media – facing the world(s) being plagued and transformed by a pandemic. (I am no longer confident if 'the world' exists. In substitution, I stand for the multiplicity of the worlds.)

Despite that social media platforms are equally if not increasingly controversial as the year before, YouTube, Twitter, Facebook, Instagram and TikTok are crucial means of social connection during COVID-19 for a great number of people. In this way, social connections and exchange are not evaporating, but rather growingly intensified. The worlds unfolded on social media are oversaturated with news, distortion, confusion, frustration, fury and hysteria. It is on social media that many people have experienced the new wave of xenophobia and political propaganda that arose from the coronavirus. Some of us have also witnessed how technophobia was spreading in the form of a conspiracy, claiming people can contract the virus via 5G exposure.

Rather than seeing social media as a collection of surreal happenings, it seems urgent to gaze into them as real as the realities. These happenings did not emerge with the COVID-19-related segregations and collapses. Instead, they have long existed in the social realities, and are brought forth by COVID-19. In this sense, today, when COVID-19 has introduced a significant body of crises and distrusts spanning across the globe, social media have become the most active and complex medium to transmit scattered thoughts into collective emotions, commotions or alienations. The alarming power of social media also bears the potential to mutate any of those feelings and attitudes into cultures, revolutions or violence.

Those realities enunciated by social media are underrepresented in mainstream art culture for long. For this art culture, these unsettling and vulgar realities are were either too peripheral or too prickly to confront. Meanwhile, for some advocating activist art, as exemplified by Lucy R.Lippard, social media are flattening the unmatched 'affects and effects' of 'face-to-face discussions and collaborations', therefore worth little for those focus on socially/politically/environmentally engaged art.[6] However, contemporary art has long been legitimating itself as a means of identifying and investigating everyday life. This every life does not — and should not — preclude a digitally-mediated one. During COVID-19, when social media become the main ways to participate in the social change, contemporary art has barely reason to shun either the social, political, cultural crises or the digital screens and networks catalysing them.

In other words, this is not perfect timing for art institution and curators to bury their heads in sands and looking back to the 'good' days when we had face-to-face art events. Neither is it the time to continue reducing social media as channels for promotion and advertisement. It is at this moment that contemporary art as cultural power-holders are expected to be sensitized, confronting the intensity and tension on social media, and the invisible yet palpable uproar behind the empty streets.

On 26th of March, Tate sent an email to the subscribers titled: 'How we're keeping connected, creative and calm'. In this email, Tate said that, 'while our doors are closed, we'll be sharing some of our favourite ideas to help you discover art you love, spark a new hobby or enjoy a quiet moment away from the headlines.'[7] However, facing the condition that hundreds of people die every day, and the national health system is in a critical situation, do we expect an art institution like Tate to teach us how to develop a hobby in calm and creative manners? If Tate has contributed to represent the identity, heritage and legacy of a nation and the globe for

6   Lucy R. Lippard, 'Is Another Art World Possible?', in Kim Charnley (ed.) and Gregory Sholette, *Delirium and Resistance: Activist Art and the Crisis of Capitalism*, London: Pluto Press, 2017, p. xviii.
7   The Tate, email newsletter, 26th of March 2020.

more than a century, how it will hold this position and reputation if it does not willing to sense the temperature of the current social and political realities?

Despite the occasional anachronism in its self-presentation, Tate is indeed well-acknowledged the power and significance of art that, '[now] more than ever, art can lift our spirits, brighten our days and support our mental health'. [8] Based on of this position, as a researcher in curating contemporary art, I would like to suggest that overloaded positivity or nostalgic attachment to physical matters (exhibition, collection, archive, etc.) may not offer people much when there are shattering worlds to reshape during and after the pandemic. What is valuable here and now, is to open up discussions to relocate art in the precarious present(s) and future(s), which are disclosed by COVID-19 and unfolded on the internet. Hopefully enough, those present(s) and future(s) in the eyes of contemporary art do not preclude the socio-political implosion ongoing on social media during COVID-19.

For the Time Being was curated by Rachel Chiodo, Sitara Chowfla, Hang Li, Esther Moerdler, Carlos Pinto, and Caroline Rosello and sought to explore the shifting responsibilities of institutions in this networked age, as part of the MA Curating Contemporary Art Programme Graduate Projects 2019 at Royal College of Art, London. The exhibition is produced in collaboration with The Photographers' Gallery. At Video Vortex XII, the documentation, website and writings of *For the Time Being* were exhibited as *Restaging For the Time Being* and was curated by Hang Li and Caroline Rosello.

References

Agorama. 'Moses the Lonely Londoner — Stream of Consciousness', http://moses-stream.agorama.org. uk/.

Grau, Max. 'Utopia's Debris', *For The Time Being*. 24 April 2019. http://forthetimebeing.co.uk/utopias-debris/.

Kametani, Tamara. 'What will be?', https://www.tamarakametani.com/#/what-will-be/.

Lippard, Lucy R. 'Is Another Art World Possible?', in Kim Charnley (ed.) and Gregory Sholette, *Delirium and Resistance: Activist Art and the Crisis of Capitalism*, London: Pluto Press, 2017.

The Tate. 'Our galleries will be closing', email newsletter, 17 March 2020.

_____. email newsletter, 26 March 2020.

---

8   The Tate, 'Our galleries will be closing', email newsletter, 17th of March 2020.

PLAYING THE REVOLUTION

PETER SNOWDON

PLAYING THE REVOLUTION

PETER SNOWDON

Between the spring of 2011 and the autumn of 2013, I spent some two and a half years making a feature-length montage film about the Arab revolutions out of YouTube videos.[1] Soon after I started working with this material, I was struck by the way in which many of these videos were the kind of videos I would have liked to make myself, if I had had the chance to be there. This was a little surprising to me, since my film work comes out of an experimental/avant-garde tradition. But I was repeatedly seeing in these YouTube videos things I recognized and valued. Specifically, I was seeing: a subjective, sometimes even gestural, camera style, worthy of Jean Rouch, if not of Jonas Mekas himself; a radical refusal of montage that both Chantal Akerman and James Benning would have been quite at home with; and, an anti-narrative, anti-dramatic approach to structure, rhythm and tension, which suggested the influence of a Jon Jost or a Wang Bing. At the same time, I was fairly sure that most of the people making these videos had never heard of these filmmakers I admired, let alone were familiar with their work.

So where was this embodied, radically subjective, radically anti-dramatic visual style coming from? And, more importantly, why were people spending their valuable time watching videos like this? After all, the fact that people film like this may be largely explainable in terms of the technological limitations of camera phones, the ergonomics of participatory street fighting, and their lack of access to, or patience with, video editing software. But that still wouldn't explain why these videos are clocking up thousands of hits on YouTube's enigmatic counter.[2] And not just the ones which do, inadvertently, resemble good raw news footage, or a handheld Hollywood action scene, but the ones I like, too: the ones where the camera is all over the place, where there is no legible information or intelligible event, the ones were nothing at all interesting happens for the first six minutes (or forever). People watch these videos — not just over-privileged researcher-filmmakers with too much time on their hands. People. Including the people who were out in the street, hoping to make these revolutions happen. This, in itself, seems to me to be a fact that deserves some attention.

The first hypothesis that suggested itself to me, and the one that I would like to explore here, is that people throughout the world, including across the Arab region, have learned to appreciate this kind of video footage, or at least to be more tolerant of it, not by attending Marie Mencken retrospectives sponsored by their local US embassy, but by playing widely

---

1   *The Uprising* (dir. Peter Snowdon, 2013), Brussels/Newcastle: Rien à Voir/Third Films, free to view at theuprising.be/Watch.

2   YouTube does not reveal the details of the algorithms it uses to count video views, on the grounds that to do so might hinder their efforts to prevent users artificially inflating view counts. The precise mechanisms are the subject of ongoing speculation, as for example at: webapps.stackexchange.com/questions/16906/youtubeview-count-how-does-it-work; atlantaanalytics.com/practicing-webanalytics/how-does-youtube-video-view-count-work/. I am grateful to Ulrike Riboni for inducting me into these mysteries.

diffused, and enormously popular, commercial video games. For the visual experience of many of these video games – and in particular, those belonging to the first person shooter genre – can be described in very similar terms: a rigorously subjective point of view, no montage as such, and a dramaturgy in which rapid bursts of extreme intensity are separated by shorter or longer periods of relatively uneventful movement and exploration.[3]

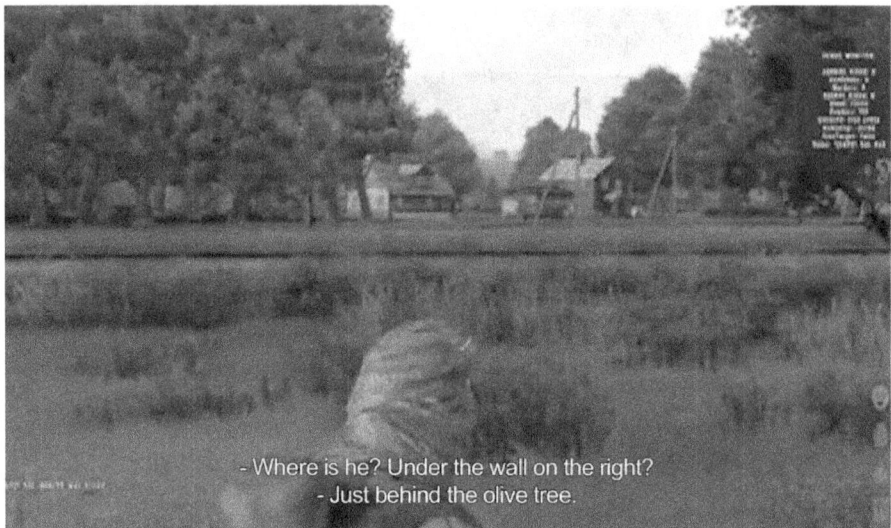

Fig. 1: Still from It's a ghost town (2013)

The formal origins of the first-person shooter have been explored by scholars, most notably by Alexander Galloway and, following him, Mathieu Triclot.[4] As Galloway points out, these visual tropes are as old as the film industry itself. But in mainstream commercial cinema they have always remained marginal, because the subjective camera and the refusal of montage (that is, the refusal to visually dramatize, or even acknowledge, the multiple points of view implicit in any scene) actually function not to promote identification between the viewer and the character, but to block it.

---

3   There is little reliable data on how many gamers there are in the Arab region, or what games they play. Most of the evidence I have been able to uncover is anecdotal. An order of magnitude contemporary with the revolutions of 2011-12 may be sensed from industry figures for 2011 which claim that 36% of the world's 1.6 billion online gamers are based in the Arab world, with Egypt providing the second largest number of them (figures from Tohme, Alexandra. 'Gaming In The Middle East', February 2011, https://www.slideshare.net/AlexandraTohme/gaming-in-the-middle-east). Important testimony can be found in Helga Tawil-Souri, 'The Political Battlefield of Pro-Arab Video Games on Palestinian Screens', *Comparative Studies of South Asia, Africa and the Middle East* 27.3 (January 2007): 536–551. Tawil-Souri's account demonstrates a widespread enthusiasm for first-person shooters in the West Bank, among girls as well as boys – an enthusiasm which was entirely confirmed by my own experience of 'passive gaming' while a regular user of several Internet cafés in Ramallah during the final quarter of 2003.

4   See Alexander Galloway, 'Origins of the First-Person Shooter', in *Gaming: Essays on Algorithmic Culture*, University of Minnesota Press, 2006, 39–69; and Mathieu Triclot, *Philosophie des Jeux Vidéos*, Paris: Zones, 2011, pp. 79–87.

In the cinema, the subjective camera is experienced as deeply alienating, so much so that it can only be tolerated in small doses, and under some narrative device which ascribes the point of view thus demonstrated not to an ordinary human being like us, but either to one who is temporarily under the influence of extreme emotion, or drugs – or to a less-than- or non-human entity, such as a psychopath, a monster from outer space, or a machine.[5] As Pascal Bonitzer once put it, extended use of the subjective camera, as in Robert Montgomery's *The Lady in the Lake* (1947), where the role of Philip Marlowe is taken by the camera itself, tends to be based on a misunderstanding of the cinema's central underlying convention, which is that 'it is not at the place of the subject that the camera operates, but from the place of the other.'[6]

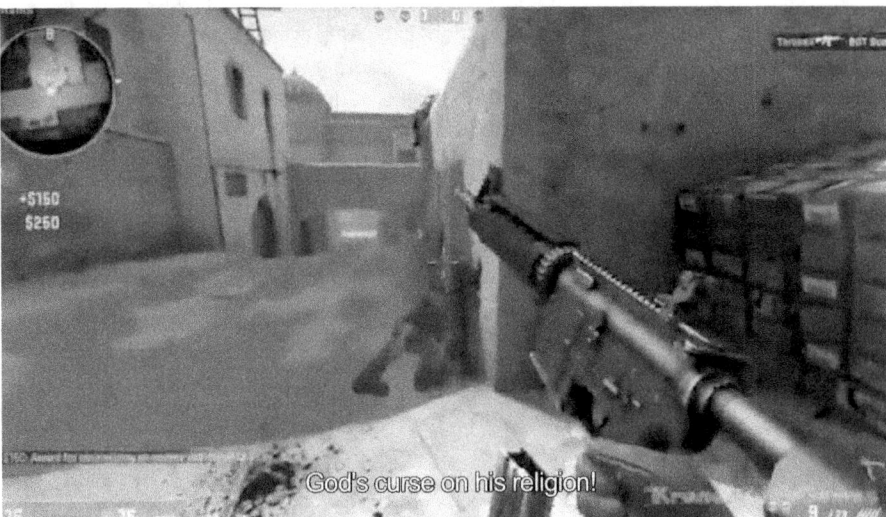

Fig. 2: Still from It's a ghost town (2013)

No way out?

Galloway proposes that what blocks identification in the cinema becomes instead a means to enhanced identification in a video game such as *Counter Strike* or *Call of Duty*, though he doesn't really explain how this might come about. Triclot however argues that, on the contrary, video games in no way neutralise or normalise the first-person point of view. Indeed, it is this constant strangeness of, and estrangement from, our largely invisible avatar that impels the player to constantly reiterated action, in the vain attempt to achieve some kind of normality or stasis.

---

5   On Arab revolutionary discourse as identifying the point of view of the people with the point of view of the machine, see Peter Snowdon, 'Game over Mubarak': the Arab Revolutions and the Gamification of Everyday Life', *Fast Capitalism* 11.1 (2014): 23-29,
    fastcapitalism.journal.library.uta.edu/index.php/fastcapitalism/article/download/300/348.

6   Pascal Bonitzer, 'Partial Vision: Film and the Labyrinth', *Wide Angle* 4.4 (1981): 58, as cited in Galloway, *Gaming*, p. 132.

But what kind of normality could one possibly hope to achieve in this way? What good will pressing buttons and joggling joysticks do, when the fundamental problem to be overcome is not that there are too many terrorists in town, or too many zombies on the loose, but that you have no legs, no real arms, in fact, no body at all, and if you have one eye, you certainly don't have two? The first-person shooter reduces the player to a monocular lens that navigates the world using a means of locomotion that is a cross between a flying carpet and a filmmaker's dolly. The mission that she confronts, ultimately, is to prove the unprovable – that she is, in fact, a human being, and not, as all the evidence would seem to suggest, a camera (or the simulation of a camera).[7]

To put it in Bonitzer's terms, what you want to do when you play, and what you rarely, or never, can do, is to escape from the psychotic subject position[8] that the virtual camera generates when we take it literally, so as to enter into a world where the reciprocity of points of view which founds your everyday sense of yourself as a functioning subject is, if not actively dramatised, then at least tacitly acknowledged. Or to put it even more simply: the fate of the first-person shooter, whether she or he shoots bullets or pixels, is always, inevitably, to be alone, when all they really want, is to be together.

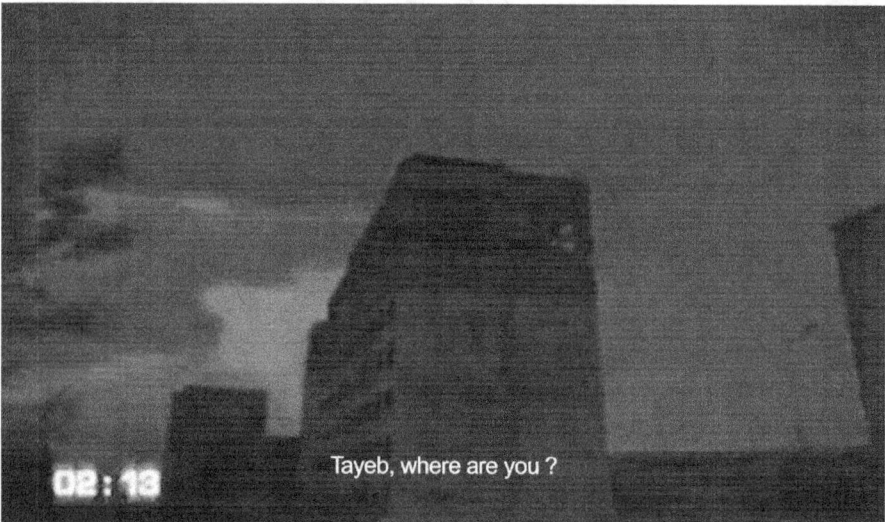

Tayeb, where are you ?

02:13

Fig. 4: Still from It's a ghost town (2013)

---

7   Triclot: 'When it comes to incarnation and our relationship to our own body, what does the FPS point of view provide us with? A mobile, outsized eye, in search of its own body and its various parts.' The result is 'a paradoxical kind of immersion, one that is deprived of any body of its own.' *Philosophie des Jeux Vidéos*, 82, 84: author's translation.

8   Compare the description of Cotard's syndrome: 'a psychiatric condition that, according to Lacan, 'belongs to the psychotic nucleus' [and which] consists in the delusional conviction according to which one doesn't possess brains anymore, or nerves, breasts, heart, stomach, blood and, sometimes, not even a body.' Fernando Tenório, 'Death of the subject: representation and real limit in the clinic of psychosis', *Ágora: Estudos em Teoria Psicanalítica* 19.3 (2016): 556. The reference to Lacan is to Book 2 of the *Seminar,* first published in French in 1978.

'Join us, o our people'

I want to suggest, then, that it is at this level that video games can help us make some sense of the role YouTube videos may have played in the Arab revolutions – to use an old-school distinction, at the level of form, not of content. And while these videos don't simply replicate the gameplay aesthetic, comparing these two media practices as first and foremost formal systems can help us think about what is unique to each of them, as well as about what each of them may have borrowed, consciously or unconsciously, from the other. To explore this subject in depth would deserve a monograph to itself. Here, I just want to make two points, one about similarity, and one about difference.

Firstly, I believe that to view these YouTube videos as they were meant to be viewed, we have to see them primarily not as documents, but as a spur to action. They are documents, of course. But the main reason they exist and are uploaded is not to document what happened, but to make something new happen: to goad us into getting up off our sofas, and away from our keyboards, and out into the streets. And their formal homology with the video games I have discussed is a sign, beyond any stylistic differences, of their functional identity. We are meant to respond to them, not with aesthetic contemplation, intellectual interrogation, or even emotional elation or despair, but by doing something in our turn. They are a move in a game, and they expect an answering move on our part.[9]

In this sense, the actions that these revolutionary videos call for are fundamentally the same as those which the video games I've discussed seek to provoke. That is, what we need to do is not to find a key, acquire a piece of equipment, or take out a hidden sniper (though there are YouTube videos from the Arab revolutions that speak to those themes, too). What we need to do is break out of the solitude that 30 years or more of this misery and contempt have imprisoned us in.[10] We need to escape from the tunnel vision of survival, and make contact with the others around us, without whose recognition – both visual and ethical – we would go crazy. We need to become human again, not through solitary acts of heroism, but by re-entering reciprocity, by finding (or composing) a community, and thus making ourselves available to others who are not simply given, but will also need to be found in their turn.

---

9   Perhaps the most explicit articulation of this overarching intention is to be found in Asmaa Mahfouz's celebrated video blog of 18 January 2011: 'Sitting at home and just following us on news or Facebook leads to our humiliation, my own humiliation… If you stay at home, then you deserve all that's being done to you. And you will be guilty, before your nation and your people. And you'll be responsible for what happens to us on the street while you sit at home… Never say there's no hope. Hope disappears only when you say there's no hope. So long (as) you come down with us, there will be hope.' Iyad El-Baghdadi, 'Meet Asmaa Mahfouz and the vlog that Helped Spark the Revolution', 1 February 2011, YouTube video, youtu.be/SgjIgMdsEuk. For a more extended consideration of this topic, see Peter Snowdon, 'The party of the couch,' in The People Are Not an Image: Vernacular Video After the Arab Spring, London: Verso, forthcoming 2020.
10   Zeinobia. '#Jan28 a small protest in Agouza', 3 March 2011, YouTube video, youtu.be/lQ1LjehDmdc.

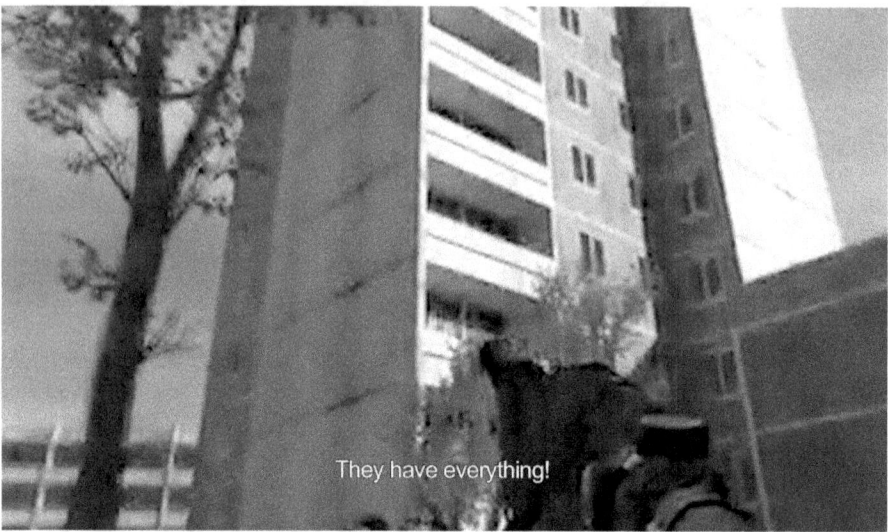

Fig. 4: Still from It's a ghost town (2013)

But there is also a fundamental difference. The kind of community, reciprocity, alterity, which these YouTube videos invoke comes to us in a different way than does the collectivity to which the lone gamer aspires. In the revolution, at keyboard is continuous with away from keyboard. A real encounter is possible, if not always practicable. To meet real people face-to-face, we don't have to step out of the game: we have to step into it. And we know this, not just because it is obviously true, but also because these videos almost always carry within themselves the evidence of its possibility. For among the many traces they bear, are the traces of encounters, meetings, moments of being together, moments in which the proof of my existence is not to be found in an act of inward reflection, but in the fact that I am able to be with, and for, others.

In even the most beautiful and poetic of the video games I have played, what I hear is always solitude calling to solitude. In these YouTube videos, we can hear the individual calling to the many, and we can also hear the many answering the individual. To quote one of my favourite come-on-down chants from Cairo on 25 January, 2011: these videos say many, contradictory things, but on one level, they are all saying the same thing: 'Join us, o our people.'[11]

That's what we hear in these videos, whether we live in Lüneburg or Latakia, in Dahklaia or New Delhi, in Aden or in Oakland. And once we've heard it, it's up to us whether we choose to answer that call, or not.

---

11   FreedomRevolution25. 'Day One of Egypt's Freedom Revolution I January 25, 2011', 24 January 2012, YouTube video, youtu.be/Co-oJUk_P_A.

Note

This text was originally written to accompany the first public screening of my video, It's a ghost town (10 minutes, 2013), on 1 March 2013 at Video Vortex #9, Leuphana University in Lüneburg. Based on an idea by my friend and editor Bruno Tracq, this video remixes gameplay videos of DayZ, Counter Strike: Global Offensive, and Call of Duty 4 found on YouTube, with four revolutionary videos from Libya, Bahrain and Syria. It does so, specifically, by transposing the soundtracks of the gameplay videos onto the camera phone videos, and vice versa. One of the ideas behind this experiment — though not the only one — was that a major difference between the use of the subjective 'camera' in these two kinds of video is in the role of sound in creating off-screen space. The soundtracks of the camera phone videos, despite — but also because of — their many limitations from an audiophile perspective, are radically open onto a world they can neither predict nor comprehend. This is not the case for the highly composed and focused sound worlds of these video games.

It's a ghost town was subsequently shown as part of the exhibition Pratiques de la distraction in the galleries of the HEAD High School for Art and Design, Geneva, in May 2019, curated by Christophe Kihm, Paul Sztulman, Dork Zabunyan and their work.master students. It is now available to view free online at: vimeo.com/61669010.

An earlier version of this text was first published in French as 'Jouer la révolution' in Smala Cinéma, 3, October 2014, 19-22. I am grateful to the participants at Video Vortex #9 for their feedback, and to Remco Roes, Hallveig Aggudsdottir, and Karolina Majewska for their comments on an earlier draft of this text. My thinking on the relationship between video games and YouTube videos from the Arab revolutions has been continuously informed by my conversations with Bruno Tracq while we were editing The Uprising together. None of these people are in any way responsible for the conclusions drawn here.

References

El-Baghdadi, Iyad. 'Meet Asmaa Mahfouz and the vlog that Helped Spark the Revolution', 1 February 2011, YouTube video, youtu.be/SgjlgMdsEuk.

Evanlapointe. 'How does YouTube video view count work?', Atlanta Analytics (blog), October 2010, atlantaanalytics.com/practicing-webanalytics/how-does-youtube-video-view-count-work/.

FreedomRevolution25. 'Day One of Egypt's Freedom Revolution | January 25, 2011', 24 January 2012, YouTube video, youtu.b e/Co-oJUk_P_A.

Galloway, Alexander. Gaming: Essays on Algorithmic Culture, Minneapolis: University of Minnesota Press, 2006.

Herr. 'How does YouTube view count work?', July 2011, question on Stack Exchange, webapps. stackexchange.com/questions/16906/youtubeview-count-how-does-it-work.

Snowdon, Peter (dir.). The Uprising, 2013, Brussles/Newcastle: Rien à Voir/Third Films, view at theuprising.be/Watch.

_____. ''Game over Mubarak': the Arab Revolutions and the Gamification of Everyday Life',
Fast Capitalism 11.1 (2014): 23-29, fastcapitalism.journal.library.uta.edu/index.php/fastcapitalism/
article/download/300/348.

_____. 'The party of the couch', in *The People Are Not an Image: Vernacular Video After the
Arab Spring*, London: Verso, forthcoming 2020.

Tawil-Souri, Helga. 'The Political Battlefield of Pro-Arab Video Games on Palestinian Screens',
Comparative Studies of South Asia, Africa and the Middle East 27.3 (January 2007): 536-551.

Tenório, Fernando. 'Death of the subject: representation and real limit in the clinic of psychosis',
Ágora: Estudos em Teoria Psicanalítica 19.3 (2016): 549-564.

Tohme, Alexandra. 'Gaming In The Middle East', February 2011, https://www.slideshare.net/
AlexandraTohme/gaming-in-the-middle-east.

Triclot, Mathieu. *Philosophie des Jeux Vidéos*, Paris: Zones, 2011.

zeinobia. '#Jan28 a small protest in Agouza', 3 March 2011, YouTube video, youtu.be/lQ1LjehDmdc.

REFERENTIALITY: VIDEO BOOK CASE STUDY

ADNAN HADZI, OLIVER LERONE SCHULTZ AND PABLO DESOTO

REFERENTIALITY: VIDEO BOOK CASE STUDY

ADNAN HADZI, OLIVER LERONE SCHULTZ, AND PABLO DESOTO

1 *after.video II*: A Video Vortex Computer Book

The second version of the *after.video* computer book, *after.video II*, will serve as proceedings of the *Video Vortex XII* conference, allowing for artists, filmmakers, academics, and participants of the *Video Vortex XII* conference to contribute to the proceedings through audio-visual materials, rather than text and image only. The DIY infrastructures of *after.video* offer a rich set of unique characteristics and affordances for offering local services to the video vortex community outside the public Internet: the ownership and control of the whole design process that promotes independence and grass-roots innovation rather than a loss of control and fear of data shadows; the de facto physical proximity of those connected without the need for disclosing private location information, such as GPS coordinates, to third parties; the easy and inclusive access through the use of a local captive portal launched automatically when one joins the *after.video II* network; the option for anonymous interactions; and the materiality of the network itself. The *after.video II* computer book, the Video Vortex XII proceedings, integrates existing FLOSS software, from very simple applications to sophisticated distributed solutions (like those under development by the P2Pvalue project, mobile sensing devices, and recent developments in open data and open hardware), allowing it to be appropriated by different non-expert users according to their respective context and use case.

after.video is a video book.[1] It is a peer-produced and collectively facilitated volume of digital video edited into a physical object — a Raspberry Pi board. The theoretical aspect of this project is articulated in the scholarly gesture of making this video book, constituted as it is of digital processes and audio-visual assemblages. It is a contribution to thinking through the world after digital video. The purpose of this project is to argue that the imaginative and intellectual work undertaken by the *after.video* contributors and participants is, or can be, a form of research. As an area of individual, social and cultural inquiry, video as a format remains somewhat under-researched.

Unlike previous experiments with hypertext and interactive databases, *after.video* attempts to translate online modes into physical matter (here a microcomputer), thereby reflecting logics of new formats otherwise unnoticed. Conceptual atoms are then re-combined differently throughout the video-book — by rendering a dynamic, open structure, allowing for access to the *after.video II* book over an 'after_video II' WiFi SSID, approaching digital video and its assemblages as a mode of inquiry based on the theories, practices and contexts used by the *after.video* participants.

---

1   Adnan Hadzi, Oliver Lerone Schultz, Pablo de Soto and Laila Shereen Sakr. *after.video*, London: Open Humanites Press; 2017.

after.video uses the mazizone.eu as a platform for the second edition of the video book, interpreting the organizational concept of hypertext for a film environment. Imagine the World-Wide-Web as a hypertext system, where all the interconnected text fragments are replaced by film. The resulting web of film fragments becomes the organizational structure and the basis for document access. In the context of academic book culture this creates a digital, potentially networkable/connective object, that can be sculpted and designed, thereby resembling a 'book' as traditionally conceived. This 'video-book' object can hold the mazizone.eu-framework and itself be used as hybrid object. Part of this hybridity is to travel/mediate between the two domains of the digital and the physical (where traditional 'books' and 'papers' reside); another hybrid quality is a dual mode existence as offline and online device — while 'offline' and non-connectivity answers to another trait associated with classical books, it also opens up to the aesthetics of maker-culture and the growing 'offline'-movement (as it still remains attached to local uses of the 'digital').

The critical and creative investigations that occur in studios, galleries, on the Internet, in community spaces and in other places where makers, activists, artists, curators, organizers, editors and post-media splinter-cells gather, are forms of research based on practices of production. Rather than adopting methods of analysis adopted from the social sciences or understanding of theory in terms of pure 'text', these research practices subscribe to the view that similar goals such as dense referencing and theoretical framing can be achieved by following different yet complementary paths.[2] What they all have in common is the attention paid to quasi-systematic modes of inquiry that privilege the role of imagination, vision and multi-modal intellectual play in constructing knowledge that is not only new, but has the capacity to transform human understanding.

Video as theory more particularly revolves around topics of a society whose re-assembled image sphere evokes new patterns and politics of visibility, in which networked and digital video produces novel forms of perception, publicity — and even (co-)presence. A thorough multi-faceted critique of media images that takes up perspectives from practitioners, theoreticians, sociologists, programmers, artists and political activists seems essential.

2 A Short History: Post-Video and Beyond

After video culture rose during the 1960s and 70s with portable devices like the Sony Portapak and other consumer grade video recorders it has subsequently undergone the digital shift. With this evolution the moving image inserted itself into broader, everyday use, but also extended it's patterns of effect and its aesthetical language. Movie and television alike have transformed into what is now understood as media culture. Video has become pervasive, importing the principles of 'tele-' and 'cine-' into the human and social realm, thereby also propelling 'image culture' to new heights and intensities[3]. YouTube, emblematic of network-and online-video,

---

2   Gabriel Menotti, Joshua Neves, Fillippo Spreafico, and Vera Tollmann, 'Pluriverses', panel at Video
      Vortex IX, Lueneburg, 2013,
      http://interlace.videovortex9.net/#i=f9a4cca3bc274e9096dd376c22d67ee3.
3   Jonathan Beller, *The Cinematic Mode of Production: Attention Economy and the Society of the Spectacle,*

marks a second transformational step in this medium's short evolutionary history. The question remains: what comes after YouTube? How might we understand a time when global bandwidth and multiplication of — often mobile — devices as well as moving image formats 're-assemble' both 'the social',[4] as well as the medium formerly-known-as video itself? What is one supposed to call these continuously re-forming assemblages? Or: how should one name the ubiquitous moving images in times when they are not identifiable any more as discrete video 'clips'? Are we witnessing the rise of Post-Video? Extended video? To what extent has the old video frame been broken?

Given the rise of networked, viral and vernacular video, with 'video drones' literally swarming into all pores of society — video has been 'diffused' in different ways: it has become an agent of change, as well as a register of governmentality; a tool of control society, as well as a carrier of a re-invented society of the spectacle;[5] a vehicle for new knowledge practices as well as a weapon. However, it has also grown into a life — or a sphere — of its own, a 'social beast' of ambivalent qualities, yet to be deciphered. Video by now functions as a non-human 'eye', capturing reality with quadcopters or deepwater gear, adding an extra-dimension to surveillance techniques — and: it is even read by machines, discovering patterns to act upon. Video 'perspectives' are now a First Person View (FPV) inserted in a soldiers helmet or a gamers' gear, to collective sights and crowd documentation, from individual views of remembrance to non-human 'views' of robots, from medical devices to military machines. This triggers a whole new wave of reflection on the role, reach and 'realities' of the (moving) image and video. For sure: No consumer product and no online media today could function and compete without video-like mini-formats; the same is true for identity creation, political discourses, let alone news. Then, on another social plane, the infrastructures of these 'extended video spheres' — from YouTube, Smart TV to satellite images, from fiber optic cables to 'image rights' — are currently and for some time to come feverishly contested and embattled.

In light of new questions of critical visibility — with Abu Ghraib, remote drone attacks, Wikileaks and the Snowden files bringing home the point to everyone — the impulses to become invisible or to make things socially visible has gained urgency. In a society whose image economies push forward new patterns and strong pressures of visibility (Skype Video, iris and facial recognition, apps like Vine or Snapchat),[6] a critique of media images and — now per-se political — representation practices, is essential.[7] That is also why it becomes more and more important to look at what is (still) rendered invisible — such as working conditions in industrial and other 'zones', while in the meantime stock video footage seem to dominate the aesthetics and

Hanover, NH: Dartmouth College Press, 2006, p. 356; Sean Cubitt, *The Cinema Effect*, Cambridge, MA: MIT Press, 2004, p. 456; Tom Sherman, 'Vernacular Video', in Geert Lovink and Sabine Niederer (eds), *Video Vortex Reader: Responses to YouTube*. Amsterdam: Institute of Network Cultures, 2008.

4   Bruno Latour, *Reassembling the Social: An Introduction to Actor-Network-Theory*, Oxford: Oxford University Press, 2005, p. 301.

5   Ralf Adelmann, *Visuelle Kulturen der Kontrollgesellschaft: zur Popularisierung digitaler und videografischer Visualisierungen im Fernsehen*, PhD diss., Ruhr University Bochum, 2003.

6   Nanna Verhoeff, *Mobile Screens: The Visual Regime of Navigation*, Amsterdam: Amsterdam University Press, 2012, p. 213.

7   Tom Holert, *Regieren im Bildraum*, Berlin: B_books, 2008, p. 340.

'realities' seen in the visual domain; meanwhile users invent strategies to interrupt predominant moving image streams and create new visual and narrative styles and cultures (e.g. remix culture, supercuts, fake videos, etc.). New actors and formerly 'peripheral' subjects, especially the so-called 'Global South', enter this new domain of networked, flowing and moving images. This raises issues regarding the need to re-negotiate, exemplified by the discourses of 'Fourth Cinema' or image politics around indigenous cultures, as well as around activist discourses on Syntagma or Tahrir Square.

We have all recently witnessed hitherto unseen political, cultural and technological revolutions through the privileged and animated channels of global video culture. These revolutions span vernacular video clips taken on millions of mobile phones, via online platforms circulating clips as special form of evidence, at ever faster rates through the fragmented global public, to ever more dramatic narrations of the political within the video-saturated domains of news, documentation, art and infotainment. In this, it has also become clear to us, as global collective, that there has been a further revolution of video itself. This revolution is a techno-visual revolution that is intrinsically tied up with the 'revolutionary' changes of global high-tech capitalism, as ruptured as high-tech capitalism might be. Indeed, video and its cultural formations have themselves become a site to experience these ruptures of global society in a concentrated and aesthetically concerted form.

3 Video Book as a Time-capsule for Future Reference

With the ubiquity of video comes not only a need to reflect on its cultural status, beyond the online video revolution as now encapsulated by YouTube and the new players of networked capitalism, but also a need to acknowledge video itself, in its multiple new vernacular forms, as an integral part of the global cultural repertoire and horizon.[8] Video might now be an integral part of the 'collective intellect' — what some call 'cognitive capitalism' and others 'transmodernism'.[9] There is now, alongside these global labels, a world of video to be theorized together with all its new interrelations, affordances and contradictions.[10]

Video, for better or worse, has become a new format for social communication and, by extension, theoretical reflection, including all kinds of 'communities of interpretation' and social movements. Video is also now a primary tool enlisted by the structures of the new 'Societies of Control'. Reality 'widely consists of images', and as a way to cut-up and reshape the world, video post-production has been generalized onto the whole of society.[11]

Video cameras are now everyday tools on our mobiles, video editing software is cheaply available, online platforms such as YouTube are plentiful, and a culture of movies and television has sunk into our collective psyche, meaning video has become a mode of expression both

8   Andreas Treske, *Video Theory: Online Video Aesthetics or the Afterlife of Video*. Bielefeld: transcript Verlag, 2015, p. 209.
9   Beller, *The Cinematic Mode of Production*.
10   Treske, *Video Theory*.
11   Nick Aikens (ed), *Too Much World: The Films of Hito Steyerl*, Berlin: Sternberg Press, 2014.

produced and consumed by a wide community of reflective and critical minds. Video is now undoubtedly 'a way of seeing',[12] and acting — some might even say it is a corporeal being.[13]

after.video therefore intends to develop a theoretically engaged series of video books that not only reflects on the disseminations and hybridizations of video and its intimate blending with our general cultural and social fabric,[14] but also features video as a medial mode of seeing, referencing and expressing, including criticism and scholarship. In this respect it follows earlier projects that also attempted to engage with video as a form of theoretical reflection: *Vectors*,[15] *Scalar, Liquid Theory TV*,[16] to name but a few. The extension of traditional textual theory into new medial modalities, particularly those concerned with the visual and video, is something that has previously been called for in several places, not least with regard to focusing on video essays as a 'stylo'[17] of choice. In this vein, *after.video* partakes in 'a second-order examination of the mediation of everyday life',[18] with a focus on video as a form, as well as a topical subject.

The *after.video* books are a time capsules for when the network (and Netflix, Popcorn Time and others) is down and for afro-futuristic,[19] satelliteless movements and other amateur space travellers. It is a historic assembly of post-cinematic media artefacts allowing future generations of media archaeologists to get a glimpse of fragments of *after.video*. The second edition of *after. video* was built on the MAZI toolkit and the capabilities offered by Do-It-Yourself networking infrastructures — low-cost off-the-shelf hardware and wireless technologies — that allow small communities or individuals to deploy local communication networks that are fully owned by local actors, including all generated data. These DIY networks could cover from a small square (e.g., using a Raspberry Pi) to a city neighborhood (e.g., the Commotion Construction Kit used at the RedHook WiFi initiative) or even a whole city (e.g., guifi.net, awmn.net, freifunk.net), and in the case of *after.video II* — the video vortex community.

References

Adelmann, Ralf. Visuelle Kulturen der Kontrollgesellschaft : zur Popularisierung digitaler und videografischer Visualisierungen im Fernsehen, PhD diss., Ruhr University Bochum, 2003

Aikens, Nick (ed). Too Much World: The Films of Hito Steyerl, Berlin: Sternberg Press, 2014.

Akomfrah, John (dir.). The Last Angel of History, 1996, London: Black Audio Film Collective.

Beller, Jonathan. The Cinematic Mode of Production: Attention Economy and the Society of the

---

12   Lorna Mills, 'The One Minutes', *Ways of Something*, view at https://vimeo.com/99135159.
13   Ingrid Richardson, *Telebodies and televisions: corporeality and agency in technoculture*, PhD diss., University of Western Sydney, 2015.
14   Francesco Casetti, *The Lumiere Galaxy: Seven Key Words for the Cinema to Come*, New York: Columbia University Press, 2015, p. 311.
15   Tara McPherson and Steve Anderson, *Vectors Journal*, http://vectors.usc.edu/journal/index. php?page=Introduction.
16   Gary Hall, Clare Birchall and Pete Woodbridge, 'Liquid Theory TV | Centre for Disruptive Media', http:// disruptivemedia.org.uk/liquid-theory-tv/.
17   Eric Faden, 'A Manifesto For Critical Media', *Mediascape* (2008), http://clients.jordanjennings.com/Mediascape/HTML/Spring08_ManifestoForCriticalMedia.html.
18   McPherson and Anderson, *Vectors Journal*.
19   *The Last Angel of History* (dir. John Akomfrah, 1996), London: Black Audio Film Collective.

Spectacle, Hanover, NH: Dartmouth College Press, 2006.

Cubitt, Sean. The Cinema Effect, Cambridge, MA: MIT Press, 2004.

Faden, Eric. 'A Manifesto For Critical Media', Mediascape (2008), http://clients.jordanjennings.com/Mediascape/HTML/Spring08_ManifestoForCriticalMedia.html

Hadzi, Adnan, Oliver Lerone Schultz, Pablo de Soto and Laila Shereen Sakr. after.video, London: Open Humanites Press, 2017.

Hall, Gary. Clare Birchall and Pete Woodbridge, 'Liquid Theory TV I Centre for Disruptive Media', http://disruptivemedia.org.uk/liquid-theory-tv/.

Holert, Tom. Regieren im Bildraum, Berlin: B_books, 2008.

Latour, Bruno. Reassembling the Social: An Introduction to Actor-Network-Theory, Oxford: Oxford University Press, 2005.

Menotti, Gabriel, Joshua Neves, Fillippo Spreafico, and Vera Tollmann. 'Pluriverses', panel at Video Vortex IX, Lueneburg, 2013, http://interlace.videovortex9.net/#i=f9a4cca3bc274e9096dd376c22d67ee3.

Richardson, Ingrid. Telebodies and televisions: corporeality and agency in technoculture, PhD diss., University of Western Sydney, 2015.

Sherman, Tom. 'Vernacular Video', in Geert Lovink and Sabine Niederer (eds), Video Vortex Reader: Responses to YouTube. Amsterdam: Institute of Network Cultures, 2008, pp. 161–168.

Treske, Andreas. Video Theory: Online Video Aesthetics or the Afterlife of Video. Bielefeld: transcript Verlag, 2015.

Verhoeff, Nanna. Mobile Screens: The Visual Regime of Navigation, Amsterdam: Amsterdam University Press, 2012.

VIDEO VORTEX #10 ISTANBUL LOG

ANDREAS TRESKE

VIDEO VORTEX #10 ISTANBUL LOG

ANDREAS TRESKE

Log.0 - Videoist

Istanbul, magic metropolis spanning two continents, recalling the fantasies of a thousand legends, a city in spheres of many realities and fantasies. Istanbul, 16 months after the Gezi Park protests, in a moment of silence. Something had happened in June 2013, which seems many years later as the echo of worldwide similarities, a call for speech, a shift towards a Brechtian radio utopia, a broadcast not of one-to-many but from many-to-many. The symbolic images of people walking over the bridge from Asia to Europe, the live video streaming of the events in the streets of Beyoğlu confirm a radical change of mediation. Mediated worlds are collapsing, or what was a mediated world has become just one of many other worlds in co-existence. A split became obvious, a split between the broadcast and the network worlds, a split in the urban scape. A new type of vision was developing.

The 10th edition of *Video Vortex* took place on October 31st and November 1st, 2014 at two locations, in Galata and Beyoglu. Thematically it circled around the pillars of art, activism and archiving. Investigating video practices and engagement on their intersections, aimed to renegotiate video in its connectivity to people and places, processes, and senses of memory and future, recalling the very close events and images of the streets of the world. The following log notes are based on fragmented personal notes and the transcript of low-quality audio recordings of the sessions by Duygu Naz after the conference. Many moments lasted short, ephemeral, can just be imagined now. The log's purpose is to recall some of it and give a protocol of the context and subjects discussed.

Log.1 – Beyğolu

The first day took place in an open cinema at SALT Beyoglu. Lewis Johnson, co-organizer of the event, opened *Video Vortex* with an introduction of Natalie Bookchin and her project *LONG STORY SHORT*.[1] Natalie had done hundreds of interviews with people at homeless shelters, food banks, and job training centers in California. The juxtaposed interviews in her project create a dialogue about poverty and displacement. The presentation on-screen mirrors isolation, editing creates a musical flow between themes, people speak next to each other, to us in the audience and each other again. A multiplicity of video diaries at the same time in multiple frames following after one another points to current modes of the digital image, visibility, and the class of the unseen, the ones who don't speak.

---

1   Natalie Bookchin, 'Long Story Short', https://bookchin.net/projects/long-story-short/, https://longstory. us, and https://vimeo.com/110819123.

The program was then followed by a screening of Rabih Mroué's *Pixelated Revolution* (2011) from Syria, introduced by Ozge Celikaslan. *Pixelated Revolution* took us back to the use of mobile phones in the streets of Syria, and the appearance and experience of the immediacy of death in front of the eyes of the filming participants, and the videos of their death shared on YouTube and the web.[2]

With Peter Snowdon present *Video Vortex* then screened his film *The Uprising*.[3] Snowdon's feature-length documentary consists of online videos made by citizens, people on the streets during the Arab Spring in Tunisia, Egypt, Bahrain, Libya, Syria, and Yemen. The montage of these amateur shots creates an interior, personal account, viewed from multiple cameras and multiple angles, building a narrative traversing an archive of a 'fragile, irreplaceable moment' of possibilities.

Log.2 - Galata

The second day of *Video Vortex* X Istanbul was set in a much more intimate round-table-setting in one of the conference rooms of SALT Galata, in a former bank in the famous Bankalar Caddesi below the Galata Tower in Istanbul, just a short walk away from the first location. The round table was set around four main themes: Starting with the first session 'Machine vision', then 'Spectacular & The Power of Images', reflecting in the third session on Video Art through the 'Video Generations', and ending the day with a discussion of practices of 'The Archive: Preserving Now & Then'. Between the sessions were interventions taken place: the first intervention connected to Brazil to Milena Szafir via skype, the second intervention was presented by Albert Figurt, and the third by Nezih Erdogan.

Log.2.1 - Machines

Ekmel Ertan opened the day with the introduction of the first round table on 'Ways Machine See', the theme revolving around the subject of machine vision, and the presentation and discussion of a video essay and written text by Boaz Levin, Adam Kaplan, and Daniel Herleth. The session aimed to explore modes of vision as a dynamic sphere. The theoretical discussion grounding the video essay traces the development of the photographic image since the inception of satellite surveillance till the digital turn, focuses on the role of photo analysis and interpretation in political processes, and expands upon the historical context within which digital images and video gained prominence. With *Last Person Shooter*, a performative video essay, machine vision was brought to the stage in a series of historical scenes reconstructed as 3D architectural models — like the assassination of Ahmed Jabari by an Israeli drone strike — navigated from a first-person perspective by an invisible protagonist.

---

2   Rabih Mroué, 'The Pixelated Revolution. Non-academic Lecture' 2013,
     https://vimeo.com/119433287.
3   *The Uprising* (dir. Peter Snowdon, 2013), Brussels/Newcastle: Rien à Voir/Third Films, fview at
     theuprising.be/Watch.

What follows takes place in a dreamlike digital desert, where the case of the Cuban missile crisis in the 1960s and its significance for the development of Satellite reconnaissance is evoked. The protagonists embody a birds-eye-view, exploring the blind spots and prejudices of such varying perspectives. Finally, the film concludes with a model and reenactment of a video shot by an American soldier in Afghanistan from a first-person perspective, which depicted the moments of his injury in battle. The dramatic moment spread virally online, reaching tens of millions of viewers, and mediating a distant war.[4]

The digital image is symptomatic of the current scopic regime. The first scene of the video of the assassination of Jabari — images of which were uploaded on YouTube, both from Palestinians as well as from the Israeli army — speaks of the proximity between different representations of collective data, the tracing or mining of geological data (which enabled that assassination), and the social media battle. Disparate devices used by different agents mining the same scene and producing a range of contradicting outputs. The reconstruction in the video essay does not spell this all out, but Jabari's assassination serves as a starting point since it seems to embody the interchangeability of these devices to link between the logic behind social networks and drones in a very direct and crude manner. The simulation of the scene serves one more visual layer with the use of slightly adequate software which yearns towards a tectonic design that is relatively purely random. The closing scene of the video is a kind of showdown, where the two voices more or less collapse into one another. A hypothesis for the attraction of the closing video online was that this is merely a result of the blind depiction of a near-death experience as many similar videos available online contain this death, injuries, etc. And, the first-person shooter encoded third-person perspective in the video, and uses the sense of aid of identification. We as viewers are shooters. We are alone together, and when the soldier cries for help for someone, we are there and absent at the same time.[5]

Log.3.1 - Cloud Intervention

Under the title 'Towards the clouding audiovisual aesthetics' Milena Szafir connected from Brazil to *Video Vortex* Istanbul. In the short performance lecture, she reflected on Brazilian mobile live streaming from street manifestations. Keywords were 'immaterial distribution of storage and means of retrieval', 'clouding audiovisual aesthetics', 'construction of meaning', and 'senses'. Milena Szafir explains:

online databases and archives [memories' shadows in the "public space" of the collective minds] provide "us our stock figures, our subliminal points of reference, our unspoken point of address" and "serve as ready-made commentaries on our contemporary and political lives"...isn't there a lack of "new" audiovisual formats to face the complexity of clouding appropriation experiences? ...How

---

4   *Video Vortex* #10 Istanbul: art, activism, and archives, Istanbul 31.10. - 01.11.2014, http://videovortex10.net/?page_id=52.

5   Duygu Naz, *Video Vortex* #10, unpublished transcript of audio recordings from the conference, 2014.

could we analyze these audiovisual online dialogues which manifest 'the desire for immediacy'!? What does happen with this emergent aesthetics after the found footage & essay film, telematic & database aesthetics!? What's about this chaotic-fuzzy cinema's grandchild as enunciate subjectivity through the intensive flow data?[6]

Log.2.2 - Fabric

The second roundtable with the theme 'The Spectacular & The Power of Images' was facilitated by Ebru Yetiskin. Participants were Oliver Lerone Schultz, Adnan Hadzi, Ersan Ocak, and Paola Barreto.

Oliver Lerone Schultz and Adnan Hadzi opened the session with the presentation of their international workshop project *Spectrals of the Spectacular* and the PirateBox file-sharing performance, which took place at the Besides The Screen conference in Brazil. The PirateBox is a 'self-contained file sharing device' for free mobile sharing. It allows to set up an anonymous wireless network in any space.[7] Through the setup of a free local network and the involvement in video sharing through the independent mobile device, Schultz and Hadzi are responding, documenting and engaging the change of video from a technology 'to something which is part of the social fabric'. Schultz and Hadzi tell us:

> We know by now, that the social is also visually constructed, that there is a struggle for "The Right to Look" and that social visions are projective, contested as well as fractal...centralized visual event streams are producing alternative visual splinters, fractions, and specters that also travel in fragmentary ways across the globe, making visible new landscapes and hidden horizons of meaning, i.e. "specters" to the current system and "mode of projection". While we are interested in the geopolitical aesthetic of a (to be) pirated reality of the "non-territories" which resist the address of the "national (interest)" and submission to the current globalized society of control and spectacle, we present some results from the *Spectrals of the Spectacular* workshop, reviewing in an exemplary fashion the particular resistances to the FIFA World Cup 2014, how they travel around and haunt the global imaginary and feed from and back to the non-aligned social intellect.[8]

In his talk 'The Power of Images' Ersan Ocak reflects on documentaries produced after the Gezi events and protests, which are mostly screened on film festivals and in NGO meetings throughout Turkey and internationally. He points out that most of these documentaries have problems corresponding to the subject views of the Gezi resisters,

6   *Video Vortex* #10 Istanbul: art, activism, and archives, Istanbul 31.10. - 01.11.2014, http://videovortex10.net/?page_id=52.

7   Jason Fitzpatrick, 'Build a Pirate Box for Mobile and Secure File Sharing', Lifehacker, 29 January 2011, https://lifehacker.com/build-a-pirate-box-for-mobile-and-secure-file-sharing-5746102.

8   *Video Vortex* #10 Istanbul: art, activism, and archives, Istanbul 31.10. - 01.11.2014, http://videovortex10.net/?page_id=52.

their personal experiences and visions leaving them as audience unsatisfied. The filmmaker is challenged not only by artistic forms of storytelling but mainly by the feeling of the participants. People are watching online up to several hours of documentation of material covering many voices raw. The filmmaker needs to provide a story in its totality. Gezi had been free time. People were feeling freedom. Even when they were tired they would continue to go and experience the movement, creating an alternative of filmmaking in an autonomous temporality without the voices of so-called 'experts'.

Following the discussion Paola Barreto took the event thematically back to Brazil again with her essay 'From Ghost Cinema to Live Cinema', describing Ghost Cinema as a specific practice or 'AV interventions' done in urban areas. Ghost Cinema consists of audiovisual materials, video footage of indigenous performances around a campfire, remixed to awake back the spirits of the place where the performance took place. Barreto points out that this could be understood as a collaborative media ritual based on shared memories becoming highly political. She particularly referred to one intervention held at Aldeia Maracanã, an indigenous terrain in Rio de Janeiro, which was under dispute since the preparation for the 2014 FIFA World Cup. In the conflict are groups who are interested in the maintenance of a symbolical and historical place clashing with the new administrators of the Maracanã Stadium and surrounding, who want to construct a parking place on the indigenous terrain.

Log.3.2 - Music Inetervention

In this intervention after the second roundtable, Albert Figurt took over the stage and the projection in SALT Galata to bring back *Video Vortex* to one of the essential forms of online video and online video performances - the Music Video. Figurt asks:

> What is a music video? A visual stream that 'illustrates' a pre-existing audio content? A short cut that follows the pace of a song? An emotional trip evocated by sounds? A video recording of people playing instruments in unusual locations? And what happens to this already slippery balance in the era of proliferating DIY video production (where a lot of famous YouTube stars are somehow musicians or music-related)? A reflection on the fruitful match of multi-tasking and multi-instrumentalism, the helical proliferation of audiovisual mash-up, the rise of video song (as opposed to the ordinary video clip, where narration or look is more important than pure expertise or creative cleverness), and ultimately on what loop-stations / audio sampling procedures/standards & covers / renovated love for theremins & ukuleles can metaphorically teach us about life [on the web?] in 2014.[9]

9   *Video Vortex #10 Istanbul: art, activism, and archives*, International Conference by The Institute of Network Cultures, Istanbul 31 October – 1 November 2014, http://videovortex10.net/?page_id=52.

Log.2.3 - Video Art

In 'Video Generations' Lewis Johnson facilitates a Turkish video artist round-up with Baris Doğrusöz, Hale Tenger, Didem Pekun under the questions: What part has video played in your practice and in what ways does this concern remembering or memory? How do archives play a part in your work? How do you think that the programmed functioning of digital archiving – of video, but also any other digitized materials – have changed ways of viewing, thinking, remembering and senses of future?

The artists spoke about their works, their entanglement with politics, the materials and textual matters, video in curated installations, strategies of resistance in three generations, the look back. While reflecting on her installation works Hale Tenger recalled especially 'Lâhavle' from 2007. From the audio recording of the session, Hale Tenger says:

> I will start first with Lâhavle. I would like to tell you about its background story. I was preparing for a show in İstanbul, and I had this project going on. It was a couple of months before Hrant Dinks' assassination. I started production of the piece, and I remember ... I was away from where the studio and where the production was going on, ... my assistant in the project, Çağla, her phone rang. She picked it up while she was driving. Her face went down, and I realized some kind of very bad news was given. I was watching her face. She put the phone down. She didn't say anything for a while, and I asked her, so what is the news, and she said Hrant Dink was shot, and he is dead. I remember I started crying. I was like crying as if I would have lost my father. Literally, it was like that. The funeral was on 19th January...As you can still hear from my voice, I was overwhelmed by those feelings. It won't go away. It took me a month. My sorrow was incomparable to the other political assassinations that I have lived since my birth time, the coup d'état...
>
> It took me quite a lot of time to understand, why I was so much hurt. Something else was going on. I liked him, not personally knowing him, I like the way he was putting his ideas, courage, and hope for peace, ... his personality. But there I was trapped. I realized that the project I was preparing, I was doing in such a way, I was looking backward because we had a period, I don't know for how long, political assassinations seemed that they had come to an end. And what struck me most, was that I was naive enough to think that they have ended, and they did not, and I was alive enough although I didn't expect much more future ...I had expectations for my daughter, so with his assassinations, what was striking me, was that this was an endless thing. There was no getting out, not even from the self, not even connecting other generations.[10]

10   Duygu Naz, *Video Vortex* #10, unpublished transcript of audio recordings from the conference, 2014.

Log.3.3 - Istanbul Intervention

Back to the images of the *Video Vortex* #10's host city, Nezih Erdogan presented his found footage film project with materials from the silent area, *Istanbul Do/Redo/Undo: Waters, Streets, Faces*.[11] *Istanbul Do/Redo/Undo* addresses the issue of making films out of existing archives and archive materials. It does not aim to create a historical awareness, rather to combine it with a contemporary perspective through music. Scenes from the 19th and 20th century bring images of people to live and places which don't exist anymore but become a new presence. The uneasiness of disappearance so Nezih Erdogan is replaced by the montage of the image and the soundtrack in a new form.

> Images from the past with sound and music of the present form a different meaning than their own; the space of the past is tied to the perception of today. The contemporary call to pray that extends into the Bosporus sky and the current voices of guilds echoing in the narrow streets create a chaotic atmosphere that resembles the lines of Ahmet Hamdi Tanpınar, neither within time nor entirely outside of it. *Do-redo-undo* is not only an English title, but it also marks the punctuation in music, the notes as they are called in Turkish 'do', 're', 'do' ('C', 'D', 'C' in English). It strives to behold the variety of sound and music along with the variety of the old and contemporary lives of Istanbul.[12]

Log.2.4 - Don't Look

The final session at *Video Vortex* #10 Istanbul was 'The Archive: Preserving Now & Then', with Ahmet Gürata, Sebastian Lütgert, Jan Gerber, E. Belit Sag, Alper Sen, Shaina Anand, and facilitated by Ozge Celikaslan, questioning:

> What are the roles of the open digital archive and the contemporary meaning of archive/archiving in Turkey as seen through the bak.ma experience? What does the participatory assemblage methodology mean in this context? What is the new role of an independent researcher or academic? Can we produce collective images and is it possible to recreate a political collective memory by visually recording political acts?[13]

Jan Gerber and Sebastian Lütgert, artists and software programmers who developed Pan. do/ra, co-founders of Bootlab and Pirate Cinema Berlin talked about the different ways in which people imagined archival projects — as online archives, software projects, and pedagogical tools and resources. Their platform Pan.do/ra offers many ways to access,

11 *Istanbul Do/Redo/Undo: waters, streets, faces* (dir. Nezih Erdoğan, 2010), https://vimeo.com/105012221.
12 *Video Vortex* #10 Istanbul: art, activism, and archives, Istanbul 31.10. - 01.11.2014, http://videovortex10.net/?page_id=52.
13 *Video Vortex* #10 Istanbul: art, activism, and archives, Istanbul 31.10. - 01.11.2014, http://videovortex10.net/?page_id=52.

sort, and subjectively organize videos and audiovisual materials. In a wiki-like structure, users can annotate clips of videos and offer therefore expanded experiences for viewers. The archive becomes a living process, always incomplete, and in 'the making'.

Ahmet Gürata introduced turkishcine.ma as an archive of Turkish films similar and inspired by the Indian version — indiancine.ma — whose main purpose is to make films accessible for research and open to the public, affording users the ability to annotate, select, search through keywords, and collaborate on interdisciplinary research projects. The archive includes about 500 films and documentaries, as well as related texts, encyclopedic data, and deep metadata. It shares the same structure as pad.ma (short for Public Access Digital Media Archive) as an open media archive, using the free open-source platform including OxJS, a JavaScript library for web applications.

bak.ma in English means 'don't look'. It is a digital archive of political movements and collectives in Turkey from Gezi to worker hunger strikes. 'Don't look' was one of the police announcements that protesters heard during the riots in the street. The archive is also built on pad.ma, and support by Lütgert and Gerber. The organizers were inspired by a writing of the Turkish writer Ulus Baker: '"Normal citizens disperse" ...This police announcement could be heard in downtown Ankara. Non-normal citizens must have been those surrounded by agents and means ready to shoot water. The state's wish was certainly to make them disappear, disperse them as soon as possible'.[14] bak.ma includes recordings of the Gezi protests collected by members of the Videoccupy Collective. The collective decided not to edit the footage, but keep its raw form and share it this way. Standard methods of recording and archiving felt to rebound political issues and the view from the inside. The archive should aim to create a personal, subjective but also collective perspective connected to the images. The perspective of the recording person would disappear.

The collective started bak.ma a year after Gezi and uploaded more than 2,000 hours of footage of the events, and additional from other events starting from 1997. The activists' goal was and is not only to preserve the recordings but also to point towards state violence and challenge governmental narratives.

Log.4 - Out

At the end of the day, Adnan Hadzi opened the discussion for a future *Video Vortex* and connected via Skype to London...

References

Baker, Ulus. 'Ölüm Orucu – Notlar', *Birikim Dergisi* 88 (August 1996), https://www.birikimdergisi.com/dergiler/birikim/1/sayi-88-agustos-1996/2285/olum-orucu-notlar/3180.

---

14   Ulus Baker, 'Ölüm Orucu – Notlar', *Birikim Dergisi* 88 (August 1996), https://www.birikimdergisi.com/dergiler/birikim/1/sayi-88-agustos-1996/2285/olum-orucu-notlar/3180.

Bookchin, Natalie. 'Long Story Short', https://bookchin.net/projects/long-story-short/, https://longstory.us, and https://vimeo.com/110819123.

Fitzpatrick, Jason. 'Build a Pirate Box for Mobile and Secure File Sharing', *Lifehacker*, 29 January 2011, https://lifehacker.com/build-a-pirate-box-for-mobile-and-secure-file-sharing-5746102.

Erdoğan, Nezih, dir. *Istanbul Do/Redo/Undo: waters, streets, faces*, 2010, view at https://vimeo.com/105012221.

Mroué, Rabih. 'The Pixelated Revolution. Non-academic Lecture' 2013, https://vimeo.com/119433287.

Naz, Duygu. *Video Vortex* #10, unpublished transcript of audio recordings from the conference, 2014.

Snowdon, Peter, dir. *The Uprising*, 2013, view at theuprising.be/Watch.

Video Vortex #10 Istanbul: art, activism, and archives, International Conference by The Institute of Network Cultures, Istanbul 31 October – 1 November 2014, http://videovortex10.net/?page_id=52.

VIDEO VORTEX CONFERENCES & AUTHOR BIOGRAPHIES

VIDEO VORTEX #7, YOGYAKARTA

Video in Indonesia: Histories, Aesthetics, Networks

Date: July 20/21, 2011

More info here: https://networkcultures.org/videovortex/past-events/7-yogyakarta-2/.

Wednesday July 20, 2011

10:30–13:00 Session 1 – Video as/in Art History

Presenters: Ade Darmawan (ruangrupa) and Agung Hujatnikajennong (Institut Teknologi Bandung and Selasar Sunaryo Art Space), moderator: David Teh (NUS).

Since the rise of Indonesian contemporary art in the 1990s, two key shifts have been identified. First, with the liberalisation of the public sphere post-Reformasi, artists have changed their focus from the national political drama to more personal and playful concerns. Second, an earlier, regional-institutional patronage has given way to more muscular market forces. Video has become a very conspicuous medium over this period. How does it reflect, contribute to, or evade these broader movements? Are there specifically 'Indonesian' ways of using the medium, or abusing it? Which are the key artists, artworks or exhibitions to have anchored video in Indonesian contemporary art? Is 'video art' a viable category, or is video simply another tool in the 'post-medium' artist's toolbox?

14:00–16:00 Session 2 – Video Aesthetics

Presenters: Aminuddin TH Siregar (ITB) and Thomas J. Berghuis (Sydney University), moderator: Andreas Treske (Yasar University).

In international art discourse, video has been theorised from many perspectives. Early on, its importance as a tool for social activism brought an emphasis on the public sphere, its place in wider processes of media democratisation. Formalist and conceptualist accounts, meanwhile – many inspired by phenomenology – hailed a new, reflexive tool in studio practice, with a special relationship to the body and performance. More recently, video's migration to the web has brought a renewed focus on the author function (recombinatory strategies, mash-up, DIY, *détournement* and tactical media). What are the best terms or theories for understanding video's aesthetics in Indonesia? Do we have the right vocabulary for a critical discussion? Should we emphasise the social or the technical? Can film or media theories be imported successfully, or should local ways of seeing lie at the core of video aesthetics?

16:30–18:00 Digest Session

(plenary, moderator: KUNCI CSC, discussant: Nuraini Juliastuti.

Thursday July 21, 2011

10:30–13:00 Session 3 – Alternative Histories of Video

Presenters: Andang Kelana and Mahardhika Yudha (Forum Lenteng, Jakarta) and Hafiz (ruangrupa and Forum Lenteng), moderator: Antariksa, respondent: Aryo Danusiri (ragam, Harvard University).

With the explosion of artistic, DIY, community and activist video in Indonesia comes the urgent need for a locally informed media history. Existing overviews, taking the lead from video's histories elsewhere, tend to privilege its relationship to broadcast and, later, to cable TV. This approach has furnished important narratives of resistance to, and infiltration of, state and then corporate media channels. But is this the whole story? Have TVRI and MTV really defined video's scope and potential? What are the medium's other industrial, artisanal or domestic contexts, and how have they informed its development? How have they shaped video access, video reception and video literacy?

14:00–16:00 Session 4 – Video Online: Impact, Effect, Affect

Presenters: Ronny Agustinus (independent critic, Jakarta); Andrew Lowenthal (Engage Media), moderator: Sujud Dartanto (House of Natural Fiber).

In Indonesia, as elsewhere, networked videos are making headlines. From celebrity sex scandals to human rights abuses, their impact can be viral, immediate and transnational. Which videos have made the greatest impact, and how? What are the crucial factors in their production, distribution, or reception? And how do the politics of the medium affect the politics of the content? This panel will pursue online video beyond the hype, focusing on specific, localised cases and contexts, asking what online videos do to the people who make them and the people who watch them.

16:30–18:00 Digest Session

(plenary), moderator: KUNCI CSC, discussant: Ferdiansyah Thajib.

VIDEO VORTEX #8, ZAGREB

The Cultures, Art and Politics of Online Video

Date: May 17th-19th, 2012

Location: Museum of Contemporary Art, Zagreb, Croatia

https://networkcultures.org/videovortex/past-events/8-zagreb/

Upload cinema Speaker: Dagan Cohen

Contemporary art and online video Moderator: Tihomir Milovac (Zagreb), speakers: Sabina Salamon (Rijeka), Seumas Coutts (Berlin), Annelies Termeer (Amsterdam).

Theoretical discourses on the contemporary shift in the digital moving image Moderator: Geert Lovink (Amsterdam). speakers: Laurence Rickels (Karlsruhe), Bojana Romic (Beograd), Riczhard Kluszchinsky (Warschaw), Andreas Treske (Izmir).

Social networks and online video in the region Moderator: Petar Milat, speakers: Aleksandra Sekulic (Beograd), Janos Sugar (Budapest) Peter Purg (Ljubljana), Sandra Sterle (Split), Damir Niksic (Sarajevo).

Techno-colonialism, surveillance and control of the distribution of the moving image Moderator: Tanja Vrvilo (Zagreb), speakers: Gabriel Menotti (London), Kuros Yalpani (Munich), Joanna Richardson (Berlin).

The perspective of online cinema Moderator: Brian Willems (Split), speakers: Jan Simons (Amsterdam), Nina Koll (Cologne) Miklos Peternak (Budapest).

Artists talk about their own work and research in online video Moderator: Dan Oki (Split), speakers: Natalie Bookchin (Los Angeles), Annie Abrahams (Paris), Gisela Domschke (Sao Paulo), Dalibor Martinis (Zagreb).

Technological aspects and new developments of online video Moderator: William Linn (Zagreb), speakers: Maarten Brinkerink (Utrecht), Miha Colner (Ljubljana), Holmes Wilson (New York).

VIDEO VORTEX #9, LÜNEBURG

Re:assemblies of Video

31.10-01.11 2013

Video Vortex #9 was conceived and hosted by the **Moving Image Lab** *and* **Post-Media Lab** *of the Innovation Incubator at* **Leuphana University** *Lüneburg, Germany.*

Online video vortices such as YouTube, are assemblages of assemblages: its infrastructure and spheres of use and production again consist of assemblages. The video sphere today is a mesh of different types of elements; we have databases, screens, interfaces, protocols and server farms. Comments, tags, lists and channels, cameras, producers, frames, users and audiences. Last, but not least, money flows, broadcasters, advertisers, property rights, eyeballs and statistics, all add to, and operate in multiple assemblages.

Currently we see new configurations of components in video culture, interacting in new ways and with loose forms of influence. VideoVortex #9 proposes that now is a time to re-engage with a structural and contextual analysis of online video culture.

We encourage critics, theorists, artists, programmers and video makers to look at:

1. Assemblages of different videos, graphics and texts, be it in material or with a view to new environments of authoring or curation. Such an approach re-poses the question of interactive multi- and hypermedia in the age of html-5, Popcorn, Apps and the likes.

2. Assemblages of content, interfaces and infrastructures, as found in platforms, with their changing forms and logics of circulation, and to scrutinize media-'flows', 'liveness', 'channels', 'archives', 'lists', and producing 'dissolving originals' and new forms of mash-ups.

3. Socio-cultural assemblages of producers, owners, curators and perceptive 'audiences'. The conditions and social realities of video- and TV-production, issues of copyright and re-organization of 'imaginary' capital evoke questions as to what extent technology, standards and protocols – and their symbolisms – are taking over the role of what before has been ascribed to 'culture'.

4. Assemblages contributing to ruptures and revolts: Indeed „the whole world is watching" different real or so-called 'revolutions': social upheavals are transmitted via video. What does it mean to be an 'observer' (individually, socially or scientifically), a 'participant' or a 'witness'? Questions of relevance, media positioning and 'real virtuality' are are gaining new urgency.

Networked video has entered a new phase and become part of major configurations. The days of pioneers and amateurs seem to be over, as do the old worlds of professional broadcasting networks: Digital technologies have professionalized production, and do-it-yourself skills have established new styles and formats. Tubes, channels and domains for mobile video are part of our everyday digital life. These tectonic shifts — from amateur and professional to an assemblage of media creators, from spectators to participants, and from a single viewpoint to parallax perspectives — have given rise to effects of a geographical and generational scope yet to be determined. The ninth edition of Video Vortex proposes that now is a time to re-engage with a structural and contextual analysis of online video culture.

Two keynotes will extend the discursive field of Video Vortex #9: Beth Coleman will re-engage local affairs with visions of networked activism, and Nishant Shah will unpack video at the digital turn as object, as process, and as a symptom of the transnational flow of ideology, ideas and infrastructure, especially in emerging information societies in the uneven landscape of globalization.

VV9 also features a number of performative lectures and thematic workshops dealing with video realities. We will follow up on the long tails of rebellion with Mosireen Collective in Cairo and Margarita Tsomou in Athens. Boris Traue and Achim Kredelbach, aka Jo Cognito, will discuss YouTube's recent forays into televisual terrain and its delegation of organizing power to commercial "networks" and media agencies. Boaz Levin will look at the way media gravitates towards im-mediating events, and Miya Yoshida will critically question familiar terminologies from "amateur" and "user" to "prosumer" and "citizen reporter."

In the run-up to the actual Video Vortex event, international video correspondents have been investigating phenomenologies of video online. After 10 joyful years of global ubiquity, the conference will also engage with reinventions of the local under conditions of digital culture. A collaboration with the local video activist collective Graswurzel.tv, whose activities are linked with antinuclear protests in Wendland (near Lüneburg), will explore mobile video in (alternative) news journalism. Artist Stephanie Hough will join with local participants to oppose tracking and other incursions into our screen lives by turning a public square into a stage for a mass lip-sync.

The future of film as it fuses with video in the digital realm, and the reconfiguration of its aesthetics, interfaces, production and distribution, will be discussed with Thomas Østbye and Edwin, the directors behind the participatory film project 17,000 Islands, and explored by Seth Keen in the domain of interactive documentary on the web. Alejo Duque and Robert Ochshorn will analyze the technological appearances and travesties of video, the soft power of codecs and compression in the information complex, and how to "interface."

A liquid publication will go live as a sourcebook shortly before VV9 and continue to expand during collaborative editing sessions at the event in Lüneburg, ultimately living on as a multifaceted publication (still available here: http://www.rmozone.com/videovortex9/).

Thursday February 28th, 2013

Confirmed speakers: Beth Coleman, Seth Keen, Edwin, Thomas Østbye, Andreas Treske, Stephanie Hough, Martin Katić, Theresa Steffens, Arndt Potdevin, Robert M. Ochshorn, Nan Haifen, Viola Sarnelli, Boris Traue, Achim Kredelbach, Dalida María Benfield, Renée Ridgway, Gabriel S Moses, Nishant Shah.

Friday March 1st, 2013

Confirmed speakers: Margarita Tsomou, Sascha Simons, Nelli Kambouri, Pavlos Hatzopoulos, Joshua Neves, Gabriel Menotti, Filippo Spreafico, Caroline Heron, Jonathan Shaw, Jan Gerber, Sebastian Luetgert, Elric Milon, Sascha Kluger, Jamie King, Stefano Sabatini, Peter Snowdon, Miya Yoshida, Boaz Levin, Azin Feizabadi, Kaya Behkalam, Jens Maier-Rothe, Jasmina Metwaly, Graswurzel.tv, Björn Ahrend, Timo Großpietsch.

Saturday March 2nd, 2013

Confirmed speakers: Vito Campanelli , Robert M. Ochshorn, Alejo Duque, Lucía Egaña Rojas, Andrew Clay, Stefan Heidenreich & Deborah Ligorio, Cornelia Sollfrank.

VIDEO VORTEX #10, ISTANBUL

VIDEO VORTEX 10 ISTANBUL - ART, ACTIVISM, ARCHIVES

BAU GALATA, DEPO İSTANBUL AND SALT GALATA

The 10th annual meeting of Video Vortex is to be hosted in Istanbul at three adjacent institutions all involved in this year's topics: art, activism and archives. The two-day event of workshops, speaker-led sessions, discussions, panels and work on show will explore how video, art and activism criss-cross questions of recording, archives and archiving, and how working with these intersections can re-motivate engagement from one to the other in important and novel ways. Video's capacities for both recording and transmission has meant that it has moved into spaces of visibility and the visual in ways that contest as well as confirm the dominant meanings and effects, across different socio-political and cultural frameworks. Video Vortex 10 will consider different issues opened up across the histories, presents and futures of video, from 'live on tape' to 'live streaming', and from one paradigm of surveillance to another, exploring the ways in which early as well as recent and contemporary video technologies and practices contest accounts of normative realities by renegotiating boundaries between the live, the recorded or the streamed, challenging repressive norms via inventive modes of archival access. The interests and values of art and activism, sometimes taken to be in conflict, converge around this renegotiation of the meanings of video and the terms of its storage and use. As forms of data gathering enable new forms of covert observation, by the agents of states and corporations, how can video interrupt or divert these processes? Video Vortex 10 Istanbul thus aims to bring together those who, working with inventive ways of accessing, classifying or 'declassifying' video recordings and transmissions are seeking to reinvent the terms of freedom, across places and spaces of cultures, processes and practices of memory, representation and senses of future.--

PROGRAM

Friday 31.10. 2014

Friday Meet Video Vortex

14:00 Opening

@ SALT BEYOĞLU

14:15 Natalie Bookchin and her project *LONG STORY SHORT*, with Natalie Bookchin, Introduction by Lewis Johnson

15:30 SCREENING

Rabih Mroué's *"Pixelated"*, introduced by Ozge Celikaslan (Koza Visual)

Syria, 2011. In the streets, right in front of the eyes of the entire world, men are shot down and film their own deaths. Images of a revolution. Revolution of the image. A captivating theatrical lecture.

Rabih Mroué @ SALT *http://saltonline.org/en/727/rabih-mroue*

16:00 SCREENING

Peter Snowdon's *THE UPRISING* and Q&A with Peter Snowdon

Saturday / Cumartezi 01.11.2014

VIDEO VORTEX 10 – ROUND TABLE

Meetings & Talks & Discussions @ SALT GALATA

09:30 Intro

Framing Video Vortex

Open Doors – "Cay ve Simit" / VORTEX #10 / Introduction to the Round Table Format / The Istanbul-Ankara Team

10:00 – 12:00 Session I

Ways Machines See with Boaz Levin, Adam Kaplan, Daniel Herleth, Facilitator: Ekmel Ertan

12:45 – 14:30 Session II

The Spectacular & The Power of Images with Oliver Lerone Schultz, Adnan Hadzi, Ersan Ocak, Paola Barreto, Facilitator: Ebru Yetiskin

Spectrals of the Spectacular (Oliver Lerone Schultz & Adnan Hadzi)

The Power of Images: Non-ficition Storytelling of the Gezi Resistance within a Co-Creative Act – Ersan Ocak

From Ghost Cinema to Live Cinema – Paola Barreto

15:00 – 15:30 INTERVENTION II

Albert Figurt

15:30 – 17:00 Session III

Video Generations. Artists Round Up with Baris Doğrusöz, Hale Tenger, Didem Pekun, Facilitator: Lewis Johnson

17:15 – 17:45 INTERVENTION III

Istanbul Do/Redo/Undo : Waters, Streets, Faces by Nezih Erdoğan

17:45 – 19:45 Session IV

The Archive: Preserving Now & Then with Ahmet Gürata, Sebastian Lütgert, Jan Gerber, E. Belit Sag, Alper Sen, Shaina Anand, Facilitator: Ozge Celikaslan. Check out: The first 5 days of Gezi – *https://bak.ma/* and *http://turkishcine.ma*.

20:00 – 21:00 Outro – Video Vortex 11 UK with Adnan Hadzi as round table facilitator

ARCHIVE BOOTCAMP ANKARA

Bootcamp with Sebastian Lütgert and Jan Gerber @ Bilkent University

Starting @ 13:40 in FB114 on Monday, 3rd (MFA Graduate Lab), Bilkent GSTMF, Merkez Kampusu

December / Aralik 2014 & January / Ocak 2015

VIDEO VORTEX EXHIBITION

Works by Yetkin Yilmaz, Ahmet Said Kaplan, David Guez, Endam Nihan, Ezgi Kilincaslan, Gonca Gumusayak, Cornelia Sollfrank, Video Occupy and others.

VIDEO VORTEX #11, KOCHI

Video in Flux--Art, Activism & Archives

23-26 February, 2017

Hotel 18, Fort Kochi & Mill Hall, Mattancherry, Kochi (Kerala/India) as part of the **Sristi Outpost,** a collateral of the Kochi-Muzeris biennale

Video technology has radically altered the way in which we produce, consume and circulate images, influencing the aesthetics and possibilities of moving image cultures, as well as yielding a rich body of scholarship across various disciplines. Given its ease of access and use, video has historically been aligned with media activism and collaborative work, further enabled by digital platforms, that facilitate transnational networks even as they exist within heightened systems of surveillance. Video has also emerged as the driving force behind the web, social media, and the internet of things. With an impressive autobiography dedicated solely to itself, video has almost become life-like. It is also a cause of vulnerability as in the case of recent hacking of web-connected cameras leading to a major network crash in America. Rapidly changing technological formats implicate the urgent need to engage with practices of archiving and curation, modes of collaboration & political mobilisation, as well as fresh comprehensions of the subject-spectator, actors & networks constituted by contemporary video and digital cultures.

Video Vortex #11 attempted to share provocations, research, speculations, video and film work that responds to current debates in film, video, media, networks, and game theory, while being particularly attentive to the implications that technologies of live video, surveillance, virtual reality, augmented reality, and artificial intelligence have for the future of video & media cultures.

Video Vortex XI, which was being held for the first time in South Asia, focuses on video theory and technology in order to highlight the particular histories of video in Asia. We are particularly interested in work that addresses the use of video in activism and political mobilisation, artistic practices, technological developments attendant to the medium (and its future), as well as the formal qualities of video in the digital post-national and post-medium context. The two day conclave included screenings, discussions, workshops and round tables and we invite proposals that addressed the following themes: histories of video in Asia, video art and activism, aesthetics of online video, video and surveillance. video archiving, infrastructures and platforms of video and emergent technologies of video and moving image Video Vortex #11 was organized by the School of New Humanities & Design, Srishti Institute of Art, Design & Technology in collaboration with the University of Bilkent, Ankara, and the Institute of Network Cultures, Amsterdam.

PROGRAM:

February 23, 2017

Introduction to Video Vortex XI: 11:00-11:30

Geetha Narayanan (Founder-director, Srishti Institute of Art, Design & Technology); Geert Lovink (Founder, Institute of Network Cultures, Amsterdam), Rashmi Sawhney (Programme Director, Video Vortex XI)

Session I: Software and the Politics of Collaboration: 11:30-12:30 (chair: Sharath Chandra Ram).

Software and its Structuring of Interactive Documentary - Fabiola Hanna (Ph.D. Candidate in Film & Digital Media, University of California, Santa Cruz)

Co-creating with my viewing public - Anandana Kapur (Ph.D. Candidate, AJKMCRC, Jamia Millia Islamia)

Session II: Samosa Breaks and Item Numbers — 12:30-1:30 (chair: Madhuja Mukherjee)

Tactical VR: Representing the Intermission in Indian Cinema - Karl Mendonca (Ph.D. Candidate in Film and Digital Media, University of California, Santa Cruz)

YouTube Sleaze: Viral Mutations of Item Numbers - Silpa Mukherjee (Ph.D. Candidate in Cinema Studies, Jawaharlal Nehru University, New Delhi)

Artist's Talk & Curated Screening: I - 2:00 — 3:00

Violent Opaque by Ray Tat (independent artist and curator, Shanghai)

Intervention I: 3:30 — 4:30

Underbelly of a City: The toing and froing between amateur and art-house films

Madhuja Mukherjee (Associate Professor, Film Studies, Jadhavpur University, Calcutta), moderated by Ahmet Gurata

Plenary I: 5:00-6:30

The video and the crowd: publics and postpublics. Ravi Sundaram (Sarai, Centre for the Study of Developing Societies, New Delhi)

Evening Programmes at The Mill Hall, 23rd February

6:30 pm: What you Don't see is what you Get (WYDSIWYG)

Artist's talk by Sharath Chandra Ram

7:00 pm onwards @ the Mill Hall

Gyrated: hula audiovisual interface by Elena Knox

Friday, 24th February, 2017

@ Hotel 18, Fort Kochi

Plenary II: 10:00-11:45

From Selfie to Mask Design, On the Politics and Aesthetics of the Online Self

Geert Lovink (Institute of Network Cultures)

Artists' Talks II: 12.00-1.00

With Ayisha Abraham & Rahee Punyashloka, moderated by Rashmi Sawhney

Deteriorating Memories: Scavenging for Home Movies in an East Bangalore Neighbourhood by Ayisha Abraham

What Does the Digital Image See? Noise Reductions, Ontological Deductions etc. by Rahee Punyashloka

Session III: Digital technologies and New Communities: 2.00-3.0 (chair: Andana Kapur)

The DIY Filmmaker in the Digital Age - Akriti Rastogi (Ph.D. Candidate in Cinema Studies, Jawaharlal Nehru University, New Delhi)

Mapping Cultural Histories of Asian Ethnic Enclaves in the Global City - Kristy Kang (Assistant Professor at the School of Art, Design and Media, Nanyang Technological University, Singapore)

Curated Screenings II: 3.00-4.00 pm

Films from Central Asia (Kyrgyzstan, Mongolia, Tajikistan) Curated by Stefan Ruso

Artist's Talk III & Titchner's Cage VR installation: 3.00-4.00

'Poly-Body Visions' by Nadov Assar (Assistant Professor and an Associate Director of the Center for Arts & Technology, Connecticut College, USA)

Panel IV: Video Theory: 4.30 – 6.00

The Autobiography of Video. A Technocentric Approach to Early Video Art - Ina Blom (Professor, University of Oslo)

<VideoTheoryII> Shiny things so bright - Andreas Treske (Professor, University of Bilkent, Ankara)

Artist's Talk IV: 6.00-7.00

House of Women (2016, 14") and an artist's talk by Michelle Williams Gamaker

Saturday, 25th February

Intervention II: 11.00-12.00 Once *within* a Time by Soudhamini V.

Curated Screening III: 12.00-1.00

CologneOFF Asia Focus curated by Wilfried Acgricola de Cologne.

Workshop with Geert Lovink: 2.00 – 5.30 Beyond the State of Internet Criticism: Lessons to be learnt for Contemporary Art Criticism

Film Screening: 5.30-6.45pm

War at a Distance (Harun Farocki, 2003, video, 58") introduced by Vasanthi Mariadass

Sunday, 26th February

Curated Screening IV: 1.00-2.00 pm

The New Museum of Networked Art's "Refugee Film Collection" curated by Wilfried Agricola de Cologne.

Curated Screenings I, II, III, IV: 2.00-6.00 pm

A programme of films on various themes related to Video Vortex XI's focus on technology, art, activism & archives curated by the Video Vortex XI team

Closing Performance @ 7pm at the Mill Hall

Networked Performances and Ubiquitious Webjaying by Anne Roqigny and her team of webjays.

VIDEO VORTEX #12, MALTA

Conference and screenings: September 26-29, 2019

Exhibition: September 13 until October 27, 2019 (in Spazju Kreattiv)

Full program: https://networkcultures.org/videovortex/wp-content/uploads/sites/8/2019/09/Final-Video-Vortex-Program.pdf

Day 1: Thursday September 26, 2019

15:00: Video Vortex Pre-Screening: Dance: Please refer to the screening pages for the detailed screening".

17:00: Opening of Video Vortex Conference

• Geert Lovink (Institute of Network Cultures, Amsterdam)

• Wilfried Agricola de Cologne: Curated screening – The W:OW

18:30: Opening Lecture & Performance

• @lbert figurt: Lecture: Desktop Horror

• Annie Abrahams, Lisa Parra and Daniel Pinheiro: Performance: DISTANT FEELINGS #6

20:00: Meet the Video Vortex Artists

• Vince Briffa and Michael Alcorn: OUTLAND

• Ryan Woodring: The oldest new structure

• Q&A with video vortex artists: Werther Germondari, Letta Shtohryn, Pablo Núñez Palma, Bram Loogman, Tivon Rice & Hang Li (together with Caroline Rosello)

Day 2: Friday – September 27, 2019

09:00: Welcome, Registration & Coffee

10:00: Session 1: Online Video Theory I

• Andrew Clay: The Extraordinary Adventures of Mr. Oakley in the Land of the Video Bloggers

• Karla Brunet: Online Video Cartography

- Ana Peraica: Disinterested and Dead: Spinning Visual Media Reporting Events

- Kathy Rae Huffman: ON/IN Time – video art from outsider to insider

12:00: Break

13:00: Session 2: Activism

- Donatella della Ratta: The vanished image: who owns the archives of the Arab uprisings?

- Aishwarya Viswanathan: Staged Fear: Real and Imagined Audiences of Mob Lynching Videos in India.

- Confusion of Tongues: Moving Membranes

- Miguel Oliveros Mediavilla: Dictature 4.0: 'La prison à plein air'

15:00: Break

16:00: Session 3: Streaming & Platforms

- Dino Ge Zhang: A Theory of Livestreaming Video

- Andreas Treske and Aras Ozgun: Narrative Platforms: Towards a Morphology of New Audience Activities and Narrative Forms

- Tomasz Hollanek: The Netflix Clinic: (experi)Mental Entertainment in the Age of Psychometrics

- Antonia Hernandez: There's something compelling about real life: early webcam tropes on current sexcam platforms

Special: ASMR workshop (parallel session on invitation only) Lucille Calmel & Damien Petitot: Soft Screens Soft Skins Soft: an ASMR workshop

18:00: Break

20:00: Video Vortex evening screening. Please refer to the screening pages for the detailed screening".

Day 3: Saturday – September 28, 2019

09:00: Welcome, Registration & Coffee

09:30: Special: Breakfast Screening

• Colette Tron: Screening: Digital images and films, what's the matter?

10:00: Session 4: Online Video Theory II

Colette Tron: Digital images and films, what's the matter?

Mitra Azar: From Selfie to Algorithmic Facial Image

Jack Wilson: PLAYING FROM ANOTHER ROOM

Chris Meigh-Andrews: EDAU Artists' Film and Video Study Collection

12:00: Break

13:00: Session 5: Experiments in Aesthetics

Dan Oki: The Absence of Telepresence

Hiroko Kimura-Myokam: Video hosting service as a presenting space and a repository

Patrick Lichty: Not Really Like Being There

Richard Misek: A Machine for Viewing: a virtual reality video essay

15:00: Break

16:00: Session 6: Workshops/lecture on tech issues

Pablo Núñez Palma and Bram Loogman: Jan Bot

Heiko Recktenwald: Montage der Sensationen

Adnan Hadzi, Simon Worthington and Oliver Lerone Schultz: VV12 after.video book

Special: ASMR workshop (parallel session on invitation only) Lucille Calmel & Damien Petitot: Soft Screens Soft Skins Soft: an ASMR workshop

18:00: Closing Ceremony

Andrew Alamango and Andrew Pace: Magna Żmien (Time Machine)

Judit Kis: Practices Beyond the SELF

Day 4: Sunday – September 29, 2019

14:00: Replay Day

SCHEDULE OF VIDEO VORTEX #12 SCREENINGS:

Day 1: Thursday – September 26, 2019

15:00: Pre-VV12 Screening: Dance

Rita Al Cunha: Error 500, 1:44, Daniela Lucato: When I dance, 67 min.,Vito Alfarano: I have a dream, 11:00.

17:00: Curated screening – The W:OW, Wilfried Agricola de Cologne, 61 min.

Day 2: Friday – September 27, 2019

20:00: Screening I: Structures

Adam Fish: Points of Presence, 18:46, Albert Merino: Bestiary, 5:10, Lotte Louise de Jong: BRB, 5:25, Esther Polak and Ivar van Bekkum: Go Move Be, 9:50, Samantha Harvey: Auto tune me, 4:31.

21:00: Screening II: Internet, Sadness, Love

Andres Azzolina: Puntomov, 15:15, Glasz DeCuir: Yes I saw an angel, 2:37, María José Ribas: Torremolinos Match, 8:51, Pedro Gomes: Mutilated Dreams, 10:22, Salvador Miranda: Aim Down Sights, 7:30.

22:00: Screening III: Myself Any Other Night

Sofia Braga: I stalk myself, 13:26, María José Ribas: Seismographical, 2:03, Zimu Zhang & Zheng Lu Xinyuan: Just like any other night, 29:33.

Day 4: Sunday – September 29, 2019

14:00: Screening I: Structures

Adam Fish: Points of Presence, 18:46, Albert Merino: Bestiary, 5:10, Lotte Louise de Jong: BRB, 5:25, Esther Polak and Ivar van Bekkum: Go Move Be, 9:50, Samantha Harvey: Auto tune me, 4:31.

15:00: Screening II: Internet, Sadness, Love

Andres Azzolina: Puntomov, 15:15, Glasz DeCuir: Yes I saw an angel, 2:37, María José

Ribas: Torremolinos Match, 8:51, Pedro Gomes: Mutilated Dreams, 10:22, Salvador Miranda: Aim Down Sights, 7:30.

16:00: Screening III: Myself Any Other Night

Sofia Braga: I stalk myself, 13:26, María José Ribas: Seismographical, 2:03, Zimu Zhang & Zheng Lu Xinyuan: Just like any other night, 29:33.

17:00: Screening IV: The W:OW

Wilfried Agricola de Cologne: Curated screening – The W:OW (ca 60 min.)

18:00: Screening V: Adam Fish: Crash Theory, 45:00.

AUTHOR BIOGRAPHIES

Annie Abrahams is based in Montpellier (France) where she has an art practice that meanders between research and performance. In her carefully scripted artworks she tends to reveal ordinary human behaviour and develops what she calls an aesthetics of trust and attention. She is interested in collaborative practices as a learning place for a 'being with'. She considers behaviour to be her aesthetic material and questions the possibilities and limits of communication in general, more specifically investigating its modes under networked conditions. https://bram.org

Ina Blom is Professor at the Department of Philosophy, Classics, History of Art and Ideas at the University of Oslo and Visiting Professor in the Department of Art History, University of Chicago. Recent books include *The Autobiography of Video: The Life and Times of a Memory Technology* (2016), *On the Style Site: Art, Sociality and Media Culture* (2007/2009) as well as the edited volumes *Memory in Motion: Archives, Technology and the Social* (2016) and *Raoul Hausmann et les avant-gardes* (2014).

Natalie Bookchin is an artist who works with video, installation, and other media. Her work is exhibited and screened around the world including at MoMA, LACMA, PS1, Mass MOCA, the Pompidou Centre, MOCA LA, the Whitney Museum, the ICP Museum, and the Kitchen in NYC, and La Virreina Center for the Image, Barcelona. Her artwork has been commissioned by the Tate, Creative Time, LACMA, and the Walker Art Center. Bookchin collaborated extensively in the 1990s and early 2000s including as part of the art/activist collective RTMark, with Lev Manovich, and on net.art projects with Alexei Shulgin, Heath Bunting a. o. Bookchin is Professor of Media at Rutgers University. She lives and works in Brooklyn, NY.

Pablo DeSoto is an architect and researcher, working at the intersection of architecture with digital media, the environmental humanities and the arts. In the 2000s he was co-founder hackitectura.net, a pioneer group of architects, computer specialists and activists. Pablo loves to make experimental books such as Fadaiat: Freedom of Movement, Freedom of Knowledge and the Video Book. He is currently affiliated researcher at Umeå School of Architecture in Sweden.

Ben Grosser creates interactive experiences, machines, and systems that examine the cultural, social, and political effects of software. Recent exhibition venues include the Barbican Centre in London, Museum Kesselhaus in Berlin, Museu das Comunicações in Lisbon, and Galerie Charlot in Paris. The *Chicago Tribune* called him the 'unrivaled king of ominous gibberish'. *Slate* referred to his work as 'creative civil disobedience in the digital age'. Grosser is an associate professor at the University of Illinois at Urbana-Champaign, USA.

Albert Figurt is an Italian videoartisan, multi-instrumentalist and independent researcher. He excretes in the environment words, notes, images, crossmedia happenings and fuzzy thoughts. A member of the VideoVortex community since 2009, he's happily obsessed with the socio/anthropological & perceptual side æffects of online video. In the past years he's been organizing *Guerrilla Film-making* and *UGCadavre Exquis* workshops, lecturing on *Screencast Narratives* and teaching American exchange students about *Non-Linear Storytelling*, *Expanded VideoEditing* and *Digital Cultures*.

Adnan Hadzi teaches at the University of Malta, co-organizer of Video Vortex #12 and co-editor and producer of the *after.video* video book. Adnan undertook his practice-based PhD on *FLOSSTV - Free, Libre, Open Source Software (FLOSS) within participatory 'TV hacking' Media and Arts Practices* at Goldsmiths, University of London. Adnan's research focuses on the influence of digitalization in media art, as well as the author's rights in relation to collective authorship. His documentary film work tracks artist pranksters The Yes Men and net provocateurs Bitnik Collective. In 2013 he released the documentary *Bitter Lemons*, mapping lemon farmers on both sides of Cyprus' no-man's land. He is currently working on a documentary on the media arts collective Mediengruppe Bitnik.

Judit Kis is an intermedia artist based in Budapest and Berlin. She studied fine art and curating at the Hungarian University of Fine Arts in Budapest and at Chelsea College of Art and Design in London. In the past few years she has participated in short residencies, workshops and exhibited her works internationally. The content of her video performances and virtual diaries are inspired by her psychological exploration of the self and by documenting and sharing the conflicts in her personal development, she invites her audience to discuss and confront their related experiences. Her works combine digital content with installations of objects from many different and innovative materials.

Patricia G. Lange is an anthropologist and associate professor of Visual & Critical Studies at California College of the Arts, San Francisco. She researches video sharing for sociality and self-expression, video ranting for civic engagement and issues of safety on social media. She is the author of *Thanks for Watching: An Anthropological Study of Video Sharing on YouTube* (University Press of Colorado, 2019) and *Kids on YouTube: Technical Identities and Digital literacies* (Routledge, 2014) and is director of the film *Hey Watch This! Sharing the Self Through Media* (2020). She was a contributor to the earlier volumes *Video Vortex Reader: Responses to YouTube* and *The YouTube Reader.* Homepage: http://www.patriciaglange.org/index.html.

Hang Li is a curator and researcher based in London and Beijing. Her research focuses on the meanings and consequences of working curatorially intersecting contemporary art and digital network technologies and cultures. With a background in curating contemporary art and architectural design, she is interested in interpreting curatorial works by considering techno-politics and multiple value systems from transnational perspectives. She is currently conducting PhD research at the Royal College of Art and working as a visiting mentor in MA Curating Contemporary Art, RCA.

Patrick Lichty is Assistant Professor of Animation/Multimedia at Zayed University, UAE. Patrick is an animator media artist, curator, and theorist exploring how media shape our perception of reality as well as the borders between the digital and the material. He is best known for his work with the virtual reality performance art group Second Front, and animator of the activist group, The Yes Men. He is a CalArts/Herb Alpert Fellow and Whitney Biennial exhibitor as part of the collective RTMark. His book, *Variant Analyses: Interrogations of New Media Culture* was released by the Institute of Network Culture. He is included in key books on Virtual and Augmented Reality, including the Oxford Handbook of Virtuality.

Geert Lovink is a Dutch media theorist, internet critic and author of *Uncanny Networks* (2002), *Dark Fiber* (2002), *My First Recession* (2003), *Zero Comments* (2007), *Networks Without a Cause* (2012), *Social Media Abyss* (2016), *Organisation after Social Media* (with Ned Rossiter, 2018) and *Sad by Design* (2019). In 2004 he founded the Institute of Network Cultures at the Amsterdam University of Applied Sciences (HvA). His center organizes conferences, publications and research networks such as Video Vortex and MoneyLab (internet-based revenue models in the arts). Recent projects deal with digital publishing and the future of art criticism.

Gabriel Menotti is Assistant Professor in Moving Images Curatorial Studies at Queen's University, Ontario. He has presented projects in events such as ISEA, the São Paulo Art Biennial, Rencontres Internationales and Transmediale, as well as written and organized a number of publications on the subject of image and technology. His latest books are *Movie Circuits: Curatorial Approaches to Cinema Technology* (Amsterdam University, 2019) *and Practices of Projection: Histories and Technologies* (Oxford University, 2020, co-edited with Virginia Crisp). He is currently working on a monograph about virtual replicas and critical cultural heritage. Together with Virginia Crisp, Menotti coordinates the Besides the Screen research network.

Dan Oki *(Slobodan Jokić*, 1965, Zadar*)* is a filmmaker, visual artist and professor of film and electronic arts. He belongs to the generation of artists who in the 1990s in Amsterdam worked with experimental film and photography, made cinematographic databases, web art and interactive video. He has presented his works worldwide, while his films and media works are part of international collections. After spending fifteen years living in the Netherlands and other countries, he returned to Croatia, where he has produced, written and directed five independent feature films. At the moment Dan Oki is doing arts related PhD research at the University of Amsterdam & The Netherlands Film Academy.

Aras Ozgun is a media studies scholar and a media artist, teaching at Cinema and Digital Media Department at Izmir University of Economics in Izmir, and at Media Studies Graduate Program of the New School for Public Engagement in New York. He studied Political Sciences (B.Sc.) and Sociology (MS) at Middle East Technical University in Ankara, and Media Studies (MA) and Sociology (Ph.D.) at the New School for Social Research in New York. He writes on media, culture and politics, and produces experimental media, photography and video works. His website: http://www.karakafa.net/.

Ana Peraica is an art historian whose research focus is on post-digital photography. She is the author of *The Age of Total Images: Disappearance of a Subjective Viewpoint in Post-digital Photography* (Theory on Demand #34, 2020), *Fotografija kao dokaz* (Multimedijalni Institute, Zagreb, 2018), *Culture of the Selfie* (Theory on Demand #24, 2017) and edited *Smuggling Anthologies, Victims Symptom (PTSD and Culture)* (Theory on Demand #3, 2009). She teaches at Danube University near Vienna, Austria, and is a visiting lecturer at Central European University in Budapest, Hungary, in addition to continuing to run a photographic studio in Split, Croatia, founded in 1932 by her grandfather.

Daniel Pinheiro was born in Venezuela and is based in Porto, Portugal. With a background in theatre, he has been exploring the concept of telematic art, using video as a tool and the internet as a platform, merging both languages into a single object of expression. In this field he aims at reflecting on the impact of technology of everyday life and the environment of the Internet as a reflection of a world where the abstract nature of this transmedia movement changes the notions of space, presence, privacy and identity daniel-pinheiro.tumblr.com

Rahee Punyashloka is a writer, visual artist, and experimental filmmaker based out of Bhubaneswar and New Delhi, India. His most acclaimed work has been the *Noise Reduction* series which had numerous screenings including in the International Film Festival, Rotterdam and Tribeca Film Festival, New York. The series investigates the material possibilities of the digital image and imagines it as various 'dramatic landscapes'. Currently he is working on a set of experimental works on the media representation of 'Dalits', a hitherto oppressed community of India, to which he belongs.

Oliver Lerone Schultz is a post-media researcher, working in transversal contexts. He studied Philosophy, History of Science and ethnography in Berlin, extended by studies in Cognitive Science and Political Economy of Industrial Societies in Berkeley. He was active in several media-activist projects and curational work, like laborB and globale-Filmfestival. Until recently he was based at the Lüneburg Centre for Digital Cultures, where — among other things — he co-initiated the Post-Media Lab.

Florian Schneider is a filmmaker who currently works in Norway. He is one of the initiators of kein mensch ist illegal at documentaX in 1997. He has realised several documentaries for the German French TV station arte in the context of thematic evenings on migration and global activism. He organised the festival Make World in 2001, started the performance and online video project Dictionary of War and has researched extensively on Imaginary Property -- a term he coined to grasp the complications of the becoming property of images and the becoming imaginary of property.

Peter Snowdon is a British filmmaker based in Belgium. His 2013 feature-length montage film, *The Uprising*, created an imaginary pan-Arab revolution out of YouTube videos. He has taught filmmaking at the University of the West of Scotland, and in the Visual Ethnography programme at Leiden University, and is currently an associate researcher at PXL-MAD School of Arts (Hasselt, Belgium). His book, *The People Are Not an Image: Vernacular Video After the Arab Spring*, will be published by Verso in September 2020.

Andreas Treske is an author, and filmmaker, writing about online video aesthetics and culture. He graduated from the University of Television and Film, Munich, where he also taught film and video post-production. He is chair of the Department of Communication and Design at I.D. Bilkent University, Ankara, Turkey. In 2015 he published *Video Theory. Online Video Aesthetics or the Afterlife of Video.* with Transcript. In 2017 the book was translated to Russian. Since 2008 he has been involved in the Video Vortex network.

Colette Tron is a Marseille-based critic. Working as a critic for the past twenty years, she has also published as a poet, using different media and languages, and questioning their function through experiments and creations. By founding the association Alphabetville (www. alphabetville.org) in 2000, she has created a place of reflection around the relations between language and the media, technic and art, aesthetic and society, and tries to articulate practice and theory in order to create a new critic and update theoretical approaches related to digital transformations in the artistic production process, and by publishing the results of this research. She has written two books and published many papers.

Jack Wilson is an Australian media theorist, cultural critic, and PhD candidate at the University of Warwick's Centre for Interdisciplinary Methodologies where he is researching conspiracy theories. He studies the media practices and cultural production of marginal digital subcultures, as well as contemporary literature, film, and electronic music. He is also a member of the Amsterdam-based research collective for the study of online political subcultures Open Intelligence Lab.

Dino Ge Zhang is a media anthropologist. He recently received his PhD from the Digital Ethnography Research Centre (digital-ethnography.com/team/zhang-dino-ge), RMIT University. He previously studied art history and media studies at University of Melbourne and anthropology at Hong Kong Polytechnic University. His PhD thesis is entitled *Zhibo: An Ethnography of Ordinary, Boring, and Vulgar Livestreams.*

www.ingramcontent.com/pod-product-compliance
Lightning Source LLC
Chambersburg PA
CBHW052308220526
45472CB00001B/34